HAND BOOK OF HERBS, MEDICINAL & AROMATIC PLANTS CULTIVATION

With Directory of Manufacturers/Suppliers of Plant, Equipments & Machineries

HAND BOOK OF HERBS, MEDICINAL & AROMATIC PLANTS CULTIVATION

With Directory of Manufacturers/Suppliers of Plant, Equipments & Machineries

Written By

EIRI BOARD OF CONSULTANTS & ENGINEERS

ENGINEERS INDIA RESEARCH INSTITUTE

4449, Nai Sarak, Main Road, Delhi - 110 006 (India)
Ph:. 91-11- 3918117, 3916431, 3920361, 3960797
Fax: 91-11- 391 6431
*** E-Mail : eirisidi@bol.net.in**
*** Website: www.startindustry.com**

Sole Distributor :

Indian Institute of Consultants, 4/27, Roop Nagar, Delhi - 110 007

PRINTED & PUBLISHED BY

ENGINEERS INDIA RESEARCH INSTITUTE

4449, Nai Sarak, Main Road, Delhi - 110 006 (India)

Ph:. 91-11- 3918117, 3916431, 3920361, 3960797

Fax: 91-11- 3916431

E-Mail : eirisidi@bol.net.in

*** Website: www.startindustry.com**

DISTRIBUTED BY

SMALL INDUSTRY RESEARCH INSTITUTE

INDIAN INSTITUTE OF CONSULTANTS

ISBN : 81- 86732-36-5

Printed in New Delhi (INDIA)

Rs. 650

Printed & Published by Sudhir Gupta for **"Engineers India Research Institute"** 4449 Nai Sarak, Main Road, New Delhi - 110 006 and Printed at Swastik Offset, Shahadra, Delhi - 32

Preface

The book ***'Hand Book of Herbs, Medicinal & Aromatic Plants Cultivation'*** *covers almost all the basic and advanced details of Cultivation. The Chapters covering in this book are Aloevera, Ashwagandha, Babchi, Belladonna, Buckwheat, Coleus, Costus, Cowhedge, Datura, Digitalis, Dioscorea, Duboisia, Foxglove, Geranium, Guggal, Honey Plant, Hop, Henna, Isabgol, Jasmine, Kalmegh, Liquorice, Lemon Grass, Long Pepper, Mint, Neem, Parrot Tree, Perwinkle, Primrose, Pyrethrum, Rauvolfia, Roselle, Rutin Bearing Eucalyptus, Rose, Senna, Steroid Bearing Solanum, Sweet Flag, Sweet Worm Wood, Valerian, Tubrrose, Tulsi, Herbs Drying, Herbs Cultivation, Spikenard, Medicinal Plant Extract etc.*

Apart from the above chapters the other most important chapter viz; Manufacturers/Suppliers of Agricultural Equipments & Implements has also been incorporated for the benifit of new entrants.

The book has been written for the benefit and to prove an asset and a handy reference guide in the hands of new farmers & well established cultivators.

Director
ENGINEERS INDIA RESEARCH INSTITUTE
Nai Sarak, New Delhi (INDIA)
E-Mail : eirisidi@bol.net.in

CONTENTS AND SUBJECT INDEX

Chapter 1

ALOE VERA

English name	:	Aloe, Barbados Aloe, Curacao Aloe, Indian Aloe, Jaffarabad Aloe
Indian name	:	Kamari (Sanskrit), Gheekanvar (Hindi) Lolesara (Kannada), Thazhai (Tamil)
Distribution	:	India, West Indies, South Africa
Uses	:	Drugs (therapeutic, purgative, vermifuge), cosmetics

Aloe species, perennial succulents belonging to the family Liliaceae, are the source of the drug aloe. Of the 275 species, there are three commerically important species which are the main sources the drug. They are: A barbadensis, Mill. (2n = 14),(A, vera toun ex Linn) which yields curacao aloe or Indian aloe or Jaffarabad aloe or Barbados aloe, which is produced in the West Indies (Curacao, Aruba, Bonaire) and A. ferox and its hybrids which yield Cape aloe, produced in South Africa and A. perryi which yields the socotrine aloe. Other aloe species (A. ofricana and A. spicata) yield aloes of lesser importance.

Aloe is obtained by cutting the leaves at their base and letting the yellow, bitter juice drain out. The water is evaporated off from the juice by heat, and the resulting light to dark-brown mass is the drug aloe. Of the two major products derived from the leaves, the yellow, bitter juice present in specialized cells beneath the thick epidermis yields the drug aloe and the parenchymatous tissue in the centre of the leaf contains a mucilaginous gel which yields aloe gel or aloe vera gel; it is currently obtained from A. barbadensis.

Aloe contains cathartic anthraglycosides as its active principles; these are mostly C-glucosides, notably barbaloin, which is a glucoside of aloe emodin. The concentrations of these glucosides vary with the types of aloe ranging from 4.5 to 25% of aloin. Other constituents present include aloesin and its aglycone aloesone (a chromone), free anthraquinones (e.g. aloe-emodin) and resins.

Aloe vera gel cotains a glucomannan which is a polysaccharide similar to guar and locust bean-gums and is believed to be the active constituent. Other constituents reported, or otherwise claimed to be present, include other polysaccharides (containing galactose, xylose and arabinose), steroids, organic acids, enzymes, antibiotic principles, amino acids, biogenic stimulators, wound-healing hormones, saponins, minerals, and so forth.

Fresh aloe gel is well known for its domestic medicinal value. For this reason, Aloe vera is also called burn, first-aid or medicine plant. When freshly obtained, the gel has the property of relieving thermal burns and sunburn, as well as promoting wound-healing; it also has moisturizing and emollient properties. The plant is used as a home remedy for these purposes. The only officially recognized use of aloe is its beneficial effects on the skin.

Aloe and aloin are extensively used as active ingredients in laxative preparations, often with other cathartics such as buckthorn, cascara and senna; belladonna extracts are often included to lessen griping. Aloin is also used in anti-obesity preparations. Aloe gel and some-times the drug aloe are used as moisturiser, emollient or wound-healer in various cosemtic and pharmaceutical formulations. Extracts of aloe or aloin are used in sunscreens, X-ray burns, dermatitis, cutaneous leishmaniasis and other cosmetic prepartions. As a food, aloe extracts are used as a flavouring ingredient primarily in alcoholic and non alcoholic beverages and in candy to impart a bitter note.

Distribution & Origin

Plants of the genus Aloe belong to the old world and are indigenous to Eastern and Southern Africa, the Canary Islands and Spain. The species spread to the Mediterranean basin and reached the West Indies, India, China and other countries in the 16th century; and certain species are now cultivated for commercial purposes, especially in some of the West Indian islands of the north coast of South America. It is also cultivated throughout India.

Plant Description

Aloe is a coarse-looking, perennial, shallow-rooted plant with a short stem, 30-60 cm high. The plants have multiple tuberous roots and many supporting roots penetrating into the soil. Aloe does not have a true stem but produce bloom-stalks. The plants generally grow close to the ground in a typical rosette shape. The fleshy leaves (about 60 cm long, 10 cm broad and 1.5 to 2 cm thick), are densely crowded, strongly cuticularized, and have a spiny margin with thinwalled tubular cells. The flowers vary from yellow to rich orange in colour and are arranged n auxiliary spikes. The flower is actinomorphic, its perianth is arranged in two whorls of 3 petals each. There are 6 stamens arranged in two whorls, the outer whorl having longer filaments than the inner whorl. The ovary is superior, trilocular with axile placentation. Most of the species are male, sterile, with scarcely any fertile pollen. The plant does not produce many viable seeds.

Varieties & Species

In India, 2 or 3 easily recognizable varieties are found, but their exact delimitations are not clear. In A. vera var. chinensis Baker, common all over the Deccan, the leaves have a distinct purple colour towards the base and the spines are not sharp. The leaves of A. vera var. littoralis Koenig ex Baker, found on the beach shingles in Madras right up to Rameswaram are smaller in size and have a dentate margin. Another variety which thrives on the Kathiawar coast, also called A. abyssinica, is the source of the Jaffarabad aloes. A. va iegata Linn. a near kin of A. vera is found in parts of Maharasha. It has large, fleshy, green leaves with sharp spines and white specks at the base of the leaves.

Soil

Aloe is a hardy plant and grows on a variety of soils. It does well in the sandy coastal to loamy soils of the plains with a pH of upto 8.5. However, water-logged conditions and problematic soils do not suit its cultivation.

Climate

Aloe is usually cultivated between March and June. The plant has a wide adaptability and can be seen growing throughout the length and breadth of the country. It is found growing in warm, humid or dry climate with even 150-200 cm to about 35-40 cm of yearly rain fall during the growing period. However, in dry regions, the crop should be provided with protective irrigation.

Preparation of Land

Before cultivation, the land should be ploughed twice and the field should be cleaned thoroughly of weeds. If required, small canals may be prepared for drainage. About 25 t/ha of cowdung manure is also added.

Cultivation

Propagation

The plants are generally propagated by root-suckers or rhizome cuttings.

Planting

The plants are planted at a spacing of 60 x 30 cm or 60 x 45 cm. About 15-18 cm. long root-suckers or rhizome-cuttings are planted in such a way that two-thirds portion of the root-sucker or rhizome-cutting should be under the ground.

Manuring

It is a newly domesticated crop and its full production technology including manurial requirments is yet to be worked out. An ad hoc basis application of a mixture of 150 kg/ha of nitrogen (N), potassium (K) and phosphorus (P) is recommended. The fertilizers are applied in the soil near the root-system, after the plants are established.

Irrigation

Soon after planting, the land should be irrigated. During the crop period, irrigation must be provided according to the moisture content of the soil. Generally, 4 to 5 irrigations per year are sufficient. However, water should not be allowed to stagnate near the plant.

Weeding

Weeding may be done twice a year and the land should be kept weed-free.

Pests and Diseases

Normally, the plant is not affected by any pests or diseases of serious nature. But recently, the leaf-spot disease caused by Altarnaria alternata and Fusarium solani has reported from India.

Harvesting and Yield

The plants are harvested eight months after planting. While harvesting, the plants can be removed manually or with the help of a tractor drawn disc harrow or cultivator. The broken rhizome part left in the soil throws out new sprouts in spring for raising the succedding crop. An aloe plantation gives a commercial yield from the second year up to the age of five years, after which it needs replanting.

The yield of the crop on a fresh-weight basis will be around 10 000-12 000 kg/ha.

Chemical Evaluation of Aloe Leaves

Aloe species are used extensively in the drug and cosmetic industry. Chemically, it is evaluated for the aloin content and aloe gel.

The lead exudate has been used for many therapeutic purposes. However, its purgative action has received the most detailed investigation. This property is ascribed as being due to the presence of certain anthraquinones. These are assayed as aloin content which is mainly barbaloin. Aloin content is assayed in aloe, in a dried form of the leaf exudate.

In order to estimate the aloin content in the leaves of one-year old plants, the whole plant may be used for chemical assay. It is recommended that plants may be selected at the time of flowering, i.e. from November to February. Transverse incisions are made on the leaves. The latex is allowed to ooze out from the leaves and is collected in a beaker. The leaf exudate is filtered and part of the exudate (1 ml) is transfered to an already weighed tube. This is dried at a high temperature and weighted. This gives the weight of 1 ml of exudate. Another part of filtered exudate (10-25 ml) is transfered to a separating funnel. This is repeatedly extracted with ethyl acetate (4 x 25 ml). The total ethyl acetate extract is filtered and evaporated at reduced pressure and low temperature ($< 50^{0}$ C). The residue is redissolved in warm water (100 ml) and a small portion (1-2 ml) is taken for chemical assay.

The second most important use of aloe is in cosmetics, in different blends. The mucilaginous pulp from the leaf parenchyma, which is mainly carbohydrate in nature, is used in skin disorders and in the treatment of burns. For the purposes of isolation and quantitative estimation of aloe gel, the portion of the leaves remaining after the removal of their exudate are out open and their mucilage is scraped out with a blunt-edged knife. This mucilage is stirred vigorously in a blender to make it into a uniform solution. This solution is strianed through a muslin cloth and filtered. A portion of this solution (5 ml) is taken in a centrifuge tube (50 ml capacity). The gel is precipitated from the extract by slowly adding acetone while stirring. This is kept overnight. The gel is obtained by centrifuging. This gel is redissolved in slightly warm water and transferred carefully to an already weighed tube. It is dried at a high temperature and weighed.

I. Introduction

Aloe vera is a genus of herbaceous, shrubby or arborescent, perennial, xerophytic succulent, found in many parts of the world. This genus however, should not be confused with the so called American aloe which belongs to the genus Agave. About four species have been introduced in India of which A. barbedensis has become naturalised in almost all parts of the country, the other species are also growing wild at some places.

It is known by different names in different languages; Bengali and Sanskrit Ghrita Kumari, Kanya; Gujarati Kumarpathu, Kunawar; Hindi-Ghee-kwar, Ghee kanwar; Kannada Kolasoare, Komarika, Mauli sara; Malayalam Kattarvazha; Marathi Koran; Oriya Kumari, Mushaboro; Tamil-Bhottu Katrazhae, Chirukatlalai, Kottadai; Telugu Kalabanda.

Aloe has a considerable demand for its medicinal and cosmetic importance. It can be easily cultivated in almost all parts of India, even under constant drought conditions. Under Unani system of medicine, aloe is known as "Ghasckumar" and as "Ghritakumari" under Ayurvedic system of medicine.

II. Distribution

Aloe is found in tropical and south Africa, Malagasy and Arabia. Of the four species which have been introduced and found in India, A. barbedensis has established itself as natural habitat in almost all parts of the country.

A. barbadensis, var. chinensis is common in Maharashtra, Karnataka, Tamil nadu, Kerala, Andhra Pradesh and Madhya Pradesh. A. barbadensis var. littoralis is found on the beach shingle in Tamilnadu upto Rameshwaram. Another variety which thrives on the Saurashtra coast is the source of Jafarabad aloe.

III. Description

It is a coarse looking perennial plant with a short stem, found in semi wild state in many parts of the country. Leaves are 30-60 cm long, erect, crowded in a basal rosette (structure and arrangement), full of juice, shining green, narrow lanceolate (pointed), long-acuminate, smooth except for spiny teeth on the margins. Scape is longer than leaves, scaly branched and flowers are yellow or orange, bell shaped, arranged in dense racemes terminating the scapes.

IV. Species

All the species of aloes are quite popular among succulent ornamental plants and because of their stiff, harsh and rugged habit they can be grown in a wide range of climate and soil conditions. Now-a-days aloe is increasingly becoming important for cosmetic purposes, besides its well established medicinal uses. Farmers can grow aloe in their barren lands, and other uncultivable areas and can enhance their income with minimum imput costs.

Few important species of aloes are briefly described here.

1. Aloe perryi (Socotrine or Zanziber aloe)

Aloe perryi has a simple stem which is 2.5 cm in diameter, scarcely rising above the ground and has crowded leaves much shorter than those of A. succotrina. It is indigenous to Socotra island. It is also found in East Africa and Arabia and has been introduced into India. The plant is suitable for growing in the limestone tracts upto an altitude of 900 m and can be readily cultivated in the driest situation and poorest soil. The drug prepared from the juice of the leaves is stomachic and tonic in small does and purgative in large doses. It is also used in jaundice, amenorrhoea, atonic dyspepsia and piles. The plant has been reported to posses mild anti tumour activity against sarcoma thirty seven.

2. A. succotina

Aloe succotina is a dichotomously branched, perennial succulent with woody stems upto 1.8 m in height and crowded leaves at the end of the branches cultivated in several parts of the country. It is used in the same way as A barbadensis. The thickened juice of the leaves is used in haemorrhoidal congestion of stomach and spleen. It is used in cases of prolapsed uterus. The colour and odour of each variety is characteristic and the taste is bitter and nauseous.

V. Climatic and Soil Requirements

As already mentioned aloes flourish in a variety of climatic conditions and even on the poorest of the soils, but need protection from frost. Well drained soil consisting of loam and plenty of broken bricks and coarse sand is preferable. During resting period (when no growth takes place) no irrigation is required and at no time soil should become sodden (with excess moisture). During the land preparation there is no need for deep ploughing as the root system does not penetrate below 20 cm level.

VI. Propagation and Nursery Raising

Propagation of aloe can be done by means of seeds or by vegetative parts such as suckers, and cuttings of new growth. Propagation by seed, however, does not ensure the progeny having the same qualities as that of parent plants since they have a tendency to hydridize under natural conditions. Artificial hybrids have been developed for commerical cultivation. As ornamental plants they are grown in pots, in beds, and in rock gardens. The potted plants need repotting after every two-three years.

Though aloe can grow under a wide temperature range, the germination of seed is found to be maximum at 21° C temperature. Seeds should be sown in the surface layers of the well prepared soil which has been filled in a pot or spread on a tray and should be covered by perlite. These pots or trays should be placed in a propagator providing heat from the bottom. Germination found to be erratic taking 4 to 24 months duration.

In summer season, gently remove off shoots at the base of a mature plants. They should be left for a day to harden them and then should be potted into pots containing two parts of compost to one part of sand mix. These pots should be watered and then left in warm place for the plants to establish themselves.

The aloe plant can be raised in the nursery from the seeds. suckers and stem cuttings. Seeds, unless they are specially crossed for hydridization, do not provide good plants. Hence, suckers or stem cuttings are mostly used for raising plants in the nurseries.

Cuttings having at least two nodes, from mature stems are planted in well prepared nursery beds which are filled with more sand and a little compost. They are planted closely in the germination beds. They are covered with sand and compost. The beds are kept moist. After some weeks the germination starts. The germinated cuttings are transferred to seedling bed and planted at one foot distance. When they are 3-5 leaf stage they are planted out into the field.

The ungerminated and rotting cuttings are disposed off safely. The sand in the germinating bed is remvoed and washed and dired to clean off all rotting fungi which may affect the new cuttings planted.

The nursery beds are partially shaded. The seedlings should be protected from stray animals, harmful insects and certain fungi that are found to be affecting cacti family.

VII. Field Cultivation

Aloe as already mentioned, can be extensively cultivated in all the dry and desert areas of our country where other forms of farming may be impossible. It can also be cultivated as intercrop. Since the plants are not affected by shading they fit in as intercrops in any orchard. In fact due to its high moisture content it is grown in the immediate surroundings of fruit tree seedlings or saplings or spalings in order to create suitable environment especially micro climate near the stem and root zone. It can be cultivated on the bunds, boundaries and sides of plots. Main cultural operations of aloe are given here.

1. Land preparation

Hardly any preparation is needed except clearing off the bushes and weeds if the cultivation is being taken up for the first time on that land. If the land is already been under some tree crops the land preparation will consists of only digging the small pits for planting the suckers. The land should be well drained.

2. Planting distance

Aloe is planted at a distance of three feet. If planted as a monocrop we can plant 4840 suckers per hectare. Distances less than three feet or more then three feet will not enable us to have optimum plant cover. Some space between the lines is required to do inter cultural and harvesting operations.

3. Planting time

Aloe can be planted throughout the year and the farmer can choose times when he is least occupied in the farm. However, from the physiological and growth habit point of view beginning of rainy season or at the end of rainy season is the best time to plant aloe suckers. Where the winter season is not that severe, aloe can be planted any time of the year and if there is severe winter plants ramain dormant during that season.

3. Planting method

The suckers or plants raisted from cuttings in the nursery are planted into small makeshift pits of 1x1x1 ft size. The pits may be dug few months before planting and left open for at least few weeks. Thereafter the pits are filled with a mixture of top soil and organic manures if available. By doing this the soil that is going to be at the root zone will be loosened and have a good condition for quick penetration of roots. At the time of planting the plants are placed in a small hole made in the loose soil in the pit and the soil all around is pressed firmly. The soil heaped on to the plant from all the sides so that water remains just around the plant not touching the plant becoase aloe is very susceptible to water logging or even high moisture content.

4. Interculture

For the first few weeks or a month the farmer shold go around in the field and make sure that all the plants are getting well established and are not hampered by any creepers of weeds. Weeding may be required periodically depending on the intensity of weed growth. The best is to pluck or cut the weeds and spread them as mulch between the lines of aloe. By this we can provide perhaps the most suitable micro-climate for the plants. The plants may require some kind of pruning and cleaning to guide its growth into more leaf production.

5. Water management

By water management proper moisture content is maintained in the soil. Aloe being very susceptible to higher moisture so, flood irrigation is not advised. Normally no irrigation is needed if there is moisture in the soil. Light furrow or channel irrigation between the lines or sprinkler or drip irrigation (which have been already set up for the other crops if it is already a cropped area) are the common irrigation methods. Under very less soil moisture conditions mulching with green leaves and stems of weeds is more than enough to protect the crop plants from excess loss of moisture through evaporation.

6. Maintenance

The maintenance and management of aloe may be considered according to the seasons: spring, summer, autumn and winter.

Spring : Give the potted plants a good supply of additional well prepared soil if needed. Spray the leaves with water and give a good feed of liquid fertiliser.

Summer : Remove the basal off shoots of a mature plant to thin down and to maintain the parent plant. Replanting of mature plants in the pots is done if necessary.

Autumn : Bring in the pots under some shade if there is any danger of frost.

Winter : Rest all pot grown plants in a cool room (minimum temperature 5° C or 40° F) and keep watering to the absolute minimum.

7. Harvesting

Mature leaves can be harvested at any time of the year. However two year old leaves are bitter as they possess better medicinal properties. The quantity of yield potential is very high though no officially recorded yields are available. the leaves are cut at the base with a knife and without injuring the stem. The cut leaves are transported to the processing plant.

VIII. Pests and Diseases

Aloe by nature is not very much susceptible to pests and diseases, however, overwatering causes rotting. So the soil mixture in the pot or the soil in the field should have good drainage facility.

IX. Uses in Folk and Traditional Medicines

On peeling the leaves, a mucilaginous gel like pulp having a typical smell and bitter taste is obtained. For use in medicine, the exudated mucilage from leaves is dried in sun where it forms a lustrous dark brown to black, hard, bitter mass. It is known as "Alva" or "Elua" or "Masasaber".

Fresh juice of leaves acts as a purgative and has cooling effect. It is used in eye-troubles and spleen and liner ailments. It has been found useful for X- ray burns, dermatitis, cutaneous lishmaniasi and other disorders of the skin.

The leaf juice forms an important constituent of a large number of ayurvedic preparations. It is also used in veterinary medicine. Fresh juice inhibits the growth of Micrococcus pyogenes var. aureus but the activity is unstable. It is reported that the frozen and dried juice heated to 80° for 15 minutes inhibited the growth of M.pyogenes, Streptococcus pyogenes, Salmonella paratyphi and Corynebacterium xerose. Ethanolic extracts of stem show anti-bacterial activity against Eschirichia coli.

The leaf extract inhibits the growth of Mycobacterium tuberculosis. The activity is attributed to the presence of barbaloin. Though the pulp of the leaves is credited with anti fertility or abortifacient activity, no-anti implantation activity was observed in the anti fertility screening tests on albino rats.

In home remedies the pulp is often pickled with black salt and ajwain and is used for treating common stomach problems such as indigestion, dyspepsia, hyperacidity, flatulence etc. The dry extract enters in the composition of many preparations used for constipation, hepatitis, dysmenorrhoea etc. "Kumari asava" prepared from the juice of the leaves and other ingredients is given to improve conditions of general debility, cough, asthma, tuberculosis etc. Other Ayurvedic preparations that have included aloe as a constituent are "Kumarika vati", Kumari paka" and "Rajah parvartini vati".

In unani systems along with ajwain, black pepper and salt it is used in "sufuf dama" for relief in asthma.

Aloe has a characteristic bitter taste and is used mainly as a purgative. It not only improves digestion but also does not lose its activity by repetitive use; it is not however prescribed for expectant women. Aloe forms one of the constituents of several proprietary laxative preparations. It is also used in early stages of tuberculosis, dyspepsia, uterine disorders and rectal fissures and as an anthelmintic, cholagogue and emmenagogue. Aloin (mixture of glycosides present in aloe) is widely used in chronic constipation. Because of the absence of resin the cathertic action of aloin is relatively milder than aloe. It is often used in combination with belladonna to overcome the tendency to griping, although action of bellodonna is rapid and brief compared to aloe. Aloin may produce renal irritation.

In USSR, aloe juice, aloe emulsion and aloe syrup with iron are in use. Aloe juice is used for treating burns, suppurative wounds and trophic ulcers. Its application results in quick cleansing of ulcers and wounds. Thick syrup of aloe with iron is effective against anaemia and the pulp of the leaves is used for rock bruises, sunburns, boils and carbuncles. In Florida, the pulp is used in ointments, cosmetic creams, lotions, shampoos and other products.

In Gujarat, the leaves and flower stalks are pickled. The leaves yield a fibre. A dye prepared from this species gives purple colour to silk, black to wool and pink to linen. Jafarabad aloe is used in lacquer work. In Kumaun, the leaf pulp is said to be eaten in times of extreme scarcity.

X. Chemical Constituents

Mixture of glycosides are present in aloe called "Aloins". Wide variations have been recorded in aloin content of different varieties of aloes as also in the different specimens of the same variety. This is due to various methods of assaying, The Aloin content and also to the fact that aloin content varies with variety. The principal constituent of aloin is water soluble crystalline glycoside barbaloin. Aloe also contain small quantities of anthraquinones. The odour is due to the presence of traces of essential oil. Resin fraction is considered by some to be of equal importance as aloin in cathartic action of the drug.

Recent reports on the chemical analysis of A. barbedensis claims the presence of seventeen free amino acids. The juice of the whole leaf, rind and pulp of aloe has been shown to contain reducing sugar, hydrolysable sugar, fructose, an oxidase, a catalase, and an amylae.

Regarding the biological activity, the purgative action of aloe is attributed to aloins. An antibacterial principal is present in aloe which inhibits growth of Mycobacterium tuberculosis which has been identified as barbaloin glycoside.

XI. Preparations and Extraction of Aloe

The term "Aloe' used in medicine stands for the dried juice which flows from the transversely cut bases of the large leaves of various species belonging to the genus aloe. For the preparation of aloe the juice is allowed to drain from the cut leaves into suitable vessels and then concentrated by evaporation either spontaneously or more frequently by boiling. The juice is colourless or yellowish to start with, but darkens due to evaporation and boiling. The nature of aloe depends upon the species from which it is prepared and the manner in which the juice is concentrated. If the juice is dried in the sun or concentrated over a low fire, it gives an amorphous opapue waxy extract called "hepatic or linery aloe". If the juice is concentrated rapidly over a strong fire, the material obtained on cooling is amorphous and semi transparent and is called "glassy of vitreous aloe". All aloes occur in both vitreous and opaque modifications.

Aloe, commonly known as "Musabbar" is a reputed purgative in the indigenous system of medicine. Three varieties of aloes are official in the Indian pharmacopoeia.

- Curacao aloe obtained from A. barbadensis
- Socotrine aloe obtained from A. perryi; and
- Cape aloe from A. ferox and its hybrids.

XII. Intercropping

Aloe is excellent as an intercrop. It can be grown in coconut gardens and between orchard trees as perennial under crop. It can be taken as an inter crop in farm forestry and social forestry. In the plantations of Jatropha, oil palm, perennial castor and in papaya plantations also it can taken as in intercrop.

Aloe can be planted in strips and in lines acroes the slope to control soil erosion. Strips of food crops are alternated with strips of aloe. Aloe can occupy the uncltivable pockets of land in a cropped area.

XIII. Soil Conservation

Aloe planted in few lines across the slope form a good belt for soil erosion control. Same way the field bunds and farm bunds may be made strong by growing aloe. The sides of the roads especially the lower side where the fresh soil is deposited can be made stable by planting aloe. All the contour bunds constructed on the slope can be fortified by aloe planting.

Chapter 2

ASHWAGANDHA

English name	:	Winter cherry
Indian name	:	Ashwagandha, Varahakarni (Sanskrit) Askandhatilli, Asgandh, Punir (Hindi) Hiremaddinagida, Panneru, Ashwagandha Kiremallinggida (Kannada) Amukkira, Amukkiran Kizhangu (Tamil)
Distribution	:	India, North Aftrica
Uses	:	Drugs

Ashwagandha (Withania somnifera Dunal.) (2n=48) is an important cultivated medicinal crop of India. It is also known as Hiremaddingagida, Panneru and Ashwagandhi in Kannada and Asgandh in Hindi. It is commonly known as Winter Cherry in English.

Ashwagandha is mentioned as an important drug in ancient Ayurvedic literature. Several Types of alkaloids are found in this plant, out of which, withanine and somniferine are important. In addition, the leaves are reported to contain five unidentified alkaloids (yield 0.09%), withanolides, glycosides, glucose and many free amino acids. The occurrence of chlonogenic acid, condensed tannin (also in the stems), and flavonoid are also reported.

The pharmacological activity of the roots is attributed to the alkaloids. The total alkaloid content in the roots of the Indian types has been reported to very between 0.13 and 0.31%, though much higher yields (up to 4.3%) have been recorded elsewhere. Many biochemically heterogenous alkaloids have been reported in the roots. In all, 13 components have been obtained chromatographically. They include choline, tropanol, pseudotropanol, cuscokygrene, 3-tigloyloxytropana, isopelletierine, anaferine, anahygrine, withasomnine and several other steroidal lactones. In addition to the alkaloids, the roots are reported to contain starch, reducing sugars, hentriacontane, glycosides, dulcitol, withanicil (0.08%), an acid, and a neutral compound. Withaniol was later found to be a mixture of two withanolides and the minor component remained unidentified. The free amino acids identified in the roots include aspartic acid, glycine, tyrosine, alanine, proline, tryptophan, glutamic acid and cysteine. The roots of the South African variety yield small amount of light-brown, pungent volatile oil.

The green berries contain a high proportion of the amino acids which include proline, valine, tyrosine, alanine, glycine, hydroxyproline, aspartic acid, cystine and cysteine. The presence of the proteolytic enzyme, chamase, in the berries may be responsbile for the high content of the amino acid.

The drug is mainly used in Ayurvedic and Unani preparations. Withaferine A has been receiving a good deal of attention because of its antibiotic and antitumor properties. It is used for curing carbuncles in the indigenous system of medicine. The paste prepared out of its leaves is used for curing inflammation of tubercular glands and that of its roots for curing skin diseases, bronchitis and ulcers. While in Rajasthan, the roots are used for curing rheumatism and dyspepsia; in Punjab they are used to relieve loin pain and in Sind for abortions. In some areas, the warm leaves are also used for providing comfort for eye diseases. However, the roots are mostly used for curing general and sexual debility.

Ashwagandha fruits and seeds are diuretic in nature. The leaves are reported to possess antihelmintic and febrifuge properties. An infucion of leaves is given for fevers. For the treatment of piles, a decoction of the leaves is used both internally and externally. The leaves are also used as a hypnotic in alcoholism. Externally, the leaves are used as fomentation for sore eyes, boils and swelling of hands and feet. As an insecticide, they are useful for killing body lice. An ointment prepared by boiling the leaves, is useful for bed-sores and wounds. The fresh leaf-juice is also applied on anthrax pustules.

An infusion of the bark is given for asthma. For the treatment of scrofula and constipation, the root is given in the form of a decoction as well. The decoction mixed with long pepper (Piper longum), butter and honey (25-50 g) and the powdered root with milk or clarified butter is used as an aphrodisiac and in seminal debility. For chest complaints, colds and chills, its decoction is recommended. The decoction along with milk and clarified butter is considered as a cure for female sterility, if taken for a few days after the menstrual period. For the treatment of bloody discharge and leucorrhoea, 45 g of powdered root with 10 g of sugar candy is given twice a day. A dose of 2 g of the root-powder along with sugar, honey, long pepper and clarified butter is given in spermatorrhoea end loss of strength. The root is considered to be very efficacious for toning up the uterus of women who habitually miscarry. An enema of the roots, with their bark removed, is given to feverish infants. The root is also said to have been used to treat snakebite.

The fruits and seeds are used in chest complaints. A paste made of the green berries with leaves and small twigs is useful for treating saddle-sores and girth-galls in horses.

Distribution and Origin

W. somnifera is found wild in grazing grounds in Mandsaur and the forest lands in the Bastar district of Madhya Pradesh, all over the foothills of the Punjab and Himachal Pradesh and Wastern Uttar Pradesh, in the Himalayas. It is also found in the wild in the Mediterranean region in North Africa. Another species W. congulans Dunal, a rigid grey undershrub, 60-120 cm high is found growing wild in Punjab, Sindh and neighbouring regions.

The crop is cultivated in an area of about 4000 ha in India, mainly in the drier parts of Manasa, Neemuch and Jawad tehsils of the Mandsaur District of Madhya Pradesh, in Punjab, Sind, Rajasthan and South India. In Karnataka, its cultivation has been reported in the Mysore district.

Plant Description

Ashwagandha belongs to the family Solanaceae. This is an erect, herbaceous, evergreen, tomentose shrub, 13-50 cm high. All its parts are clothed with whitish, stellate hairs. Branching is extensive, the leaf is ovate, entire, thin, its base is cuneate and is densly hairy beneath. The flowers are bisexual, greenish or luird yellow, axillary, in clusters of about 25 forming umbellate cymes, sessile or subsessile. The fruit is a berry, 7 mm across, red, globose, smooth, enclosed in an inflated, membranous, somewhat 5-angled, pubescent, persistent calyx. The fruits turn orange-red in colour when they mature. The seeds are yellow in colour and reniform in shape. The flowering season is from July to September and the ripe fruits are available in December.

The commercial drug consists of the dried roots of W.somnifera which occur in small pieces, 10.0 to 17.5 cm long and 6.12 mm in diameter. The base of the stem is also used. The pieces are darkbrown with a creamy interior. They are straight, unbranched and conical. The main roots bear fibre-like secondary roots. Their outer surface is buff to greyish-yellow with longitudinal wrinkles. The stembases are thickened, cylindrical and green and have longitudinal wrinkles. The roots have a short and uneven structure, a strong odour and a mucilaginous, bitter and acrid taste. The young tuberous and older roots have distinct macroscopic and microscopic characters.

Varieties

A variety named 'Jawahar Asgandh - 20' has been released from a single plant selection from the Jawaharlal Nehru Krishivishwa Vidyalaya, Regional Agricultural Research Station, Mandsaur, under the Medicinal and Aromatic Plants project. This variety has recorded the highest dry root yield, consistently, over the others.

Soil

It grows successfully in sandy loam or light-red soils with good organic matter and drainage. Under such soil conditions, it is also easy to dig the roots out without damaging them. A soil pH range of 7.5 to 8 is ideal.

Climate

Ashwagandha prefers a subtropical climate. It is planted during the late rainy season and prefers dry weather for its successful growth. In these conditions, 1-2 late winter rains are enough for its roots to develop fully. Places which receive 660-750 mm of rainfall are suitable for its cultivation.

Cultivation

Propagation

The crop can be grown by directly sowing the seeds into the field, as well as by raising seedling and transplanting them.

Direct Sowing

In this case, the seeds are sown directly in the main field by broad-casting. Since it is largely grown as a rainfed crop, the sowing is determined by the monsoon. After receiving one or two showers, the field is thoroughly prepared, divided into plots of convenient sizes and the seeds are sown during the second week of July. A seed rate of 10-12 kg/ha is required for this method of planting.

Nursery Raising and Planting

When the seedlings are to be raised for transplanting, they should to be sown in well-prepared, raised nursery beds. About 5 kg of seeds are required to proved enough seedlings for sowing one hectare. To avoid nursery diseases, the seeds are treated with Dithane M-45 at the rate of 3 g/kg of seeds before sowing. The seeds in the nursery beds are sown in lines spaced at 5 cm and covered with light soil. The germination commences within 6-7 days of sowing and in about 10 days after sowing it is complete. When the seedlings are 6 weeks old and sufficiently tall they are transplanted in 60 cm-spaced rows, 60 cm apart in well-prepared land.

Manures and Fertilizers

The ashwagandha crop does not require heavy doses of manure and fertilizers. In Madhya Pradesh, where it is grown on a commerical scale, no fertilizers are applied and the crop is cultivated on only residual fertility. Studies at the Indore Research Station have showed no effects of nitrogen and phosphorus on its root yield.

Interculture

The directly sown crop is thinned at 25 - 30 days to maintain a plant population of 20 000 to 25 000/ha. Hand-weeding at 30-day intervals helps to control the weeds effectively.

Diseases and Pests

Insects

There are no known serious pests infesting this crop.

Diseases

Seed rotting, seedling blight and leaf blight are common diseases affecting Ashwagandha. They reduce the plant population drastically, ultimately reducing the yield. Their incidence can be minimized by treating the seeds before sowing with Captan at the rate of 3 g/kg of seeds, followed by spraying the crop with Dithane M-45 at the rate of 3 g/l of water when the crop is 30 days old. The spray should be repeated at an interval of 7-10 days if the disease is not controlled.

The other diseases reported on this crop are seedling mortality or die-back. When the conditions are humid and the temperature is high, seedling mortality becomes serious. The diseases can be minimized by the use of healthy seeds and pretreatment of seeds with Thiram or Dettan (3-4 g/kg of seeds).

Harvesting and Drying

Harvesting starts from January and continues till March (150-170 days after sowing). The maturity of the crop is judged by the drying out of the leaves and the berries turning red. The entire plants is uprooted and the roots are separated from the aerial parts by cutting the stem 1-2 cm above the crown. They are then transversely cut into smaller pieces of 7-10 cm for drying. Occasionally the roots are dried as a whole. The berries are plucked from the dried plants and are threshed to obtain the seeds.

Grading

The dried whole roots undergo cleaning, trimming and grading before despatch. They are beaten with a club to remove the adhering soil and the thin lateral roots and rootlets. The main taproot may be cut into transverse pieces. The entire product is then carefully hand-sorted into four grades, based on the thickness and uniformity of the pieces.

A-grade : Root pieces up to 7 cm in length, solid, with 1-1.5 cm diameter, they should be brittle and pure white on the inside.

B-grade : Root pieces up to 5 cm in length, solid, with a diameter of less than 1 cm, the roots should be brittle and white on the inside.

C-grade : Root pieces upto 3-4 cm in length, side branches solid, with a diameter of 1 cm or less.

Lower grade: Small root pieces, semi-solid, very thin and yellowish on the inside.

Yield

An average yield of 300 to 500 kg/ha of dried roots and 50 to 75 kg/ha of seeds can be obtained.

Extraction Procedure

(i) Extraction of total withanalides from leaves

The leaf extract of ashwagandha exhibits marked activity against bacterial infections. The ground leaves are used in Ayurveda for the treatment of carbuncles, ulcers and painful swellings. These properties are due to the presence of several steroidal compounds. From the crude methanolic extract of the leaves, five crystalline sabstances have been isolated for the first time by A Yarden and L Lavie in 1962. One of these substances is withaferin-A, which is a C-28 steroid, with remarkable antibacterial properties. Abraham et. al. later obtained withaferin-A and related compounds. Withanolides (Steroidal Lactones) structures related to withaferin-A have been so far isolated from various chemotypes of the plant.

In order to estimate the withanolides by the TLC method, the leaves are collected, washed and dried in the oven. Dried leaf powder is extracted with alcohol in a Soxhlet extractor. The solvent is removed and the extract is defatted with petroleum ether. The residue is again dissolved in methanol and spotted on an activated silica gel plate. The plate is run in Benzene: Ethyl acatate mixture (90:10).

The colour of the spots are developed by iodine vapour. Nine clearly visible spots of withania steriods (withanolides) are seen on the plate. The R values of the spots are calculated and percent composition of various spots are worked out by preparative TLC method followed by Colorimetric estimation.

(ii) Preparation of alkaloid concentrate from roots

The root is described in early and modern Indian literature as a curative for many ills. Early chemical investigations of the root, established the presence of nearly seventeen nitrogenous bases. The total alkaloid content in the root was found to be within the range of 0.21 to 0.33%. Previously, the powdered root was used for treatment, but it is difficult to take large quantities of the powder orally, due to its bitter tasteConsidering thidLooking at this, the alkaloid Considering this, alkaloid concentrate from the withania root which contains a higher percentage of alkaloids may be useful for the chemical industry. Thus, a smaller quantity of the drug can be taken in tablet or capsule form.

To prepare the concentrate, 10 g of dried root-powder (dried at 60^0 C for 24 hours) is placed in a 500 ml stoppered, conical flask. A 100 ml of 1% solution of sulfuric acid (H_2 SO_4: water, 99|:1) is added and mixed well. The stopper is placed and the flask is kept overnight. The next day it is shaken in a horizontal shaker for about half-an-hour. The resulting mass is filtered by suction or the material is centrifuged for about 20 minutes at 6 000 to 8 000 rpm. The supernatant liquid is collected in a clean 250 ml beaker. The residue is again treated with 40 ml of 1% H_2SO_4 in the centrifuge tube and centrifuged in a similar manner. This process is repeated twice and 150 to 160 ml of supernatant liquid isd collected in the beaker. This syrupy, turbid solution contains a mixture of alkaloids, starch and other impurities. The residue is tested to see whether it is alkaloid-free, otherwise one more washing can be done. The pH of the solution may be within the range of 1.5 to 2.5.

For removing starch and other impurities, the solution is made alkaline by adding a small amount of calcium hydroxide powder by continuous stirring. The lime is added slowly which gradually changes the pH of the solution. Stirring and mixing should not stop at this stage. When the pH becomes neutral, the starch and other materials get precipitated. Let it settle for few minutes. Add a pinch of lime and centrifuge the solution.

The starch and other impurities get settled in the bottom of centrifuge tube and a clear solution of alkaloid with a neutral pH is obtained. This step should be done quickly and an extended contact with lime must be avoided.

The solution obtained from centrifugation is concentrated on a Thin Layer Rotary Evaporator till it becomes semi-solid and can be stored in bottles for further use as withania root alkaloid concentrate.

The concentrate prepared has nearly 6% alkaloid. The concentrate can be spotted on a silica gelG TLC plate after dissolving in methanol; taking n-butanol: HCL (98.2), colour is developed with modified Dragendorff Reagent. Eight spots of major alkaloids are clearly visible on the TLC plate which are similar to the spots developed by the alkaloids obtained from the solvent extraction, providing that this procedure has extracted all the alkaloids from the powder.

Chapter 3

BABCHI

English name	:	Babchi seeds
Indian name	:	Vakuci, Bakuci (Sanskrit), Bakuci Babchi (Hindi), Bavanchigida (Kannada) Karpogam, Karpokkarisi (Tamil).
Distribution	:	India Tropical/Subtropical regions of the world
Uses	:	Drugs

Psoralea corylifolia Linn, commonly called Babchi, is a medicinal plant belonging to the subfamily Papilionaceae of the Leguminaceae family. The seeds of babchi are used in the indigenous system of medicine in the treatment of leucoderma, leprosy and psoriasis. The seed is surrounded by a sticky, oily pericarp which contains coumarins, of which Psoralen and Isopsoralen are therapeutically important. Besides treating psoriasis, psoralin is being investigated as a cure for several diseases including AIDS. It is also used in the treatment of intestinal amoebiasis and the healing of wounds and ulcers. There are several reports in literature on the antimicrobial, antifeedant and insecticidal activities of babchi, suggesting other possible uses.

Distribution

The genus Psoralea, is widely distributed in the tropical and subtropical regions of the world. Out of the four species occurring in India, the seeds of Psoralea corylifolia Linn, alone are used in medicine. This species has a large distribution in the South-eastern districts of Madhya Pradesh and

Uttar Pradesh from where commercial collections are being made. In addition, it has a wider distribution in parts of Rajastan, Andhra Pradesh, Bihar and Gujarat and related semi-tropical grasslands in the country.

Plant Description

Babchi is an erect, annual herb, that grows 30-60 cm tall under natural conditions and up to 160 cm under cultivation. The plant branches profusely; its stem and branches are covered with conspicuous glands and white hairs. It bears simple leaves, broadly elliptic, rounded and mucronate at the apex. The axillary, solitary inflorescence (raceme) comprises 10 to 30 flowers with a hairy pedicle. The calyx is 3-4 mm long and hairy outside; the corolla is bluish-purple, nearly twice as long as the calyx (7-10 mm), zygomorphic, with depending imbricate aestivation; its 'standard' is 6 mm long, orbicular, clawed and glabrous. The stamens, numbering 10, are diadelphous; the carpel is small and unilocular. It bears a single-seeded pod which is indehiscent and the pericarp is usually found adhering to the seed.

Babchi is a self-pollinated crop. The initial flower-bud opens in about 17-18 days. The flowers open in two flushes, once early morning and again in the evening. Anther dehisces about one hour before the stigma becomes receptive. Its chromosome number (2n) is 20 and 22.

Soil

In nature, it is found growing on a variety of soils ranging from sandy medium loam to black-cotton soils. However, sandy loam soil with good organic matter is the best for its growth and yield. It also tolerates a wide variation in soil pH, but too acidic and too alkaline soils should be avoided.

Climate

The crop prefers dry tropical regions with a comparatively warmer type of climate for its successful growth and yield. It is generally grown as a rainy season crop with the onset of the monsoons. It is a hardy plant and grows well in areas with low to medium rainfall during the summer months. Under Bangalore conditions, the crop sown in the month of June has yielded the best.

Land Preparation and Sowing

The field should be prepared to make good seed-beds, by light ploughing followed by two harrowings before the onset of the monsoon season. The seeds are dibbled in rows, preferably 45-60 cm apart, keeping plant-to-plant spacing around 30-45 cm, depending upon the fertility of the land. A seed rate of 7 kg will be enough to cover a one hectare area.

Cultivation

Propagation

Babchi is propagated through seeds. The seeds have a problem of dormancy due to the hard seed-coat and germination is invariably poor (5-7%). The germination percentage can be improved by breaking the dormancy by the mechanical puncturing of seed coverings or by treating the seeds with sulphuric acid for 50 minutes. A pretreatment of seeds in 1% sulphuric acid has been found efficacious; the sulphuric acid should be washed off by repeated washings in water before the seed is sown.

Manure and Fertilizers

The crop responds well to the use of organic and inorganic fertilizers. It has been noted that the basal application of Farmyard Manure (FYM) at 20 t/ha gives a good initial growth and increases the seed yield significantly. Besides, a fertilizer dose of 100 kg N, 60 kg P and 50 kg K/ha is recommended. Of this, half a dose of N and a full dose each of P and K is given as a basal dose, while the remaining 50 kg N/ha is applied in one dose as a top-dressing after 45 days of sowing.

Irrigation

Since it is mostly grown as a rainy season crop, the irrigation requirement of babchi is moderate. However, after the rainy season is over (June-September), the crop may be irrigated fortnightly. About 6 to 8 irrigation may be given until the crop is finally harvested.

Interculture

The field must be kept free from weeds by regular weeding as and when required. In all, about 2 to 3 hand-weedings are necessary during the early period f growth after which, the plants cover the ground densely providing practically no opportunity for the growth of weeds.

Pests and Diseases

The plant is sufficiently hardy and free from pests. However, under Bangalore conditions, the Lepidopteron insects, viz. the leaf folder (Archips micaceana) and two defoliators (Helicoverpa armigera and Papilio polytis) have been found to cause considerable damage to this crop. These insects can be effectively controlled by spraying monocrotophos @ 1.5 ml/l of water.

Among the diseases, the powdery mildew is the only disease of a serious nature noticed on this crop. This disease can be controlled by spraying wettable sulphur @ 3 g/litre of water at weekly intervals.

Harvesting and Yield

The crop takes about 7-8 months from the time of sowing to reach maturity. As the seeds continue to mature over the growing plants continuously, the seed-picking will commence from mid-December onwards to the end of February. In all, 4 to 5 pickings are usually taken. At maturity, the single-seeded fruit turns brownish-black and emits a mild odour.

A average yield of about 2 t/ha of dry seeds may be obtained.

Introduction

English name : Bengal quince

Family : Rutaceae

Vernacular names

S.No.	Language	Vernacular name
1.	Bengli	Beal, Bel,
2.	Hindi	Beal, Bel,
3.	Marathi	Beal, Bel,
4.	Gujarati	Bili
5.	Kannada	Bela, bilva
6.	Malayalam	Koovalam, Vilvam
7.	Oriya	Belo
8.	Sanskrit	Bilva, Sriphal
9.	Tamil	Bilva, Vilvam
10.	Telugu	Bilavamu, maredu
11.	Urdu	Bel

Bael is highly valuable in Ayurvedic medicine. It is a moderate size, slender, aromatic tree, growing wild through out the deciduous forest of India. It is extensively planted near Hindu temples for its leaves and wood which are used for worship and for its edible fruits. Though the tree is planted in gardens, temples and private dwellings, no regular plantations are found of it is never grown systematically. Due to its ability to grow in poor, stony and alkaline soils, it is recommended for reclamation of waste lands and also for wind breaks in Northern India.

II. Occurence and Distribution

It is commonly found throughout India specially in dry hilly areas, gardens, road sides, and also cultivated in other places in India. It grows wild throughout the deciduous forests of India ascending to an altitude of 1,200 m in western Himalayas and also occurring in Andaman Islands. Bael tree in its wild state occurs commonly in the sub-Himalayan tracts and also in the dry deciduous forests of Central and Southern India.

The tree is generally found scattered in Bahraich distt of Uttar Pradesh. However it occurs gregariously in pataches of varying extent. It can withstand various types of soil, climatic conditions and a pH range of 5 to 10. It is drought hardy and is found in dry localities unfavorable to the majority of species. It is fairly frost resistant and can withstand as low temperature as 7^{0}C, Although it grows in open forests, it is capable of standing a fair amount of shade. In its wild state the tree occurs in regions where the absolute maximum shade temperature varies from 40^0 to 46^0 C, the absolute minimum from 0^0 to 7^0 C, and annual rainfall ranging from 570 to 2,000 mm.

III. Description

It is moderate size, slender, aromatic tree, 6.0 - 7.5 m in height and 90-120 cm in grith, with a somewhat fluted bole of 3.0 - 4.5 m and spines are straight, strong and axillary on branches. Bark is soft, corky, light gray, exfoliating in irregular flakes.

Leaves are alternate, foliate occasionally digitately five foliate. Leaflets ovate or ovate-lanceolate, crenate, acuminate, lateral sesslie, terminal long petioled.

Flowers are large, greenish white, sweet scented in short axillary panicles.

Fruits are globas, grey or yellowish, rind woody, seeds numerous, oblong, compressed, embedded in sacs covered with thick orange-coloured sweet pulp.

It flowers during April-May and fruits ripen during March-April.

IV. Properties and Uses

Part used are Fruits, seeds, leaves, bark and root. It is 'Madhura', palatable, Kashaya, pacifies deranged 'pitla", benficinal in deranged 'Kapha', fever diorrhoea, appetizing and gastric stimulant. Different parts of the tree have their own medicinal importance.

A. Leaves

The fresh leaf juice in doses of 8 to 16 gm is given with honey as a mild laxative in fever, catarrh and asthama. The leaf juice is mixed with black pepper and given in dropsy (a disease marked by excessive collection of a watery fluid in the tissues or cavities of the body) with constipation and Jaundice. A decoction of the leaves is a febrifuge (agent used for reducing fever) and expectorant. It is particularly used for asthmatic complaints. A hot poultice of the leaves is applied to the eyes in opthalmia, to the head in delirium (extreme mental distrubance marked by excitement restlessness and rapid succession of confused ideas) of fevers, to the chest in acute bronchitis and to inflamed part of the body. Fresh leaves are used in West Bengal as a remedy for beriberi (A defnciency disease caused by lack of vitamins especially B1).

B. Fruit

The fruit is of considerable medicinal value when it just begins to ripen. The ripe fruit is aromatic, astrigent, cooling and laxative. The unripe or half ripe fruit is astrigent, stomatic (a drug that strengthens the stomach and promotes it action), antiscorbutic (a drug which prevents or cures scurvey), and digestive. The fruit is said to act as tonic for heart and brain. It is best given in sub-acute or chronic cases of diarrhoea and dysentry and in irritation of the alimentary canal. It is a useful adjunct inthe after treatment of bacillary dysentry as it helps to remove constipation which hinders the healing of ulcerated surfaces of intestine. The ripe fruit is prescribed in intestinal disorders and certain terms of dyspepsia (indigestion), characteriized by alternate constipation and diarrhoea. A Shortbet of the ripe fruit is given for chronic constipation and dypepsia.

An extract of the fresh half ripe fruit is given in doses of 2-4 gm repeated many times a day. An extract made from sundried slices of the unripe fruit is given in doses of 4-8 gm. As a tonic the powder of the dried pulp is given in 0.85 gm 1,0 gram doses; as an antiscorbutic and febrifuge in 1.1 to 1.25 gm doses; as a nauseant and anti dysentric in 5 gm to 8 gm doses.

The ripe fruit is eaten fresh. The ripe fruits are woody large, spherical upto 20 cm in diameter, oblong or pear shaped, with smooth or tuberculate surface. The peripheral part within the rind is fleshly and chambers are full of viscours, translucent pulp slightly sweet. The pulp diluted with water and added with requisite amount of sugar and tamarind forms of delicious cooling drink, commonly known as Sherbat. The tender green fruit is utilized for making a preserve (morabba) which occupies an important place in the food industry of the North India. The fruit is rich in pectin but poor in acid and hence does not give a good jelly unless extra acid is added. Due to the presence of seeds and mucilage in the pulp, the ripe fruit cannot be eaten comfortably. Also due to the presence of oxidative enzymes, the pulp readily turns brown on exposure. To enhance its palatability and homagenity, it is necessary to add water to the pulp (upto 50% of the pulp) and heat it upto 70°C with constant heat to kill the harmful germs. The mass is then sieved while hot to separate the seeds, mucilage and fibre and is cooled immediately to prevent loss of flavour. The pulp, thus obtained is smooth, uniform and can serve as a base for various food products, like bael fruit squash, jam, and fruit necter, etc.

C. Root and bark

The root and the bark are used in the form of a decoction as a remedy in meanchchcholia, intermittent favers and palpitation of the heart. Root is one of the ingredients of "Dashmula", a common Ayurvedic formulation, particularly useful in loss of appetite and puerperal diseases (the problems which arise in period between child birth and the return of the womb to its normal condition). The rootbark has been used particularly in intermittent fevers and also as a fish poison.

V. CHEMICAL COMPOSITION

Since all the parts of the Bael tree are showing medicinal properties. Their chemical composition is given here separately.

A. Leaves

Alcoholic and aquous extracts of the leaves are reported to possess cardiotonic effect, like digitalis on amphibian and mammalian heart. The alkaloid, aegiline, present in the leaves is efficacious in asthma. The leaves contain four new alkaloids viz, O-halfordinol, N-2-ethoxy-2-ethylcinnamid, N-2 methoxy-2-ethylcinnamid, besides aegelenine and aegeline. Condensed tannins, pholobatannins, flavan-3-ols, leucoanthocyanins, anthocyanins, flavanoid glycosides, skimmianine and y-sitosterol are also present.

On steam distillation the leaves yield an essential oil. The essential oil has broad spectrum of anti-fungal activity comparabled to that of 0.5% Hamycin.

B. Fruits

Analysis of the fruit gave the following average values: moisture 61.5%; protein 1.8%; fat 0.3%; Carbohydrate 31.8%; and fibre 2.9%. Besides the following are present in small amounts (mg/100 gm); Calcium,85.0; phosphorous, 50.0; iron 0.6; thiamina, 0.13; riboflavin 1.2; niacin, 1.1; oxalic acid 18.7; and Vit C; 8.0 and; Carotene, 55 microgram/100 gm.

The fruit contains allo-imperatorin, marmelosin which are identical with imperatorin and B-sitosterol. It contains marmelide, an isomer of impertorin, which exhibits tyrosinase accelarating and tryptophan pyrrolase-inhibiting affect in Bufo melanosticus. The presence of psoralin, a powerful germination inhibitor and tonnic acid is also reported.

The fruits yield 2% of dried, water soluble gum. Hydrolipis of the gum gave; galactose 20:4; aralrinose, 10.7; D-galacluronic acid 25.2% and traces of rhamnose.

C. Seeds

The seeds yield an oil (34.4% on dry weight basis). The fatty acid composition of the oil is as follows; palmitic 16.6; stearic 8.8%; Oleic 30.5%; linoleic 36.0%; and linolenic 8.1%.

D. Roots and root bark

The roots contains auraptine, marmin, umbelliferone and lupeol. The alcholic extracts of the root gave psoralen, xanthotoxin, dimethoxy counmarin, scopoletin, lembamide, umbelliferone, marmesin, marmin, skimmlamine, and a glycoside identified tentatively as skimmin. The presence of decursinol an alkaloid haplopine, skimmianine, y-jagarine, marmesin, marin, xanthotoxi, umbelliferone and lupeol is also reported from the root bark.

VI. Conclusion

Our experience with nature and our knowledge about its flora and fauna have, with the inceasing urbanisation and consequent changes become almost nil. Urgent need is there, to realise the importance of plant like Bael, All parts of this tree have medicinal value and can be utilised for curing away diseases. Therefore it is also economically important.

Chapter 4

BELLADONNA

I. Introduction

Belladonna (Atropa belladonna) belongs to the family Solanaceae. A genus of herbs, distributed in Europe and Asia. One species A. acuminata is endemic to India and valued for its alkaloids where as A. belladonna L, the European species has been successfully introduced and is cultivated for its alkaloids in Himachal Pradesh and Kashmir.

In different languages and at different places it is known by different names as given in table.1.

Table. 1 : Vernacular names of Belladonna

S.No.	Language/State	Name
1.	Bengali	Yebruj
2.	Hindi	Angur shefa, Lukmuna, sagan gur
3.	Kannada	Nati belladonna
4.	Himachai	Pradesh Jhakra
5.	Kashmir	Mait-brand
6.	Punjab	Angur-shefa, suchi
7.	Bombay	Girbuti

The genus name Atropa has been derived from "Atropos" the Greek goddess of death. This name was given on the basis of wide use of the drug as a poison by the Greeks and the Romans. The word belladonna is derived from the Latin word "bella" meaning beautiful and "donna" means woman. This nomenclature has been adopted because of the fact that in olden days the Italian ladies used the berries of the plant as cosmetic to dilate the pupil of their eyes.

The medicinal value of belladonna was discovered accidentally when Daries, a drug clerk in Hamburg, inadvertently rubbed an extract of the plant into his eyes. This led to the discovery of the local action and mydriatic (pupil dilator) properties of Belladonna.

Leaves of Belladonna were at first included in the British Pharmacopoeia as a drug in 1809. The roots were accepted as a drug only in 1880. The commerical drug is obtained from the leaves, tops and roots of A. belladonna and A. acuminata often referred as Indian Belladonna. Although in most of the countries of the world the drug is obtained from A. belladonna, in India all the belladonna comes from the plantations which are a mixture of A. belladonna and A. acuminata

II. Distribution

Atropa belladonna occurs naturally in central and southern Europe. It is also found growing in calcareous soils in England and Greece. It is cultivated in a number of countries including England, Germany, Poland, Czechoslovakia, Hungary, Russia, USA and India.

It is found in the western Himalayan ranges extending from Kashmir at altitudes of 1,800-3,600 m to adjoining hills of Himachal Pradesh up to 2,500 m. Belladonna occurs chiefly in the valleys of Jhelum. Chenab and Kishanganga rivers and the forests of Bhadarwah and Kishtwar in Jammu and Kashmir in Himachal Pradesh, it occurs in the Kangra reserve forests, the Kulu forest division in Kinnaur, and the Narkanda forests in Simla hills. In Uttar Pardesh it is found growing near Chakrata and in West Bengal near Darjeeling.

III. Botany

Atropa belladonna is a perennial herb up to 1.5 m tall with a strong root system. The lower part of the stem may be either simple or bear three directional branching. The young stem is covered with greenish trichomes and may be greenish of reddish violet in colour. Leaves are ovate or oblong ovate, 7.5 x 10.0 cm, entire, accuminate narrowed to a petiole, alternate, or in pairs of which one is smaller than the other. Flowers are large bell-shaped, upper part brownish violet or purple or golden brown with violet brown veins. Fruits are globular, slightly bilobed, shining purple-black, subtended by enlarged calyx lobe.

Atropa acuminata is a tall perennial herb 0.7 to 1.5 m in height with dichotomously branched system. Leaves are green or olive green in colour,

7-18 cm in length and 3 to 7 cm in breadth, oblong gradually tapering towards the base and apex. On flowering branches the leaves are in pairs. Flowers are auxiliary, dirty yellowish in colour, campanulate, occurring singly or in groups of two to four. Fruits are globular and purple black in colour.

Both the species are more or less similar except for the shape of leaves and colour of flowers. On upper branches each leaf is accompanied by a small stipule like leaf.

Belladonna is a hexaploid plant with 2n = 72 (x=12). Most of the cultivated strains are being obtained from wild races in Europe and India. Tetraploids have been obtained but they have not been found to be useful. A number of mutants obtained through chemical mutagens have also not been found of any practical value. Selection work has been done in Russia and it claimed that stains having up to 1% alkaloids have been obtained.

IV. Chemical Composition

Both the leaves as well as root of the plant contain total alkaloide from 0.3% to 1 per cent. About three-fourth of the total alkaloids is present in the form of L-hyoscyamine, the reminder being hyoscine (scopolamine) and atropine. Atropine is present in the fresh plant only in traces and is formed by racemization during extraction of the drug. Small but varying amounts of other alkaloids like apoatropine, belladonnine, and cuscohygrine are also present. According to the British pharmacopoeia, the leaves and roots should not contain less than 0.4% total alkaloids calculated as hyoscyamine.

All parts of the plant contain alkaloids, but the alkaloids are produced in the roots only and are traslocated through stem. Though only the leaves and the roots are used commercially, other parts especially the seeds could also prove to be promising source of alkaloids. The roots give better yield of alkaloids than the leaves, but in the first year of planting they are very thin and are not suitable for commercial extraction.

There is a great variation in the content of total belladonna alkaloids as also of individual alkaloids due to several factors-both intrinsic and extrinsic. The plants raised in sunlight contain 50% more alkaloids than those growing in shade. The single-stemmed plant yielded higher percentage of alkaloids than the multi-stemmed ones. The alkaloid content which is maximum in the roots, stems and leaves at the time of flowering, progressively decreases at the fruit bearing stage (November in India). The leaves of the plants whose flowers have been removed earlier contained 0.7% alkaloids whereas those with flowers intact contained only 0.5 per cent. Young tissues are richer in alkaloids than the mature ones. The terminal leaves contain maximum quantity of alkaloids and the Basal ones the minimum. The presence of trace elements like iron, manganese, cobalt and particularly copper in the leaves appears to increase the accumulation of alkaloids.

Nitrogeneous fertilizers, especially ammonium nitrate, increased the total alkaloid content. Calcium, potassium and phsophorus manuring increases the yield of the alkaloids only to a slight extent. Tetraploids obtained by colchicine treatment or branch chimeras contained more alkaloids.

The various occurring in belladonna roots, leaves and seeds are listed in table 2.

Table 2 : Alkaloids of Belladonna roots, leaves and seeds

Plant part	Alkaloids
Root	1-hyoscyamine and its N-oxides, atropine, hyoscine (atroscine, scopolamine), apo-atropine, (atropamine), belladonnine, bellaridine, cuscohygrine.
Leaves	1-hyoscyamine and its N-oxides, atropine hyoscine and its N-oxide, apo-atropine, belladonine, noratropine, apo-scopolamine, norscopolamine, scopadonine, nicotine.
Seeds	1-hyoscyamine and its N-oxides, atropine, hyoscine, apo-atropine, noratropine, aposcopolamine, norscopolamine.

Atropine has wide applications. As an antispasmodic substance it relaxes smooth muscles in alimentary and bilary tracts (as in peptic ulcer), in urinary tract (as in tanesmus infaction), in uterus (or in dysmenorrhoea) and in bronchi (as in asthma).

It acts as an antisecretary agent to reduce sweating, as in nightsweat, and to reduce salivary and bronchial secretions.

As a mydriatic, it dilates the pupil and paralyses for examination and postoperative condition.

By vagal inhibition, atropine increases heart rate and thus acts as a cardiac stimulant. To reduce tremor and rigidity as in case of "Parkisonism" atropine serves as a central "abtusoasmodic" agent. Scopolamine is used principally for central effects to reduce tremor, and rigidity in "Parkinsonism" as a sedative often in connection with morphine (twilight sleep); as a preanaesthetic mediation and in motion sickness.

V. Soil and Climate

Belladonna is a temperate plant and grows well in deep fertile soils of medium texture which are rich in humus. Heavy clay soils, which are water logged, should be avoided. In temperate climates the plants behave as a perennial and gives maximum yield of herb and alkaloid. It can also be cultivated as a winter crop in subtropical areas like northern India but under such conditions only one crop can be obtained and the plant behaves as an annual as it dies during the summer months and the yields is poor because of limited number of harvests of leaves. Belladonna crop also requires protection from strong sunlight.

VI. Propagation

Population of belladonna in the existing plantations is heterogeneous comprising A. acuminata, A. belladonna and a hybrid of these two species. Morphologically, they are distinguishable. Atropa belladonna is a herb 30-70 cm in height with divaricate branching near the base, 8-20 cm long leaves and purple flowers. The hybrid is 40-90 cm in height with divaricate branching at the base, ovate to ovate lanceolate 11-22 cm long leaves and yellow flowers flowers with purple tips.

Recently belladonna has been grown by tissue culture methods for production of atropine. The excised root tips, 1.0 cm long are grown in ascptic conditions in the laboratory in modified street and McGregor's nutrient solution at 28^{0} in the dark. The dry weight of the excised root tips increases steadily with the process of culture period. The root tipe synthesize @ 45% atropine when cultured on revised Murashige and Skoogs nutrient medium.

The plants are heterogeneous due to cross pollination and there is considerable variation in growth habit and alkaloid content. Treating the seeds with chemical mutagens and radiation increases the variability and widens the scope for increasing the alkaloid content and the herb yield. The plant can be propagated from seeds or from cutting of the young shoots or from fleshy root stocks. Large scale cultivation is however most successful with seeds under tropical conditions. The seeds are very small, brownish black and are obtained by crushing the berries. They show poor germination due to the hard, thick and waxy seed coat, an inhibitor present in the seed coat and an internal membrane enclosing the rudimentary embryo. Seeds pre-treated with sulphuric acid, ethyl alcohol or petroleum ether give better germination than the un-treated ones, but the plants from treated seeds are stunted and their allkaloid context is only 40%, that of the plants from untreated seeds. Treating the seeds with gibberallic acid (40 ppm for 24 hours) or thiourea (0.5-2%) improves germination without affecting the alkaloid content. Surface sterilization of the seeds by fungicides like captan, agrosan GN, dithane-45 or agallol before sowing reduces seedling mortality due to damping off.

VII. Nursery Raising

Although belladonna has been cultivated by direct sowing, raising of the nursery gives the cost results. Before making the beds, the land should be tilled well so as to give a fine tilth. Raised nursery beds should be made surrounded by drainage and irrigation channels. Well-rotten farm yard manure or sheep manure should be mixed in the top 10 cm of the soil. Seeds should broadcasted on the surface of the beds at the rate of 200 of seed per square meter. Use of heavy seed rate is essential for getting good stand. Although a number of authors have suggested that germination of belladonna seeds require special treatment, experience in Kashmir has shown that belladonna seeds germinate readily, if planted properly at the proper time. The broadcasted seeds should be covered with a layer of well rotten leaf compost of farmyard manure and soil. Alternatively the beds can be covered with a mulch of rice straw or wheat straw. The beds should be irrigated with a sprinkler. After the seeds have sprouted, the mulch should be removed. The beds should be kept free of weeds by frequent hand weeding and irrigated frequently. The best time for raising the seedlings is early summer (May-June) or autumn (Septermber-October). Planting the seedlings are ready for planting in the field after 8-12 week the ideal time for planting in field is early spring (March-April) or autumu (October-November). Generally seedlings raised in autumn are planted in spring and those raised in summer are planted in autumn.

Seedlings should be planted at a distance of 50-60 cm in rows kept 60-70 cm apart. It is always safer to plant the seedlings on ridges as it avoids water logging and facilitates irrigation.

VIII. Manures and Fertilizers

Studies in Europe and India have shown that belladonna responds well to fertilizer application. Nitrogenous fertilizers give good response. However, application of nitrogen beyond a certain level does not affect the alkaloid content. It is always better to give a balanced fertilizer of nitrogen, phosphorus and potash in order to get a good crop. Normally, a basal dose of 20 kg/ha nitrogen, 60 kg/ha phosphorus and 50 kg/ha potash should be applied before planting. Three top dressings of nitrogen at the rate of 20 kg/ha per application at an interval of six weeks give good results under Indian conditions. This prectice should be followed during the first year. 60 kg/ha nitrogen in 2 split doses should be applied in succeeding years. Trace elements have also been found to affect growth.

IX. Irrigation

Belladonna has a high water requirement and it should be irrigated frequently during the dry period. Normally 6-7 irrigations are required in Kashmir valley during the dry months from June to September. While irrigating care should be taken to avoid water-logging.

X. Inter-culture and Weed Control

The plant require frequent inter culture to keep the soil loose and to control weeds. The common weeds found with belladonna are Stachys germanica Lin. Verbascum thapsus linn, Senecio spp, Phytolacca acinosa and Brassica species. Repeated weeding and hoeing should be done. Normally 3-4 weedings and hoeing are required during the growing season. The weeds can also be removed by pulling them out before flowering. Inter culture can also be carried out by a tractor. However, hand weeding is practicable in hilly areas on small terrains.

XI. Diseases and Insect Pests

Belladonna is affected by a number of diseases. Most important diseases are root rot and leaf spot.

Root rot is caused by a fungus Phytophthora nicotianae. The symptoms consist of soft rot of roots and the stem just above the ground level. In severe cases the plant topples over and dies. This happens mostly in wet conditions.

Root rot is also caused by Pythium butleri is the only serious diseases in India which causes considerable damage to plantations in Kashmir every year. Plants at very early stage of growth are affected. In young seedlings the fungus causes preand post-emergence damping off. This can be controlled by fumigation of the soil by methyl bromide and treating the seeds with captan would reduce the damage and increase crop yield. Older plants when affected suffer from wilting and finally die. If the affected plants are pulled up, the cortex of the roots and the lower parts of the stem is found to have a brownish soft rot.

In order to reduce the dying it is better to plant healthy seedlings raised on seed beds which are fumigated with methyl bromide. It is better to avoid planting belladonna continuously on the same plot. After a 3 year crop of belladonna, the field should be planted with a crop like rye or wheat, which should be flowered by a 5 year crop of pyrethrum.

Leaf spot is caused by the fungus Ascophyta atropae. The disease is characterized by appearance of small roundish brown spots on the leaves. In severe cases the leaf spots cause blighting of the leaves. The disease can be controled by spraying of blitox.

Cutworms (Agrostes flammetra) does considerable damage in nursery and young plants in the fields. The attack is severe in early summer months of April–May when the seedlings and young plants are cut at ground level. The pest can be controlled by treating the seed bed with Aldrin just before planting and treating the soil with a solution of chlordane (1:19) 2 weeks after germination of the seedlings.

XII. Harvesting and Storage

Belladonna grows vigorously during summer and rainy seasons. In autumn and winter, the plants start shedding leaves.

The subterranean parts resume growth with the advent of spring. In the second year the plants start flowering.

Belladonna yield two crops of leaves during the first year of growth. In the second and subsequent years it gives 3 or 4 leaf crops. The roots are however, dug out after the third or fourth year of planting. Harvesting hegins with the first sign of flowering when the alkaloid content in the plant is at the peak. The plants are cut in August, about 30 cm above the ground with a sickle or a cutter, while in the autumn they are cut 3 cm close to the ground. Cutting at 30 cm height ensures quick regeneration of leaves and more leaf content and elimination of woody branches having low alkaloid content. The plants are irrigated and fertilized immediately after harvest so that they put out new shoots again. The harvested crop is cropped into pieces, particularly the young herbaceous shoots, and dried by spreading in the sun in thin layers. Losses upto 30% can occur if the material is dried in thick layers. The material is periodically raked to ensure uniform drying to retain the green colour of leaves and also to prevent decomposition of alkaloids by enzymatic action. Drying at 40 for 24 hours ensures complete drying. Hot air is sometimes employed for drying. The woody stems are discarded and the dried material is stored in gunny or polythene bage; in well-ventilated sheds. Under humid conditions, material absorbs moisture resulting in the lowering of alkaloid content. Lumps of calcium chloride kept in store rooms help to avoid such moist conditions.

XIII. Yield

The yield of leaves from a uniform belladonna crop varies between 500 and 600 kg/ha in the fist year and reaches upto 750 kg/ha in the subsequent years. At Seoni and Chaubatia (U.P) yield upto 1,500 kg/ha is recorded in experimental trials. Grown as a winter annual in the plains of Jammu, the crop yields 1,440 kg of leaves (dry weight) and 240 kg of root (dry weight) per hectare. The ratio of stem to leaf in the harvested leaf crop is 50:50 by weight.

In temperate climate the roots are dug out by ploughing after the third or fourth year of planting. They are washed and cleaned and cut into short pieces of 10 cm, the thicker ones are sliced lengthwise. They are dried thoroughly in the sun or by artificial heat. The yield of roots is 160 kg/ha.

The drug (belladonna) consists of cylindrical pieces of the roots upto three cm thick, occasionally branched, sliphtly contorted and with a short tough fracture. They are pale brownish grey and longitudinally wrinkled. Pieces with the crown are 3-9 cm in diameter at the top, and have bases of 4-12 aerial stems. The powdered root is grey to light brown in colour. It has a characteristic odour and a sweetish taste which later becomes bitter.

The drug from the leaves, called belladonna herb has a slight odour and a somewhat bitter ad acrid taste. It consists of the dried leaves; the powdered leaves are greenish yellow. Sometimes flowers with short pedicles, immature fruits and seeds are found in the dung.

XIV. Uses

In traditional Indian systems of medicine, the plant is not used much, except as a substitute of Datura, for external application to relieve pains and internally for relief in cough, asthma, and other bronchial troubles but in modern medicine, alkaloids from it are extensively used in ophthalmology and as a sedative.

It is used in unani preparation "Habul Khaskhash" for cough and cold. Belladonna is used mainly as extract, tincture or plaster and it has been rarely used as a source of pure alkaloids. Recently use of total alkaloids has become common Various preparations of belladonna are employed in medicines, mainly because of anticholinergic action of tropane alkaloids. In case of diseases of respiratory tract like asthma and whooping cough it is used to check glandular secretion and spasms of the bronchial tube. Similarly for the same purpose it is also used in intestinal disorders, peptic ulcers, coitic pain, pain of urinary bladder and kidney stones to check spasms and pain as well as glandular secretion. It is also used in case of epileptic conditions parkinson's disease, night sweats and bradycardia. In suitable doses it is also used as sedative and in the form of plaster and ointments it is used as an anti-inflammatory agent. It is often used as antidote for opium and muscarine poisoning. The dried leaves are smoked as an antispasmodic. The root is generally used externally and not internally, it is used as an anodyne (drug which relieves pain) for rheumatism (pains in muscles, joints and certain tissues), neuralgia (pain felt over a nerve) lumbago (rheumatism of muscles at back) and local inflammations.

XV. Conclusion

India imports the crude drug as well as its alkaloids prepared from Belladonna. Sometimes there is a problem of adulteration. The roots of Althaea officinalis are sometimes mixed with belladonna roots but they can be distinguished on the basis of their fracture and absence of starch in the exposed surface. The leaves of Phylolacca acinosa which grows side by side with belladonna in nature, often mixed with or substituted to Belladonna leaves. It can be detected in commercial samples by its ovate leaves and hollow stems.

Previously, most of the belladonna was obtained from the forests of Jammu and Kashmir and the crude drug was exported. Now the plant is becoming extinct in Kashmir forests. The most economic method of propagation is raising a nursery through seeds and transplanting it in the field. Farmers should undertake belladonna as a crop and earn profit as well as help in fulfilling the annual demand of drug which is extimated to be more than 800 quintals.

More Details :

Family	:	Solanaceae
English name	:	Belladonna, Deadly Nightshade
Indian name	:	Angurshefa, Luckmuna, Kotu, Phaphra (Hindi)
Species and varieties	:	A. belladonna Linn. (Deadly Nightshade)
	:	A. acuminata Royle (Indian Atropa)
Distribution	:	India, England, Europe, US, USSR
Uses	:	Drugs

Belladonna (Atropa), belonging to the family Solanaceae, comprises four species of medicinal plants. Out of these four species, the commercial drug is obtained from the leaves, flowering tops and roots of A. belladonna Linn. commonly called Deadly Nightshada and A. acuminata Royle, often referred as Indian Atropa or Indian Belladonna. The genus name Atropa has been derived from Atropos the Greek goddess of death, whereas, the word belladonna is dervied from the Latin word Bella meaning beautiful and Donna meaning woman. Although in most of the countries of the world the drug is obtained from A. belladonna, in India all the Belladonna comes from plantations which are a mixture of A. belladonna and A. acuminata.

The leaves and roots of belladonna contains tropane alkaloids whose concentration varies from 0.13 to 0.7% (the average is 0.45%).

A. belladonna contains alkaloids, chiefly 1-hyoscyamine and small amounts of atropine, its optically inactive isomer, and small amounts of hyoscine (scopolamine). In addition, there are small quantities of volatile bases, such as pyridine and N-methyl-pyrroline. The leaves also contain B-methyl esculetin (scopoletin), succinic acid, asparagin, etc.

A. acuminata leaves contain 0.45% hyoscyamine and non-alkaloidal volatile bases not greater than in A. belladonna. The roots of A. acuminata contain 0.20-0.8% hyoscyamine (0.47% is the average) and non-volatile alkaloids (0.4%).

Belladonna leaves were included in the British pharmacopoeia in 1809. The roots, however, were accepted as a drug only in 1880. Belladonna leaves are widely used for the manufacture of tinctures, extracts and plasters. The drug serves as an anodyne, sedative stimulant, antigalactogogue, antidiuretic, mydriatic or anti-asthmatic, antispasmodic and anti-inflamatory. It is also used for relief from whooping cough, in the treatment of renal and bilary colic, in stomach disorders, to stop sweating, in opthalmology to cure gastric ulcers and as an antidote for depressing poisons such as opium, muscarine and chloral hydrate. The roots are primarily used in the external treatment of gout, rheumatism and other afflictions. It is also used in the treatment of epilepsy, Parkinson's disease and bradycardia.

Origin and Distribution

A. belladonna is indigenous to Southern and Central Europe and naturalized in Southern England. It is cultivated for its drug in Central Europe, England, the USSR, the United States and Northern India. A. acuminata is found in a natural state in the Western Himalayas extending from Kashmir to Simla and the adjoining areas of Himachal Pradesh. Its chief habitat in Jammu and Kashmir state are the forests of Sindh, Jhalum, Lidder and Chenab Valleys. It is also cultivated in some places in the Himalayas.

Description of the Plant

A. belladonna (2n=72, hexaploid) is an erect, herbaceous plant, 150 cm high, with a long, cylindrical, branched, fleshy, creeping, perennial root, varying from 2.5 cm to several centimeters in width, yellow-brown externally, white within. The plant is shrub-like with spreading slender, cylndrical, sometimes slightly downy, often purplish, branches. The leaves are alternate, but on the upper branches, each leaf is usually accompanied by a small, stipule-like leaf. The blade is ovate, pointed, entire, soft, with conspicuous veins and frequently with a purplish mid-rib which may be hairy beneath; 7.5-22.5 cm long, 5.0-10.0 cm wide and petioles of 0.6-3.75 cm. The flowers, borne singly in the leaf axils, are large, bell-shaped, the upper part is brownish-violet or purple or golden-brown with violet-brown veins. The fruits are globular, slightly bilobed, shiny purple-black, subtended by an enlarged calyx-lobe. The fruit is a berry and it reaches 1.25 cm in diameter and is two-celled and contains many kidney-shaped seeds embedded in a pulp which is somewhat sweet and yields a purple juice. In the variety Lutea, the leaves and stems are yellow-green.

A. acuminata is a tall perennial herb, 70 to 150 cm in height with a dichotomously branched stem. It closely resembles A. belladonna. It has a large taproot with lateral rootlets 6 inches or more in length and of 1-2 cm thickness. The leaves are green or olive-green in colour, 7.5-21.5 cm long and 4-9 cm in breadth. The flowers are brownish-yellow with greenish veins and are borne singly or in groups of two to four. The fruits are globular and purple-black in colour.

Varieties

There are no named varieties reported under this crop but the workers at the Regional Research Laboratory, Srinagar, have selected plants containing 0.60% alkaloids in A. belladonna.

Soil

Belladonna grows well in slightly acidic, deep, fertile soils of medium texture, which are rich in humus. Heavy clay soils which are water-logged should be avoided.

Climate

Belladonna is a temperate plant. It behaves as a perennial in temperate climates and gives maximum herbage and alkaloid yield. In subtropical areas it can be grown as a winter crop. However, the plant behaves as an annual as it dies during the summer months and hence the yields is poor.

Land Preparation

The land is prepared well and brought to a fine tilth with the help of tractors and organic manure at the rate of 25 t/ha, to begin with, is mixed with the soil.

Cultivation

Propagation

The crop is propagated through seeds extracted from the berries, usually collected from September to November. About 4 kg of seeds will be required to raise seedlings for one hectare of land. The germination is very poor and it takes 3-6 weeks for the seeds to germinate. Hence, the seeds may be treated with 80% sulphuric acid at the time of sowing for 2 minutes to improve germination. Stratification of seeds on wet sand under 5 to 12^0 C or 2 to 2^0 C for 10-40 days has given a high percentage of germination in other countries. Vegetative propagation by root-division from 3-4 year old belladonna plants is also suggested by the Drug Research Laboratory, Jammu and Kashmir.

Nursery Raising

Belladonna has been cultivated by driect sowing. but raising them in the nursery gives the best results. The nursery may be raised from the second week of May to the end of autumn (September to October) and in summer under sufficient shade. Before making the nursery beds, the land should be ploughed well so as to give a fine tilth. Raised beds of 3 m X 1 m size may be made, surrounded by drainage and irrigation channels. Well decomposed FYM or sheep manure should be mixed in the top 10 cm of the soil. Seeds pretreated with fungicides like dithane M-45 or Agallol (10 g/kg of seeds) may be mixed with fine soil in a 1:40 ratio to ensure uniform sowing and broadcast (@ 200 g seeds/m^2) in the nursery-beds and covered with a layer of FYM and then with straw. The beds must be watered immediately after sowing with a watering can and daily therafter. The seeds normally germinate within 3 weeks with a good germination percentage, and the seedlings will be ready for planting in the main field when they attain a height of 15-20 cm after about 8-12 weeks.

Broadcasting

About 20 kg seeds are required for sowing one hectare of land by broadcasting.

Transplanting

The ideal time for planting in the field is early spring (March-April) or autumn (October November). Generally, seedlings raised in autumn are planted in spring and those raised in summer are planted in autumn. Seedlings are planted at a spacing of 50-60 cm in rows about 60-70 cm apart. It is always safer to plant the seedlings on raised beds with 1 m-wide strips or ridges as it avoids water-logging and facilitates irrigation. The field may be irrigated immediately after transplanting.

Fertilizer Application

Belladonna is an exhausting crop, hence a basal dose of 25-40 kg N, 40-60 kg P_2O_5 and 30-50 kg KO_2/ha is supplied. An additional dose of 60-80 kg N is applied in 3-4 split doses as a top-dressing at monthly intervals after every harvest. The application of heavy doses of nitrogen gives a good crop of leaves and also increases their alkaloid content.

From one year after planting, a basal dose of nitrogen and phosphorus should be repeated every year in the beginning of the spring season (March April), which is followed by a top-dressing of nitrogen. Micronutrients have been found to affect the growth. It is better to irrigate the field after each application of fertilizers, if there is no rain.

Irrigation

Belladonna has a high water requirement and it should be irrigated frequently, once in 10-15 days during the dry period. Normally, 6-7 irrigations are required during the dry months. Care should be taken to avoid water-logging.

Interculture and Weeding

The crop should be kept from weeds by frequent weeding and hoeing. One hand-weeding is necessary when the plants are young. A tractor-drawn cultivator or hoe may be employed for later weeding.

Pests and Diseases

Pests

Among the insects, cut-worms (Agrostis flammetra) cause considerable damage to young plants. The other insects noticed on this crop are the potato beetle and flea beetle. The attack is severe in the early summer months (April to May), when the seedlings and young plants are cut at the ground-level. The pests can be controlled by treating the seed bed with Aldrin just before planting, and treating the soil with a solution of Chlordane (1:19) 2 weeks after germination of the seed.

Diseases

A species of Phytophthora, a root fungus, causes havoc in European belladonna plantations. Whereas, in India, Pythium butleri causing root-rot is the only serious disease-causing organism to the belladonna plantations. Plants at every stage of growth are affected. In young seedlings, the fungus causes pre-and-post emergence damping-off of the seedlings. This can be controlled by fumigation of the soil with methyl bromide and treating the seeds with Agallol or Captan. Older plants, when affected, will wilt. After a 3-year crop of belladonna, a crop rotation may be followed by planting the field with a crop like rye or wheat which should be followed by a 5 year crop of pyrethrum. The fungus Ascochyta atropae causes leaf-spot disease, whose symptoms are the appearance of small, roundish, brown spots on the leaves. In severe incidence, blighting of leaves is noticed. The disease can be controlled by spraying Blitox (3 g/l of water). Pythium spp. is reported to cause damping-off of the seedlings, for which drenching of the field with 0.1% Dithane M-45 is recommended. Belladonna mottle virus has been observed on A. belladonna, for which the vectors are not known. Uprooting the plants and burning them in isolation or burying them deep are the control measures suggested.

Harvesting

The first harvest of leaves is available three months after planting. The initial yield is poor because of the fewer number of branches; the yield of leaves increases after the first cutting. Harvesting should be done as soon as the shoots start flowering, as it is the period when the alkaloid content is higher. The leaves are cut with the help of a cutter (pruning scissors) about 30 cm above ground-level as against 7.5 cm above ground-level, done earlier. During the first year, 3 to 4 crops of leaves are obtained. Usually, the crop will be retained for 3 to 4 years, after which new planting may be taken up.

Drying

The leaves are dried imediately after harvest under the shade or sun or on wire racks, taking care to see that the dried leaves remain green. The leaves may also be dried with artificial heat, with or without fans for air circulation. The harvested leaves are spread in thin layers and turned frequently while drying. The woody stems are discarded before drying. Caution: Prolonged drying reduces the alkaloid content.

The roots are harvested after 3 years. After harvest, they are washed, cut into 4-inch long splits, length-wise if thick and shade-or sun-dried. The dried crop is pressed bydraulically into large hessian cloth bags and stored in a cool, dry place away from light, or are transported right away to processing units.

Yield of Herb and Roots

During the first year, an average of 6 q/ha of dry herb is obtained. The yield increases to 12 to 15 q/ha during the 2nd and 3rd year. The yield of dry roots will vary from 1.7 to 3.35 q/ha.

Chapter 5

BUCKWHEAT

English name	:	Buckwheat
Indian name	:	Kutu (Hindi)
Distribution	:	India, Central Asia, Europe, France Russia USA
Uses	:	Drugs, Food and vegetable crop Livestock and poultry feed

The genus Fagopyrum, belonging to the family Polygoneaceae, has three important species, of which Buckwheat (Fagogyrum esculentum Moench) is an important medicinal plant, commerically grown for Rutin. The other two species of this genus, F. cymosum and F. tararicum, are cultivated for fodder and sometimes their leaves are cooked and eaten as spinach or as amaranthus. It is considered as an excellent crop for soil-improvement, particularly for virgin lands or for poor soils which do not support any other cereal crop. By its spreading habit and vigrous growth, it smothers weeds and forms an excellent cover. It acts as a soil-binder preventing soil erosion during heavy rainfall. It also produces a large quantity of green biomass can be incorporated into the soil as green manure. All the three species also yield grain which is used as flour for bread-making. The plant is, however, in no way related to the real wheat and it is only a pseudo-cereal. In USA and Russia, the grains are mostly used in the manufacture of livestock and poultry feed.

Buckwheat came into the limelight in 1946, as the most promising and economical source of rutin. While the leaves and flowers are rich in rutin, the seeds have none. With the growing importance of rutin as a medicine to treat the harmful effects of X-rays, it may be of use to persons exposed to dangerous atomic radiations. In addition, rutin is used in the treatment of increased capillary fragility which is associated with hypertension a condition which sometimes reults in the bursting of blood vessels in the brain, leading to apoplexy or retinal haemorrhage and causing partial or complete blindness. It is useful in a variety of haemorrhagic conditions which include certain types of purpura, i.e. bleeding from the kidney, heridatary haemorrhagic telangiectasia and haemophilia. It has been used with success as a prophylactic treatment against gangrene due to frostbits. Rutin injection with certain miotics is useful in galucoma, and in combination with dicummarol in the treatment of retinitis. It also prevents the weakening of capillaries due to drugs such as salicylates, arsenicals, thiocyanates, sulphadiazines and gold salts. The usual dose is 20-30 mg repeated 3-4 times/day for several weeks.

Distribution and Origin

Buckwheat is said to be a native of Central Asia and is cultivated in various countries as a food or fodder crop. In Europe, Russia, USA and France it constitutes one of the main food crops. In India, it is grown as a grain crop in the higher altitudes (600 3 650 m) of the Himalayas (from Kashmir to Sikkim) and in the Nilgiris, but more often as vegetable crop in the lower mountain ranges.

Plant Description

It is an annual herb growing up to 80-160 cm in height. The leaves are alternate, acute and 2.5-7.5 cm long; flowers are produced in auxiliary or terminal cymes and are pinkish white in colour, fragrant, diamorphic and highly self sterile. The fruit is of 3 colours, ranging from silvery-grey to brown or black.

Soil

The crop can be grown on a variety of soils, but it thrives best on well-drained sandy or loamy soils. It does not grow well on poorlydrained, heavy or acidic soils.

Climate

A moist, cool climate is ideal for its optimum growth. It is a quick growing crop, requiring 7 to 9 weeks from seed to seed. A monthly average temperature of 18 to 30^0 C seems to be satisfactory. As it is a photosensitive crop, flowering is very erratic and sometimes plants as small as 6 to 8 cm are seen flowering, hence the period of cultivation should carefully be chosen for its optimum production. In most places in India, early September to early December seems to be the best, during which period at least two crops can be cultivated in the same field. A crop sown in the last week of October takes 46 days to reach maturity with an appreciable plant height of 47 cm. Crops sown four weeks earlier and later than the above period of sowing, resulted in poor total fresh and dry weight of herb and crude rutin content.

Therefore, it is suggested that when buckwheat is intended to be introduced into a new region or area, field trials should be conducted with staggered planting at narrow intervals to find the most suitable season for successful crop production.

Cultivation

The crop being a short duration, medium-sized annual and sensitive to water-logged situations and a poor competitor with weeds, thorough prepration of the land so that it is free of weeds is necessary. The land must be thoroughly ploughed 3 to 4 times and brought to a fine tilth by harrowing. The field is divided into plots of convenient size (4 to 6 sq m) for the proper distribution of irrigation water. The soil within the plots is levelled. F. esculentum requires a seed rate of 60-80 kg/ha whereas, for the other two varieties, 40-50 kg seeds/ha is sufficient. The seeds are line-sown with a spacing of 20 cm between rows and 10 cm within each row. The most favourable temperature for germination is found to be 35° C. In the crop sown between December and January, there are chances of delay in germination due to frost.

Manures and Fertilizers

The field is moderately manured with well-rotted FYM. An application of 50 kg N and 40 kg each of P and K/ha is found to be adequate for a good crop. Half the quantity of nitrogen along with the full dose of phosphorus and potash are applied as a basal dose. The remaining half-dose of nitrogen is applied 4 to 5 weeks later.

Irrigation

It is generally grown as a rainfed crop with one or two protective irrigations, if required.

Interculture

The crop is kept weed-free by frequent hoeing and weeding in the early stages of growth.

Pests and Diseases

Insect Pests

No major insects affect this crop

Diseases

A few bacterial and viral diseases are noticed on this crop and are not of a serious nature. However, leaf blight which appears during flowering or even at earlier stages of growth, causes some damage to the crop. Initial symptoms start with minute spots on leaves which quickly develop and coalesce to from bigger patches, which turn into blight and finally result in leaf-fall and the drying up of the plant. The leaf blight disease can be controlled effectively by spraying 0.2% copper oxycholoride, whenever the disease is noticed.

Harvesting and Yield

The best stage for harvesting is 40 to 50 days after sowing and when the plants begin to bloom. Harvesting should, however, be done well before grain-formation, if the crop is intended for rutin production. Delayed harvesting causes a sharp decline in rutin content from 6.0 to 3.8%. The period between blooming and seed-setting being short, close observation is required to enable harvesting the crop at the proper stage. The crop at this stage which would have generally attained a height of 60 to 70 cm is cut and harvested above ground-level.

Post harvest Drying of the Crop

As the stems are hollow and the leaves contain 88 to 90% moisture, sun-drying is slow and may also lead to fermentation and enzymatic action leading to a loss of rutin. Dehydration technique by artificial rapid drying of the leaves is the best suited method. A process for rapid dehydration of leaves using an alfalfa drier has been developed for obtaining leaf-meal rich in rutin and stable under ordinary storage conditions for at least a year.

Yield of Fresh Herb and Rutin

An average yield of 5 000 - 6 000 kg herb/ha is considered satisfactory.

Chemically, rutin (C_{27} H_{30} O_{16}) is a flvanol-3-O-di-glycoside, a greenish-yellow, crystalline powder obtained from the leaves and flowers of buckwheat plants. The dry herb yield per hectare is around 500 kg. The leaf to stem ratio is 0.6:1, the crude rutin being 4.9%. Thus, 100 kg of fresh herb, on an average, yields 10 kg of dry herb.

Chapter 6

COLEUS

English name	:	Coleus
Indian name	:	Pashan Bhedi (Sanskrit), Patharchur (Hindi) Makandiberu (Kannada)
Distribution	:	India, Africa (tropical ea'st), Arabia, Brazil Egypt, Nepal, Pakistan, Sri Lanka
Uses	:	Drugs

Coleus barbatus Syn: Coleus forskohlii Brig, belonging to the family Lamiaceae, is one of the most significant potential medicinal crops of the future as its pharmacopeical properties have been discovered only recently. The tuberous roots are found to be a rich source of forskolin (syn. Coleonol) which is being developed as a drug for hypertension, glaucoma, asthma, congestive heart failures and certain types of caners. The plant is well known throughout the country and is known as Pashan Bhedi in Sanskrit, Patharchur in Hindi Garmalu in Gujarati and Maimnul in Marathi. In Egypt and Africa, the leaves of C. barbatus are used as an expectorant, emmenagogue and diuretic while its foliage is empolyed in treating intestinal disorders, and it has been used as a condiment in India for a long time. The tuberous roots of this plant, resembling a carrot in shape and brown in colour, are the commercial parts.

Origin and Distribution

The crop has been distributed all over the tropical and sub-tropical regions of India, Pakistan, Sri Lanka, tropical East Africa, Brazil, Egypt, Arabia and Ethiopia. In India, it is found in the subtropical Himalayan regions from Kumaon to Nepal, Bihar and the Deccan Plateau of Southern India. It is cultivated in parts of Ragasthan, Maharasthra, Karnataka and Tamil Nadu in an area of about 2 500 ha.

Plant Description

Coleus barbatus (2n = 30) is an aromatic perennial plant 0.5 m tall with thick tubers and with very showy bluish to pale lavender coloured flowers, arranged in whorls on a long spike like racemes. The entire plant is aromatic (whether fresh or dried). The leaves and tubers have quite different odours, the latter being reminiscent of, but quite different from, ginger.

Member of the genus Coleus, have square stems, branched, the nodes are often hairy. The leaves are usually pubescent, narrowed into petioles. The flowers, borne on racemes, are perfect, the calyx is fine-toothed and deflexed in the front. The pale-blue corolla is bilabiate, the lower lobes are elongated and concave. The ovary is four-parted and the stigma is bilobed. Coleus-flowers are cross-pollinated by means of wind or insects. The species has four didynamus, with declinate stamens where filaments unite as a sheath at the base. The roots are tuberous, fasiculated, up to 20 cm long and 0.5-2.5 cm thick, they are conical, fusiform, straight, orangish and strongly aromatic.

Varieties

A selection from Karnataka, K-8, is reported to give 0.5% forskolin and a higher tuber yield.

Soil

It thrives best in porous and well-drained soils with a pH ranging from 5.5 to 7. It does not require very fertile soils and can be economically be grown on soils with marginal fertility. The red, sandy loam soils of Karnataka are ideal for the cultivation of this crop.

Climate

Coleus is a crop of the tropics and is found growing well on barren hills at an altitude of about 2 400 m, under tropical and subtropical conditions. In India, it is grown mainly in Belgaum (the Sahayadri mountain range of Karnataka) and in Gujarat. The climate here is humid with a RH ranging from 83 to 95% and a temperature of 10-25° C. The annual rainfall is 100-160 cm, mainly between June-September. It is also found to perform well in less humid and warmer regions of South India like Coimbatore, where it is grown as an irrigated crop.

Cultivation

Propagation

Coleus can be propagated by seeds as well as by stem-cuttings. However, propagation through seeds is little difficult and slow and should be used only for the breeding of new varieties. Whereas, propagation by cuttings is very easy and economical to raise this crop on a large scale.

Nursery Raising

The viability of the seeds being very poor (8-10%), a sufficient quantity of fresh seeds has to be sown in well-prepared nursery-beds to obtain good germination. Regular care about watering, weeding and plant protection of the nursery should be taken. In about 15 to 20 days, the germination is completed. When the seedlings are 45 days old and have attained about 8-10 cm height, they are ready for transplanting.

Vegetative Propagation

Vegetatively the crop is propagated through terminal cuttings. Normally, 10-12 cm long cuttings comprising 3-4 pairs of leaves, are sown in already prepared nursery-beds and regular care about shading and watering is taken. The cuttings establish well in the nurseries and there is no problem in their rooting. After about a months time, when the cuttings have produced sufficient roots, they are transplanted to the main field.

Planting

In most areas, the crop is planted during June-July at the onset of the Southwest monsoon. Before planting, the field is ploughed deep soon after the of pre-monsoon showers and brought to a fine tilth. Further, the land is prepared into ridges and furrows at a spacing of 60 cm and the rooted cuttings or seedlings are planted 20 cm apart within the row.

Manures and Fertilizers

Studies conducted at TNAU, Coimbatore, to standardize the nutritional requirement of this crop have shown that it responds well to the application of N, P and K combination of 40 kg N, 60 kg P_2O_5 and 50 kg KO_2/ha was found to be optimum for obtaining the maximum fresh (120 t/ha) and dry (3.982 t/ha) tuber yield from this crop. Half the dose of N the whole P and whole K may be applied as the basal dose followed by the remaining half

N, 30 days after planting as top-dressing.

Irrigation

The first irrigation is given immediately after transplanting, if there are no rains. During the first two weeks after planting, the crop is irrigated once in three days and, thereafter, weekly irrigation is enough to obtain good growth and yield.

Weeding

Due to the frequent irrigations during the initial stages, there is a lot of competition from weeds. In order to obtain economic yields, frequent weeding during the early growth period is desirable.

Diseases & Pests

Pests

The leaf-eating caterpillars, mealy bugs and root-knot nematodes are the important pests that attack this crop. These insects can be controlled by spraying the plants and drenching their roots with 0.1% methyl parathion, while nematodes can be controlled by the application of carbofuran granules at the rate of 20 kg/ha.

Diseases

Among the diseases, bacterial wilt is the major one. The spread of wilt can be controlled by spraying and drenching the soil adjoining the affected plants with 0.2% Captan solution immediately after the appearance of the disease and later after a week's interval.

Harvesting and Yield

Flowers if any should be nipped off during the growing period to obtain more biomass of roots. The crop is ready for harvest 4 1/2 to 5 months after planting. The plants are loosened, uprooted, the tubers separated, cleaned and sun-dried for the extraction of 'forskolin.'

On an average a yield of 1 500 - 2 000 kg/ha of dry tubers may be obtained. However, if proper cultivation practices are applied, a yield of up to 2 500 kg/ha of dry tubers can be easily obtained.

Chapter 7

COSTUS

English name	:	Costus
Indian name	:	Chanda (Sanskrit), Kebu, Keyu (Hindi) Kondige (Kannada), Kostam (Tamil)
Distribution	:	India Indo-Malayan region, Nepal
Uses	:	Drugs

Diosgenin, widely used as a starting material in the commercial production of steroidal hormones, is chiefly obtained from certain species of Dioscorea of which Dioscorea deltoidea constitutes the main Indian raw material. This source, however, has limitations in ensuring large supplies on a sustained basis due to its restricted distribution in a few localities in the northwest Himalayas and poor response to domestication. It has become necessary to search for an alternative botanical source which could be easily cultivated under a wide range of agroclimatic conditions and provide the industry with raw-material at a comparative low price and on a sustained basis. A number of plants were found to contain steroidal sapogenins, but none could satisfy all the criteria of such a sustitute. The report of the presence of diosgenin in the rhizomes of Costus speciosus, (Family: Zingiberaceae) raised hopes of developing such a source, as the plant was widely distributed in India. Diosgenin is further synthesized into sex hormones and steroidal drugs which are widely used for their antifertility, anti-anabolic and anabolic, properties in family planning and health programmes all over the world.

Distribution & Origin

Costus speciosus (Keon) SM is among the five species of stout, perennial herbs indigenous to the Indo-Malayan region. Two varieties of C. speciosus, viz. nepalensis found only in Nepal and Arunachal Pradesh and var. argyrophyllus having a wide distribution in India, have been described.

Plant Description

The plant has broad, lanceolate, dorsally silky leaves, borne spirally on stout, erect or sometimes ascending stems. The flowers are white, with a large in-curved lip. These are clustered in terminal globose heads, characterized by large and shiny brown or red bracts. Both diploid (2x = 18) and tetraploid forms occur in nature. C. speciosus perenniates through underground rhizomes which lie a few centimetres below the soil surface, the rhizome is differentiated into nodes and internodes. The vegetative activity above the ground lasts for about 7-8 months. Stems sprout during the month of April, flowering commences during July and continues till the end of September and the fruits ripen during the middle of November, after which the leaves are shed and the majority of the canes start drying up. The underground portion remains dormant from December to March.

Soil

The plant can be grown on a variety of soils ranging from coastal alluvium to the heavy, brown, forest type. It grows more luxuriantly on alluvial soils which have a sandy to clay loam texture with a pH of 5.7 - 7.5.

Climate

It can be grown from sea-level to about 1 500 m elevation. But the areas situated at elevations between 400 and 600 m above mean sea-level, having a subtropical climate with an annual rainfall ranging between 1 000 and 1 500 mm, produce good quality material. A well-marked dry period between monsoon precipitation reults in higher diosgenin content in naturally occuring plant populations. Coastal regions and regions with high annual rainfall and humidity throughout the year bear poor quality raw material in terms of diosgenin content.

Land Preparation

The land is ploughed 2-3 times and the soil is brought to a fine tilth. FYM @ 15 t/ha is applied and mixed well with the soil and furrows are made 50 cm apart.

Cultivation

Propagation

Although the plant can be propagated from seeds, stem cuttings and rhizomes, commercially it is being propagated only through rhizome cuttings. The selection of rhizomes for planting is, however, important. The rhizomes have a number of nipple-shaped buds, most of them being concentrated around the stem scars and the tips. The formation of buds on the rhizomes is poor during April. The cuttings of rhizome pieces for propagation should have at least two viable buds. Rhizome pieces weighing around 40 g should be selected. About 2 000 to 2 400 kg of fresh rhizomes are required for planting a hectare of land.

Planting

The rhizome pieces are placed at a depth of 8-10 cm taking care to place the eye buds facing upwards, horizontally, in rows 50 cm apart and covered with soil. The crop is irrigated immediately after planting. Thick-sized pieces sprout slowly only after 40-45 days of planting. This is due to the eye-buds being dormant on these rhizome pieces which take a longer time to develop, especially in the case of the crop planted in April. After 70-75 days about 90-95% sprouting is obtained.

Dessication of young sprouts has been observed during the hot summer months, necessitating a liberal water supply during this period. The best period of planting is from the 3rd week of April to the 3rd week of May. Rhizomes planted during June and July complete germination within 60 days, but yields obtained are low as the crop has a shorter growth period in the first year before dormancy sets in. The active vegetative growth period of the crop is from July to mid-September and the maximum turberization takes place between September to November. The effect of planting on ridges versus flat beds indicates that there is no significant difference in yield due to the method of planting although a slighly higher yield of fresh rhizomes was obtained from the crop planted on ridges.

Manures and Fertilizers

It is a rhizomatous crop and to compensate the biomass production, heavy manuring is required. In a trial conducted at Vallanikkara, Kerala, the tentative optimum dose for obtaining the maximum yield of diosgenin was observed to be 45 kg N, 30 kg P_2O_5 and 30 kg K_2O along with 15 t/ha of

FYM. The FYM and a half-dose of P and K are applied in 2 split doses at 20 and 60 days from the time of planting the remaining half dose of P and K is given along with the second dose of N after the 60th day of planting.

Irrigation

The crop requires a liberal supply of water for its successful growth. The crop planted during April and May requires irrigation at least two to three times a month till the outbreak of the monsoon. As September to November is the period of maximum turberization, at least two irrigations should be given in this period. During the dormancy period (December to March) if winter rains are scanty there is a need for irrigation. If moisture conditions are adequate,it has been observed that the crop sprouts towards the end of March or early April. With a liberal supply of irrigation during the hot summer months an excellent crop growth is observed. Thus, for a crop to be harvested after a period of 17 to 18 months, 14 to 17 irrigations are required.

Weeding and Interculture

One weeding during the sprouting period of the crop followed by two more, keeps the crop fairly free of weeds. During the period of active vegetative growth (July to September) most of the weeds are suppressed. If the monsoon is erratic, at least one more weeding is required.

Weeding once or twice during the dormant season helps in better sprouting of the crop during the next season. During the second year of the crop, the inter-row space between the plants is covered up by the canes and only two to three weedings are necessary before the crop is harvested in August or September.

Diseases & Pests

There are no major pests which affect this crop. However, the following are some diseases which are observed to affect the crop.

1. Rhizome rot

It is caused by Phytophthora solani and develops very quickly from July to August, in the rhizomes kept in storage after the harvest. Initially, the symptoms start from the tip of the injured portion of the rhizomes. Subsequently, the rhizome becomes light-brown and gives off an offensive odour.

Properly harvested rhizomes without injuries can be stored for a long time. No chemical control has been worked out.

2. Pythium rhizome rot

The disease is caused by Pythium spinosum. In this disease, the infection in the plant starts from the injured portion of the rhizomes and in later stages the rhizomes turn dirty brown in colour, the leaves become yellowish-brown and finally dry off.

The prudent selection of rhizomes from the healthy crop and dipping the rhizomes in fungicidal solutions like Benlate, Bavistin or Dithane Z-78 has been recommended to control the disease.

3. Leaf blight

It is caused by Curvularia paradisii. It is very severe from July to September. The symptoms develop on the leaf laminae as small, spherical to irregular spots, light-brown in colour, and in the advanced stages they become dark-brown. The upward curling of young leaves is very common. In the advanced stages, all the leaves fall off, leaving bare stems in the field. This pathogen can be effectively controlled by spraying 0.3% Dithane M-45 at fortnightly intervals.

Harvesting and Yield

It is observed that the diosgenin content is maximum when the crop is in an active stage of vegetative growth, and when it is about 16-17 months old. Two operations, viz. harvesting the aerial shoots and digging out the rhizomes, are required to complete the harvesting in costus. After harvesting the aerial shoots the most satisfactory and economical method of dig out the rhizomes is to run the tractor-drawn cultivator cross-wise twice or thrice over the field and simultaneously collect the uprooted rhizomes manually. A negligible amount of damage is caused to the rhizomes during this operation. The harvested rhizomes are spread out for a few day and the mud adhering to the rhizomes is removed or alternatively the rhizomes are washed under a jet of water from the tubewell discharge pipe.

The rhizomes have to be chopped and dried before the diosgenin can be extracted. Hand-chopping is time-consuming and costly so chopping by mechanical means is employed. Several methods have been tried, but the ordinary wheat thresher with a little modification is found satisfactory for chopping the fresh rhizomes. Very finely chopped material dries quickly

(2-3 days).

A yield of 28 to 30 t/ha of fresh rhizomes may be obtained in the 1st season's crop (8-9 mongs) harvested in the dormant season, but the diosgenin yield will be poor on account of low recovery. the crop should therefore, be harvested after 17-19 months of planting for a better yield of fresh rhizomes and diosgenin content. From the second season's crop (17-19 months), there is a yield of 50 tonnes of fresh rhizomes from which 75-125 kg of crude diosgenin may be obtained.

Chapter 8

COWHEDGE

English name	:	Common Cowhedge
Indian name	:	Atmagupta, Kapikacchuh (Sanskrit) Gonca, Kaunc Kivacc (Hindi) Turachi Avare Nasugunnikayi (Kannada) Punaikkali Punaippidukkan (Tamil)
Distribution	:	India, Andaman and Nicobar Islands Sri Lanka
Uses	:	Drugs

Mucuna pruriens (L) DC(=Syn. M.prurita Hook), commonly called cowhedge, is an annual, herbaceous climber belonging to the family Leguminceae. The black-seeded variety of this plant contains L-DOPA [L-3,4 digydroxy phenylalanine] which is a non-protein amino acid and the aklaloids mucunine and mucunadine. The seeds also contain glutathione, mulhingallic acid, a number of alkaloids including nicothine, prurienine, prurienidine and five bases designated as P, Q, R, S and Y. The seed-kernel oil contains sitosterol and lecithin. Biotransformation of L-tyrosine to DOPA has been shown in suspension cultures. Besides 5-hydroxyptamine and a proteolytic enzyme-mucanin are present. This crop is gaining commercial importance because L-DOPA at 60 g/day in 3-4 divided doses is an anti-Parkinsonian and hypertensive drug. The percentage of this chemical on a crude-weight basis is about 4% and in crystalline form 2 to 2.5%. In addition, the seeds have fats, sterols, alkaloids and other amino acid. The plant is said to have antidiabetic properties also. The seeds are astringent, nutritive and have shown hypoglycaemic activity in albino rats. They are also used as an aphrodisiac, as a nervine tonic in scorpion stings, for leucorrhoea, spermatorrhoea and menstrual disordes. Generally the seeds are given as a powder in doses of 30-40 g or in the from of a decoction. The roots are pungent stimulant, diuretic purgative and tonic. They are recommended for diseses of the nervous system such as facial paralysis etc. An ointment made from the the root is used for the treatment of elephantiasis. Besides, the roots are prescribed in fever powdered and made into a paste and applied to the body in dropsy a strong mixed with honey is given for cholera also.

Distribution

In India 14 species are found in the foothills of the Himalayas, the plains of West Bengal, Madhya Pradesh, Karnataka, Kerala, Andhra Pradesh, Uttar Pradesh the Andaman and Nicobar Islands and Sri Lanka. Amongst these M. pachylobia and M. utilis are cultivated for their young leaves and pods which are used as a fodder and a vegetable, respectively.

Plant Description

Mucuna is an annual climber. The leaves are pubescent, 3-foliate. Its flowers are 2.5 - 3.7 cm long, purple coloured and are borne in racemes. The fruit is a pod, 10-12 cm long, covered with brown to grey stinging hairs. The seeds are 5-6 mm in size, small, white, black or mottled and number 4-6 in each pod.

Soil

The crop can be grown on a wide range of soils, but well-drained sandy to clayey loam soils are best suited.

Climate

This plant can withstand drought and can be grown in tropical and subtropical climates. Under favourable conditions, the plant grows vigorously. It is sensitive to frost and should not be grown in frostprone areas.

Season

The crop can be grown both under rainfed and irrigated conditions. The rainfed crop is sown in June with the onset of the monsoon and the final harvesting is done in December. As am irrigated crop it can be grown throughout the year. But the best season for sowing the crop is August and the harvesting of this crop is usually done in January-February.

Land Preparation

The field is ploughed well 2-3 times and brought to a fine tilth. About 10 t/ha of FYM is applied to the soil at the time of the last ploughing. Finally, ridges are made along the contours with a spacing of 60 cm between the ridges.

Caltivation

Propagation

The plant is propagated by the direct sowing of seeds. About 50 kg of seeds are required for sowing one hectare of land.

Sowing

The seeds are sown on the inner sides of the ridges (opened at every 60 cm) 60 cm apart, provided that support is given to the plants. If support is not given to individual plants the seeds can be sown 45 cm apart in 60 cm rows. A basal irrigation may be given before sowing. The seeds germinate in about 7-10 days after sowing.

Fertilizer Application

The crop should be supplied with 100 kg N, 80 kg P and 40 kg K/ha. Phosphorus is applied as a basal dose along with FYM. The entire quantities of N and K are applied in two equal, split doses when the crop is 30 and 60 days old.

Staking of Plants

Mucuna is a twining annual, hence artificial supports are provided to the vines to get the best yields. Each vine can be supported with sticks 150 - 180 cm high or tied to an overhead trellis (similar to the type used in Dioscorea) by gunny twines. This method, however, is expensive.The choice of material for the support depends upon the materials available and the cost. Sticks or parts of shrubs will also serve the purpose.

Irrigation

For an irrigated crop, before sowing, a basal irrigation should be given. A second irrigation should be given after the germination of the seeds. Further, the crop is to be irrigated after each top-dressing of fertilizers. The crop needs about 4-6 irrigations from November to December at intervals of 20-25 days. Sometimes, maize or jowar are grown as an intercrop.

Pests and Diseases

No serious incidence of pests or diseases has been reported in this crop except towards the end of the season. At that time, occasionally leaf eating insects and Cercospora leaf spot are noticed. The crop can be protected from these insects and diseases by two sprays of Malathion at 2 ml along with the Dithane M-45 at 1.5 g/l at 30 days of growth and another at 90 days of growth.

Harvesting and Yield

The plants start flowering after about 45 days growth. Flowering in this crop is continuous and pods mature periodically. Hence, the dry pods are harvested 3 to 4 times in the season. The pods are sun-dried after harvest. Due to the sun-drying, the pods will break open. Then, the seeds are separated from the husk by winnowing.

Under rainfed conditions, if the crop is left on the ground without staking the plants a seed yield of 1 500–1 750 kg/ha can be expected. Whereas, under the same conditions, if staking is provided to the crop a seed yield of 3 000–3 750 kg/ha can be obtained. In irrigated crops with proper staking the seed yield will be around 5 000 kg/ha.

Chapter 9

DATURA

English name	:	Thorn apple
Indian name	:	Dhatturah, Dhusturah (Sanskrit) Dhattura, Kaladhattura (Hindi) Ummatti (Kannada) Ummattai (Tamil)
Distribution	:	India, Africa, Asia, Europe, Mexico, South America, USA
Uses	:	Drugs

The genus Datura, belonging to the family Solanaceae, consists of annual or perennial herbs, shrubs and trees growing mostly in the warmer parts of the world. Out of the 15 species reported from the world, 10 species are found in India. Some of them like Datura stramonium and D. innoxia are weeds. They are narcotic, poisonous when used in large doses, and medicinal in small doses.

Some of the Datura species contain alkaloids, rich in scopolamine, hyoscyamine and metaloidin. Out of the 10 species reported in India, 3 species, namely, D. stramonium, D. innoxia and D. metal, are important drug plants.

1. DATURA STRAMONIUM L. SYN. D. TATALA L. (JIMSON WEED) STINK WEED, MAD APPLE, THORN APPLE, STREMONIUM

Origin and Distribution

It is believed to be a native of South America and is found growing on the hills throughout India up to an altitude of 2 400 m. It is a common weed in many parts of the world. This crop is commercially cultivated in the USA and Europe with a view to obtain a drug of uniform potency. In India it is cultivated in the hills of Uttar Pradesh, Himachal Pradesh, the Kashmir Valley and some parts of Karnataka.

Description of the Species

It is a glabrous or farinose annual, usually 90 cm high, but attaining a height of 180 cm or more in rich soils. The stem is erect with spreading branches. The leaves are pale-green, ovate or triangularovate 12.5-15 cm long and irregularly toothed. The flowers are large, 7.5 to 20 cm long, white or violet, the capsule is erect, 7 x 3.5 cm, ovoid, thickly covered with sharp spines and dehiscing into 4 valves. The seeds are numerous and reniform. Its chromosome number is 2n=12 and it is a diploid.

Parts of Economic Importance

The leaves and flowering tops are important. The roots, fruits and seeds also contain alkaloids.

Uses

Stramonium is obtained from the dried leaves and flowering tops of D. stramonium. It has a characteristic disagreeable odour and a bitter, unpleasant taste. Stramonium contains 0.3 to 0.5% of tropane alkaloids, chiefly hyoscyamine and small quantities of atropine and scopolamine (hyoscine).

Stramonium is a narcotic, an antispasmodic and anodyme and is used chiefly to relieve the spasms of bronchitis or asthma. The leaves may be made into cigarettes or smoked in a pipe, with or without tobacco, to relieve asthma. They are also used in the treatment of Parkinson's disease. The alkaloid content of different parts of D. stramonium is as follows.

Leaves	Stem	Roots	Fruits	Seeds
0.41-0.45%	0.25%-0.26%	0.21%	0.46%	0.19%

II. DATURA INNOXIA. MILL. SYN. D. METEL AVETT (2N=24)

Distribution & Origin

It is a native of Mexico, and is also found growing in the Western Himalayas, the hilly regions of the Western parts of the Deccan Peninsula, and a few other places in India. D. innoxia and D. metel are found mainly distributed in the states of Punjab, Haryana, Rajasthan, Gujarat, Andhra Pradesh, Maharastra, Karnataka and Tamil Nadu.

Species Description

It is a coarse bushy annual attaining a height of 90–120 cm. The leaves are dark-green, ovate, often somewhat cardate, about 12.5 cm long and 7.5 cm broad. The flowers are white and fragrant; about 7.5 cm long. The furits are ovate, conical, about 5.0 cm long and 3.75 cm in diameter, opening at the top into 4 valve-like forms, exposing a long central column bearing numerous light-brown seeds and emits a heavy, narcotic odour.

Parts of Economic Importance

All plant parts, i.e., leaves, flowering tops, fruits and seeds, contain the alkaloid.

Uses

In is used in India for the same purposes as D. stramonium. It is of interest as a possible source of the alkaloid, scopolamine, which is used as a pre-anaesthetic in surgery and childbirth, in opthalmology, and for the prevention of motion sickness in the form the of its salt, hyoscine hydrobromide.

The alkaloid content of the different parts of this species is as follows.

Leaves	Stem	Roots	Fruits	Seeds
0.25%	0.3%	0.39%	0.12%	0.23-0.25% (0.2-0.35%)

III. DATURA METEL L. SYN. D. FASTEROSA L. D. ALBA NUS, D. FASTEROSA VAR. ALBA NUS, DEVILS TRUMPET, BLACK DATURA

Distribution and Origin

It is a native of Asia or Africa. It occurs throughout India and is occasionlly grown in gardents.

Description of the Species

It is a subglabrous, spreading herb sometimes becoming shrubby. The leaves are triangular-ovate in outline and unequal at the base. The flowers are 17.5 cm long, often double or triple, white, violet, reddish-purple or purple on the outside and white within. The fruits are globose, tuberculate or muricate; borne on a short thick peduncle, the capsule dehisces irregularly exposing a mass of closely-packed, light-brown, flat seeds, which nearly fill the interior.

Parts of Economic Importance

All the plant parts contain the alkaloid.

Uses

Used for the same purposes as D. innoxia and D. stramonium.

The alkaloid content of the different parts of this species is as follows.

Leaves and Stem	Roots	Fruits
0.12%	0.10%	0.20%

Varieties

Two improved varieties of D. metel have been evolved by RRL Jammu. They are :

a) PRL-Purple

This is a early flowering type and the entire plant is purple with dark-green leaves. The yield is about 240-290 q of green herb and 18-24 q/ha of seeds. The alkaloid content varies from 0.24 to 0.36% in the leaves and 0.12 to 0.19% in the seeds.

b) RRL Green

A late maturing type, the entire plant is green with light-green leaves. The yield is 210 q of green herb and 1 500-2 000 q/ha of seeds. The alkaloid content varies from 0.24 to 0.28% in the leaves and 0.098 to 0.128% in the seeds.

Soil

Daturas can be grown on a variety of soils but prefer rich alkaline or neutral, clay, loamy soil or those tending to saline-alkaline reaction, rich in organic matter, for their successful growth and yield. Clayey, acidic and/or water-logged soils do not suit this crop.

Climate

Datura is grown in the warmer parts of the world. It can be grown up to an altitude of 2 400 m. The plant is sensitive to frcst and sheltered situations. Open areas with bright sunshine are, therefore, preferred for their cultivation. In the plains, the plant cannot withstand high rainfall or high temperature. Locations with an annual rainfall of 100 cm and a temperature range between 10-15^{0} C in winter and 27-28^{0} C in May-June are ideal for its cultivation.

Season of Sowing

i) D. innoxia is grown as a winter or spring crop and the seeds are sown in October or in late Jaunary, respectively.

ii) D. metel is grown as summer crop and the seeds are sown in March.

iii) D. stramonium is grown in temperate areas like the Kashmir Valley. The seeds are sown in March-April and in November in the North Indian plains. The seedlings are transplanted to the field in May-June in terperature areas and in November-December in subtropical areas.

Land Preparation

The land in ploughed 2-3 times followed by planking. Weeds and stubble are removed and FYM with a basal dose of fertilizers is incorporated into the soil during the land preparation.

Cultivation of Datura Species

Propagation

Daturas can be grown directly through seeds or by transplanting nursery-grown seedlings.

Nursery Raising

The nursery-beds are prepared by mixing well-rotted FYM into the beds. The seeds are sown by the broadcast method on the beds and covered with a layer of sand and FYM. The beds are kept moist by spraying water. About 2 kg of seeds are required to raise seedlings for planting one hectare.

Problem of Seed Germination

The germination of datura seeds is low and irregular due to the presence of an inhibitor. Seed germination can be enhanced by soaking the seeds overnight in water and washing them repeatedly 2 to 3 times with fresh water before sowing. The seed germination can also be hastened by alternate exposure to freezing and thawing. This treatment makes the seed coat weaker.

Direct Sowing

The seeds are sown in rows 45-60 cm apart and covered with soil. About 7-8 kg of seeds are sufficient of sowing one hectare. The seeds start germinating within a fortnight and in a month's time the germination is complete. Weeding and thinning is done when plants are 10-12 cm high, keeping a plant-to-plant distance of 30-45 cm within the rows.

Transplanting

In the case of the crops raised by transplanting, the seedlings are transplanted when they are 8-12 cm tall and possess four leaves, at a distance of 30-45 cm in rows which are 45-60 cm apart. A spacing of 75x75 cm is recommended for obtaining higher yield and alkaloid content of seeds, for the crop planted in December and January.

Manures and Fertilizers

Daturas respond very well to the application of manures and fertilizers. In a study conducted at the University of Agricultural Sciences, Bangalore, it was found that the application of 10 tonnes of FYM along with 60-90 kg of N, 30-40 kg of P_2O_5 and 40-50 kg of K_2O are optimum for obtaining higher herbage and alkaloid yield in D. stramonium. A half-dose of nitrogen and the full dose of phosphorus and potash are applied at transplanting, and the remaing half-dose of nitrogen can be given after two months of transplanting. For D. innoxia, the application of FYM @ 2 t/ha before sowing planting, 80 kg N and 90 kg P_2 O_5/ha during the vegetative growth is recommended. Phosphorus applied at the time of sowing is also reported to give better yields. The alkaloid content is reported to be affected by micronutrients.

Irrigation

The first irrigation is arranged immediately after the sowing or transplanting, if there are no rains. The subsequent irrigations may be given at intervals of 8-10 days depending upon the weather conditions, till the final harvest.

Weeding and Hoeing

The first weeding and hoeing are done when the plants attain 10-12 cm height, i.e., about one month after transplanting, and the second hoeing and weeding are done after two months.

Chemical Weed Control

Dimid (diphenamid) @ 5 kg/ha applied a few days before the crop emergence, provides effective weed control and improves crop growth and yield.

Pests and Diseases

Pests

No major pests have been reported on this crop in India. However, thrips act as vectors in transmitting the mosaic virus, which can be controlled by spraying a suitable insecticide like Metasystox (1.5 ml/lit).

Dieseases

In India, the plant is very hardy and is not affected by any serious disease. However, some of the important diseases observed elsewhere are :

i) Wilt

This disease is caused by Sclerotium rolfsii. Infested plants show initial symptoms of drooping leaves and finally wilting of the entire plant. The characteristic browning and rotting has been observed in the roots and the collar region of the infested plants. No control measure is suggested for this disease. However, field sanitation and crop rotation are recommended.

ii) Root and foot-rot

The causal organism for this disease is Corticium solani. Seedlings show symptoms of damping-off and the plants are killed within few days in the nursery. In mature plants, the leaves become yellow and there is drooping of apical parts. The infested portion at the soil surface becomes dirty brown in colour and the tissues get separated from the bark. Young seedlings can be saved by drenching them with a solution of copper funigicide (0.3%) in the nursary.

iii) Leaf spot

This disease is casused by Alternaria tennuissima in D. metel and D. innoxia. The disease begins with the characteristic dark-brown spots of various sizes, which are round to oval and sometimes irregular i shape. The spots gradually enlarge with concentric rings and become necrotic at later stages, which leads to the withering and drooping of the leaves. No control measure has been worked out for this disease, on this crop.

iv) Viral diseases

Several viral diseases like Distortion mosaic, Enation mosaic, Rugose leaf curl, Little leaf and Mosaic have been reported under this group of crops. Some of the control measures recommended to control them are : uprooting the affected plants from the nursery as well as from the main field, the use of seeds from disease-free fields and control of vectors like thrips (mosaic virus) and plant hopper (rugose leaf curl) by spraying any suitable insecticide.

Harvesting and Yield

1. D. stramonium

The crop is ready for harvest 6-7 months after sowing. While harvesting the entire plant is cut when the fruits are mature but green, and partially dried in the sun or in the shade. The leaves are stripped and separately dried. The seeds are shaken off from the capsules when the fruits begin to burst. An output of 11.2-17 q/

ha of leaves and 8 g/ha of seeds may be expected.

2. D. innoxia

In India, this species is grown for its seeds. The crop is ready 6-8 months after sowing for the final harvest. Plantations raised in winter (October) and spring (late January) start flowering by the middle of February and by the beginning of April, respectively (5 months after sowing). The time required for the fruits to muture is one month after flowering. Fully-grown fruits, when still green, are plucked by hand 2-3 times before the final harvest which is done by cutting the whole plant with a sickle from the base, by the end of May in the former case and by the end of June in the latter case (approximately 8 months after sowing in case of the winter-sown crop and 6 months in the case of the spring-sown crop).

The harvested fruits are spread out under the sun until they open. The open fruits are threshed with a stick to separate the seeds, which are dried in the sun and packed in gunny bags when fully dried. A yield of 1 200-1 700 kg/ha of dried seeds is obtained, with an alkaloid content varying from 0.2 to 0.35%.

3. These plants attain optimum vegetative growth as well as the highest percentage of alkaloids by July (5 months after sowing), when the first harvest is taken. All the tender branches along with the leaves are cut. The herbage is dried in the shade immediately. The harvested plants regenerate and two more harvests are taken, with a second harvest in late August and a third harvest in October. In the last harvest plants can be cut from the base, if a ratoon crop is not desired. Besides foliage, a sizeable number of fruits are also harvested as and when they ripen. A yield of 240-290 q/ha of green herb and 18-24 q/ha of seeds is obtained from the variety RRL purple and a yield of 210 q/ha of green herb and 15-20 q/ha of seeds can be obtained from the variety, RRL-Green.

Chapter 10

DIGITALIS

Family	:	Scrophulariaceae
English name	:	Foxglove
Indian name	:	Tilpushpi (Sanskrit)
Species and	:	Datura Purpurea varieties D. lanata Ehrh.
Distribution	:	India the British Islands, Canada Western Europen France Germany Hungary Mexico UK,USA and some Asian countries
Uses	:	Drugs

Digitalis commonly known as Foxglove, belongs to the family Scrophulariaceae. There are many species under the genus Digitalis of which D. purpurea L and D. lanata Ehrh. are the most important for their glycoside content, used in life-saving medicines. The leaves of the recommended varieties are a rich source of digitoxin, an active cardiac glycoside. Besides the leaves also contain digitoxin and gitoxin. Other important glycosides are digitoxigenin glucodigitoxigenin-bis-digitotoxoside glucogitaloxigein-bisdigitoxoside, glucovatromonoside, glucogitoroside, glucolanadoxin varadoxin, stropeside and anthraquinone. Digitalis is used mainly for its effect on the cardiovascular system, i.e. increasing the force of systolic contractions and the efficiency of a decompensated heart. It is used as a myocardial stimulant in congested heart failure, auricular flutter and rapid auricular fibrillation. In the case of burns, it is more selective in preserving the cells severely injured by heat.

Presently, the major portion of the raw material required by leading pharmaceutical industries in India is being met by imports. The price of digitoxin amounts to crores of rupees. In view of the importance of the crop for its glycoside content, improved cultivation practices have been developed through a series of experiments conducted at Solan and Kodaikanal.

Origin and Distribution

Digitalis is a native of Western Europe the British Islands and the erstwhile USSR countries. The crop is being cultivated in France, Germany, UK, Hungary, USA and other Asian countries over centuries for medicinal purposes. It has been introduced as an ornamental plants throughout North America, Canada, Mexico Central America and Asia.

The northern states like Jammu and Kashmir, Himachal Pradesh and the hilly and elevated areas in South India have vast potential to produce a sufficient quantity of leaves and seeds to meet the demands of the pharmaceutical industries in the country.

Description of the Plant

Digitalis (2n=56) is a family of herbaceous, erect, branched biennials attaining a height of 60-90 cm in nature. The leaves are simple, exstipulate, alternate, opposite or whorled. The flowers are zygomorphic, bilipped, pentamerous, hypogynous and bisexual with 4-5 partite bracts. The sepals are gamosepalous and lobed, there are 4 petals which are gamopetalous, bilipped, sometimes spurred and with imbricate aestivation. There are 2-4 stamens. The anthers are bithecate, hairy, dehiscing by longitudinal slits and epipetalous. The ovary is bicarpellary, syncarpous, superior with many ovules and a single or bilobed style. The stigma is bilobed and the fruit is a capsule. Digitails is a insect-pollinated plant, bees being the main pollinators.

Varieties

The strain E.C. 115996 has been reported to give a higher foliage yield with high glycoside content. This parent material has been used in crossing and selection amongst progenies to identify a few promising selections, namely D-76 D-21 DYF and DPF, which have consistently given higher yields over the years.

Soil

Foxglove requires a well-drained, sandy loam soil, rich in organic matter. III-drained and water-logged conditions are detrimental to the crop. Clay and sandy soils are also harmful. While-lime rich soils are essential for proper growth and glycoside content in the leaves of D. lanata it is harmful for D. purpurea which requires acidic soils.

Climate

The crop prefers a warm climate. The two important species, viz. D. purpurea and D. lanata, that are suitable and promoted for commerical cultivation in India, perform best in a temperature ranging between 20^0 C and 30^0 C. The growth and development of the plants as well as the content of their active principles is maximum; furthermore, the seed germination is best in this temperature range. For the luxuriant growth of the crop, well-distributed rainfall and good sunshine during winter are ideal. It is found growing successfully up to an altitude of 200 m above mean sea-level (MSL).

Season

The time of planting is very critical for this crop. The best planting period is mid-April in cooler regions like Solan (Himachal Pradesh) and the second fortnight of July at Kodaikanal (Tamil Nadu). Planting in August in the other hilly regions with a higher elevation in South India, registered a higher yield of leaves and glycoside content.

Land Preparation

As the crop is a biennial, the field preparation should be thorought. Plough the land 4 to 5 times using a disk and harrow, remove the weeds and bring the soil to a fine tilth. Incorporate the FYM during the final ploughing for thorough mixing with the soil. Divide the field into plots of convenient size (2 to 3 sq m) distributing the water evenly.

Cultivation

Propagation

Digitalis is propagated from seeds, either by direct seeding (linesowing/ broadcasting), or by first raising the seedlings in a nursery and then transplanting them.

Seed Material

Seeds produced in the Solan and Chamba distrits (H.P) are the best for the successful cultivation of this crop in India. About 1 500 seeds weigh one gram. Fresh seeds should be used for sowing, since the seeds lose viability after two years of harvesting. The seed should be presprouted to hasten germination by soaking them in water and incubating them at about 30° C for 2 to 3 days. About 5-8 kg of seed is required for directly seeding one hectare, while for nursery raising just 1 to 2 kg of seeds will suffice.

Direct Sowing

The field, thus prepared, can be used for direct seeding by linesowing at a depth of not more than 2 cm to avoid failure of seed germination. A spacing of 45 cm between rows and 30 cm between plants in a row are maintained in both methods of planting.

Nursery Raising and Transplanting

Raised nursery-beds (10-12 numbers) of the dimension: 3 m long, 1 m wide and 10 cm high are prepared. The soil for the nursery beds is enriched by organic matter. To each bed, 3 to 4 basketfuls of welldecomposed FYM is incorporated and the land is brought to a fine tilth. The seeds are sown in lines 4-6 cm apart; the surface of the bed is covered with a 1 cm layer of sand. The beds are irrigated lightly every evening with rose-fitted cans. The seeds germinate in 15-20 days and the seedlings will be ready for transplanting about 35 to 45 days after sowing, when they have attained a height of 8-10 cm.

The field is kept ready by preparing ridges and furrows at a 45-60 distance. When the seedlings attain a height of 8-10 cm (35 to 45 days after sowing) they are transplanted to the main field at a spacing of 30 cm apart, in rows.

Manures and Fertilizers

FYM is applied at the time of land preparation while fertilizers are applied in the furrows and incorporated in the soil thoroughly immediately after transplanting. The application of 40-60 tonnes of well-decomposed FYM along with 100-150 kg N, 50 kg P_2O_5 and 25-30 kg K_2O is the optimum. One-fourth of the nitrogen supplemented in the form of calcium ammonium nitrate, along with a full dose of P and K should be applied at the time of planting. The remaining N is applied in 3 split doses, i.e. first top-dressing at 60 days after transplanting, the second and thrid dose is applied at 1 1/2 to 2 month intervals thereafter. The application of N, P and K is repeated following the above schedule during the second year also. The glycoside content has been found to increase by application of trace elements like molybdenum and magnesium.

Irrigation

During summer (April, June and July), the crop is watered at an interval of 7 to 10 days, then 2 to 3 irrigations will be sufficient each month until the dormant period which sets in by November. The first harvest is done just before that. Then one or two irrigations a month will be required till the new leaves are formed. Weekly irrigations are recommended till the leaves mature. However, during the monsoon watering can be suspended as there will be sufficient precipitation to take care of the crop.

Interculture and Weeding

Weeds, by competing for light, moisture and nutrients and also acting as host for many diseases and pests cause a drastic reduction in leaf yield. Hence, the crop must be kept completely free of weeds by either chemical or manual weeding. During the rainy season, handweeding is preferred. During summer as well as after each harvest hoeing should be attended to. At least two hoeings before the first harvest and another afterwards are important.

Pests and Diseases

The occurrence of insect pests is not serious. Leaf blight caused by Alternaria spp. is a common disease of foxglove. Brown spots appear on the leaves, which enlarge, covering the entire leaf surface and killing the foilage in a few days. Spraying any copper fungicide at the rate of 0.1 to 0.2% effectively controls this disease.

Occasionally, there is an occurrence of curly top, a mosaic and a broad-bean wilt virus. In addition to the chemical control, destroy the alternate hosts and control the vectors in the vicinity. The affected digitalis plants should be pulled out and destroyed.

The other diseases of this crop reported from Europe are antheracnose caused by the fungus Collitotichum fuscus two types of leaf spots: one caused by Septoria digitalis and the other by Phyllosticta digitalis, and crown rot caused by Botrytis cineria.

Harvesting of Leaves

While harvesting leaves, attention has to be paid to aspects like the age of the leaves, the time of the day and the length of the leaves. These points are important with respect to the glycoside content. The cardio-activity of the leaves is higher in species like D. purpurea and D. lanata, when the leaves are harvested during the hotter part of the day. The glycoside content in the leaves is highest around midday and the lowest at midnight, since the glucoside, quickly disintegrates in the dark. The leaves are well developed when they attain 8-10 cm length and are ready for the first harvest about 5 months after planting. The subsequent harvests will be at a 1½ to 2 months. Interval thin, afterwards, during the first year of the crop. The plants undergo dormancy after the last harvest. In the second year, the crop can give two harvests, besides seed production. The first harvest of leaves in the second year will be in March-April approximately about 3 to 4 months after the 1st harvest of the previous year. The final harvest will be about 2 months later. Although the crop is biennial and the leaves are potential glucoside yielders during both the years, it is suggested that the crop is grown as an annual for leaf production, unless meant for seed production in which case it can be grown as a biennial.

Processing of Leaves

Drying and storing the leaves are the other important activities. Great care should be exercised to prevent the loss of the active ingredients. In hotter regions, the drying process is easy and economical, as natural solar energy can be utilized for drying by spreading the leaves in layers on clean yards and turning them over occasionally to obtain a minimum moisture content. This may take 2 to 3 days on hot days. The alternate method is dehydration, by passing hot air at 50-60° C over the leaves and upturning them. This process should, however, be at the appropriate temperature and with the minimum timelag. Fermentation of leaves during drying should be avoided by turning the leaves occasionally and exposing them to the heat source, otherwise, enzymatic activity leads to the deterioration of glycosides. Higher temperatures beyond 70° C will also lead to a loss of active ingredients.

Storing the leaves after drying is yet another factor to take into account for carefully preserving the glycosides. The dried leaves should be stored in airtight containers like polythene bags with some dehydrating substance such as silica gel or activated alumina. The bags should be kept in a cool and dry place.

Yield of Leaves and Glycoside

The variety, EC 115996, gives a higher glycoside content of 0.65-1.20% It gives a higher foliage yield of 15 t/ha on a fresh-weight basis and about 3 tonnes on dry-weight basis.

Estimation of Total Glycosides in Leaves

For this purpose, 5 g of powdered dry sample of Digitalis leaves is taken and added to 80 ml of alcohol (20%) shaken for 6 hours and filtered. The residus is again extracted two times, each time using 80 ml of alcohol (20%) and with chloroform (20 ml x 5) in a separating funnel. All the chloroform extracts (lower layers) are combined, transferred to a conical flask and dried over anhydrous Na_2SO_4 the Chloro from layer is decanted into a R.B. Flask Na_2SO_4 is washed with chloroform (15 ml x 3) and the washings are added to the main chloroform bulk and the chloroform is evaporated to dryness. The dried residue is dissolved in a mixture of $CHCl_3$: MeOH @ 1:1 and filtered the filtrate is evaporated to dryness over a water-bath on a weighed watch-glass and the residue weighed as the total glycoside content.

Chapter 11

DIOSCOREA

English name	:	Greater yam Asiatic yam
Indian name	:	Alukam (Sanskrit) Chupri alu, Khamalu (Hindi) Perumvallikilanku Kappan Kaccil (Tamil)
Distribution	:	India Africa, Asia Europe Mexico South America, USA
Uses	:	Drugs

Steroidal drugs alone constitute about 6% of the total production of pharmaceuticals. They are one of the costliest and most important medicines used throughout the world. Because of their antifertility propertis, they have gained tremendous importance in the health and family planning programmes of the developing countries. Diosgenin, a steroidal sapogenin obtained from the rhizomes of various species of Dioscorea (Family : Diascoreaceae) is the major base chemical for several steroid hormones including sex hormones, cortisones, other corticosteroids and the active ingredient in the oral contraceptive pill. The other important sapogenins found are yamogenin, botogenin and kryptogenin. Minor sapogenins like pannogenin and tigogenin are also found in certain cases. It is estimated that the world production of diosgenin is 1 000 tonnes and of other precursors is 1 200 tonnes.

Botany

Plants of the genus Dioscorea, commonly called medicinal yams, are perennial, climbing herbs with tubers or rhizomes. Approximately 600 species have been reported to occur throughout the world, mostly in tropical and subtropical regions and to a limited extent, in temperate regions also. Of these, only 15 species are known to contain steroidal sapogenins, chiefly Diosgenin. Out of the various species tested D Composita Hemsl. and D.

Floribunda Mart and Gal. found growing wild in Central America and D. Deltoidea Wall, found in the North-western Himalayas are the main species from which diosgenin is extracted commercially. All the three species are dioecious.

Species and Varieties

1. D. deltoidea Wall (2n=20)

It is an indigenous species found growing wild in the North-western Himalayas. It produces very slender vines and is very weak. It is propagated by tuber pieces but tthe regeneration of tubers is so slow that it takes about 7-10 years to fully develop even in its natural habitat of temperate regions. Hence,s the cultivation of this species on a commercial scale is not attractive to farmers.

2. D floribunda Mart and Gal. (2n=36)

It is a native of Mexico (Central America) and is grown in Karnataka, Goa, Assam, Meghalaya and the Andaman Islands. This species can be very easily propagated from tuber pieces and seeds. The plants is dioecious in nature, a robust climber twining to the left. The branches are thick and it produces yellow, compact tubers at a shallow depth. The leaves are petiolate and spirally disposed on the stem. The male flowers are solitary or in groups of 2-3 dark-brown or green and sessile with 6 stamens. The male spike is short and solitary, with 6 staminodes and a hypogymous stigma with a bifid apex (divided into two). The diosgenin content varies from 2-7% depending upon the age of the tubers. The seeds germinate within 3-4 weeks and produce vigorous seedlings that establish well in the field.

Three varieties of D. floribunda have been released for cultivation. The varieties FB(C)-1 strain and Arka Upkar were released from the Indian Institute of Horticultural Research (IIHR) Bangalore, while Pusa-1 by the Indian Agricultural Research Institute (ICAR) New Delhi. These three varieties adapt well to tropical and subtropical regions. The salient features of these varieties are as follows.

FB (C) 1

This is a composite strain from introduced clonal material from Central America. The plants are vigorous and relatively free from pests and diseases. The tuber yields is 20 000-25 000 kg/yr (1 kg/plant) or 60 000 kg for a 2-year old crop (2.5 kg/plant). The diosgenin content of the dired roots varies from 2.5 to 3%.

Arka Upkar

A high yielding clonal selection from FB (C)-1 with intense darkgreen leaves and a vigorous growth. The tuber yield exceeds 6 000 kg (in a 2-year-old crop) and the diosgenin content ranges from 3.5 to 4.0%.

Pusa-1

A selection from germplasm with a tuber yield of 1.5 kg/vine after 18 months.

3. D. composita Hemsl. (2n=36)

This species is also a native of Mexico and has been domesticated in several tropical countries. It is a robust climber, twining to the left, which produces large thick leaves. The underground protion comprises of thick, fleshy branching tubers which are long, white in colour and grow deep. This species is mostly propagated from seeds rather than from tubers, as the rotting of tubers is pronounced.

Other important sapogenin-bearing species are D. friedrichsthali R.Kunth D. spiculiflora Hemsl, and D. prazeri. Prain and Burk.

Soil

Dioscorea can be grown in several types of soils. Light or sandy soils require heavy irrigation and fertilization, whereas heavy clay soils restrict tuber growth and harvest and often create water-logging. The best yields are obtained in medium loam and in deep soils which are rich in organic matter. In red soils, the best growth has been observed for both D. floribunda and D. composita. It tolerates wide variation in soil pH but highly acidic and highly alkaline soils should be avoided.

Cilmate

The different species of Dioscorea are found growing in different climates, but while D. floribunda and D. composita are more suited to the tropics, D.

deltoida is reported to be a suitable species for temperate locations. It grows well in the temperate regions of Kashmir and Himachal Pradesh.

Preparation of Land and Planting

The field should be ploughed and harrowed several times, levelled properly and drainage channels should be made. Since yams have a high requirement of organic matter for good tuber formation, a sufficient quantity (20-25 t/ha) of FYM is incorporated at the time of land preparation. A spacing of 45 x 30 cm for a 1-year-old crop and 60 x 45 cm for a 2-year-old crop in D. floribunda is found to be optimum under irrigated conditions. For planting, deep furrows are made at 60 cm distance and sprouted tubers are planted in furrows at 5 cm depth. After sprouting is completed, earthing up is done, utilizing the soil from the ridges. D. compsoita and D. deltoidea are reported to give higher yields at spacings of 60 x 30 cm and 30 x 70 cm, respectively.

Cultivation

Propagation

The yams can be propagated either by seeds rhizome pieces or stem-cuttings. In India commercial plantations are raised from tuber-cuttings. Seed progeny is variable and takes a longer time to start yielding tubers, compared to plants raised from tubers. The choice of propagating material will depend on the cost of planting and the prevailing climatic conditions of the region.

a) Propagation from Tuber Pieces

This crop grows best from tuber pieces. Tubers or rhizomes are divided into approximately 50-60 g pieces for planting. The growth of plants is slow and the yield lower if smaller pieces are used for planting. There are 3 tupes of pieces (1) Crowns (stem end), (2) Medians (middle portion) and (3) Tips (distal ends). Crowns produce new shoots within 30 days of planting, while the others take nearly 100 days to sprout. Besides, the crown portion contains less diosgenin compared to the median and the tips, hence the latter can be used for the extraction of alkaloids and the former can be used for propagation. But, if there is a shortage of planting material, the median and tips can also be used for planting.

In order to avoid the rotting of tubers (before sprouting), only healthy tubers should be selected. the healthy tubers must then be dipped in benlate fungicide (0.3%) for 5 minutes followed by dusting the cut ends with 0.3% benlate powder before planting or storage.

Before planting the tubers directly in the main field, they should be stored in a moist, well-aerated rooting medium until shoot growth commences. The benlate-treated tuber pieces should be kept in raised beds in the shade, covered with sand and watered daily. After 30 days the sand may be removed and the sprouted crowns taken out and planted in the field. The median and tip portions are again covered with sand and watered regularly. Subsequently, after 60-75 days when they have completely sprouted, they can also be planted in the field.

Season of Planting

The tuber pieces can be planted either in February-March or June-July. In Karnataka, February, March planting is better. And for medians and tips it is better to plant from the middle of January because they take more time to sprout compared to the crowns. The new sprouts will grow vigorously during the rainy season which commences from June.

b) Propagation by Seeds

Propagation through seeds is much more successful in D. floribunda and D. composita, as compared to the other temperate species. The seed has a wide membranous wing that can be removed without affecting germination. The seeds can be sown either in raised beds in the shade (with a mixture of loamy soils and FYM) or in polythene bags (filled with sand soil and FYM @ 1:1:1). The planting depth should not be more than 1.25 cm and frequent watering of the beds is essential. The seeds germinate within three weeks and are ready for transplanting in 3-4 months. The seedlings should be supported immediately.

The best season for transplanting the seedlings to the field is just before the start of rains, i.e. in June in South India, but in North India this can be done at any time except during the winter.

Seed Production

Since dioscorea is a dioecious plant, female and male plants should be grown close to obtain the seeds. Under South Indian conditions, excellent seed set is noticed. Flowering starts from August and the seeds mature from December to February. The pods turn brown and dehisce along with the upper margin. The harvested seeds should be stored in airtight plastic bags where they will remain viable for 3-5 years.

c). Propagation by Stem cuttings

D. floribunda can be propagated by stem cuttings with 80% success. The vines should be raised from 50-100 g tuber pieces in the green-house. One or two month-old vines, are taken and cut into single node cuttings, each with one leaf. They are planted in sand-beds keeping the leaf blade above the sand. Before planting, the cuttings should be treated with 1 ppm 2, 4 D and 0.1% benlate for 4 hours. The beds should be watered regularly. After rooting, the cuttings are transplanted to polythene bags and produce about ten leaves in a period of two months.

Propagation of D. floribunda can also be done by air-and ground-layering. Application of NAA at 100 ppm was found to be most effective for getting 80-90% rooting.

d) In Vitro Propagation

Single node leaf cuttings of D. floribunda, when used as explants, give 100% rootings when grown in vitro. In D. deltoidea, both single nodes and apices have been successufuly used as explants for propagation. Shoot apices explants are reported to produce full fledged plants after 90-100 days. In vitro-raised single node cuttings were ready for planting in the field after 50-60 days.

Provision of Support

The vines need support for their optimum growth as this exposes the maximum number of leaves to the sunlight. The system tried successfully at Bangalore consists of 2 m-high, stone pillars spaced 9 m apart in the field. Galvanized wires (Nos. 6 and 8) are used on the boundaries and the intercnnecting wires can be of 12 gauge thickness. The vines are supported on coir ropes tied to the wires and pegged to the ground by wooden stakes.

Fertilizer Application

Yams respond very well to fertilizer application. A fertilizer dose of 300 kg N, 150 kg P and 150 kg K/ha, has been found to be optimum for a one-year old crop of D. floribunda. The entire quantity of P should be applied as a basal dose while N and K are given in four equal split doses at bimonthly intervals commencing from 2 months after sprouting. For D. deltoidea, for a 4-year-old crop the recommended fertilizers under Kashmir conditions are 40 kg N, 80 kg P_2O_5 and 60 kg KO_2 in split doses at an interval of one month from the time of planting in the first year and the same quantity in the second year. In the third year, only N at 30 kg/ha has to be applied in two split doses. For increasing the tuber yield and diosgenin content, the application of S, Ca and Mg has also been recommended.

Irrigtion

The crop needs irrigation frequently during summer months. An interval of 4 to 5 days in summer and7 to 10 days in winter is desirable for the proper growth and development of this crop and for economic yields.

Interculture

In the initial stages, yam plantations require more frequent handweeding than in the later stages. Chemical herbicides have also been tried, but are not recommended commercially. Studies have revealed that it is feasible to intercrop medicinal yam with short duration crops like cowpea, cluster beans and kidney beans where irrigation is available. This practice not only minimizes the growth of weeds but also gives additional returns. Apart from this interopping also helps in reducing the requirement of nitrogen as the crops recommended above are leguminous.

Intercropping

Cowpea, cluster beans and french beans are the recommended intercrops for Dioscorea.

Plant Protection

Pests

The two important pests affecting this crop are aphids and red spider mites which can easily be controlled by spraying 0.5 -1.0% of Kelthane (1 ml/l) or Rogor (2 ml/l). Cut-worms are also reported to damage this crop.

Diseases

No major disease has been reported to affect this crop. The only disease which affects the crop is the rotting of D. floribunda tuber pieces during storage in sand-beds. This can be controlled by treating the tubers with

0.3% benlate solution. Leaf spot disease, caused by Drechelera sorokiniana, is also reported to occur in D. composita, resulting in defoliation and death of the seedlings. The disease can be effectively controlled by spraying Benlate (0.1%). Besides, Cercospora, Remularia and late blight caused by Phytophthora infestans are reported from Tamil Nadu and can be controlled by Dithene Z-78 (0.3%) or any other copper fungicide. Collar rot of seedlings, which is a nursery disease, can be effectively controlled by spraying Brassicol (0.5%).

Duration of the Crop and Yield

The diosgenin content of the tubers tends to increase (within certain limits) with age. Studies have shown that the growing of D. floribunda as a two-year crop is economical. An average yield of 15 to 20 t/ha of fresh tubers can be obtained during the first year, and up to 40 to 50 t/ha during the second year. The diosgenin content of the tubers tends to increase, on an average, from 2.5-3.0% in the first year to 3.0-3.5% in the second year. The cost of cultivation is, however, much less during the second the second year.

Harvesting and Marketing

Experiments have shown that D. deltoidea should be harvested only after three years to get the optimum yield from the crop with the maximum diosgenin content. Similarly. D. floribunda should be kept at least for two years in the field for viable yields.

Generally, the tubers are harvested during February-March. Harvesting can be done by manual labour with pickaxes. The tubers are harvested when the plants are in a dormant condition to obtain the maximum yield of diosgenin.

In studies conducted on the effect of gamma radiation on tuber yield and diosgenin content of D. floribunda, it was found that radiation decreases the tuber yields, but the diosgenin content showed a wide range of variation. The diosgenin content in 1 2 and 3 treatments was 2.6, 3.6 and 2.8%, respectively, against 2.9% in the control.

A number of drug companies, using diosgenin as raw material, are interested in buying this crop grown on a contract basis. On the basis of the prevailing market conditions with dry tubers, a net profit of about Rs. 30 000/ha in a one-year-old crop and Rs 60 000/ha in a two-year-old crop can be obtained.

Chapter 12

DUBOISIA

English name	:	Corkwood tree
Indian name	:	Bendumăra (Kannada)
Distribution	:	India, Australia (Queensland), New Caledonia Japan, Northern and Central New South Wales
Uses	:	Drugs

Duboisia, belonging to the family Solanaceae, is a subtropical shrub endemic to the Australian region. It is commonly called the 'corkwood tree' and is represented by three species, viz.: D. myoporoides D. leichhardtii and D. hopwoodii. The leaves of the first two species are rich in hyoscine and hyoscyamine, whereas the third one contains tobacco alkaloids, nicotine and nor-nicotine. Recently, the roots of D. hopwoodii have been found to contain substantial amounts of hyoscyamine and hyoscine. Hyoscine, hyoscyamine and atropine are used extensively in medicines throughout the world because of their mydriatic, antichloinergic and antispasmodic action. Hyoscyamine and atropine are used in respiratory diseases like asthma, intestinal disorders, colic pain and peptic ulcers. Hyoscine is used for the treatment of motion sickness and asthma.

The leaves contain a complex of tropane alkaloids including hyoscine (scoplamine) hyoscyamine, nor-hyoscyamine, valeroidine tigloidine poroidine isoporoidine isopelletierine, and anabasine. The constituents vary not only with the stage of growth, but also with the geopraphical location. The total alkaloid content of the leaves has been found to vary from 2.75 to 4.90% of which hyoscyamine was 56.7% hyoscine 23.3% and other alkaloids 20.0%. On an average, the plant gives a crop containing 3% of total alkaloids.

In the wood of the young root, tropine is the principal alkaloid, with smaller amounts of vatropine, hyoscyamine and valeroidine. The root-bark possesses hyoscine, atropine, tropine and apohyoscine; while the wood of the mature roots contains hyoscyamine hyoscin, apohyscine tropine and tetramethyl putrerscine. These alkaloids and valtropine occur in the mature root-bark.

Distribution

Duboisia grows wild on the borders and open woodlands along the east coast of Queensland and Northern and central New South Wales. It is indigenous also to New Caledonia. It is commercially cultivated in Australia, mainly in the Queensland area, from where it is exported to Europen contries for further processing. It is also grown in Japan and India. Duboisia was first introduced in India at the Forest Research Institute, Dehra Dun and is being grown as a commercial crop in Karnataka, Andhra Pradesh, Madhya Pradesh and Maharastra.

Description of the Plant

D. myoporoides (2n=60) is a shrub or small tree occasionally attaining a height of 40 ft. When cut down or burnt, the plant produces numerous suckers from the roots which form dense clumps. The bark is grey, corky, fissured, and the wood is light in weight. The leaves are alternate 6-10 cm in length, petiolate, ovate-oblong to broad lanceolate, blunt-tipped and tapering at the base. the inflorescence axillary with terminal cymes, dichasial to begin with and showing a tendency to scorpioid cymes. The flowers are small, bell-shaped white or pale-lavender or lavender-streaked, pedicillate and actinomorphic. The calyx has 5 persistent sepals. The corolla has five petals, is tubula R and shows green streaks at the throat of the corolla. The androecium has 5 epipetalous stamens, the gynoecium is 2-celled with many ovules and axile placentation. The fruit is a berry 5 mm wide black and juicy when ripe, containing 5-6 seeds. The seed are small and kidney-shaped, one plant contains about 500 seeds.

D. leichhardtii (2n=60) is also a small tree or shrub reaching a height of 17ft. The leaves are generally shorter and more slender than those of D. myoporoides 5-10 cm long, oblong lanceolate or ovate, blunt-tipped, tapering at the base and entire.

The flowers are borne on terminal broad panicles, fairly leafy at the base bell-shaped with flaring, narrow long, pointed lobes, much more conspicuous than the lobes in D. myoporoides; the calyx is small, with short, broad teeth. The fruit is oval in shape, 6 mm long with 6-12 seeds which are kidney, shaped and have a pebbly surface.

Varieties

There are no varieties available in this crop. However a hybrid of D. leichhardtii and D. myoporoides has been developed. Higher alkaloid yields are observed in crosses, where the female parent is D. myoporoides.

Soil

It can be grown on a wide range of soils, but it grows best in welldraned, medium-to-light-loamy soils, with a neutral pH.

Climate

It is a subtropical plant. Hence it requires a moderate climate where the winter and summer temperatures are not severe. Areas with an avarage annual rainfall of 100 cm, well distributed rhoroughout the year, are ideal. Heavy rainfall is harmful to the crop.

Preparation of Land

Land is ploughed to a depth of 20-25 cm about 2-3 months before planting. The soil should be worked to a good tilth to eradicate weeds.

Cultivation

Propagation

Duboisia can be propagated from root-cutting, terminal shoot, cuttings and seeds. But in commercial plantations, propagation by seeds or terminal cuttings is practiced.

Raisting the Nursery

Duboisia is propagated by seeds. The seeds are usually sown from February to April. The seeds are washed to remove all the pulp and dried in the sun before being used for propagation.

They are sown in sterilized soil in nursery beds under 60% shade or seedlings can also be raised in polythene bags containing a mixture of fine sand and FYM in equal proportions @ 2 seeds/bag. Pre-treatment of seeds with gibberellic acid reportedly gives better germination. The seeds are soaked in 250 ppm gibberellic acid at about 40^{0} C for about 24 hours.

The seeds are then thoroughly washed in fresh water dried in the sun and can be used for sowing after about six weeks. The seeds sown in nursery beds or polythene begs start germinating from about the 12th day and by the 18th day about 10% of the seeds germinate. Nearly about 60% of the seeds germinate in about 40 days. Therefore it is very essential to keep watering the nursery to ensure good germination. The seedlings raised in polythene bags are thinned maintaining 1 plant/bag. The seedlings are ready for transplanting when they attain a height of about 25 cm and are 3 months old. About 250 seedlings are required for planting one hectare of land.

Transplanting

After the land is prepared, pits of 30 x 30 x 30 cm are made at 2m x 2m spacing. The soil is mixed with the recommended dose of manure and fertilizers and made ready for transplanting. Healthy seedlings are planted in each pit, taking care to see that the seedlings are planted at the same depth as in the nursery bed or polythene bag to avoid crown rot. Planting is usually done in the dry period. The field must be irrigated immediately after transplanting.

Manures and Fertilizers

At the time of land preparation FYM @ 20 t/ha may be incorporated into the soil. Prior to transplanting, 20 kg N, 40 kg P_2O_5 and 49 kg KO_2/ha should be mixed well with the soil. Subsequently N @ 20 kg/ha is given to the crop at bimonthly intervals. Manure and fertilizers are supplied to the crop in the same dosage as above during the second and subsequent years of growth.

Irrigation

Plants should be watered frequently in the initial stages. The frequency is gradually reduced and when the crop is well established irrigation once in about 15 days is sufficient during the dry period.

Interculture

Clean cultivation is a prerequisite; weeds are usually controlled mechanically. Grass-cover crops are sown after the leaf harvest.

Pests and Diseases

Pests

The major pests are the flea beetle leaf-eating ladybird beetle, brown olive scale trunk borer and green caterpillar. The crop can be sprayed with 0.2% Malathion whenever the insects are observed.

Diseases

No serious diseases have been reported in the crop. However, a viral infection causing leaf yellowing has been noticed in the plains of North India.

Harvesting and Processing

The plants are harvested after about 6 months of transplanting. The main as well as the side branches are cut at a height of about 1 m, retaining about 20% of the leaves on the plant to encourage profuse branching. Two harvests are possible during the first year, and three harvest a year can be had from the second year onwards. The plants are likely to yield well for at least five years, after which, replanting should be done.

The leaves are separated and spread out for drying in the shade which takes 2-4 weeks in warm weather, and are packed in gunny bags after drying.

Yield

The average yield of fresh leaves per harvest is about 2 kg/plant which on shade drying, reduces to about 0.5 kg. The fresh herbage yield is 10 t/ha in the first year and 15 t/ha from the second year onwards. This, on shade drying, gives about 2 tonnes of air-dried leaves in the first year and 3 tonnes from the second year onwards.

Chapter 13

FOXGLOVE

Introduction

Foxglove is a hardy herb grown in many parts of the country. Its leaves are a rich source of glycosides like digoxin, digitoxin gitoxin etc. which are cardio active. With an adoption of proper agro-techniques, high glycoside content of 0.65 - 1.20% can be extracted from the leaf cuttings. The price of digitoxin used in the international market is very high, upto Rs.22,620-kg while digoxin costs 17,267 per kg and the total cost of raw-material imported from foreign countries comes to crores of rupees. If the pharmaceutical industries take up the manufacture or extraction of these glycosides sufficient quantities of seeds and raw materials can be produced in the country, leading to a considerable saving in foreign exchange.

Scientifically it is called as Digitalis which owes its origin from a Latin word "Digitus" means finger. Due to the finger like corolla of its flowers, foxglove is named so. It is also known by several common names such as American foxglove, dead men's bells, dog's finger, fairy fingers, fairy gloves, finger flower, folk's glove. lion's mouth, ladies glove and purple fox glove.

II. Origin and Distribution

Although the medicinal value of foxglove was recognized in 18th century it is said to be in cultivation since 16th century in Europe. Hence, Europe is considered its place of its origin. It is introduced into our country as an ornamental plant and is not indigenous to India. The two important species that are found in our country are Digitalis purpurea and D. lanata.

Both the species are well distributed through out Europe. The species D. purpurea is grown in U.K., Egypt, Japan, India and North America where as D. lanata is found in U.K ,U.S.S.R ,Holland and both the species are produced commercially in Holland.

In our country the hilly regions of Northern India, such as Himachal Pardesh and Kashmir, Darjeeling in West Bengal and Nilgiri hills in Tamil nadu are the chief cultivators of these species.

III. Morphology

The botanical features of the species are described here.

A. Digitalis purpurea

The plant is biennial and rarely perennial. It is an erect herb and grows to a height of 45-150 centimeters. The stem is simple or slightly branched. The leaf arrangement is alternate and they are ovate or lanceolate to broadly ovate in shape. Normally size of the leaves is 10-40 cms long and 4-15 wide. The leaf margins are not smooth but serrated or dentate having a winged petiole.

The flowers are 5-8 cms long having multi-lobed corolla. The colour of the flowers is pinkish purple with deeper purple spots hence the name Digitalis purpurea.

B. Digitalis lanata

This species is a biennial or perennial. The leaves are alternately arranged generally 5-15 cms long and 4.5 cms wide. The leaf margin is entire and ciliate in the basal half of the leaf and becomes wavy towards the apex. The leaf surface is glabrous. The leaves are sessile (without petiole) and the stem is simple. The flowers are yellowish-white with or without purplish net work.

IV. Chemical Composition

The chemical composition of commonly cultivated species of Digitalis is mentioned here.

A. D. purpurea

The leaves contain several glycosides in relatively lower concentrations of 0.2-0.45 per cent. The principal glycoside in this species is digitoxin which is extracted commercially. Other glycosides are gitoxin gitaloxin, digitin and digitalin. Variations are seen in digitoxin content (0.15 to 0.79 g/kg) and gitoxin content (0-0.7 g/kg) from the normal concentrations. Presence of tannin,s inositol, deteolin, fatty matter and many acids are also observed. A new cardiotonic glycoside named digicorin has been isolated from leaves.

B. D. lanata

The glycosides that are present in the dried leaves Of D. lanata are called lanatosides. The concentrations of lanatosides is higher than D. purpurea which ranges from 1-1.4 per cent. The principal glycoside is digoxin and other important ones are digitoxigenin, gitoxienin and digoxigenin. These active components are less toxic than that of D. purpurea. Sugars like D digitoxose D-glucose and D-digitalose are also present in this species.

V. Climate

Foxglove prefers warm climate well distributed rainfall and good sunshine during winter. However well distributed rainfall during summer and winter months is beneficial for the luxuriant growth of the crop. Even at an altitude of 1,200 mts above the mean sea level the plant grows upto 45-60 centi meters.

VI. Soil and its Preparation

The plant requires well drained, sandy loam soil rich in organic matter and exposed to sunlight. Sandy, clay and water logged soils are unsuitable to its growth. It thrives well in both acidic and alkaline soils. The plant of D. purpurea yields good glycoside content in an acidic soil, while D. lanata gives improved yields in alkaline soil. The field should be prepared by two or three ploughings. After this the soil should be pulverized by harrowing followed by planking.

VII. Nursery Raising

Nursery beds should be prepared having soil rich in humus. Seeds produced at Solan and Chamba districts of H.P. can be used successfully for raising this crop. The quantity of seed required to raise a nursery for one hectare of land is 8 kilo grams. They are sown in lines at a row spacing of 15 centi meters. Good quality seeds should be used as older one lose their viability. The seeds should be covered gently with 0.5-1 cm thin layer of soil and light irrigation should be done. The seedlings are ready within 35-40 days after sowing. Soaking of seeds at 30 degrees centigrade for two days hastens the germination.

VIII. Transplantion

The time of planting is very critical in this crop. It ranges between mid April–July and depends on the location of the crop. Delay in planting effects the yield adversely. If possible the transplantation should be done in the evenings or on cloudy days avoiding scorching heat of sun. When the seedlings attain a height of 8-10 cm they are transplanted by keeping a spacing of 45cm between the rows and 30 cms between the plants in the same row. For proper establishmeent of seedlings light irrigation after transplanting is essential.

IX. Manures and Fertilizers

By proper manuring practices 32-49% increase in yield can be observed. Foliage yield considerably improves by NPK fertilization. Well rotten fermyard manure is applied at a rate of 40-60 tonnes per ha before transplanting. Fertilizers should be used one and half to two months after germination. Addition of 100 kg nitrogen, 50 kg phosphorus and 25 kg potassium per ha is beneficial. One fourth nitrogen should be supplemented in the form of calcium ammonium nitrate or urea along with full doses of phosphorus and potassium at the time of planting. Remaining nitrogen should be applied in three equal splits. First dose at 60 days of transplanting, second dose after the first harvest in November and last dose after the dormant season i.e. in Feburary. The second and third plucking are taken after these periods.

The highest content of digoxin was recorded under the agro climatic conditions of Shillong with the combination of NPK at the rate of 200,100 and 100 kg per hectare.

X. Irrigation

In summer between April to June, the crop should be irrigated 3-4 times each month, whereas in September October 2-3 irrigation are sufficient before the dormant session sets in by November. However after the first harvest (dormant season) it is necessary to give 1 or 2 irrigations a month, till the new leaves are formed. Later on weekly irrigation is recommended till maturity.

XI. Hoeing and Weeding

Motha (Cyperus rotundus) doob (Cynodon dactylon) and baru (Sorghum halepense) are the predominant and persistant perennial grasses occurring in the crop field. Hand weeding during rainy season is important to control the weeds. Pulverizing the soil and removing the weeds in between rows by equipment is hoeing. It should be done during summer and after each harvest. At least two hoeings before the first harvest and two after it important.

XII. Diseases

Leaf blight caused by Alternaria sp. is a common disease of foxglove. Brown spots appear on the leaves. They enlarge covering the entire leaf surface and killing the foliage in a few days.

Spray of any copper fungicide at the rate of 0.1-0.2 percent effectively controls this disease.

Occasionally, there is the occurence of beet-curly top and broad-bean wilt viruses.

XIII. Harvesting

Cutting of individual leaves is not economical. Cutting of entire plant 10-15 cms above the soil is recommended. But as in most of the areas leaf cutting only practiced, leaf harvesting is described here.

The age of harvesting the leaves require special attention to get maximum content of glycosides. Three to four pluckings can be taken. Irrigating the crop after each plucking encourages proper re-growth. Flowering in this species takes place in first week of May. For Plucking of leaves month of August is considered to be the best. However harvesting of leaves for the first year crop ws found to be better in months of July to October whereas for second year crop May to July was found to be right time for harvesting. Daytime between 11 to12'O clock was found to be best suited for plucking. If harvesting of leaves during first year crop gets delayed than the second year crop becomes weak. Leaves should be plucked when they are 8-10 cm long.

Long leaves (excluding petiole) should be initially plucked from the first year crop in October-November followed by second harvest after 105 days and third harvest after 150 days. Spring harvest yields almost double glycoside content than autumn harvest. The leaves are plucked by hand, by twisting them or breaking off by hand, or with the help of a blade without damaging the thick fleshy leaf stem. The lower basal leaves of yellow or brown colour are rejected and the upper smaller leaves of the stem are left unharvested. Generally, 75 percent of the total leaves per plant are harvested at a time.

After 2-3 pluckings the crop is left for seed and the shoot bearing capsules. The capsules can be harvested when they turn brown.

XIV. Yield

From one hectare about 600-700 Kg of dry leaves are obtained. By following appropriate cultivation practices, a farmer can fetch Rs. 12,000 - 25,000 per hectare and can boost his income even with small holdings in the hilly terrains provided somebody is to organize the production and marketing.

In recent experiments high foliage yield of 152 and 156 q/ha was obtained on fresh weight basis 31 and 28 q/ha on dry weight basis at Solan (Himachal Pradesh) and Kodaikanal (Tamilnadu) respectively. The glycoside content was lesser at Kodaikanal than at Solan. The total annual demand of the drug obtained from foxglove in India is estimated as more than30 quintals.

XV. Drying and Storage of Leaves

Drying of leaves is an important factor to prevent the loss of glycosides. Thus, to retain their active principles, the leaves should be dried either in shade or artificially. The collected leaves are spread under the shade in layers on the ground and left for drying for 36-48 hours. The ideal temperature should be between 30-40 drgrees centigrade. Leaves are turned occasionally to prevent rotting and also fermentation. Moisture at this stage may cause harm to the yield. If the weather is moist/humid then drying is done in oven artificially at about 50^0 to 60^0 C temperature. Drying in oven, however, results, in marked deterioration, especially when the temperature is high. Once the leaves are dried they are stored in air tight containers, polythene bage and kept in cool and dark place. Normally to avoid any bacteria on leaf during storage washing of the leaves prior to drying is recommended.

The total glycoside content of the leaves deteriorates when they are left exposed to the open air especially during rainy and summer season. If the leaves are plucked dried and stored carefully, their quality remains good for years. Drying causes 70% loss in weight and, drying done in hot air oven lends to 25% loss in glycoside content of leaves.

XVI. Uses

Leaves are the parts used for medicinal purposes. The dried leaves of the plant constitute the drug. The leaves must be dired at about 60° C temperature as soon after collection as possible.

The main use of this drug is in heart diseases. The drug promotes and stimulates the activity of all muscle tissues. It is used in cases of congested heart failure.

Digitalis forces more blood into the coronaries and improves the nutrition of the heart. When blood circulation gets impaired and dropsy (a disease marked by an excessive collection of a watery-fluid in the tissues or cavities of the body) sets in Digitalis hepls in restoration and regulation of the function of the heart. It improves the blood supply to the kidney and thus promotes urination and removes obstructions in kidneys.

Digilalis is used in some ointments for local application on wounds and burns. This drug however has some cumulative toxic effects and causes headache, giddiness, etc. These side effects must be watched.

It is important to note that this plant is a poisonous plant. this drug is not to be used with impunity in the home but only under medical supervision. Even touching the plant of D. purpurea with bare skin has been known to cause rashes, headache and nausea.

XVII. Conclusion

Considerable efforts are necessary to spread the cultivation of medicinal plants. New cultivars suited for different regions and systems of farming need to be evolved. Many medicinal plants can be fitted into multiple cropping system involving food and cash crops. We are all aware that the medicinal plants and their derivatives-processed items as well as active principle can be important foreign-exchange earners.

Chapter 14

GERANIUM

English name	:	Geranium
Indian name	:	Geranium (Hindi) Pannirsoppu Pannir patre (Kannada) Geranium (Tamil)
Distribution	:	India, South Africa, Belgium, China, Congo Egypt, Franc,e Madagascar, Morocco, Reunion Istands, Spain, former USSR countires
Uses	:	Cosmetics Perfumery

Oeranium (Pelargonium graveolens L. Herit.) is one of the important aromatic plants, yielding an essential oil which is highly priced for its very profound and strong rose-like odour. The plant is also known as rose geranium. The chief constituent of the oil are geranial and citronellol. The oil also contains a βpinene, βpinene, βterpinene, myrcene, phellandrene, limonene, cis-ocimene, trans ocimene, p-cymene, terpinolene-cis-roseoxide trans-rose oxide menthone, trans-linalool, iso-menthone, caryophyllene, geranyl acetate, nerol, geranyl formate, geranayl butyrate and geraniol.

The pure geranium oil is almost a perfume by itself and blends well with all other perfumes. It is widely used in scenting soaps and for the isolation of rhodinal which forms part of most high-grade perfumes. India is importing more than 20 t of this oil from other countries to meet the local demands of the Indian perfumery industries, in addition to an indigenous production of only about 20 t of oil annually.

Origin and Distribution

Geranium is native of the Cape Province in South Africa. It is commercially cultivated in France, Belgium, Spain, Morocco, Mada gascar, Egypt, Reunion

Islands, Congo, China, India and the former USSR countries. The world production of geranium oil is estimated at 250-300 t whereas the demand is more than 500 t annually. The first planting of a high-yielding Pelargonium graveolens introduced from Renuion island was grown at Yercaud by a French planter, in the early twentieth century. From that time onwards it has been cultivated as a commercial crop, but only in high altitude areas with a milder climate. However, the crop also comes up well in the South Indian plains. Presently it is being commercially cultivated mainly in the Nilgiris and Kodaikanal Hills of Tamil Nadu and in and around Bangalore in Karnataka in an area of about 2 000 ha.

Description of the Plant

The commercial oil of geranium is obtained from Pelargonium graveolens, L. HERIT. (2n=88) of the family Geraniaceae. There are about 600 species of the genus Pelargonium many of which possess an agreable odour. Other species like P. radula P. fragrance are of lesser importance and have not attained any commercial significance.

Geranium is a bushy aromatic plant. The stem is cylindrical woody at the base, pubescent, green when young and turning brown with age. The leaves are alternate, stipulate, simple with 5 primary lobes and secondary lobes and densely pubescent. The leaves are highly aromatic in nature. The inflorescence is umbellate and hairy. The flower is bisexual, hypogynous, with a pink corolla, the two posterior petals are larger with reddish, purple markings. There are 10 stamens the filaments are subequal, united at the base; the anthers are 7, dithecous and shed easily. The overy is hairy superior pentacarpellary and syncarpous; the style is hairy, breaking up distally into five stigma.

Varieties

1. Algerion or Tunisian

   This type of geranium is slender with flowers of a dark pink colour. It is being grown in the Nilgiris and is unsuitable for wet conditions. This variety yields 50-60% more oil with a more delicate odour than that of the Reunion type.

2. Reunion or Bourbon

   Grown in the Nilgiris and Anamalais, the plant is more sturdy with light-pink flowers and more suitable for wet conditions. The soil content is higher during the summer months from April to June. The terminal portion with 6 to 12 leaves contains more oil than the middle and basal portions.

In the evaluation trial of the Algerian and Reunion types, PG-7 and PG-20 respectively, at the Horticulture Research Station, Kodaikanal, the clone PG-7 recorded 0.3% essential oil and 2.32 ml of oil per plant, and has been released under the name 'KKL-1.' The Indian Institute of Horticultural Research (IIHR) Bangalore, has found 'Sel-8' a Reunion type as the highest yielder under Bangalore conditions and has recommended it for cultivation. 'Hemanti', 'Bipuli', and 'Kunti', are the other varieties released by the CIMAP, Lucknow, for cultivation in the plains of North India. Kelkar Ooty and IIHR Sel-8 are the other varieties available in this crop.

Soil

Geranium is a shallow-rooted crop and as such, it requires a welldrained porous soil. The crop is found to perform well in red lateritic soils with a pH of 5.5-8.0 though a calcium rich porous soil is the best.

Climate

Geranium can be grown in temperate, subtropical and tropical climates at various altitudes from 1 000 to 2 200 m. It thrives best in subtropical climate with a temperature ranging from 5°C to 23°C. However, temperatures below 3°C will kill the plant. Warm winters coupled with mild summer temperatures and well-distributed annual rainfall ranging from 100-150 cm is ideal. However, heavy rainfall results in water-logging, causes root-rot and stunted growth. It has been observed that it grows equally well at much lower altitudes and tolerates higher temperatures upto 43° C in the plains when grown under irrigated conditions.

Propagation

Geranium is easily propagated by cuttings since there is no seed setting in geranium vegetative propagation is a must. Terminal cuttings about 20 cm long and consisting of about 8 nodes are the best suited material for propagation as they give 80% rooting even without any treatment. Howeve,r the middle portion and basal cuttings are reported to give poor rooting, which can be improved by treating them for 6 minutes with growth regulators like IBA or IAA at 200 ppm. Thus a rooting of 80% and 65%, respectively, can be obtained.

The cuttings are planted in raised beds 3 m long and 1 m wide. The soil should be well mixed with powdered FYM. The cuttings are planted closely at a spacing of 8-10 cm. Before planting the cut end of the cuttings are dipped in 0.1% Benlate solution. Before root initation, temporary shade is provided and the beds are watered regularly. The nursery is sprayed with a 0.2% Urea solution at biweekly intervals and the cuttings strike roots in 40 days. After about 60 days, the cuttings are ready for transplanting. They can also be rooted in polythene bage, which helps to avoid damage to the root system while while planting in the main field. This practice ensures a high percentage of success in the field.

Recently its propagation through leaf petioles has also been reported to give a good rooting percentage (75%) which will help to multiple this plant in larger numbers than the traditional method of propagation using 20 cm-long cuttings. The CIMAP Lucknow has developed a protocol for large-scale production of geranium calliclones and plants have been obtained under field conditions with improved oil-yield and quality.

Planting and After care

About 30 000 cuttings are required for planting an area of 1 ha. Before planting the land should be properly prepared by ploughing (disc) and brought to a fine tilth. Ridges and furrows are made, the application of fertilizer and irrigation should be done a day prior to planting. The cuttings are carefully dug out from the nursery and planted at a spacing of 60 cm x 60 cm. They must be irrigated immediately after planting. Irrigation is continued on alternate days for about 10-15 days and then reduced to twice a week. The schedule is modified during the winter and summer months at intervals of 7 to 10 days, depending on the situation through geranium tolerates short periods of drought water-logging of the crop must be completely avoided. The crop growth is slow initially; weeds should therefore be removed periodically. Intercropping of cowpea or black gram is benefical during the log phase and they do not affect the geranium crop.

It has been experimentally observed at the CIMAP, Lucknow, that polyhouse cultivation reduces weed infestation the number of irrigations and produced less weed biomass.

Manures and Fertilizers

Prior to transplanting the cuttings 10 t of good quality FYM, 35 kg N, 35 kg P_2O_5 and 3 kg K_2O/ha are incorporated into the soil in the form of urea, super phosphate and muriate of potash. A second dose of nitrogen at 35 kg/ha is applied about 2 months after the first application, Further, nitrogen is given in two equal split doses for each harvest-the first dose being just after the crop is harvested and the second two months later. Altogether, 210 kg/ha/yr of N is applied to the crop in six equal doses to cover three harvest. Application of 30 kg N/ha (15 kg/ha as basal and 15 kg as a foliar spray with 1% urea solution 45 and 90 days after basal application) is reported to inrease herhage yield and oil yield by 447% and 140%, respectively, over the control.

In addition the application of 20 kg/ha of zinc sulphate and 10 kg/ha of boron has been reported to increase the herbage yield. Similarly, an application of copper (20 kg/ha) and molybdenum (30 kg/ha/year) in four split doses after each harvest has been found to increase the yield by 37%.

Harvesting

Geranium is harvested 4 months after transplanting when the leaves begin to turn light-green and exhibit a change from a lemon like odour to that of rose. However this requires careful observeation and experience. The crop should be harvested using a sharp sickle and sent for distillation immediately. The use of a sharp sickle is important as it minimizes the jerks, pulls and damage to the crop while harvesting. After every harvest, hoeing, fertilizer application and irrigation are done according to the schedule. The plant then puts forth fresh shoots, grows faster and reaches the next harvesting stage in 4 months. Thus, a total of 3 harvests can be expected in a year. Since it is a perennial crop, a good harvest can be obtained for 3-6 years. Cultivation under polyhouse conditions is reported to reduce the harvest time by 21 days.

The essential oil is distributed over the green parts of the plant, particularly in the leaves. The oil content is higher during the summer months, from April to June. The terminal portion with 6-12 leaves contains more oil then the middle and basal portions.

Yield

The quality and yield of oil will be better if the crop is harvested at the appropriate time of maturity. For a higher yield, a good plant population in the field is necessary. A minimum of 25 000 plants should be maintained in a hectare in a year which, in turn, may yield 15 kg of oil on ditillation. The recovery of the oil ranges from 0.08 to 0.15%, depending upon the season of harvest and type of material. Cultivation under polyhouse cover is reported to increase herb and oil yields upto 53% over the conventional planting of the geranium crop.

Distillation of Oil

The freshly-harvested terminals are used for the distillation of oil. The plant material is stacked near the stills for about 12 to 24 hours. This results in a slight fermentation and splitting of the glycosides, which increases the yield of oil. The oil is extracted by a simple distillation method. The herbage is tightly packed in a still over the perforated grid and tamped down tightly and the still-head is clamped shut. The steam is generated in a separate boiler and conveyed to the still. The oil volatalizes and escapes along with the steam vapour, which is later condensed by passing it through a condenser with running cold water. The condensed oil is separated from the water by the differential density method and clarified by filtering it with activated carbon.

Chapter 15

GUGGAL

English name	:	Indian Bedellium tree
Indian name	:	Gugguluh Mahisakah (Sanskrit) Gugal, Guggul (Hindi) Gukkulu ,Mahisaksi (Tamil)
Distribution	:	India ,Africa, Asia, Australia, Bangladesh, Pacific Islands, Pakistan
Uses	:	Drugs Perfumery

Guggal or the Indian Bedellium tree is Commiphora mukul (Hook ex Stocks) Engl. Syn. Balsomodendron mukul, a small tree belonging to the family Burseraceae. This plant is a source of Indian Bedellium, a oleo-gum-resin obtained by incision of the bark. The resin occurs in vascular or stalactitic pieces, paleyellow, brown or dull-green in colour with a bitter aromatic taste and balsamic odour. The oleo-gum-resins are mixtures of resin (about 61%) gum (about 29.3%), volatile oil (about 1.45%) and occasionally combined with other substances, mainly myrcene, dimyrecane and polymyrecene. It has ketonic and non-ketonic fractions. The ketonic mixture constitute about 12% of ethyl acetate soluble neutral part which consists of 8 steroids. Two of these steroids Z-and-e gugalsterone, constitute 2% of the gum resin and are responsible for the lipid-lowering activity of guggal. Non-ketonic fractions exert a synergistic action of the biological activity of the ketonic fractions. The ethyl acetate extract of guggal has been named 'guggulipid.'

The resin is largely used as incense and as a fixative in perfumery and in medicine. In indigenous medicine, it is used as an astringent, antiseptic, stomachic, carminative and digestant. The oleo-resin causes an increase of leucocytes in the blood and stimulates phagocytosis. It acts as a diaphoretic, expectorant and diuretic and is said to be a uterine stimulant and an emmenagogue as well. It is highly effective in the treatment of obesity, arthritis, indolent ulcers, week and spongy gums, pyorrhoea, alveolaris, chronic tonsilitis and pharangytis, ulcerated throat, and chronic dyspepsia. Inhalation of the fumes of burnt guggul is recommended in hay fever acute and chronic catarrh,-chronic laryngitis, chronic bronchitis and phthisis. It is an ingredient of ointments for ulcers.

Distribution & Origin

The genus Commiphora, which has 165 species, has its origin in Africa and Asia and is widely distributed in the tropical regions of Africa, Madagascar, Asia, Australia, Pacific Islands, India, Bangladesh and Pakistan. Four species occur in India. These are : C. agollochoa Engl; C. stocksiana Engl; C. mukul Hook ex stock and C. berryi (Aen). Engl. The genuine guggal gum is derived from C. mukul. In India, this species is distributed in the states of Rajasthan, Tamil Nadu, Assam, Gujarat, Maharastra and Karnataka.

Plant Description

A small tree or shrub up to 3-4 m high, the branches are crooked, knotty, aromatic and end in sharp spines. The bark is papery and peels in strips from the older parts of the stem. The leaves are sessile alternate or fascicled, 1-3 foliate, the leaflets are glabrous. The terminal is sessile or subsessile obvate serrate 1-5 cm long, 0.5 to 2.5 cm broad, lateral, when present, sessile, serrate or entire. The plants are dimorphic, one having bisexual and male flowers and the other having female flowers with staminodes. The bisexual and male flowers are sessile, 3-5 mm long, usually red and rarely pinkish-white. The flowers appear in groups of 2 or 3. The calyx is fused with the disc basally, it is tubular or urceolate, 1-2 mm long. The petals are reflexed, acute, 3-5 mm long and 1 mm broad. There are 8 stamens very rarely 10; 3-5 mm long. The disc is conspicuously toothed. The ovary is 2-loculed with a sessile 2-lobed stigma. The fruit is ovoid up to 1 cm-long drupe, red when ripe and the mesocarp is yellow. When it is ripe it splits into two.

Varieties

About 26 cultures designated by the name of the places from where they are collected are being evaluated at Anand, in Gujarat, from 1981 and a variety named 'Marusudha' which is the highest yielder, has been released for cultivation.

Soil

Guggal is not grown on a commercial plantation scale anywhere. But the plants are found growing naturally in arid tracts of Western India over sandy-to-silt loam soils which are poor in organic matter but rich in several other minerals. Faster growth of the plant is observed in soils which have moisture-retaining capacity. An average soil is suitable for its cultivation.

Climate

The plant has a wide adaptability and is found growing in arid regions under varying conditions. Its small, leathery leaves and thick bark, covered with a white waxy coat over the stem, helps it to withstand desert conditions. It prefers a warm, dry climate for a good yield of oleo-gum-resin.

Land Preparation

The land is prepared well in advance of the rainy seson by 2-3 ploughings and laid out plots of convenient sizes. Pits of the size 0.5 x 0.5 x 0.5 m^3 are dug at a spacing of 3 to 4 m, in rows. The pits filled with FYM and topsoil and mixed with Aldrin (5%) to prevent any damage to the plants due to termite attack.

Cultivation

Propagation

Guggal can be propagated by seeds and vegetatively through stem-cuttings. Air-layering has also been successful in this plant. In literature the protocol for meristem culture is also available.

i) Propagation by Seeds

This is not a common method of porpagating this plant, because the seed germination is slow and is also very poor (5%) due to the presence of the hard seed-coat. To achieve a good rate of germination the seeds mechanically scarified with sandpaper and are kept under running water for 24 hours. The seedlings may be raised in polythene bags during the kharif season and, after hardening may be planted in the main field.

ii) Propagation by Stem-cuttings

About 15-20 cm long and 10 mm thick semi-hardwood cuttings are taken and the cut end is treated with IBA or NAA growth, regulator solutions and planted in well-prepared and manured nursery beds during the months of June and July. The beds are irrigated lightly after planting and regularly therafter. The cuttings sprout in 10-15 days, they grow well and are ready for planting in the main field after 10 to 12 months, during the next rainy season. The percentage of rooting in stem-cuttings is around 80 to 94%.

Planting

The rooted cuttings are planted in the pits during the rainy season. As the plants grow, they are trained properly by cutting the side branches.

Fertilizer Application

This crop has not shown good response to fertilizers except to lowlevel or nitrogen fetilization. Hence urea or ammonium sulphate at 25/50 g/bush is given twice a year before irrigation.

Irrigation

Providing light irrigation during the summer season supports good growth of the plants.

Intercultivation

Interculture is confined to one weeding and hoeing in the early stages of growth. But the soil has to the stirred around the bushes twice in a year. This practice of soil-stirring is found to increase the growth of plants.

Diseases and Pests

Guggal plants are attacked by a leaf-eating caterpillar Euproctis lanata Walker; white fly-Bemisia tabaci, which sucks the sap of leaves as a result of which the leaves turn yellow and finally drop off. The rooted cuttings also suffer from termite attacks in the early stages of growth.

The diseases noticed on this crop are leaf-spot cuased by Cercospora spp. and bacterial leaf-blight.

Gum-tapping and Yield

The plants attain normal height and girth after 8 to 10 years of growth when they are ready for tapping. For tapping the gum which is present in the balsam canals in the phloem, bark-deep, i.e., a shallow, incision is made on the bark. If the incision incised is too deep, the plant either dies or yields little resin in the following years. While making the incision a small quantity of guggal gum mixed with water may be applied to the incised place using a prick chisel. The sharp end of the chisel is dipped in the guggal solution and an incision is made on the bark carefully. Usually the incision is made after November but before April. The resin is collected at an interval of 10-15 days. Weather conditions influence the success of obtained gum.

The yield of gum-resin from each plant is about 700-900 g.

Separation of Resin from Gum

The resin can be separated from the gum either by not expression or solvent extraction at 120-130^0 C. The yield by the former process is about 10% less than that obtained by solvent extraction (61%). The purified resin is transparent in thin films but translucent or even opaque in bulk. It is completely soluble in most of the organic solvents and in castor oil drying oils and turpentine and mixes well with vegetable waxes, stearic acid and resin.

Pruning of Plants

In experiments conducted by CIMAP Lucknow on guggal plants obtained from the arid regions of Gujarat and Rajasthan, it has been demonstrated that guggal stems pruned in May contain the maximum amount of guggal sterons (0.06%). This method saves the plant from drying and ultimate death, which was a result of the extraction procedure adopted earlier.

Chapter 16

HONEY PLANT

English name	:	Honey Plant
Indian name	:	Madhugida (Kannada)
Distribution	:	India, Abyssinia, west Africa, Egypt, Europe, France, Germany, the Mediterranean Region, Switzerland
Uses	:	Drugs

Honey plant (Ammi majus L) belonging to the family, Apiaceae; Umbelliferae, is an important medicinal plant indigenous to Egypt. Its seeds constitute the principal commerical source of xanthotoxin. The other constitutents of the seed are: bergapten isopimpinellin, isoimperatorin, oxypeucedanin, heraclenin, oxypeucedanin hydrate, sexalin, pabulenol and three other compounds, and the synthetic psoralens: xanthotoxol, bergaptol, imperatorin, heracelin, heraolenol and sexalin. Around 16 psoralens have been obtained from A. majus; thus, this species is one of the richest known source of linear furocoumarins. Xanthotoxin is commonly used in the treatment of vitiligo or leucoderma and in formulations of suntan lotions. The xanthotoxin content in the fruit is about 0.4% and additional quantities of it can be prepared by converting the imperatorin persent in the fruits by chemical means. The plants is reported to be biennial in its natural habitat, but behaves as an annual under cultivation in India.

Distribution and Trade

The plant is indigenous to Egypt and is widely distributed in Europe the Mediterranean region, Abyssinia and West Africa. The plant is reported to have been first introduced in India along with A. visnaga by the forest research institute, Dehradun, in 1955, by the courtesy of the UNESCO. It is being successfully grown in the temperate and subtropical regions of Himachal Pradesh, Uttar Pradesh, Gujarat, Tamil Nadu and Karnataka. Although the recent statistics on the area, production, import and export details of this crop are not available, but according to Singh (1963), France Switzerland and the Federal Republic of Germany alone require about 400 t/yr of Ammi majus fruits and part of this requirement is being met by the exports from India. On the other hand India has been importing xanthotoxin worth about two lakhs annually.

Description of the Plant

It is an annual herb attaining a height of 80 to 120 cm. It has a long taproot and a solid, erect stem. The leaves are decompound lightgreen alternate variously pinnately divided, having lanceolate to oval segments. It bears auxiliary and terminal compound umbles of white flowers. The fruits are ribbed, ellipsoid, green to greenish-brow when immature, turnning reddish- brown at maturity. The odour of the fruit is slightly characteristic of terebinthinate and becomes strong on crushing. The taste is slightly bitter and extremely pungent. The chromosome number is 2n=11.

Varieties

Only two varieties: 'Suttons and Monoica' are reported in this corp.

Soil

It can be grown on a variety of soils, but thrives best in well-drained sandy loam to clay loam soils containing a moderate amount of organic matter. Any soil which is saline, alkaline or water-logged is unsuitable for its cultivation.

Cilmate

The plant requires a mild, cool climate in the early stages of growth and warm and dry weather at maturity. Recently, its successful cultivation in some subtropical parts of the country has also been reported. It does not like heavy rainfall during its growing period, and under such conditions the yields are considerably lower.

Cultivation

Propagation

The crop is propagated by seeds. They can be either sown directly into the main field or by transplanting the seedlings. Since the directly seeded crop takes a longer time in the field, involving higher inputs on irrigation and weeding the crop is usually raised by transplanting the seedlings.

i) Nursery Raising and Planting

The seedlings are raised in well-prepared nursery beds of 1 x 3 m in size. Before sowing, a mixture of equal quantities of calcium amonium nitrate and single super phosphate at the rate of 150 g per bed is added and mixed well with the surface soil. About 1.5 to 2.0 kg of seeds will be enough to raise seedlings for 1 ha of land. After sowing, the seeds are covered with a mixture of FYM and soil mulched and watered. The beds are kept moist by light irrigations every day.

The seeds start germinating after 7-8 days of sowing. At this stage the mulch is removed and the beds are kept free of weeds and watered continously. The seedlings are ready for transplanting after about 8 weeks.

For transplanting the seedlings are carefully removed to avoid any damage to the roots. They are transplanted in well-prepared land at a spacing of 45 x 30 cm or 45 x 60 cm in the main field.

ii) Direct Sowing

However, where the area is very large and there is a scarcity of labour, direct sowing may be preferred. A seed rate of 12kg/ha is recommended when the the crop is to be raised by direct seeding. Since the seed is very small, it is mixed with fine soil or sand in a ratio of 1:10. The seeds can be sown in furrows at 45 cm apart, from August to the middle of September. If there are no rains within a week of sowing, the field should be irrigated liberally. The seed starts germinating after a fortnight and it taken about a month to complete the germination for the whole field. When the seedlings develop true leaves and are 8-10 cm in height, thinning is done so that plant-to-plant distance in a row is maintained at 30 cm.

Manures and Fertilizers

The crop has been found to respond well to the application of manures and ferilizers. A fertilizer dose of 100 kg N, 115 kg $P_2 O_5$ and 30 kg $K_2 O$/ha has been repoted as optimum for the crop. This is in addition to 20-25 tonnes of FYM. The manure and half of the N the full dose of P and K are applied in furrows before transplanting. The rest of the N is given as a top-dressing after thinning when the plants have started branching.

Irrigation

Ammi majus is a herbaceous crop and the availability of moisture has a direct effect on its growth and productivity. Hence it should be irrigated frequently during the dry period. The first irrigation is given immediately after transplanting and afterwards at an interval of 8-10 days. Since the crop is quite sensitive to excess moisture, care should be taken to avoid water-logging.

Interculture

As the crop is very sensitive, it is necessary to keep the plots weedfree at the initial stages. Once they grow, they cover the whole plot and thus there is very little scope for the other weeds to compete. About 2-3 hand-weedings will be enough to keep the weeds down. In large-scale plantations, two hoeings should be given to keep the soil mellow and free from weeds.

Pests and Diseases

A bright yellow mosaic disease in the form of a ring or line or patterns on the leaves has been reported from Lucknow for the first time on this crop. Several fungi are known to cause damage to the fruits during storage. Aspergillus ochraceus was observed to cause heavy damage to xanthotoxin during the first month of storage while Fusarium oxysporum causes damage to A. niger and A. flavus and during the first three months of storage and drastically reduces the xanthotoxin content.

Harvesting and Yield

Ammi majus is a 5-6 months' duration crop. When sowing is done during the months of August-September the crop starts flowering during the months of November-December. The flowering and maturity of seeds is spread out over about a month.

Studies have shown that the mature brown coloured fruit contains only 0.4% xanthotoxin; whereas, when harvested at the mature green stage, it gave 0.72% and in immature green fruits, it was as high as 1.0%. However, the mature green stage, of harvesting is recommended as in the case of the immature green stage there is a considerable reduction in the total yield of the crop. The other advantage of harvesting at this stage is that the loss of the crop due to seed -shattering which occurs when the seeds have turned brown, can be minimized.

While harvesting, the umbels are hand-picked individually by cutting the plant at its middle. The cut umbels are kept in loose bundles and staked till the fruits are dry. The fruits are later separated by threshing and winnowing.

On an average, the crop may yield about 900 to 1 200 kg/ha of dry seeds.

Chapter 17

HOP

I. Introduction

Hop (Humulus lupulus) is a native of the northern temperate zones cultivated commercially especially in Northern Europe, North America and Chile. Roman records from the 1st Century AD describes hops as a popular garden plant and vegetable, the young shoots being sold in markets to be eaten rather like asparagus. Hops gardens did not become widespread in Europe until the 9th century. In Britain the hop was a wild plant and used as vegetable before it become one of the ingredients of beer. It was not until the 16th century that the word hop and the practice of flavouring and preserving beer with the strobiles or female flowers of the hop were introduced into Britain by Flemish immigrants and relaced traditional bitter herbs such as alehoof and alecost.

During the reign of Henry VIII, parliament was petitioned against the use of hop as it was said that it was a wicked weed that would spoil the taste of drinks, ale and endanger the people. Needless to say the petition was thrown out. The use of hops revolutionised brewing since it enabled beer to be kept for longer. Hops have also been used as medicine for at least as long as for brewing. The flowers are famous for their sedative effect and were either drunk as a tea or stuffed in a hop pillow to sleep on.

II. Climate and Soil

This crop grows well under humid temparate conditions. Soil should be in fine tilth, fertile and well drained. It grows on any type of soil but loamy soils rich in humus suit well. Though it can tolerate moisture stress conditions to some extent, areas with fair distribution of rainfall throughout the year are favourable for its cultivation.

III. Species

Hop commonly known in English as Hop, belongs to family Moraceae (Cannabinaceae). The genera have two species Humulus lupulus or common hop and H. lupulus Aureus which is commonly known as golden hop. The hop vine is a perennial climbing plant many angular rough stems, grows up to six metres long from a branched rootstock. The leaves are rough, opposite, cordate, serrate and three to five lobed. The floweres are yellowish green; the male flowers are arranged in hanging panicles whereas the female in catkins. The name hop usually refers to the scaly, conelike fruit that develops from the female flowers.

1. H. lupulus Linn. (Common hop)

It is a hardy, perennial, a herbaceous climber growing to a height of six metres. The male plant has yellowish flowers, growing in branched clusters and the flowers are without sepals and have five petals and stamens. The female plants has tiny, greenish yellow scented flowers hidden by big scales. The scales become papery when the fruiting heads are ripened. These are the flowers which are harvested for beer. The mild green leaves have 3-5 lobes and with sharply toothed edges. The stems are hollow and are covered with tiny hooked prickles. These enable the plants to cling to shrubs trees etc always in clockwise direction.

2. H. lupulus 'Aureus' (Golden hop)

It is hardy perennial herbaceous climber which grows to a height of six metres. The main difference between this plant and common hop is that the leaves and flowers are much more golden which make it very attractive in the garden and in flower arrangements. It has same properties as common hop.

IV. Propagation

The hop can be propagated by seed, cuttings or splitting the roots.

A. Seed propagation

If you grow hop from seed you will not know the gender for two to three years which is the time it taken before good flowers are produced. Obtain the seeds from a reliable source and sow them in summer or autumn. The seeds are of medium to large size as such sowing should be done with good spacing. One seed per hole is sufficient while the dibbled hole is closed afterwards with the compost. If the seeds are sown in trays, then cover the trays with polythene and leave somewhere in cool place for germination. Germination can be very erratic. If the seeds are not fresh, you may need to give hot/cold treatments. Caution is to be taken not to mix seeds from wild hops in commercial hops as they may contaminate crop.

Cutting of stems

Softwood cuttings should be taken in spring or early summer from the female plant. Choose young shoots and take the cuttings in the morning, as they will loose water very fast and wilt.

C. Splittings of roots/stems/suckers

In the spring session dig up and divide the roots stems and suckers of extablished plants. Replant one metre apart against the support splitted portion of roots/stems/suckers. Before planting after digging the different branches along with suckers and roots are splitted and kept ready for replanting.

V. Land Preparation

The site in which the crop is going to be sown should be ploughed and harrowed in order to get a fine tilth. The land is levelled by planking to avoid water accumulation at one point. The field should be provided with good drainage system. Preparation for line sowing can also be made during land preparation itself.

VI. Manures and Fertilizers

At the time of ploughing, it is beneficial to add 10-12 tonnes per hectare of farmyard manure which add organic matter to the soil. It also require nutition in the form of nitrogen, phosphorus and potassium as they are the major nutrients. According to soil testing report, the dose of fertilizer is recommended. Generally around 30 kg nitrogen, 18-20 kg phosphorus and potassium per hectare can be applied.

VII. Planting

For successful planting the site should be sunny and open, the soil needs to be rich in humus and dug deeply. It is not generally necessary to tie the plants if a good support is available. The plant will need thinning and training to entwine where the plant is to be grown. The plant suffers from die back in winter. Cut the plant in autumn to ground level (just above) and fertilize it with manures and fertilizers including compost. The plant will again sprout out into a new vine or climber. If we want to raise a crop from seed, sowing of the seed late in the summer will result in good germination. In autumn cut back the remaining growth to the ground. The plant requires irrigation and care so that it should not get trampled.

VIII. Pot Culture

The plant is to be cared and maintained throughout the year. In spring the roots can be divided and these separated rooted stems and suckers are grown in well composted containers. Repotting can be done by changing the plants from small pots to bigger pots. Give the plants a good supply of manures, fertilizers and compost. Bring containers into a cool place. There is no need for any protection during winter season.

IX. Irrigation

This crop can be grown under rainfed conditions. But irrigation facilities should be available in anticipation of monsoon failure. Irrigation will boost up the yield tremendously. If there are no rains after sowing then first irrigation should be given after one week and then according to requirement water should be provided. As everybody knowns appearance of wilt is a sign that plant require irrigation.

X. Weed Control

Weeding can be done manually or chemically. It is essential to do weeding every now and then to keep the field free of weeds. These weeds if allowed to grow not only empower the crop but also contaminates the quality by imparting its own odour to the plants.

XI. Pests and Diseases

Very few diseases and pests attack the plants. The most common disease is hop wilt. If this occurs, dig up and burn the plant to control the wilt disease. Do not replant hop in that area at least for a few years. Leaf minor can sometimes be a problem. Remove the infected leaves immediately to control the pest. The golden variety sometimes suffers from sun scorch. If this appears it is better to prune for new growth and also changing its position if possible in the following season would help in controlling this.

XII. Harvesting

Pick young fresh female flowers and side shoots in spring. Collect young fresh leaves as required. Collect ripe female flowers in early autumn. Dry and use them within a few months, otherwise the flavour becomes unpleasant. The leaf can be used to make a brown dye. If you live close to a brewery it is worth chatting them up in each autumn for the spent hops which makes either a great mulch or a layer in a compost heap.

XIII. Medicinal Properties

Hop tea made from the female flowers only is recommended for nervous diarrhoea insomnia and restlessness. It also helps to stimulate appetite dispel flatulence and relieve intestinal cramps. A cold tea taken an hour before meals is particularly good for digestion.

It can be useful if combined with fragrant valerian for coughs and nervous spasmodic conditions. Recent research into hops has shown that it contain a certain hormone which accounts for the beneficial effect of helping mothers improve their milk flow. To make a hop pillow, sprinkle hops with alcohol and fill a small bag or pillow case with them. Hops bracts and flowers of female plants forming a leafy conical inflorescances are (stobilus) collected before fully matured. Because brown glandular hairs of bracts are more active having bitter principle and volatile oil which stimulates appetite, acts as an antibiotic and regularises menses. Antibiotic activity of drug decreases rapidly with age. Estrogenic extract of hops contain estradiol which can be used for cosmetics, in face creams and effective against dermatophytes in skin preparations such as deodorants or soaps.

Bitter substances in extraction are iso-alfa, gamma and beta acids (lupulones), Y-acids (humulinones) and delta acids (hulupones) Lupoxes a and b and lupdoxes A and B are active against Bacillus subtilis.

XIV. Other Uses

Pistillate inflorescences are spike-like in appearance and are borne in leaf axils of either main stem or more frequently lateral branches. These are known as strobiles cones or burrs and constitute the commercial hop. Inflorescences are composed of scales covered with glandular hairs which produces bitter principle an important ingredient in brewing of beer and other beverages and gives beverages its characteristic aroma and taste. In spring young shoots are boiled and eaten like asparagus. The male flowers can be cooked and used as salad.

Chapter 18

HENNA

Family	:	Lythraceae
English	:	Henna, Egyptian Privet, Cypress Shrub
Indian name	:	Medhini, Madayantika, Nakharanjani (Sanskrit) Mehandi, Heena (Hindi), Goranti (Kannada) Mailenanti, Marutani (Tamil)
Species and	:	Lawsonia inemmis L.
varieties	:	Hina, Hajni
Distribution	:	India, Australia, Egypt, Iran, Madagasca,r Pakistan Persia, Sudan
Uses	:	Cosmetics, Drugs, Dyeing Ornamental purposes Perfumery

The henna of commerce is the dried leaf of Lawsonia inermis L. belonging to the family Lythraceae. The plant is widely cultivated as an ornamental and dye plant. The aqueous solution is orange in colour and shows a green fluorescence. The principle colouring matter is' lawsone.' Besides lawsone, the other constituents present in henna are gallic acid, glucose, mannitol, fat, resin (2%), mucilage and traces of an alkaloid. The steam-distillation of leaves will yield 0.01-0.02% of an essential oil called Henna or mehndi oil. The flowers have a strong aroma and yield and oil consisting mainly (90%) of α and βionones (ratio 1:4) a nitrogenous compound and a resin. The seeds also yield a non-drying, viscous oil and roots yield a red colouring matter.

From ancient times, henna has been employed as a cosmetic dye for the hair beard and eyebrows and as a personal adornment for colouring and making intricate design on the palms of the hands, the soles of the feet and the fingernails. The tails and manes of horses are sometimes dyed with henna which is also used for colouring leathers ad skins. More recently, there has been an increase in its usage as a hair dye in Western Europe and North America. Prior to the widespread availability of synthetic dyestuffs, henna was also employed as a dye for textiles. For its use as colouring material, henna powder is made into a paste with water and applied. Henna leaves are also used medicinally as a prophylactic against skin diseases. They have astringent properties. They are used externally in the form of a paste or deccotion against boils, burns, bruises and skin inflammations. The alcoholic extract of the leaves show anti-bacterial properties also. Henna or mehndi oil is used in perfumes and embalming. The seed-oil is used for anointing the body. The wood is of minor utility it is used for tool-handles tent-pegs and other small articles.

Origin and Distribution

Henna is indigenous to the area between the Islamic Republic of Iran and northern India and has been introduced throughout the tropics subtropics and warm temperate regions. Large-scale cultivation of henna for the sake of the leaves which yield the dye is confined to India, Egypt and Sudan and to some extent in Persia, Madagascar, Pakistan and Australia. It is grown as a hedge-plant throughout India and as a commercial dye crop in Punjab, Gujarat, Madhya Pradesh and Rajasthan.

Description of the Plant

Henna is a glabrous much-branched shrub or small tree with a greyish brown bark. The leaves are opposite, subsessile, elliptic or broadly lanceolate, entire, acute or obtuse, often macronulate. The flowers are numerous, small, white or rose-coloured fragrant and occur in large, terminal, pyramidal, panicled cymes. The capsule is globose, about the size of a pea, with numerous pyramidal, smooth seeds.

Varieties

Since the crop is generally propagated by seeds, very little is known about he cultivated varieties. However, the known varieties are 'Hina' and 'Hajni.' The first one is little more robust, reaching a height of 6 m and produces fragrant white or rose-red flowers, : whereas, the latter is more the colouring type.

Soil

The plant is found growing on a variety of soils ranging form light loam to clay loam, but does best on heavy soils which have good amount of organic matter and are retentive of soil moisture, with no drainage problems. It is found growing on soils with a pH range of 4.3 to 8.0.

Climate

Henna is a hardy plant and can tolerate a wide range of climatic conditions. However, the plant prefers a hot and dry climate with a temperature range of 20-30^0 C for its successful growth. It also withstands quite a wide range of moisture fluctuations and, hence, is found growing in areas with an annual rainfall ranging from 20-42.5 cm.

Land Preparation

The land is well prepared with 2 or 3 ploughings until a fine tilth of soil is obtained. FYM is incorporated into the soil at the time of final ploughing.

Cultivation

Propagation

Henna is raised through seeds as well as through cuttings. The former method is usually preferred. The seed rate used is about 10 kg/ha. The seeds have a hard coat and are kept under a moist cloth for 8-15 days till they sprout (the average germination being 20%). The sprouted seeds are then mixed with fine sand and sown by broad-casting in a well-prepared nursery-bed during the month of March. The seed-beds are kept moist and free from weeds.

Manuring

In order to obtain a good growth of leaves and flowers the land is supplied with 40t/ha FYM and 40 kg/ha N at planting and a similar quantity of nitrogen is applied thereafter in 2 split doses, annually.

Irrigation and Interculture

In order to obtain better establishment of the transplanted seedlings, daily irrigation for about a week is necessary. Later on, up to one year, the plants should be irrigated whenever there is a long, dry spell. Regular irrigation even to the adult trees is beneficial in obtaining higher yields. The field should be kept free of weeds and occasionally ploughed. When the crop is grown under rainfed conditions, the fields are bunded during the rainy season to conserve moisture.

Pests and Diseases

Pests

Some of the insect pests like termites ants and mites are reported to damage the crop. Dustings the crop with Aldrex is recommended as preventive measure.

Diseases

The crop is sufficiently hardy and not very prone to diseases. However, some of the diseases reported are black-rot disease caused by Corticium koleroga and leaf spot a bacterial disease caused by Xanthomonas lawsonieae.

Harvesting and Yield

Usually in the third year, the plants begin to yield the leaf crop and continue to give economic yields for the next 25 years or so twice a year in April-May and October-November. While harvesting the plants are cut close to the ground, dried in the shade and the leaves are separated by threshing.

Under rainfed conditions, for dense planting, the dried leaf-yield in the first year may be around 200 ka/ha while over the second, third and fourth year the yields normally range from 1 000 to 1 500 kg/ha with irrigation and heavy fertilizer treatment, plus three croppings a year. Yields in excess of 2 000 kg/ha can be obtained in the peak years.

Grading

In India, Henna in trade is graded as Delhi, Gujarat (also known as Bombay) and Malva. Henna is Delhi quality is marketed in the form of powder and the principal marketing centre is Faridabad. Gujarat henna is available in the form of leaves and is exported from Bombay. Malva henna is the produce of Rajasthan the main trading centre being Bhawani Mandi near Kotah; it is marketed in the form of powder.

The quality of henna powder is determined by its colour, purity and fineness.

Chapter 19

ISABGOL

English name	:	Blond psyllium, Spogel seeds
Indian name	:	Snighabijah, snigdhajirakah (Sanskrit) Isabgol, Isabgul (Hindi) Iskol Isphogol (Tamil)
Distribution	:	India, West Asia, West Pakistan, Persia Mexico Mediterranean Regions
Uses	:	Drugs

Plantago is a large genus of herbs and subshrubs, distributed mostly in the temperate regions and a few in the tropics. It comprises of about 200 species, of which 10-14 are natives of India. Plantago ovata Forsk (Syn. P. isphagula Roxb). commonly known as Isabgol or blonde psyllium or indian plantago or psillium in commerce, is important for its seeds and husks which have been used in indigenous medicine for many centries. Because of the superior quality and yield of its seeds it has replaced the French psyllium, P psyllium Linn, in the world market. In fact, France now depends on India for its requirements.

It derives its name from two Persian words, 'asp' and 'ghol' meaning a horse ear, referring to its characteristic boat-shaped seeds. Plantago is from Latin, meaning 'sole' of the 'foot' and refers to the shape of the leaf, psyllium is from the Greek, meaning 'flea' in reference to the colour size and shape of seeds (flea seed) and ovata refers to the ovate shape of the leaves.

The husk of the seed is the economic part and is separated by a physical process. The seed-husk contains a colloidal mucilage (30%), mainly consisting of xylose, arabinose, galacturonic acid with rhamnose and galactose, etc. The seed also contains some oil and small amounts of glycoside acubin and tannin. The husk has the property of absorbing and retaining water and therefore it works as an anti-diarrhoeal drug. It is beneficial in chronic dysentries of amoebic and bacillary orgin. It is also used for treating constipation and intestinal disorders because it works as calorie-free fibre food, promoting regular bowel movement. It is reported to have no adverse side-effects.

The seed has also cooling and demulscent effects and is used in Ayurvedic, Unani and Allopathic systems of medicine. The seeds and husks are used to cure inflammations of the mucous membranes of gastro-intestinal and genito urinary tracts, duodenal, ulcers, gonorrhoea and piles. It can also be used as a cervical dilator for the termination of pregnancy. In addition to these medicinal uses, it has a place in dyeing, calico printing in the ice-cream industry as a stabilizer, also in confectionery and cosmetic industries. The seed without the husk, which contains about 17-19% protein, is used as cattle-feed.

Distribution, Area and Production

The plant is indigenous to Persia and West Asia, extending up to the Sutlej Sind and West Pakistan. The plant has also acclimatized well in Mexico and the Mediterranean regions.

At present, the Isabgol crop has acquired the place of the 'dollar earner' crop of north Gujarat, where it is being cultivated on about 50 000 ha with production of 40 000 tonnes. It has now been introduced in Southern Rajasthan, Punjab and, to a very small extent, in Maharastra and Uttar Pradesh. Experimental cultivation at Bengalore has been quite successful. The quality of husk and yield is comparable to the crop grown in Gujarat. About 75-80% of the total annual produce of north Gujarat is exported which brings crores of rupees of foreign exchange annually. India continues to hold a monopoly in its production and trade in the World though India enjoy the monopoly in production and export of Isabgol, hardly 50% of the requirement of the USA is being met. In view of its s ustained demand, there is still scope to increase the area and production and to intensify its cultivation. Therefore, if India is to retain its monopoly in the production of this important foreign exchange earning commodity, there is an urgent need to evolve high-yielding strains and to examine suitable locations for growing this crop in other states of the country.

Description of the Plant

P. ovate (2n=8), belonging to the Plantaginaceae family is a stemless or short-stemmed, highly cross-pollinated annual herb which attains a height of 30 to 40 cm has alternate, leaves, which clasp the stem strap-like, recurved, 7.5 to 2.5 cm long, narrow-varying from less than 6.0 mm to 12.0 mm in width, tapering to a point, three-nerved, entire or toothed, coated with fine hairs. The flower are white, minute, four-parted. The capsule is ovate, 8.0 mm long 2-celled, the top half lifting up when ripe, releasing the smooth, dull, ovate seeds which are 1.8 to 3.8 mm long, pinkish-grey brown or pinkish-white with a brown streak on the convex surface. the seeds are covered with a translucent membrane, known as the husk, which is odourless and tasteless. When soaked in water the whole seed appears hugely swollen because of the expansion of the mucilage in the husk. The husked seeds are dark-red and hard.

Another species P insularis Eastw. is closely related to P. ovata and is different from it in having rachis villous, the trichomes half-as-long ot longer than the bracts, the bracts being pubescent, rarely glabrous the membranous wing of the basal bract is as wide as or wider at the apex than at the base.The filaments and style are red, pick or white the corolla mid-vein is often reddish.

Varieties

Gujarat Isabgol-1 (GI-1) and Gujarat Isabgol-2 (GI-2) are the two varieties of this crop released by the Gujarat Agricultural University. Both these varieties were identified, evaluated and recommended for cultivation based on their yield performance alone, and none of these varieties have any markers by which these can be distinguished. Another variety 'Niharika' has been released by the CIMAP, Lucknow, as a high yielding variety.

Soil

It is an irrigated crop which grows well on light soils. Heavy soils and those with poor drainage are not conducive to the good growth of this crop. A silty-loam soil, having a soil pH from 4.7 to 7.7 with low nitrogen and moisture content, is reported to be ideal for the rich growth of these plants and high yield of the seeds.

Climate

Isabgol thrives in warm temperate regions. It requires cool, dry weather and is sown during the winter months. Sowing, during the first week of November gives the best yields. Early sowing especially with a higher seed rate, makes the crop vulnerable to downy mildew diseases; whereas, late sowing provides a shorter period of growth in winter along with the possibility of seed, shattering due to summer rains in April-May. At maturity if the weather is humid, its seeds shatter, resulting in reduced yield. Heavy dew or even a light shower will proportionately decrease the yield, sometimes even leading to a total loss of the crop. The temperature required for maximum seed germination is reported to be between 20^0 and 30^0 C.

Cultivation

Land Preparation

The field must be free of weeds and clods and should have a fine tilth for good germination. The number of ploughings, harrowings and hoeings depend upon the soil conditions, the previous crop and the degree of weed infestation. About 10-15 t of FYM/ha is incorporated into the soil at the time of the last ploughing. The field should be divided into suitable plots of convenient size depending upon the texture of the soil, the slope of the field and the source and quantum of irrigation water. For light soils with even contours a plot size of 8.0 x 3.0 m is convenient.

Seeds and Sowing

For a high percentage of germination the seeds should be taken from the crop harvested at the end of the preceding season. Older seeds tend to lose viability under ordinary storage conditions. The seeds at the rate of 4-8 kg/ha are sown after treating them with any mercurial seed-dresser at the rate of 3 g/kg seed, to protect the seedlings from a possible attack of damping- off.

The seeds are small and light. Hence before sowing, the seed must be mixed with a sufficient quantity of fine sand or sieved FYM. The seeds are broadcast, because sowing in lines at different spacings does not increase the seed yield significantly. After broad-casting, the seeds are swept over lightly with a broom to cover them with some soil. The broom however should be swept in one direction only, to avoid deep burial of the seed and for uniform germination. The sowing should immediately be followed by irrigation. Germination beings four days after sowing. If delayed it should be stimulated by another watering.

Fertilizers Application

Isabgol does not require the application of heavy doses of fertilizers. A fertilizers dose consisting of 50 kg N 25 kg $P_2 O_5$ and 30 kg K_2O/ha, has given the maximum seed yield under Bangalore conditions. The full dose of P and K along with half of the N is given as a basal dose at the time of sowing itself, and the second split dose of N is applied as a top-dressing after one months of sowing. For other areas a basal dose of 25 kg N and 25 kg $P_2 O_5$/ha is recommended. A top-dressing of 25 kg N/ha is given 32 days after sowing.

Irrigation

Immediately after sowing, light irrigation is essential. First, irrigation should be given with a light flow of water otherwise, with a fast current of water, most of the seeds will be swept off to one side of the plot and the gemination and distribution will not be uniform. The seeds germinate in 6-7 days. If the germination is poor, a second irrigation should be given. Later on, irrigation are given as and when required. The last irrgation should be given at the time when the maximum number of spikes have reached the milk, stage. The crop requires totally 6-7 irrigations for good productivity in medium sandy soils.

Interculture

The first weeding is done after about 20-25 days of sowing. Since the crop is sown by broadcastings, hand-weeding is a very costly operation. Ordinarily, 2-3 weedings within two months of sowing will help to keep the weeds under control.

Pests

Insect Pests

Sometimes white grube and termites damages the crop by cutting off the root. These can be controlled by broadcasitng phorate 10G.@ 10 kg/ha before the last ploughing. Aphids also attack this crop and can be controlled by spraying 0.2% Dimethoate.

Diseases

Downy Mildew

It is a major disease of this crop which is caused by Peronospora plantaginis and P. alta. The extent of the damage depends upon the intensity of the disease. Normally, this disease appears at the time of spike, initiation. The first symptom is small patches on the leaf which spread throughout the leaf, completely destroying it and thus affecting the yield. The disease intensity will be very high in humid weather or when the dewfall is high it is very difficult to keep the disease under control once it has affected the crop extensively. Hence, as a prophylactic measure it is suggested to spray one of the following fungicides whenever the weather becomes cloudy and humid.

1. Bordeaux mixture (6:3:100) at the rate of 600 to 800 l/ha.

2. Copper oxychloride Dithane M - 45 Dithane Z-78 or any other copper fungicide at the rate of 2.0 to 2.5 g in 1 litre of water.

3. The antifungal antibiotic, Aureogungin. The fungicide should be sprayed 30 days after sowing, followed by two or more sprays at an interval of 15-20 days.

The crop is also sometimes affected by the damping-off-disease, caused by Pythium ultimum, Rhizoctonia solani and Fusariumoxysporum. Wilt is reported to be incited by P. ultimum F. oxysproum and F. solani. Another disease of minor importance the powdery mildew which appears at flowering time, is caused by Erysiphe cichoracearum.

Harvesting and Processing

Blooming begins two months after sowing and the crop is ready for harvest in February-March (110-130 days after sowing). When mature, the crop turns yellowish in odour and the spikes turn brown in colour. The seeds are shed when the spikes are pressed slightly. At the time of harvest the atmosphere must be dry and there should be no moisture on the plant otherwise harvesting will lead to considerable seed-shattering. Hence, the crop should harvested after 10 a.m.

The plants are normally cut at the ground level or are uprooted, depending upon the texture of the soil. The harvested plants are transported to the threshing yard bundled in large cloth pieces and spread out. After 2 days, they are threshed with the help of a tractor or bullocks. Threshing should preferably be done during the early morning hours to facilitate the easy separation of the seed from the spike. Sometimes, water is sprinkled over the heap for easy threshing. Care should be taken not to sprinkle excess water lest it should spoil the qualtiy of the produce. Its straw is used as cattle feed. The plants are threshed and winnowed and the seeds sieved until they are clean. The seeds may be marketed whole or the husk may be sold separately. To remove the husk, the cleaned seeds are passed 6 to 7 times through stone-grinders, sieved and screened through several grades of mesh to sort according to fineness. Most of th exported husk is of the grade designated as 70 mesh. The highest quality husk is white with no particles of the red kernels. The husk seed ratio is 25:75 by weight . It costs about Rs 2-8 million (at 1978 prices)·to establish an industry for processing about 8 t of seeds per day.

Yield

Gujarat Isabgol 1 variety yields 800-900 kg of seeds/ha. The new variety, 'Gujarat Isabgol 2' has a potential to yield a 1 000 kg of seeds/ha. Increased yield can be obtained in this crop by spraying cycocel (CCC) at 25 mg/l. twice at the seedlings stage and just before the heading stage.

Analytical Methods

The isabgol husk is used for its mucilage content mucin or mucilage are generally acidic mucopolysaccharides. They are usually attached to proteins to form proteoglycans, in which the polysaccharides make up most of the weight. Normally, mucin consists of recurring disascharide units each of which contains a derivative of an aminohexose, usually D-glucosamine or D-galactosmine. The polysaccharides isolated from mucin are slippery and lubricating proteogulcons fo mucous. These are jelly like ground substance or intercellular cement. There is scanty information available regarding the composition and qualtiy of the mucilage of isabgol. For screening of isabgol germplasm it is necessary to test the isabgol mucilage for its quantity and quality parameters. To study the swelling capacity of the husk 1 g of husk is put in a 50 ml centrifuge tube and 40 ml water is added to it. After mixing the contents the tube is kept overnight. The next day the tube is centrifuged for 5 minutes at 5000 R.P.M. when the gel settles down and a clear liquid is separated on top the volume of gel is measured that is 34 ml, which shows the swelling capacity to be 1:34.

Chapter 20

JASMINE

English name	:	Arabian jasmine, Common jasmine Catalonian jasmine, Needle flower jasmine Sambac jasmine Spanish jasmine Tuscan jasmine
Indian name	:	Jati, Magadhi, Malati, Mallika, Sucimallica, Yuthika (Sanskrit) Bel, Chemeli, Jati, Juhi, Juyi, Mogra (Hindi) Jajimallige, Gundumallige, Mallehoo (Kannada) Kotimalligai, Kuadu, malligai, Malligai Peechi, Usimalligai (Tamil)
Distribution	:	India
Uses	:	Cosmetics Flavouring Perfumery

Jasmine (Jasminum spp)., belonging to the family Oleaceae, constitutes a group of plants which are commercially grown for their fragrant flowers and essential oil. Several types of jasmine oil and perfume extracts from flowers are available in the markets, such as concrete absolute and pomade. The French and Italian jasmine absolute is reported to contain benzyl benzoate, benzyl alcohol, βenzaldehyde and eugenol. The other trace/ additional constituents include farnesol, bergamotene, nerolidol, p-cersol benzyl acetate (65%), linalool (15%) indole (2.5%) cis-jasmone (3%) methyl anthranilate (1.5%) geraniol (10%) terpineol (5%) cis 3-hexenyl benzoate nerol, benzoic acid, 5-hydroxy, jasmonic acid lactone, iso-phytol, phytol, tetramethyle hexadecanol geranyl linalool, phytyl acetate methyl palmitate, methyl linoleate, methyl jasmonate cis-pent-2 enyl pentanolide vanillin methyl heptone, 6, 10 14-trimethyl pentadecan-2-one, methyl-N-acetyl anthraniate and methyl-N-methylanthranilate.

Jasmine flowers are used in garlands and strung into decorative wreaths for hair adornment, for religious offering and a small quantity is used for the production of hair oils and attars. Jasmine concrete and absolute is used in high-grade perfumes. Almost all high-quality perfumes contain at least a small quantity of jasmine oil. The absolute blends with every floral scent imparting smoothness and elegance to the perfume composition. Jasmine oil is used for perfuming expensive soap and cosmetics, mouthwashes and dentifrices salts and tobacco. The oil is also used in incense and deodorants alcoholic washings of concrete are used in handkerchief perfumes. The odour of jasmine flowers cannot be imitated by any known synthetic aromatic or natural isolates, thus giving it a unique status in the perfume world. Hence jasmine oil and perfume extarcts are in good demand in the world market and have a great export potential.

Description of Species and Varieties

Jasmine are climbing, trailing and erect shurb; there are both evergreen and deciduous species. The leaves are opposite or alternate simple trifoliate or pinnate the leaflets are entire. The flowers are white, yellow rarely reddish, sometimes solitary more often in cymose culsters of three to many usually fragrant, the Corolla is tubular with four to nine lobes. There are 2 stamens; the ovary is 2, loculed with 1-4 erect ovules. The fruit is a berry and black in colour.

Important Jasmine

1. J. AURICULATUM VAHL.

It is commonly called 'Juhi' vasanta mallige, 'Parimullai' Co-1 mullai etc. It is a twining shrub with small shiny leaves with auricles. The flowers are white, sweet-scented borne in pubescent, compound many flowered flat cymes and they open early (6-7 p.m). The fruits are black in colour when ripe. The flowers are very light and about 26 000 flowers weigh one kilogram. From its flowers usually attar is prepared and the essential oil is extracted. The essential oil recovery from the flowers varies from 0.24 to 0.42%. No. 24, LR and SR were reported to be high-yielding selctions compared to the local parimullai.

It flowers from April to December with its peak flowering in May followed by September.

2. J. GRANDIFLORUM LINN. (SYN. J.OFFICINALE FORMA GRANDIFLORUM)

It is commonly known as French, jasmine, Spanish, jasmine, Catalonian, jasmine, Chemeli, Jagi, Ajjige, Mallige etc. It is a semicreeper, having pinnate leaves, with 3 to 5 leaflets of equal size. The flowers are large white reddish beneath, delightfully fragrant and are bone in lax, axillary or terminal cymes and they open early (6-7 a.m). Due to triploidy (2n=39) the flowers are highly sterile. It bears flowers from June to September. It is largely used in the production of essential oil. The essential oil content of the flowers ranges from 0.24 to 0.42%. The following are some of the improved cultivars of French jasmine.

CO-1 Peechi

This improved cultivar yields about 10 t/ha/year of flowers containing 0.29% concrete and 25 kg/ha of concrete yield. This cultivar was released by the Tamil Nadu Agriculture University Coimbatore through selection from the material obtained from Lucknow.

Arka Surabhi (Pink pin)

This strain contains 0.35% concrete and is reported to yield about 10 t/ha of flowers and 35 kg/ha of concrete. This variety has been released by the IIHR, Bangalore. Thimmapuram and Coimbatore are the other varietes under cultivation.

3. J. SAMBAC (LINN) AIT

It is commonly known as Mallika, Bela, Mogra, Motia or Gundumallige. The plant is a sub-erect shrub. The leaves are simple opposite cordate to oblong, almost sessile and dark-green in colour. The flowers are white very fragrant, borne in solitary or 3-flowered terminal cymes and they open late (8-9 p.m.). The calyx has 5-9 teeth which are linear, subulate, the corolla lobas are narrowly oblong, acute, obtuse or arbicular, the carpels are black when ripe.

About 22 varieties are known to be under cultivation in different parts of India, of which Gundumalli, Madanban, Iruvatchi, Kasturimalli, Soojimalli, Palmapur, Motia, Mogra and Hazara are important.

The flowers from this species are mostly used for garlands and at a few places for making oils and attars.

Soil

Jasmine can be grown on a wide range of soils. Well-drianed, rich, sandy loam, red loams and clay loams with a pH ranging from 6.5-7.5 is ideal for their cultivation.

Climate

The optimum conditions for the successful cultivation of jasmine are warm summers and mild winters with plentiful water and sunny days. Some species require cool, humid weather. Jasmines do well from locations at sea-level to an elevation of 600 - 1 200 m. The best season for planting is from June to August. A well-distributed annual rainfall of 80 to 100 cm is found to be congenial.

Land Preparation

The soil should be thoroughly preparad and kept free from weeds before planting. Pits of 45 cm are prepared, depending on the type of soil and are exposed for a week. They are filled with top-soil mixed with about 10-15 kg of well-rotted cattle manure. Aldrin (10 g/pit) may be added to the soil in the pit to prevent the attack of termites. A planting distance of 1.5 cm x 1.5 m is recommended for J. auriculatum and J. sambac while J. grandiflorum is planted at a spacing of 1.8 to 2 m.

Cultivation

Propagation

Jasmines was usually propagated by cuttings and layering. Seed propagation, though uncommon, is necessary for crop improvement through planned hybridization. Multiplication through suckers, grafting, budding and tissue culture has also been found successful.

Seed Propagation

Interclonal variations in seed germination have been reported in J. auriculatum and J. grandiflorum and also among other species. Higher temperature and humidity hastens the germination and maximum germination has been reported in sawdust and sphagnum media.

Vegetative Propagation

a) Layering : Layering has been the made of vegetative propagation in jasmines until recently. Simple layering is attempted during June -July in North India and from June to December in South India. This method of multiplication, however, involves more time and restricts the number of plants propagated from a bush. For preparation of layers well matured, one- year old shoots are selected and are buried in the soil 10-15 cm deep after making a shallow tongue-like cut in the portion that is to be buried. The roots form in 90-120 days.

b) Cutting : This is the easiest method of propagation which has been attempted in certain species particularly those grown on a commercial scale. There are however several factors like the type of cutting, rooting medium environmental conditions etc. which influence root formation in cuttings. Sand vermiculite moss and a mixture of these are some of the commonly used media for root formation in cuttings of jasmine. The highest percentage of rooting and the largest number of roots were recorded in cuttings of J. auriculatum planted in coarse sand followed by a mixture of sand and moss (1:1 or 1:3) and vermiculite. The treatment of cuttings with growth regulating substances (Indole Butric Acid-400 ppm) before planting has been found very useful for promoting root formation. Cuttings which are 22-25 cm long with 3 or 4 eyes are obtained in March. The cuttings are buried morethan 5 cm. deep in the rooting medium and are spaced 7 cm apart. The cuttings will be ready for transplanting into the main field after 4 to 5 months of planting in the rootings media. In the French jasmine shoot-tip cuttings have been found to be better than semi hardwood cuttings. Close media sachet or CMS technique and a media-less sachet techniques also have been devised to regenerate jasmines.

c) Micropropagtion : Successful callus proliferation from a culture of buds petals, anthers, internodes and peduncles, and the regeneration of plants from stem apices have been achieved. Apical and ancillary buds, selected from plants, can be cultured in Murashige and Skoog's medium. Outside the dormant period, axillary buds responded to treatments in a similar manner to the apical buds which were active throughout the year.

Planting

The best time for planting is during July and August and from the end of January to February in North India, while in South India planting is done any time between July to December. After planting, a light irrigation is given to the plants.

Manures and Fertilizers

Nutritional studies have revealed that the application of different nutrients markedly improve the growth, flowering and oil content. The application of N, P and K at 120:240:240 g/plant along with 20 kg of FYM applied in six splits: once immediately after pruning in January and again in March, May, July, September and November, is recommended for optimum growth and yield under South Indian conditions. For North Indian conditions, the application of 20 kg of FYM per pit after pruning in Junuary and again in July and August is recommended. This is to be followed by 25 g ammonium sulphate or 10 g of urea per plant before each irrigation from January to April. About 250 g of super phosphate and muriate of potash should be given per plant in split doses from May to July. Split doses have been found very useful in improving the growth, flowering and oil content. Treatment with N as foliar spray at 30 g/plant is reported to be more economical than the conventional method of applying N at 120 g/plant through the soil.

Pruning

Pruning is an important practice for the manipulation of growth and flowering as it influences growth, flower-bud initiation differentiation and ultimately, the flower production. Plants pruned between 17th Demember and 17th January produce the maximum number of branches and the highest yield of flowers. Normally, irrigation is withheld prior to pruning and plants are pruned to half their original length, including the dead and diseased branches. All the leaves are stripped off. Following pruning, all the cut ends are smeared with Bordeaux paste to prevent infection. The height of pruning depends on the species. In French jasmine, 15th December pruning at 90 cm length maintaining 9 to 11 shoots registered the maximum production of shoots and a high flower-yield. In some places chemical defoliants like paraquet dichoride pentachlorophenol, potassium chloride and sodium chloride are employed instead of annual pruning.

Irrigation

Sufficient moisture in the soil is necessary for proper growth and flowering in jasmine. Normally, plants are irrigated once a week in the summer months. After flowering, no irrigation is normally required till after the next pruning and manuring. Though there is a 30% saving of irrigation water through the use of sprinklers, there is also a 10% reduction in the flower-yield.

Irrigation at 60% ASM is reported to increase the flower-yield by 20.33% over the control.

Weeding and Hoeing

Weeds cause enormous losses to the jasmine crop and increase the cost of cultivation. Manual weed control is effective if attended to at the appropriate time, but this is very expensive. Chemical weed control is comparatively economical, convenient and efficient in eradicating weeds with one or two applications. Treatment with Oryzalin has been reported to control weeds for 10 weeks on silt loam soil.

Good vegetative growth and flowering of jasmine is also said to occur with the application of this chemical. Mulching also reduces the weed population.

After pruning the soil 15-30 cm from the main stem around the bushes should be stirred up to a depth of 15 cm. This should be repeated every two to three months.

Intercropping

In the first two years when the plants are small vegetables like tomatoes and ornamental plants can be grown as intercrops. These can provide some additional income to the growers.

Harvesting and Post-harvest Handling

The plants start flowering six months after planting. The bearing of flowers gradually increases and, from the 3rd year onwards, commercial yields are obtained. The stage of harvest depends on the use of the flowers to be harvested. For fresh flowers, fully developed, unopened flower-buds are hand (picked early in the morning. While, for the extraction of concrete only fully opened, freshly) picked flowers are required. Any delay in picking results in the gradual reduction of the concrete yield. Care should be taken to see that the flowers are not badly handled, wrinkled or damaged during harvest and transport. Generally, in warm weather and ample sunshine the flowers are more heavily scented than in cool or rainy weather.

Longevity of Flowers

The stage of harvest and pre-and-post harvest handling, markedly influence the quality of the picked flowers. They are treated with certain chemicals like boric acid, aluminium sulphate and silver nitrate to prolong the shelf-life of the harvested flowers up to 72 hours against 48 hours under normal conditions. The fragrance of the fresh flowers also remains unchanged for a longer period due to the treatment.

Packaging

Althrough no standard grades are available for jasmines, the flower-buds are generally graded according to their shape, size and freshness before packing in boxes or baskets for marketing. Corrugated cardboard boxes are the best packaging material for distant markets while bamboo baskets may be used for local markets. The packaging should be functional economical and attractive besides being acceptable in markets. Harvested flowers should be given the cold treatment before packing.

Distillation of Oil

A poor yield is obtained when the flowers are steam-distilled. Hence, the steam-distillation method is not commercially used. The chemicals responsible for the odour of the oil are captured through a method called 'enfleurage' which is widely used in India for the production of jasmine attars. The method involves soaking of Sesamum indicum L (sesame) seeds in water to remove their covering and then drying them in the sun. Then, the fresh jasmine flowers and the dehusked sesame seeds are spread in thin layers, one over the other for 10 to 12 hours daily. The exhausted blossome are replaced with fresh flowers and this process is repeated for 5 to 7 days till all the dehusked seeds are saturated with perfume. The ratio is 1 kg seeds 3 kg fresh flowers. The perfumed seeds are distilled and the vapours of jasmine are absorbed into sandalwood oil for the production of attars. In other countries, jasmine is obtained by solvent extraction, which is a more modern method and recovers practically all the odour constituents and is economical as well. The solvent used is either petroleum ether or hexane. The solvent is recovered by vacuum-distillation and the residue constitutes the concrete, which is purified by extraction with 95% alcohol whereby the jasmine absolute is obtained 'Jasmine concrete' is a yellowish brown, waxy mass with an odour of jasmine flowers. It is partly soluble in 95% alcohol. The absolute on the other hand is a viscous clear yellowish- brown liquid possessing a delicate odour of fresh jasmine flowers.

Yield

The flower and concrete yield in jasmine's vary considerably according to the species and cultivars and management practices. The flower-yield and concrete recovery in J. grandiflorum ranges from 0.25 to 0.30% whereas,

J. auriculatum gives a higher recovery of concrete : between 0.28 and 0.36% while J. sambac which is mainly grown for flowers yields a lower percentage of concrete the recovery ranging from 0.1 to 0.19%. It is to be noted that the concrete from J. grandiflorum alone has an international market. The cultivar, Co. 1 Peetchi is the highest yielder, producing over 10 t/ha flowers with an estimated concrete, yield of 20 kg the recovery being 0.29%. The flower, yield of various cultivars in kg/ha are given below.

Cultivars	Ist Year	IInd Year	IIIrd Year	IVth Year
J. auriculatum	1250	2 500	5 000	10 000
J. grandiflorum	125	3 750	10 000	11 000
J. sambac	1250	2 500	500	7 500

The life of a jasmine plantation is between 10-15 years. It is advisable to replant the whole plantation after every 15 years.

Chapter 21

KALMEGH

English name	:	King of Bitters, Chiretta
Indian name	:	Bhunimbah Kirta (Sanskrit), Kalmegh (Hindi) Nelaberu (Kannada), Nilavembu (Tamil)
Distribution	:	Indian, Bangladesh, China Sri Lanka, Thailand
Uses	:	Drugs

Kalmegh (Andrographis paniculata Nees). belonging to the family Acantaceae, is one of the nineteen species of the genus Andrographis, which is indigenous to India and has been used in Indian systems of medicines since time immemorial. The plant is also known as 'Rice betters' in West Indies and King of bitters' or 'Chiretta' in England. The fresh and dried laves of kalmegh and the juice extracted from the herb are official drugs in Indian pharmacopoeia.

The whole herb is the source of several diterpenoids of which the bitter water-soluble lactone andrographolide is important and is distributed all over the plant body in different proportions. The leaves contain the maximum (2.5%) andrographolide content while the stem contains a smaller amount (2.0%) of this active principle. In addition, the plant is an important source of the flavonoids, sespuiterpenes, phenylpropanoids. The roots contain the flavonoids andrographin, panicotin, aplegenin-4-7-dimethyl ether mono, methyl wightin and hydroxy 7,8,2, 3-trimethoxy flavone and sitosterol. In Japan, several flavonoids named as andrographidin A,B,C,D,E,F, have been extracted from the roots and their content varies from 0.015 to 0.15%. Sesquiterpenes like paniculide A,B and C, have been reported to be obtained from the callus tissues. Phenyl propanoid eugenol has also been recorded in the aerial parts of the plant. The diterpenoid and sesquiterpenoid compounds occurring in A. paniculata have been referred to as paniculides and andrographolides. Besides the flavonoids, caffeic acid chlorogenic acid and dicaffeoyloquinic acids are also present in this plant.

Kalmegh forms the principle ingredient of a household medicine called Alui extensively used in West Bengal for general debility and for certain forms of dyspepsia amongst adults and infants. The expressed juice of the leaves is prescribed with cardamom cloves and cinnamon in the form of globules to infants for relief from bowel complaints irregular stools and loss of appetite. The plants is considered to be highly efficacious against chronic malaria and often used as a substitute for Swertia chirata. In India the entire plant is used to treat snakebite. The hot water extract of the whole plant is used for acute jaundice where the powder is mixed with garlic and 2 g of this mixture is given orally with buttermilk for four days and also as febrifuge and as an antidysentric agent while the extract of the dried-leaf is used to treat stomach worms the hot water extracts of the dried leaf and stem is used as a stomachic, febrifuge and tonic, while the fresh leaf-juice along with the leaf-juice of Azadirachta indica and Tinospora codifolia are used to cure cholera. The roots are used as antipyretic, alternative and cholagogue agents. The decoction of the plants is used in some cases of anemia. In Thailand, the decoction of the dried leaf is used against high blood pressure. While in Bangladesh, the hot water extracts of leaf and stem are prescribed as a powerful tonic.

The common ayurvedic drugs are Kalmeghasva and 'Kalmeghnamayas Haub', the main constituents of which are A. paniculata besides Trikatu (Piper longum, P. nigrum and Zingiber officinalis) Cyperus scariosus Triphala Embelia ribes Plumbago zeylanica and Lauh Bhasm (organo, metallic salt of iron).

Distribution

It grows wild as an undershrub in tropical moist deciduous forests. The plant is found in the plains throughout India and Sri Lanka. It is also reported from certain parts of China Thailand and Bangladesh. In India it is distributed in the States of Andhra Pradesh, Assam, Bihar, Karnataka, Kerala, Madhya Pradesh and West Bengal.

Botany

It is an annual herbaceous or shrubby recumbent or erect plant 0.3-1.0 m high. The branches are sharphy quadrangular, often narrowly winged towards the apical region. The leaves are petiolate, 5-8 cm long and 1-1.25 cm broad lanceolate and acute. The flowers are small, solitary, in panicles with a rose-coloured corolla which is hairly externally. The filaments are flattened, hairy on the upper part and the anthers borne at the base. The fruit is 20 mm long and 3 mm broad, linear-oblong and acute at both ends. The seeds are numberous yellowish-brown and glabrous.

Soil

Kalmegh is a hardy plant and can be grown on a variety of soils. In the native state, it is found growing in clayey to sandy soils in various locations. However sandy loamy soil rich in organic matter is good for its growth and yield. Soils with water logged conditions and problematic soils are not suited for its cultivation.

Climate

This crop comes up well in tropical and subtropical regions. However, cooler climates with well distributed rainfall are ideal. Under natural conditions, this crop is found growing abundantly in moist, shady places and sometimes in dry forests also. Studies at Bangalore have shown that the best season for planting this crop is during the month of June when it has the maximum growth and gives the highest yield of herb.

Propagation

Kalmegh is propagated either by seeds or cuttings. However, for commercial purposes the crop is raised from seeds as it is not only easy but economical compared to the vegetatively grown crop.

Seed Propagation

Seeds are either sown directly in the main field or nursery raised seedlings are transplanted. About 400 g/ha of seeds are required for sowing. While for raising the seedlings the seeds are sown in polythene bags filled with a mixture of soil, sand and organic manure in 1:1:1 proportion. The seedlings can also be raised in nursery beds of 3 x 1.5 x 0.15 m size. The nursery beds are mixed with well rotted, powdered cattle manure @ 20 kg/ m^2. The seeds are sown in lines 5 cm apart in the nursery beds. The beds or polythene bags are watered daily. The seeds germinate in about 8-10 days and the seedlings will be ready for transplanting into the main field when they are 45-50 days old.

Land Preparation

The land is prepared well by repeated ploughing and planking and brought to a fine tilth. FYM @ 25 t/ha is mixed well into the soil at the time of the last ploughing. The land is laid out into plots of convenient sizes along with irrigation channels for easy management.

Sowing/Transplanting

For direct sowing, furrows are made at a distance of 30 cm and about 3-4 seeds are sown in each spot maintaining a distance of 15 cm between two plants while the seedlings are transplanted at a spacing of 30 x 15 cm or 15 x 15 cm. Studies have shown that in order to get the maximum herb yield, a spacing of 15 x 15 cm is the best.

Application of Manures and Fertilizers

Kalmegh responds very well to the application of manures and fertilizers. Besides the application of about 25 tonnes of FYM a fertilizer dose of 75 kg N, 7 5 kg P_2O_5 and 50 kg K_2O is required for a crop of one hectare. Of this, 50% N and the entire dose of P_2O_5 and K_2O is given as basal dose and the remaining 50% N is used as a topdressing 30 days after sowing or transplanting.

Irrigation

As kalmegh is mainly grown as a rainy season crop in the areas with well distributed rainfall hardly any irrigation is given. However in case of long dry periods, the crop is irrigated initially at 3-4 days interval and later the interval is increased to one week, depending upon the weather conditions.

Weeding

Kalmegh is a small herbaceous shrub and therefore the competition with weeds during its initial stages of growth should be avoided by keeping the land free from weeds. The first weeding is done after about 20-30 days of planting. After this, one or two weedings are done after 60 days of sowing to keep the weeds under control during the initial stages of crop growth. Later weeding follows every harvest.

Pests and Diseases

Kalmegh is a hardy plant and is not attacked by any pests and diseases of a serious nature.

Harvesting and Yield

The crop is ready for the first harvest after about 90 to 120 days of sowing when the plants start flowering. At this stage they are harvested by cutting the plants at the base, leaving about 10-15 cm of the stem for regeneration.

The field is given a top-dressing of N and irrigated after every harvest for regeneration. The regenerated plants are ready for harvest in about 60 days of the previous harvest. Totally, 2 to 3 harvests can be made in a year. Sometimes, the whole plant is also harvested after about 6 months. After harvesting, the plants are dried under shade for 3-4 days before storage.

The average yield is about 2 to 2.5 t/ha of dry herb.

Chemical Evaluation

To estimate the andrographolide content the coarsely powdered drug (10 g) accurately weighed is transferred to a Soxhlet extractor and extracted with 200 ml of alcohol (95%) for six hours. The extract is concentrated to about 50 ml 30 ml of distilled water is added to it.

The soluton is extracted with two 25 ml portions of benzene and the benzene layer is rejected. Distilled water (20 ml) is added to the aqueous layer. The combined aqueous solution is then extracted with three 25 ml portions of ethyl acetate, which is sufficient to extract all the bitter principles. The combined ethyl acetate extract is treated with anhydrous sodium sulfate and then filtered through a cotton plug into a 10 ml beaker. The cotton plug is again washed with 5 ml ethyl acetate. The residue collected in the beaker is dried to constant weight on a water-bath and weighed as andrographolide. The values are expressed in per cent andrographolide.

Chapter 22

LIQUORICE

English name	:	Liquorice
Indian name	:	Yastimadhu, Madhukah (Sanskrit) Jetimad, Mulahati (Hindi) Atimadhura Yestimadhuka (Kannada), Atimaturam (Tamil)
Distribution	:	India ,Afghanistan, North Africa, Asia Western China, Southern Europe, France, Germany, Greece, Hungary, Italy, Pakistan, Spain, Syria, Yugoslavia
Uses	:	Confectionery, Drugs, Tobacco

Olycyrrhiza glabra Linn. is a hardy perennial herb and undershrub belonging to the family Papilionaceae. As its roots are very sweet, it is popularly called liquorice. In Greek, glycyrrhiza means 'Sweet Root'. In India it is known as Jethimadh, Yasthimadhu, Jesthimadhu or Mulahati. It has been known in pharmacy for thousands of years as an important medicinal plant. In Hindu medicine, it is a principal drug of the Susruta, in China also it was considered as an important drug. The Egyptians Greek and Romans utilized it for medicinal purposes and, liquorice maintains its place of importance even in present day medical and pharmaceutical sciences.

The dried, peeled and unpeeled underground stems and roots constitute the drug. Its extract contains about 5-20% saponin, like glycoside glycyrrhizin, which has a healing effect on peptic ulcers. It also contains coumarine compounds herniarin and umbelliferone and the flavours liquiritin, liquiritigenin, isoliquirtin and isoli quirittgenin. The glycosides, liquiritoside and isoliquiritoside are also present. A few of the reputed uses of the drug are demulscent mildly laxative expectorant and it is an important constituent of all cough and catarrh syrups throat lozengen and pastilles. Mustong, a preparation in which one of the constituents is G. glabra improves sexual inadequacy. It is also known for its analgesic anti-inflammatory and anticonvulsive properties. Recent investigations have shown its growth and inactivation of virus particles. Large quantities of liquorice are used in confectionery and in tobacco blending. the extrect is reported to lend sparkle and aroma to beer.

Distribution & Origin

Liquorice is distributed in the subtropical and warm temperate regions particularly in Western China, parts of Asia Minor, Persia, the Asian Republics of the erstwhile USSR and Afghanistan. It is also distributed in the warmer parts of the Mediterranean region of North Africa, Spain, Italy Yugoslavia, Greeca, Syria, Hungary and South Russia. It is cultivated in Italy, France, Russia, Germany, Spain and China. Although the origin of liquorice is attributed to regions from Southern Europe to Pakistan and Northern India none of the liquorice yielding species occur in India. In an effot to curb import, substitution attempts have been made to cultivate liquorice in several places in India notably Baramulla, Srinagar, Jammu, Dehradun, Delhi, Anand, Indore and Bangalore and it has been found to come up successfully in quite a few places. Presently India is importing the drug on a considerable scale (5 000 - 10 000 t) from Iran, Iraq, Afghanistan Burma and Singapore.

Plant Description

Liquorice (2n=16) is a perennial herb or undershrub attaining a height of 1-2 m with long, cylindrical burrowing rootstock and horizontal creeping stolons which are 1.5-1.8 m in length. The leaves are alternate pinnate with 9-17 ovate yellowish-green, leaf-lets about 2.5-5.0 cm long. The flowers are borne in erect auxiliary 1.25 cm long. The seed pods are maroon 3 cm long oblong, pointed, flattened and contain 2-4 kidney-shaped seeds. The chromosome number is 2n=16, and the plant is self-pllinated. The root system is highly branched and confined to the upper crust to the soil it consists of a short tap-root with a large number of rhizomes.

Varieties & Species

a) Glycyrrhiza glabra var. Typica Regel. and Herd: This is called Spanish liquorice. It attains a height of 120 to 150 cm and bears typical papilionaceous flowers of a purplish-blue colour. The underground portion consists of long roots and thin rhizomes. The principal root divides just below the ground into several secondaries which penatrate the soil to a depth of 120 cm or more. A considerable number of stolons are given off, which attain a length of 150 to 180 cm and run near the surface. The concentration of glycocide ranges from 6-10%. It is cultivated in Spain, Italy, England, France, Germany and the USSR. It fetches a higher price in the market and is the sweetest of all.

b) Glycyrrhiza glabra var. glandulifera Waldst and Kit. It is also called Russian liquorice. The root system is shallow, but grows into a large stock; the rhizomes grow over a long distance without stolon development. It is rich in glycyrrhizin (10-14%), but the sweet taste is accompanied by a perceptible but mild bitterness owing to the presence of liquiritin and isolquiritin.

c) Glycyrrhiza glabra var. violaceae Boiss: This is called Persian liquorice. It bears violet flowers and is grown in Iran and Iraq, in the valleys of the Tigris and Euphrates. The plant produces thick, hard and lumpy roots and is considered inferior in quality.

Varieties

Through an evaluation trial of 14 accessions of G. glabra from different countries at Anand, Indore and Haryana a Russian collection EC-111236 has been released as 'Haryana Mulhati No. 1' by the Haryana Agriculture University for cultivation. It has long broad and dark-green leaves and produces approximately 200 cm-long roots at harvest. This variety is resistant to leaf-spot disease and gives 70-80 g/ha of roots at 3 years with 7.5% glycyrrhizic acid. An accession, EC-21950, has been identified at the All India Co., ordinated Research Project on Medicinal and Aromatic Plants, which is said to be tolerent to the root-rot disease.

Soil

The plant requires a soil with a minimum of 1 m depth for the proper growth and development of the root system. Loamy soils of light texture with a pH of 6 to 8.2, are ideally suited for high biological and economic productivity. Deep moist soils, particularly on the banks of rivers, subject to periodical inundation, are also suitable. Liquorice is one of the plants which can withstand salinity without affecting its growth and active principles.

Climate

Liquorice prefers a warm and dry, subtropical climate with well-defined winters, to induce the translocation of food to the rhizomes. Heavy rains or frost affects its growth adversely. The plant thrives in locations receiving

50-100 cm rainfall annually, supported with irrigation.

Cultivation

Propagation

Different varieties of Glycyrrhiza glabra are perpetuated by seeds and cuttings of both root and stem and by tissue culture.

Seed Propagation

Though the plants can be grown from seeds this is seldom practised because of the germination problem. It is was found that treatment of seeds with 0.0025 to 0.005% of succinic acid, combined with scarification (in sand), increased laboratory and field germination. The treated seeds are drill- sown 15 cm apart in raised nursery beds (1 x 3 m) that are well prepared and manured. The germination starts after 15 days and is completed within a month. The seedlings are picked out when they are 10-15 cm high and planted in the main field.

Tissue Culture

Rapid clonal multiplication of Glycyrrhiza glabra L. using auxiliary bud culture has been reported. The technique has also been standardized for transplanting test-tube grown plantlets to the field.

Clonal Propagation

The traditional method of perpetuation is by utilizing the cuttings prepared form the old crowns of the lifted roots, cut into pieces of 10-15 cm length. The plants are also produced from runners or underground stems which are prepared into cuttings of 10 cm long, each with 2 buds. These cuttings are kept in moist sphagnum moss for about 8-10 days and afterwards, when their buds start sprouting, they are planted in the main field.

Preparation of Main Field and Planting

The crop is usually grown continuously on the same land. Uprooting of the plant is done in October-November and this disturbs the soil to depth of 80 to 100 cm. The soil is then levelled and planting ridges 60 cm wide and 30 cm apart are marked out. The rows are enriched with FYM and the soil from the intervening spaces is swept up to cover the manure to form rounded ridges whose summits are about 37 cm along the furrows. The planting is done in March or early April. The setts are planted in groups of 3, 30 cm apart in rows. The central planting material of every alternate groups is an old crown which is placed at the top of the ridge with the two other setts (root-cuttings) on either side of the ridge approximately 30 cm apart. The crowns are covered with 5 to 7 cm of wet soil. Dry conditions at planting time and for the next few months give the conditions required for a good crop. If cold weather prevails in May or June, 20 to 40% of the setts may fail to grow.

Manures and Fertilizers

In order to obtain good growth and development of the roots, the field must be liberally manured. Compost or FYM @ 10-15 t/ha is enough to meet the requirements. However, there is difficulty in getting organic manure in such large quantities, hence, a fertilizer dose at the rate of 40:40:20 kg/ha per year is recommended for application in the form of urea, superphosphate and muriate of potash. Of these, a full dose of superphosphate and potash are applied as a basal dose at the time of planting. Whereas nitrogen is applied in three split doses i.e., at planting after six months and one year of growth respectively. Since the crop remains in the field for 3-4 years, every year the same dose has to be reapplied.

Irrigation

Regular irrigation is necessary until the cuttings put down roots and establish themselves. Later, the watering may be done at intervals of 8-10 days for 5-6 months and afterwards as and when required. Once the plants are established they need no special attention as the crop is fairly drought resistant.

Intercropping and Weeding

The crop occupies the land for a period of 4 to 5 years, and the growth is slow during the first 2 years. Thus, intercropping by planting carrots, potatoes or cabbage between the ridges, with the additional inputs required by the intercrop is recommended. The field may be hoed periodically to keep down the weeds.

Pests and Diseases

Pests

Termites cause a lot of damage to young plants during the dry period.

Aldrex at the rate of 25-30 kg/ha can be given during the last ploughing/ harrowing to control termites. Cotton ash weevil (Myllocerus undecimpunctatus) is reported to cause injury to leaves and this insect can be controlled by spraying Metasystox (1.5 ml/L).

Diseases

The crop is found to be infected by root-rot disease. The roots and stolons of the affected plants turn soft ad pulpy, 5 kg/ha Brassicol (or drenching the soil with 6:3:100 Bordeaux mixture) is applied during February to control the disease effectively. Rhizoctonia bataticola, Sclerotium spp., and Fusarium spp. causes root-rot, collar-rot and wilt diseases. Soil treatment/aerial spray of Bavistin or Benlate (0.05%) is reported to control these diseases.

Cercospora cavarae is reported to cause leaf-spot disease. To control the disease spray 0.4% Bavistin (4g.,50.w.p. in 10 litres of water). However one protective spray should be given one-and-a-half to two months after planting. The other fungi which are reported to cause leaf-spot diseaes are Alternaria tenuis, Septoria glycyrrhizae or Phyllosticta glycyrrhizae. Uromyces glycyrrhizae causes leaf-rust. Leaf-blight is another serious infection which can be controlled by foliar spraying of Blitox (0.2%) 3 to 4 times, at an interval of 5 days.

Harvesting

The crop is ready for uprooting about 3 to 4 years after planting and just before the plants have borne fruit. The plants are lifted in autumn (November-December) after the rains. A trench about 60 cm deep is first dug at the side of the ridges then, by working inwards, the soil is loosened from the roots so that they can be pulled out easily. The aerial parts are cut and removed. The broken root-parts are left in the soil and new sprouts are thrown out in spring and, for raising the succeeding crop, only the gaps need to be filled with rooted cuttings.

Processing

Roots and underground stems are cut into 15 to 20 cm-long pieces, 1 to 2 cm in diameter and are dried alternately in the shade and sun, this may take several months. The drying process reduces the weight to 50% and the moisture from 50-60%. Artificial drying can also be done at 30-40° C by using mechanical driers.

Yield

The yield depends upon the soil fertility variety the climate and cultivation practices. An yiedl of 5 t/ha of roots, plus 14-20 t/ha of trimmings is considered satisfactory.

Analytical Method

The principal constituent of liquorice is glycyrrhizin which has a characteristic sweet taste. The other constituents are glucose (3.8%), sucrose (6.5%), mannite, starch, asparagine, resins, volatile oil (0.03-0.06%) and the colouring matter isoliquoricin.

Glycyrrhizin ($C_{42}H_{62}O_{16}$, m.p. 205) occurs as Ca or K salts of glycyrrhizic acid. On acid hydrolysis, it yields glycyrrhizic acid ($C_{30}H_{46}O_4$, a triterpenoid aglycon) and manuronic acid.

i) Analytical procedure for Glycyrrhiza glabra

The shredded roots of liquorice are stirred with 10 times its volume of distilled water for 4 to 6 hours, keeping the temperature at 60° C. The pH of the suspension is maintained between 6.5 to 7.0 by adding ammonium hydroxide. The suspension is centrifuged and the supernatant is separated. The extract, thus obtained, is evaporated in vacuum to about 75% of its volume. Ten percent concentrated sulphuric acid solution is added to this suspension with constant stirring. The supernatant liquid is discarded. the precipitate comprising fo crude glycyrrhizic acid left in the beaker is taken up in distilled water and the pH of this suspensionis brought to 4.0 by adding the required quantity of ammonium hydroxide/ sodium carbonate/potassium carbonate. This suspension is stirred for 4 to 6 hours, and transferred to a centrifuge tube. The suspension is centrifuged till a clear supernatant is obtained. The supernatant is discarded and the residue left behind is suspended in distilled water and its pH is brought to 6.0 by adding ammonia. The material is again centrifuged and the supernatant is discarded. The precipitate is dried and extracted with absolute alcohol. Alcohol is evaporated on a water-bath and dried in a vacuum oven to obtain active glycyrrhizic acid. The recovery of active glycyrrhizic acid under this procedure is 7 to 8%.

ii) Determination of crude fibre content in Glycyrrhiza glabra roots

The residue left after the water extract is taken and processed as below for the determination of crude fibre content. Otherwise, about

2 g of the powdered sample is weighed and treated with ether on a funnal to make it free from fat.

The fat-free residus is transferred to a 400 ml beaker containing 100 ml of 2.5% $H_2\ SO_4$ and 100 ml of boiling water a mark is made on the beaker with a glass pencil to represent the level of the mixture in it. The contents are brought to boil and the boiling is continued for exactly 30 minutes. During the boiling it is stirred with a glass rod to mix the contents and to remove particles from the sides of the beaker. The volume of the liquid is kept constant by the addition of hot water from time to time.

At the end of 30 minutes, the beaker is removed, the contents are filtered immediately through a wet piece of linen cloth and the residue is washed with hot water till it is free from acid.

All the residue from the cloth is then transferred back to the original beaker. The linen is washed with hot water, added to 100 ml of 2.5% NaOH solution and the volume is brought up to 200 ml by the addition of boiling water. The contents are boiled as before for exactly 30 minutes, stirring with a glass rod and keeping the volume constant by the addition of hot water the beaker is removed and the contents re-filtered immediately through the same linen cloth. All the residue is transferred to the cloth with a jet of hot water. The residue is washed with hot water 3 times, than with dilute 1% HCL solution and again with hot water till it is free from acid. Finally, the residus is washed once with 95% alcohol and once with ether.

Quantitatively, the whole residue is transferred to a clean dry crucible previously weighed. The residue is dried in the oven at 100° C to constant weight. It is cooled in a dessicator and weighed. The residue is ignited completely, till white or greyish white ash is obtained. It is cooled in a dessicator and weighed again. The difference in the two weights represents the weight of crude fibre. The glycyrrhiza roots possess about 15 to 20% of crude fibre.

Chapter 23

LEMON GRASS

I. Introduction

The name Lemon grass is given to it because of the presence substance called citral in its oil extracted from leaves. The oil is obtained by steam distillation of the leaves of species of Cymbopogan. The oil from C. flexuosus is referred to as East Indian Lemon grass oil whereas that from C. citratus is designated as West Indian lemon grass oil. Both type of oils contain 75-85% of citral but West Indian Lemon grass oil is inferior in quality as its solubitlity in 70% alcohol is less.

Lemon grass has been used in different types of medicine in India for more than 2000 years. However, the first distillation of this grass in India was started around 1890 from the wild grass from Kerala Most of East Indian lemon grass oil is produced in India, and West Indian lemon grass oil is in Guatemala.

II. Distribution

Both the species of lemon grasses are extensively found in India. The C. flexuosus is indigenous to the Malabar Coast of India, and is cultivated in India. C. citrus is indigenous to South East Asia and Africa, and is cultivated in Gutemala, Medagascar, Comoro Island, Brazil, China and Indonesia,. West Indies name to lemon grass sp. C. citrus is misnomer as it is not indigenous to West Indies. It was introduced there afterwards a third species C.Pendulous wats is recently introduced in India and is a much more hardy than the previous two.

III. Botany

Lemon grass belongs to the Graminae family. Two well known species, Cymbopogon flexuosus and C. citratus are widely cultivated all around in the world. Recently a third species C. pendulus is also introduced in India for distillation.

A perennial, densely tufted, aromatic, tall grass stem underground shoot, oblique, with ringed segments. Leaves in dense clusters, coarse, linear, terminating in long bristly point firm glaucous, green, leaf blades 3 ft long or more, 1/2 inch broad, leaf bases, cylindrical, tightly clasping each other, upto a foot long, smooth, slightly leathery, cinnamon coloured on the inside. Flowers at the nodding have branched panicles.

IV. Soil

Lemon grass is adapted to a wide range of soils, but welldrained sandy loam and medium loam soils support good growth of the plant. Although it prefers neutral soils, it can also be cultivated in moderately alkaline soils with pH upto 8.5. Lemon grass can also cultivated on the marginal and submarginal soils of poor fertility.

V. Climate

It is a tropical plant and growns well in humid areas with bright sunshine and high humidity with well distributed rainfall. However, it can also be cultivated in sub tropical areas which do not have frost. But in the subtropical area yields are lower than the tropical areas.

VI. Propagation

Lemon grass can be propagated through seeds or vegetatively by splitting the culms. Vegetative propagation gives better results as it enables to maintain the genetic purity of the clones. Vegetative propagation has also been found to give better yields.

A. Seed propagation

When propagated from seeds seedlings are raised in nursery by sowing in May and June.

1. Seed nursery

About two kg of seed is sufficient for planting of one hectare of land. Seed beds are prepared slightly raised at convenient elevation and after the soil is well pulverised. The seeds are sown in lines about 15 cm apart and covered with light layer of soil and irrigated. When the seedlings are 6-8 weeks old they can be transplanted.

2. Transplanting

The seedlings are transplanted in July and August during monsoon period. The seedlings are transplanted at a distance of 40 cms. from plant to plant and 60 cm. apart rows.

B. Vegetative propagation

Vegetative propagation gives better yields. For vegetative propagation clumps are dug out and divided in slips. One or two slips are planted in holes at a distance of 45 cms. from plant to plant and 60 to 70 cms. row to row spacings. Ideal time of planting is rainy season i.e., July, August. However, it can be planted in February and March in North Indian plains, where adequate irriagation facilities are available. Before planting soil is ploughed thoroughly to have good tilth.

VII. Fertilizers and Manurers

Lemon grass is a leafy crop and hence responds well to fertilizer application. In soils of average fertility a mixture of 30 Kg. each of nitrogen, phosphate and potash per hectare is offered at the time of planting, as a basal dose. This can be followed by 60 Kg. nitrogen as a top dressing in 2 to 3 solit doses during the growth period. At the time of preparation of soil, farmyard manure and woodash at the rate of 2-5 tonnes/hectare has been found very useful in Kerala. In eastern India, higher doses of fertilizers of 60 Kg. of nitrogen 55 kg of phosphate and 30 kg. of Potash Per hectare is applied to get higher yields in central and South India higher doses of Phosphate has not given any good results Micronutrients application has been found to be beneficial in Kerala.

VIII. Irrigation

In areas with well distributed rainfall, no irrigation is required as the plant tolerates the intermitted periods of droughts. In comparatively dry areas, 3 to 4 irrigation are required. In north Indian plains it is advisable to grow lemon grasses with 4-6 irrigations.

IX. Interculture and Weed Control

In lemon grass about 2 to 3 seedlings are required to control weeds during the first 6 months of its growth. Weeding should be followed by interculture (loosening the soil) by a cultivator which may be either tractor drawn or bullock drawn. Application of organic mulch consisting of lemon grass or citronella grass is useful in controlling weeds. The mulch should be applied after two handweeding operations. When the slips are well established, Herbicides eg. Diuron 15 Kg/ha and Oxyfluorfen 0.5 Kg/ha have been found useful in controlling integrated method of weed control.

X. Diseases and Pests

Lemon grass is resistant to attack of diseases and insect pests under normal conditions and no plant protection measures required. However, a number of diseases and pests are reported from various regions.

A. Diseases

The most important diseases are grassy shoot, leaf blighter smut.

1. Grassy shoot disease

It is prevalent in several parts of India, especially in Kerala. This is caused by excessive proliferation of shoots and shortening of leaves giving the typical appearance of little leaf or witch's broom type of disease. The disease is caused by the fungus Balansia sclerotica.

2. Leaf blight

It is caused by Cotletotrichum graminicolu. The disease appears in the form of small bronish spots on the leaf, stem and enlarges into large brown patches.

3. Smut

It is caused by a fungus, Tolysporium christensenji. The symptoms appears in the form of conversion of flowering panicles into black powdery mass. Seeds and flowers are converted into smut spots.

Other minor diseases includes curvularia leaf spots helminthospotium leaf spots, cochliobolus leaf spot and Rhizoctoniza leaf blight.

B. Insect pests

The most important insect pests are scale insects white flies and spotted bugs.

1. Scale insect (Duplachionapsis diverges)

This insect produces yellow spots on the stem and sucks the sap from the leaves and stem.

2. White Fly (Tetraleuroles semi leunanaria)

This insect sucks sap from the leaves causing chlorosis and withering away of leaves. The insect can be controlled by 0.5% Dimenthoate.

3. Spotted Bug (Clovia Bipunctata)

This bug is predominantly found in Kerala. The nymphs of these bugs attack young leaves causing crinkling. It can be controlled by 0.05% Quinolphos.

XI. Harvesting and Processing

The first harvesting of lemon grass is done between 4 to 6 months after planting and the subsequent harvests are taken at an interval of 3 to 4 months depending upon fertility of the soil temperature, and humidity. In north Indian plains, two harvests are taken during the first year and three harvests are obtained during subsequent years, while in tropical areas, 4 or 5 harvests are obtained in subsequent years. The crop is maintained in the field for 5 to 6 years, and after that it is pulled out and rotated with other crops. Harvesting is done by cutting the leaves with sickle about 10-15 cms above the ground level.

The grass should be allowed to wilt for 12-24 hours before distillation. The oil is extracted from the grass by distillation of the leaves. Steam distillation gives better yield of oil and higher citral content as compared to other types of distillations. In order to get better distillation and save energy and fuel, it is better to chop the leaves before distillation. The distillation is completed within 2-3 hours. The oil content in the leaves is variable ranging from 0.3 to 0.8 per cent. Yield of oil depends upon the fertility of the soil and distillation time. An average oil yield of 50-60 Kg/ha is obtained in the first year and 80-100 Kg/ha in the subsequent years. However under good management conditions yield upto 200 Kg/ha can be achieved. After distillation the oil is made free from moisture and stored in galvanized iron or aluminum containers.

XII. Chemical Constituents and Uses

The main constituent of East Indian lemon grass is Citral which is about 75-90%. Minor constituents are linalool, geraniot, citronellol, nerol, 1-8 cinole ,citronellal, linalyl acetate, geranyl acetate alpha-pinene-limonenes Caryoplylene, Ocimene, terpenolene methyl methylheptenone, 2-nonanone and alpha-termineol.

West Indian lemon grass contains citral A (41%) citral B (32%) and myrcene (12%) as main constituents. The minor constituents are alpha-pinene beta pinene, delta-3-corene, dipentene, beta-phallandrene, para-cymene methyl- heptenone, citronellol, beta-clemene, beta-caryophyllene citronellyl, acetate, gernyl acetate gerniol, elemol, beta caryoplyllene oxide, citronellol and geranial.

Jammu lemon grass of C. pendulus contains citral A (30-50%) and citral B (20-30%) as main constituents. The minor constituents are alpha-pinene Canphene, beta, pinene, Car-3 O myrcene, dipentene, phellantrene, para cymene, methyl, hepthenone, citronellol, linalool, beta caryophyllene citronellyl acetate, geranyl acetate, geraniol beta, elenol and beta cuminyl oxide.

Lemon grass oil is used as such in scenting detergents, washing soaps and other home products. It is mainly used to isolate citral which is used both as a perfume as well as flavour. Betaionene a by product of citrals is also converted into Vitamin A.

The tea made from the leaves lemon grass is a stomachic tonic, diaphoretics, diuretic and refrigerant. A paste of the leaves made with buttermilk is applied to eradicate ringworm. The grass is generally used in the form of an infusion. A decoction of the grass is used locally over rheumatic joints, lumbagos and sprains. It is valuable sotmachic for children, with aromatics, it is given as diaphoretic and stimulant in catarroh, and febrile conditions. With black pepper, the infusion is used in congestion and neuralgic forms of dysmenorrhoea, disordered mensuration, vomitting, diarrhoea, and dropsical condition caused by malaria.

Lemon grass oil is carminative antipasmodic stimulant and diaphoretic.

XIII. Conclusion

Lemon grass is a perennial, densely tufted, aromatic tall grass which yields a valuable oil used in medicines and as tragarent. This has been used as medicine for the last thousands of years, but its commercial extraction only started in the last 100 years. Since its cultivation is easy it can be commonly grown on all type of lands, with an economical profit. The two species eg. East Indian lemon grass and West Indian lemon grass are being cultivated in a larger areas. A third species viz. Cymbopogon pendulus is a new introduciton and since it is a hardy crop it can be grown on the adverse soils and climatic conditions. Lemon grass cultivation is a quite profitable introduction in the small farmers cropping systems.

Chapter 24

LONG PEPPER

English name	:	Indian long pepper Long pepper
Indian name	:	Pippali Magadhi (Sanskrit) Pipli, Pipal (Hindi) Hippali (Kannada) Pippili Tippili (Tamil)
Distribution	:	India, Andaman and Nicobar islands, Inddonesia, Malaysia, Nepal, Philippines, Sri Lanka, Timor
Uses	:	Drugs, Spice

Long pepper is obtained from the unripe spikes of Piper longum Linn, a slender, aromatic, perennial climber belonging to the family Piperaceae. The spikes of this plant contain the alkaloids piperne (4-5%) and piplatin, and two new alkaloids one of which is designated as alkaloid A and which is closely related to pellitorine; and three more new alkaloids piperolactum A piperolactam B and piporadione. The roots contain the alkaloids, piper longuminie (0.2-0.25%) and piper longumine (0.02%) besides piperine. Further purification of piper longumine has yielded six known alkaloids cepharadione B, cepharadione A, cepharanone B, aristolactam A 11, norcepharadione B and 2 hydroxy 1 methoxy 4 H dibenzoquinoline 4,5 (6 H) dione); lignins, viz; pluriatilol, fargosin, sesamin, asarinine, guineensine and pipercide. Besides, the dried spikes on steam distillation, yield 0.7% essential oil with a spicy odour resembling that of pepper and ginger oil.

The root is pungent, and has heating, stomachic, laxative, antihelmintic, carminative properties, improves the appetite; is useful in bronchitis, abdominal pains, diseases of the spleen, and tumours. The unripe fruit is sweetish, cooling and useful in biliousness.

The ripe fruit is sweet pungent, a stomachic, aphrodisiac alternative laxative, antidiarrhoeic, antidysenteric is useful in vata and kapha asthma bronchitis abdominal complaints, fevers, leucoderma urinary discharges, tumours, piles diseases of the spleen, pains, inflammations, leprosy, insomnia, jaundice, hiccoughs, tubercular glands and reduces biliousness (in the Ayurvedic system of medicine).

The roots and fruits are used in palsy, gout and lumbago. The root has a bitter hot and sharp taste. It is used as a carminative, a tonic to the liver, stomachic, emmenagogue, abortifacient aphrodisiac, haematinic, diuretic, digestive and as a general tonic, useful in inflammation of the liver, pains in the joints, lumbago, snakebite, scorpion-sting and night blindness (in the Unani sytem of medicine).

In the Travancore region an infusion of the root is prescribed after partiurition to help in the explusion of the placenta. It appears to partake, in a minor degree of the stimulant properties of the fruit.

As an alternative tonic, long pepper is recommended for use in a rather peculiar manner. An infusion of three long peppers is to be taken with honey on the first day then for ten successive days. The dose is to be increased by 3 peppers every day so that on the tenth day the patient will take thirty at one dose. Then the dose is to be gradually reduced by 3 daily and finally the medicine is to be stopped. Thus administered, it is said to act as a valuable alternative tonic in paraplegia, chronic cough, enlargements of the spleen and other abdominal viscera. Long pepper is used in the composition of several snuffs; boiled with ginger mustard oil, butter-milk and curds it forms a liniment, used in cases of paralysis. In the Konkan region the roasted fruits are beaten up with honey and given to treat rheumatism; they are also given powdered with black pepper and rock salt (2 parts of long pepper and 1 of salt) in half tola doses.

The dried immature fruit and the root in the form of decoction are extrensively used in acute and chronic bronchitis attended with cough and found to give gradual relief in all such cases.

Distribution & Origin

Long pepper is a native of the Indo-Malaya region. It is found growing wild in the tropical rainforests of India, Nepal, Indonesia, Malaysia, Sri Lanka, Timor and the Philippines. Indian long pepper is mostly derived from the wild plants, but is also grown in small area in the Khasi hills the lower hills of West Bengal, Eastern Uttar Pradesh, Madhya Pradesh, Maharastra Kerala, Karnataka and Tamil Nadu. It occurs wild in the forests of Andhra Pradesh and in the Andaman and Nicobar Islands as well.

Plant Description

Piper longum Linn. (2n=24,48,52,96) is a slender, climbing, under-shrub creeping and rooting below. The young shoots are downy; the leaves are 5-9 cm long, 5 cm wide, ovate, cordate with broad rounded lobes at the base sub-acute, entire, glabrous. The plant bears unisexual flowers in solitary, erect spikes during or just after the rainy season. The male spikes are larger, slender and are 2.5 to 7.5 cm long, while the female spikes are 1.25 to about 2 cm long when in flower, growing to about 3 cm when in fruit. The berries are ovoid, yellowish orange, sunk in thick rachis about 0.25 cm in diameter.

Wild Species and Varieties

The Indian long pepper appears to be derived from two or three species, including the one which is imported from Malaysia and Indonesia. It is a product of either P. longum or P. pepuloides, while the java long pepper is from P. officinarum DC. (Syn. Chavica officinarum Miguel). The long pepper of English commerce is chiefly the produce of the java variety.

In different agroclimatic regions of the country, a number of geographical races exist. The Assam, West Bengal and Nepal races are the most popular among them. The West Bengal type is the Gol Thippali (round ball type). The Maharastra type is Pipal Nonsori. The races found in Assam are Asali (true) and Suvali (female in Assamese).

Under the All India Co-ordinated Research project on Medicinal and Aromatic Plants, a selection from Cheemathippalli, which bears female type spikes possessing the highest spike weight and total yield has been released under the name 'Viswam' from the Kerala Agriculture University for cultivation as a intercrop in irrigated coconut plantations.

Soil

It flourishes well in a rich, well-drained loamy soil. It is also cultivated on a large scale in limestone soil below the Cherrapunji region. Laterite soils, rich in organic matter content with good moisture holding, capacity are also suitable.

Climate

The plant requires a hot, moist climate and an elevation between 100 and 1 000 m (330-3 330 ft) for its cultivation. At still higher elevations, the yield will be low. It can be successfully grown even in areas which receive heavy rainfall with high relative humidity. In its natural habitat, the plant is found growing as an undershrub. Hence it should be grown under partial shade with 20-25% shade intensity.

Land Preparation

The land should be ploughed 2-3 times and levelled properly. Then, raised beds of size 3 m x 2.5 m are prepared in which pits are dug at a spacing of 60 cm x 60 cm. The pits are filled with soil mixed with 100 g/pit of well-decomposed FYM or compost. In under to avoid water stagnation in the pits and beds, channels are made to drain excess rain water.

Cultivation

Propagation

Long pepper is propagated through seeds suckers or cuttings or by layering of mature branches at the beginning of the rainy season. The establishment percentage at 3-5 noded rooted cuttings is reported to be very high. The suckers establish very well in heavy rainfall areas. Vine cuttings can be rooted in polythene bags filled with common pot mixture. The nursery can be raised during March and April. In the nursery, mealy bugs often attack the roots of the rooted cuttings. This can be avoided by mixing 10% DP with the potting mixture. Similarly excessive irrigation may lead to Phytophthora, wilt of rooted cuttings. Irrigation should be done on alternate days to avoid dampness and also to control the wilt disease. The cuttings planted in March-April will be ready for planting in the main field by the end of May.

Planting

The rooted cuttings or suckers are planted in the pits at the rate of 2/pit with the onset of the monsoon. The pits are gap-filled one month after planting.

One year after planting each plant is reported to bear 7 primary and 6 secondary roots with lengths of 12 and 7 cm, respectively. Long pepper is planted as an intercrop with subabul, eucalyptus and coconut in different parts of the country.

Manuring

This crop needs heavy manuring. Nutritional studies at the University of Agricultural Sciences Bangalore have shown that the application of 20 T FYM along with 50 kg N 20 kg P_2O_5 and 70 kg K_2O/ha is required for optimum growth and yield of the crop. Of this, 50% N and the entire dose P_2O_5 and K_2O is given as a basal dose and the remaining N is given as a top-dressing.

Irrigation

The crop should be irrigated once a week if it is grown as a pure crop. In case the crop is grown as an intercrop with other crops, the irrigation provided to the main crop is sufficient. The sprinkler system may be adopted for economizing irrigation water. In Kerala, it is the unirrigated crop which has shown more vigour and hardiness than the irrigated crop. It is observed that summer irrigation will induce continuous spike formation during the off-season.

Interculture

In the first year of planting, weeding is done when weed growth is noticed in the beds. After the application of FYM to the beds, earthing-up is done from the channels. Once the crop grows and covers the interspaces of the bed it is difficult to do any interculture operations.

Mulching

When the crop is not irrigated during summer the beds may be mulched with dry leaves or straw.

Pests and Diseases

Pests

Mealy bugs infest the roots of plants and suck its sap. The infested plants look stunted in growth. The severity of this insect is greater in summer. The insect can be controlled by the application of a systemic insecticide like Rogor. Helopeltis theivora is another insect whose adults and nymphs feed on tender foliage causing necrotic leisions around the feeding punctures and leaving shot-holes on the lamina. Application of neem kernel extract at 0.25% concentration will control this insect.

Diseases

During the monsoon season, the fungus Collitotrichum spp. causes leaf and vine rotting. This fungus and Cercospora spp. cause necrotic spots and blight on leaves during the warmer months. Sometimes these two organisms may cause partial or total crop loss. A spray of Bordeaux mixture at 1% concentration during May and 2 or 3 sprays subsequently, during rainy season, is the suggested control measure. Besides this a virus-like disease leading to yellowing and crinkling of the leaves with stunted growth of plants is also reported. the affected plants produce spikes of reduced size and inferior quality.

Harvesting Drying and Yield

The spikes are picked from the vines six months after planting. The spikes will be ready for harvest 2 months after their formation on the plants. The spikes should be picked when they are blackish-green and most pungent. If the spikes are not picked at this stage, there is a greater loss of pungency in Bengal, picking is done annually in January while in Kerala the spikes picked 3 to 4 times a year. The harvested spikes are dried in the sun for 4 to 5 days until they are perfectly dry. The green to dry spike yield is around 400 kg/ha. The yield increases thereafter up to 3 years and it will be about 1 000 kg/ha during the third year. After three years the productivity of the vines decrease and they should be replanted.

Besides the spike the thick parts of the stem and roots which have medicinal value also be harvested from 18 months after planting. While harvesting the stems are cut close to the ground the roots dug up cleaned and heaped in the shade for a day after which they are cut into 2.5 to 5 cm long pieces. The average yield of roots is 500 kg/ha.

Grading

The dried thicker parts of the stem and roots are called piplamool. There are three grades of piplamool. Grade I with thick roots and underground stem it fetches a higher price Grade II and III which consists of either roots stems or fragments.

Chapter 25

MINT

Family	:	Lamiaceae, Labiatae
English name	:	Mint
Indian name	:	Pudina, Putiha (Sanskrit), Pudina (Hindi & Kannada), Putina (Tamil)
Species and	:	Mentha arvensis (Japanese mint)
varieties	:	M. Piperita L. (Peppermint) M. spicata L. (Spearmint) M. spicata L. (Spearmint) M. citrata Ehrh. (Bergamot mint) Himalaya, Kalka, Shivalik, Kosi, Gomati EC-41911, Kukrail, Kiran, MSS-1 MSS, 5, Punjab spearmint-1
Distribution	:	India, Brazil, Paraguay, USA
Uses	:	Cosmetics, Culinary purposes, Flavouring Perfumery

Mints are a group of perennial herbaceous plants, belonging to the family Lamiaceae, Labiatae, which yield essential oil on distillation. The various species of mints which are commercially cultivated in different parts of the world are; Japanese mint or corn mint or field mint (Mentha arvensis subsp haplocalyx Briquet var. Piperscens Holmes var. Javanica), peppermint (M. piperita L), spearmint or garden mint or lamb mint (M. spicata L) and bergamot mint or orange mint (M. citrata Ehrh).

Distribution

Mint is believed to have originated in the Mediterranean basin and from there, spread to the rest of the world by both natural and artificial means. Among the mints, Japanese mint is cultivated on a large scale in Brazil,

Paraguay, China, Argentina, Japan, Thailand, Angola and India. Peppermint is grown in the USA, Morocco, Argentina, Australia, France, USSR, Bulgaria Czechoslovakia, Hungary, Italy, Switzerland and on a small scale in many European countries. USA is the major producer of peppermint and spearmint. Bergamot mint is a native of Europe and has been naturalized in eastern USA. It grows successfully in the temperate and subtropical region of India. In India, Japanese mint is grown mainly in the Terai region (Nainital, Badayun, Bilaspur, Rampur, Moradabad and Bareilly), extending to parts of the Indo Gangetic Plains (Barabanki and Lucknow) and parts of Punjab (Ludhiana and Jalandhar) in North-western India.

The total area under mint cultivation, which is mostly confined to Uttar Pradesh and the Punjab, is around 10 000 ha.

Description of the Species of Mint

M. arvensis (Japanese mint) is a downy perennial herb spreading by root-stocks which creep along the ground or just under the surface and root at the nodes. There are three horticultural varieties : one with reddish-purple stems and broad obtuse leaves and other two having green stems broad or narrow leaves and with purplish-green stems and narrow leaves, respectively. They have rigid branches, pubescent, 60-90 cm tall. The leaves are lanceolate to oblong, 3.7-10 cm long, sharply-toothed, or shortly petiolated and hairy. The flowers arranged in cymes which are usually sessile and rarely pedunculate. The flowers are purplish and minute. The calyx is 2.5-3.0 mm long, deltoid, acuminate the corolla is white to purple and 4-5 mm long.

M. piperata spreads by a system of branching underground rootstocks and grows to a height of 45 to 90 cm (1 1/2 to 3 ft). The square branching stems are dark-green (Var. officinalis sole sub var. pallescens Camus) to deep-purple in colour (Var. officinalis sole sub var. rubescens Camus) and bear opposite, broadly lance-shaped, slightly toothed leaves of a deep-green colour 2.5 to 5 cm (1 to 2 in) long. Small purplish flowers are borne in terminal spikes on the main stem and braches, from June to September.

M. citrata grows up to 30-60 cm height, with decumbent branches and erect ends. The leaves are 1.25-5.0 cm long thin bronzy-green, petiolate, smooth, broadly ovate to elliptical and the apex is obtuse. The flowers are purple, appearing in the upper axils on short dense terminal spikes. The calyx is glabrous with subulate teeth; while the corolla is glabrous and about 0.5 cm long. M. citrata is a hybrid between M. aquatica and M. uiridis.

M. spicata (2n=41) propagates by stolons, from which 30-60 cm erect ascending branches arise. The leaves are sessile, smooth, lanceolate or ovate-lanceolate sharply serrate smooth above and glandular below the apex is acute and up to 6.5 cm long. The flowers are sharply pointed long and narrow and, hence, the name spearmint is attributed to the plant. The calyx teeth are hirsute or glabrous and the corolla is about 3 mm long.

Another variety of spearmint known as scotch spearmint (M. cordiaca (S.F.Gray Baker) is cultivated in the USA to a limited extent.

M. arvensis was first introduced in India in 1954 by the Drug Research Laboratory, now the RRL, Jammu and Kashmir ;whereas, peppermint was introduced in India during the British period on a very smal scale. Scientific experiments were started in 1959 in the Kashmir Valley. The bergamot mint was introduced into the country at the RRL, Jammu and Kashmir in 1959 and spearmint during the colonial period at the Regional Centre of the CIMAP, Pantnagar.

Varieties

A) Japanese mint

Himalaya (MAS-1) : It is a selection released by the CIMAP Lucknow which contains 0.8 to 1.0% oil (FWB) with 81% menthol content and a low congealing point. Thus, 65% of it can be easily removed by chilling. The yield of oil is around 290-293 kg/ha, which is predominantly high. This variety has a higher regeneration capacity in the second and subsequent harvests and, also, delay in harvesting time does not affect the oil production and quanlity. This variety is highly resistant to rust, leaf-spot and powdery mildew diseases.

Kalka (Hyb 77): It is a tall, vigorous variety evolved by the CIMAP Lucknow, through crossing MAS-1 and MAS-2. It produces 762 g of fresh herb and 468 kg/ha of oil, containing 81.5% menthol. It is highly resistant to leaf spot, powdery mildew and rust diseases.

Shivalik : It was introduced from China and released by the CIMAP, Lucknow. The plant has a compact, bushy growth with thick, leathery leaves. It compares very favourably with other cultures in high oilyield and menthol content in the oil.

Ec 41911: This is a progeny selection of an interspecific cross between M. arvensis x M. piperita. It is less affected by rain root-rot and aphids and is reported to yield 236.5 g/ha of herbage and 12.2 kg/ha of oil, with a menthol content of 70%.

B) Peppermint :

Kukrail : This is an high yielding variety developed and released by the CIMAP Lucknow.

C) Bergamot mint

Kiran: This is a mutant selection developed by mutation through gamma irradiation at the CIMAP Lucknow. It has a high oil content and quality. This variety can yield 239 kg/ha of oil with 48% linalool, over 172 kg/ha oil and 39% linalool in parent cultivars.

D) Spearmint

MSS-1: This is a selection from the spearmint cultivars introduced from USA. This variety was released by the CIMAP, Lucknow. It gives a fresh herbage of 535 q/ha and yields 253 kg/ha of oil in 3 cuttings containing 60% carvone.

MESS-5: It is a selection from MSS-1 made at the CIMAP Lucknow. This variety has an yield potential of 600 q/ha of fresh herb and 349 kg/ha of oil from 3 cuttings. The carvone percentage in the oil is 70%.

Punjab spearmint 1: This variety is a clonal selection made at the CIMAP Lucknow. This variety has an erect quadrangular purplegreen hairy stem. It produces 209 q/ha of herb with 0.57% oil and can yield 119.29 t/ha with 68% carvone.

Arka and Neera are the recently released variaties from CIMAP Lucknow.

Chemical Composition and Uses

Japanese mint (M.arvensis)

Japanese mint is a primary source of menthol. The fresh leaves contain 0.4-6.0% oil. The main constituents of the oil are menthol (65-75%), menthone (7-10%) and menthyl acetate (12-15%) and terpenes (pipene, limonene and comphene). The menthol content of the oil varies, depending on the climatic conditions. Generally, it is higher in tropical regions. Menthol is used in the flavouring of a large number of pharmaceutical and oral preparations like toothpastes, dental creams, confactionery, beverages and other items like tobacco, cigarettes and pan masala. Menthol itself finds extensive use in medicine (usually in combination with eucalyptus oil) in the treatment of nasal and bronchial catarrh; it is also occasionally employed as a carminative and as an analgesic in the treatment of neuralgia and rheumatism.

Peppermint (M. piperita)

The fresh herb contains essential oils ranging from 0.4 to 0.6%. The constituents of peppermint oil are almost similar to japanese mint oil. However the menthol content is lower in peppermint oil and varies between 35-50%. The othe rconstituents are menthyl acetate (14-15%) menthone (9-25%) menthofuran and terpenes like pinene and limonene.

Peppermint oil is one of the most popular and widely used essential oils. It is usually considered an arvensis type of oil and is used in the flavouring of pharmaceuticals and oral preparations like toothpastes, dental creams mouthwashes, in cough drops, chewing gums, confectionery and alcoholic liqueurs. Medicinally, it is an excellent carminative and gastric stimulant. When applied externally, it acts as a mild analgesic.

Bergamot mint (M. citrata)

Linalool and linalyl acetate are the main constituents of Bergamot mint oil. The oil is used directly in perfumes. Cosmetic preparations like scents soaps after-shave lotions and colognes also contain this oil.

Spearmint (M. spicata)

The principal constituent of spearmint oil is carvone (57.71%) and the other minor constituents are phellandrene, limonene, L-pinene and cineole. The oil is used mostly as a flavouring in toothpastes and as a food flavouring in pickles and spices, chewing gum and confactionery, soaps and sauces.

Seasons

In the plains planting is done during the winter months, whereas in temperate climates planting is done in autumn or spring from the last week of December to the first week of Marck or from the first week of

January to the third week of February. Late planting always gives poor yields.

Soil

Medium to fertile deep rich in humus is ideal for the cultivatioin of mint. The soil should have a good water-holding capacity but water-logging should be avoided. A pH range of 6-7.5 is best.

Climate

Japanese mint can be grown in all tropical and subtropical areas under irrigation. However it does not tolerate damp winters which cause root-rot. A temperature of 20-25° C promotes vegetative growth but the essential oil and menthol are reported to increase at a higher temperature of 30° C under Indian conditions. Peppermint and spearmint cannot be grown profitably in tropical and subtropical areas, especially those areas with very high summer temperatures (41° C) and the ideal yield is obtained only in humid and temperate conditions like in Kashmir and the hills of Uttar Pradesh and Himachal Pradesh. Open sunny situations without excessive rains during the growing period are congenial for the good growth and development of the oil.

Bergamot mint can be grown both in temperate as well as subtropical areas. However the yield is higher in temperate climates.

Land Preparation

Mints require thoroughly ploughed, harrowed, fine soil. All the stubble of weeds should be removed before the crop is planted. Manuring may be done at the time of land preparation by adding FYM @ 25 to 30 t/ha. Green manuring may also be done before the mint is planted. Sun-hemp (Crotalaria juncea L) is an ideal green manure crop. Mints are planted on flat land or ridges. Hence, flat beds of convenient sizes or ridges are made according to the spacing recommended.

Cultivation

Propagation

Mints are propagated through the creeping stolons or suckers. In the case of peppermint and bergamot mint, even runners are planted. Stolons are obtained from the previous years planting. A hectare of well-established mint, on an average, provides enough planting material for ten hectares.

About 400 kg stolons are required for planting one hectare of land. The best time for obtaining stolons is during the months of December and January.

Planting

The stolons are cut into small piaces (7-10 cm) and planted in shallow furrows about 7-10 cm deep with a row-to-row distance of 45-60 cm, manually or mechanically. While planting on ridges the stolons are planted half way down on the inner sides of the riges. The plot is irrigated immediately after planting.

Fertilizer Application

Mint responds very well to a heavy application of nitrogenous ferilizers. the increase in herbage by the application of phosphorus is not as remarkable as in case of nitrogen. Generally, nitrogenous fertilizers @ 80-120 kg P and K at 50 kg P_2O_5 and 40 Kg K_2 O/ha is required for a good crop of mint. However in M. arvensis an increase of up to 160 kg N/ha and, in M. piperata 125 kg N/ha has given increased fresh herbage and essential oil yield. An amount of 100-120 kg N/ha is recommended for producing the optimum herb and oil-yield in M. citrata under Pantnagar conditions. A split application of 75 kg N/ha in combination with P at 60 kg P_2O_5/ha is recommended under Kodailkanl conditions. Potassium application has no significant effect on herb and oil -yield. In M. spicata the maximum herb, yield is obtained with the application of 100-120 KGN/no Nitrogen may be applied in three split doses at 1 1/2-2 and 3 months after planting and the third dose after the first harvest of the crop.

Boron deficiency reduces both the yield of green herb and the essential oil in peppermint. Increased yields of herb menthol. content and essential oil content in peppermint have been obtained by using a combination of boron and zinc fertilizers. Visual symptoms have been documented for some cultivars of Japanese mint towards Fe and Zn deficiencies. With respect to Zn, the crop response was maximum at 20 kg/ha of Zn applied at planting. Similarly, experiments conducted at the CIMAP, Lucknow, have shown that the application of 20 kg/ha of sulphur will increase the herb and oil-yield in M. spicata. Among the different sources of S, calcium sulphate was best followed by ammonium sulphate and elemental sulphur.

Irrigation

The water requirement of mint is very high. Depending upon the soil and climatic conditions, the crop is irrigated 6-9 times before the first monsoon.

The crop requires three irrigations after the monsoons during September, October and November. Sometimes another irrigation is required during winter, if the plant is dormant and there are no winter rains to encourage proper growth of the underground stems. Experiments conducted at Pantnagar have revealed that fifteen irrigations are required to get the maximum herb and oil-yield in japanese mint. When mints are grown in temperate climates only 3-4 irrigations during the period from July to October are required.

Interculture and Weed Control

Uninterrupted weed growth causes about 60% reduction in herb and oil yields. Hence, mints require weeding and hoeing at regular intervals in the early stages of crop growth. One hand-weeding is required after the first harvest. Sinbar is the only herbicide which controls a large number of weeds effectively when applied a as post-emergence spray @ 1 kg/ha. However, combining organic mulch with a combination of 0.5 kg/ha of Oxyfluorfen herbicide and weeding or application of Pendimethion herbicide at 1 kg/ha and weeding, are found to give excellent weed control throughout the crop growth. Dalapon (4 kg/ha) or Gramaxone (2.5 l/ha) as post-emergent spray: Diuron(2kgA.1/ha) or terbacil treatment 2Kg.A.i/ha) as preemergent treatment are also recommended for chemical weed control in mints.

In low temperature areas the plant become dormant in November. In order to give a perennial crop (of 3 years only) in peppermint, recultivation is done either in autumn (November-December) or in spring (March-April). When peppermint is grown as a perennial crop the first year crop is called 'Row mint' while the second and third year crop is called 'Meadow mint'. This practice is not followed in other mints which are to be planted every year.

Crop Rotation

Crop rotations help to maintain a reasonable control on weed growth preserve the fertility of the soil and to obtain higher returns from the land. The following crop rolations are in practice in Uttar Pradesh (a) Mint, maize potato (b) Mint, early paddy and potato and (c) Mint, late paddy and sweet pea. Whereas in Punjab, the farmers practice mint, maize and rape seed/ mustard and mint-maize and potato or mint and paddy rotation.

The recommendation for the Teral region of Uttar Pradesh is a 2 year rotation of mint summer fallowing or millet (fodder) followed by mint on poor fertility lands and mint, wheat, paddy and mint on medimum fertile lands.

Pests and Diseases

Insect Pests

A large number of insect pests attack mints. Among them the important ones are the leaf-roller, pyralid, the hairy caterpillar and termites.

The caterpillar of the leaf-roller (Syngamia abruptalis Walk) attacks the mint crop during August-September. This can be controlled by spraying systemic insecticides like Monocrotophos or Dichlorovas (1 ml/l). The larvae of the army worm-pyralid (Laphygma exigua Hub). bore into the plant and eat the leaf-buds during February-April. The spraying of a systemic insecticide like Monocrotophos will also control this pest.

The attack of the hairy caterpillar (Diacrisia obliqua Walk) during the months of April-May causes rapid defoliation. This can be controlled by spraying 5% Dipterex. During the dry months termite attacks are often observed. These can be effectively controlled by the application of 3% Heptafan @ 50 kg/ha to the soil before planting. Other pests like cut-worm (Aulucophora favicollis) also cause damage to the crop. They can be controlled by spraying Thiodon. Nisia atrovenosa is the new pest reported on this crop. Effective control of this pest can be achieved by spraying Monocrotophos.

Nematodes like Pratylynchus scribneri, Belonolaimus longicaudalus and Dolichodorus heterocephalus, severely, damage the foliage yield of mints. These nematodes can be effectively controlled by the application of Fenamiphos @ 1.2 kg/ha to the soil.

Diseases

Rust, powdery mildew, wilt, leaf-blight and stolon-rot are the five fungal diseases which have been reported to affect mint to a significant extent under Indian conditions.

Rust is caused by Puccinia menthae Pers, which results in severe leaf-shedding. Erysiphe cichoracearum DC causes powdery mildew which is a major disease. These two diseases can be controlled by spraying Hexasul (wettable sulphur, 0.4%) and Karathane. In Japanese mint, stolon-rot is caused by Macrophomina phaseoil Hob. Ashy and also by Thielavia basicola which adversely affects the production of stolons and mentha oil. Dithane

M-45 (0.3%) and Brassicol (0.5%) can be used to control the disease.

A new, leaf spot disease caused by Corynopsora cassicola (Berk and Curt) has also been reported. Severe wilting of Japanese mint during the months of February and March is observed in different parts of India.

Harvesting

Japanese mint is generally harvested after 100-120 days of planting, when the lower leaves start turning yellow. If the harvesting is delayed the leaves start falling resulting in loss of oil. Further harvesting should be done in bright sunny weather. Harvesting consists of cutting the green herb by means of a sickle 2-3 cm above the ground. A second harvest is obtained about 80 days after the first harvest and the third one afer about 80 days from the second harvest. Whereas in peppermint spearmint and bergamot mints which are grown in temperate climates, the first crop is ready by the end of June and the second in September or October.

Yield

A good crop of Japanese mint can give as high a yield as 48 t/ha of fresh herb. However the average yield of mints from three cuttings is 20-25 t/ ha. The fresh herb contains 0.4% oil.

Distillation of Oil

Mint oil is obtained by distilling either the fresh or the dry herb. The distillation is done both in primitive and modern stills in the former the principle of water and steam-distillation is followed while in the latter steam generated in a separate boiler is employed. The stems are removed from the dried material prior to distillation, becoause they constitute 30 to 50% of the material and contain only traces of the oil.

The average yield of oil is 50-70 kg/ha. Although bergamot mint as well as Japanse mint give an average yield of 70-100 kg/ha the yield of peppermint oil is lower with an average of 50 kg/ha.

Storage of Oil

Mint oil is a light and golden-coloured, motile liquid and it should be completely free from moisture before storage. It is stored in large steel, galvanized steel or aluminium containers, filled up to the brim to protect against any air remaining inside and placed in a cool storage godown, away from light and humidity.

Chapter 26

NEEM

English name	:	Neem tree, Margosa tree, Indian Lilac
Indian name	:	Nimbah, Prabhadrah (Sanskrit) Nim Nimb (Hindi) Bevu (Kannada) Vembu Vepam (Tamil)
Distribution	:	India, Africa, Central and South America, Andamans, Australia, Bangladesh, Carribean, Fiji, Indonesia, Haiti, Malaysia, Mauritius, Myanmar, Niger, Pakistan, Puerto Rico Sri Lanka, the Middle East Sudan, Thailand, Virgin Islands
Uses	:	Drugs, Fertilizers, Insecticides

Neem, Azadirachta indica A. Juss (Syn Melia indica Brand and M. azadirachta Linn), is one of the most valuable and yet the least exploited of tropical trees, belonging to the Indian lilac, white cedar, paradise tree, chinaberry or crackjack in various places.

The neem tree has great potential for agriculture, industrial and commercial exploitation because of its multiple uses such as firewood, timber and in pharmaceutical and entomological preparations. Every part of the tree from its roots, trunk, bark ,leaves, flowers, fruits ,seeds, sap and gum are known to have some use and have a place in the traditional folklore and medicine (especially in the Ayurvedic and Unani systems of medicine), so much so it almost plays the role of a village dispensary in this land.

The leaves are reported to contain minerals like calcium magnesium, iron and phosphorus; protein; vitamina A; crude fibre carbohydrates; fat and alkaloids like quercetin, nimbosterol βsitosterol, azadirachtin, nimboflavone and nomicinol. Medicinally, its leaves are used to cure many diseases of the bladder, kidney, eyes ,and skin, for the explusion of intestinal worms, and with honey for curing jaundice, boils and urticaria.

The flowers are reported to contain nimbosterol, kaempferol, quercetin, myrcetin, nimbosterin, nimocetin, fatty acids and a highly pungent essential oil. The dry flowers are considered as a stimulant, tonic and stomachic. The flowers are useful in some cases of atonic dyspepsia and general debility. The bitter oil extracted from the flowers is useful in skin diseases.

The trunk bark contains a resin, nimbin, nimbinin, nimbidin, essential oil, tannins the bitter principle margosine desa-acetyl nimbin, inorganic phosphorus, sulphur and iron. The bark is a bitter tonic, astringent and antiperiodic. It is usually prescribed in the form of a tincture or an infusion. The bark preparations are useful in fever thirst, nausea, vomiting, skin diseases, scorpion and snakebites. The bark is also used as a vermifuge the aqueous extract is reported to cause immobilization of human and bovine spermatozoa. The oil of the bark possesses a marked antibacterial spectrum against Gram ve and Gram+ve bacteria. The fresh, tender twigs are used to clean the teeth particularly in cases of pyorrhoea.

The heartwood of the tree is slightly aromatic and is reported to yield nimatone, tannins inorganic calcium potassium and iron salt. Besides, two esters of sitosterol and 24-methylene cycloartanol have been found in the petroleum extract.

The pericarp of the fruit is rich is carbohydrates and constitutes a promising substrate in methane gas generation. The seeds contain calcium, magnesium phosphorus, an amorphous morgosopicrin, diacetylnimbin, thionemone, azadirachtin salanin, nimbin, and vilasimin, azadiracthtol, nimbine,6-deacetyl nimbinine, nimbanidol, nomolicinol, salannotide, meliacin-4-epinimbin nimlin and desacetyl nimbin. The processed seed-meal contains all the essential amino acids. The seed-kernel contains about 45% fo fixed oil called neem oil. The oil is non-drying, bitter and greenish-yellow to brown in colour and has a strong,. characteristic, garlic-like odour. The bitter principles of hte oil are nimbidin, nimbin and nimbidol. The other active principles of the oil are salannin meliantriol azadirachtin 7-acetylneotri -chilenone, azadiradione, azadirone, 6-desacetylembinene, 17 epiazadiradione, epoxyazadiradione, framinellone, genunin, meldenin, melianone, nimbanidol, nimbidinin, nimbinene, nimbinin, nimbolide, nimbolin, salannol, vepinin and volasinin. The oil contains 34 lipid associates and 48 fatty acids also. The oil displays a stimulative, antiseptic, an alternative effect when used for massage of the body and is said to possess anti-inflammatory properties. At the same time, it is an active remedy against boils and ulcers. The oil has proved to be remarkably effective in infections like ringworms, itches, erysipalis, urticaria and scrofula. In veterinary surgery the oil is used for foul sores and it has shown antidiabetic activity in rats. Medicinally, the oil is employed as an antihelminthic, useful in bleeding gums, pyorrhoea and asthma. It is used externally as a stimulant in convulsions and collapse from fevers cholera and fits. The oil finds use in the Siddha system of medicine also. It has antifertility and antibacterial effects. Several pharmaceutical preparations like liquors, emulsions, ointments, liniments, as well as medicinal cosmetics like creams, lotions, soaps, shampoos, hair-tonics, toothpastes and gargles have been prepared with nimbidin and with the salts of the acid derived from it. Of the salts, sodium nimbitinate has so far been used for injection purposes. Nimbidin is reported to be efficacious in the treatment of skin diseases such as warts extensive and persistent dandruff, furunclosis, arsenical dermatitis, scabies and saborrhoeic dermatitis. Nimbidin is also known to exhibit pronounced anticholinergic, diuretic, antihistamine, antinicotinic anti ulcer and moderately sedative effect in experimental animals. The oil is used in manufacturing a good number of insecticides as well.

Neem-cake is obtained after expressing the oil from the seeds. The cake represents 80% by weight, of the whole seed. The cake contains oil (91.8%), nitrogen (6%), magnesium (0.88-1.3%), calcium (0.47-1.02%), sulphur (1.6%), proteins (37.5%) carbohydrates (25.6%), fibre (5.8%) and ash (5.4%) Besides, it also contains 110 ppm boron and tannic acid. The cake finds extensive use in crop production as an organic manure.

The gum exudes from the bark in the form of clear, bright, ambercoloured tears or fragments. It is found mixed with gumghatti. The gum contains water (13-15%), ash (3%), galactose (12%), pentosans (26%) some albumins and oxidase. The gum is a non-amphotric, polyelectrolyte and behaves like a lyophilic colloid. On hydrolysis the gum yields, αarabinose, αfructose D- galactose and D-glycoronic acid. The gum also contains glucosamine and 19.8% proteins. The proteinaceous component of the gum contains 18 amino acids. The gum is prized medicinally as a stimulant, demulscent and tonic. It is useful in catarrhal and other affections which are accompanied by great weakness.

A sweet liquid, neem toddy, is occasionally obtained as an exudation from the upper parts of the trees or by exposing a healthy-looking root cutting through it and placing a vessel beneath to receive the exuding liquor. It has the unpleasant odour of neem and contains sugar (6.5%) and albuminous and gummy matter (6.5%). The neem sap (toddy) exuded by the roots has been reported to contain glucose, sucrose, gums and protein. Its ash contains iron, aluminium and calcium. The toddy or fermented sap of the tree is useful as a refrigerant, nutrient and alternative tonic. It is of great service in some chronic and long-standing cases of leprosy and other skin diseases, tuberclosis, atonic dyspepsia and general debility. The presence of amino acids particularly tryptophan in fairly high concentrations is important in relation to the therapeutic value attributed to the exudate.

Various neem products, either in combination with each other or in combination with other plant products, are also used to cure many diseases.

Distribution & Origin

Neem is believed to be a native of upper Burma and possibly of the Siwalik, Deccan and other parts of South India. It is widely distributed in tropical Africa Australia, the Andamans, Pakistan, Sri Lanka, Myanmar, Malaysia, Indonesia, Bangladesh, Thailand, Middle East, Sudan, Niger, Fiji, Mauritius, Central and South America, the Carribean, Puerto Rico, the Virgin Islands Haiti and other places. The largest known plantation of nearly 50 000 trees is at the Arafat Plains, en routs to Mecca in Saudi Arabia, for providing shade to the Haj pilgrims. In India, it is cutlivated all over. It grows wild in the Siwalik Hills, in the dry forests of Andhra Pradesh, Tamil Nadu and Karnataka. The tree is well suited for afforestation. According to one report in 1991, India has approximately 14 million neem trees and has an annual potential to produce 0.1 million tonnes of neem oil and 0.15 million tonnes of neem-cake from 0.45 million metric tonnes of seeds.

Plant Description

Neem is a large glabrous tree 7 to 20 m high with a straight trunk. The branches spread widely and form a oval crown. The trunk attains a girth of 1.8 to 2.7 m. The bark of the trunk is 1.2 cm thick, furrowed longitudinally and obliquely, dark grey outside and reddish-brown inside.

The sapwood is yellowish-white, the heartwood is red or brown especially the inner part. From insisions in the trunk near the base made in spring issues a quantity of sap often flowing for weeks.

The leaves are alternate imparipinnate, 22 to 38 cm long, the leaflets are 9 to 13 in number, nearly opposite, shortly petiolate, 2.5 to 7.5 cm long. The leaflets have unequal sides, are ovatelanceolate, sometime falcate deep and sharply serrated, accuminate and glabrous.

The inflorescence is an axillary panicle. The flowers are white, with a strong smell of honey, especially at night, pentamerous, on short slender pedicles with short, scatttered hairs. The bracts are minute and deciduous. The calyx is small, flat,-5-fid connate at the base, the lobes are orbicular. The corolla has five petals which are free, spatulate, narrow at the base and deflexed, and up to 1.5 cm long, the stamens are 10 in number, situated at the base of a hypogunous disc. The filaments form a long culindrical tube. The ovary is 3-celled, with 2 ovules in each cell, the style is slender; with 3-5 stigma. The fruit is a drupe ovoid-oblong 1.25 to 1.75 cm long smooth greenish yellow when ripe one-or sometimes two-celled. The seed is ex-albuminous, elliptical and reticulate outside. The germination is eipgeal. The chromosome numbers as determined by metaphrase plates of meiosis of the pollen the mother-cells are 14 in number. They are the haploid or n-chromosomes. The flowers appear from March-May and the fruit ripen during June-August.

Soil

Neem grows even in a nutrient deficient soil. It grows well on moist dry stony, clayey or shallow soils including moderately saline and alkaline soils compact clays and lateritic cruts. However silty flats clayey depressions and land prone to inundation are not conducive to its growth. It tolerate a soil pH of up to 10.

Climate

The tree is very hardy and can survive high temperatures and altitudes between 50 and 100 m and little rainfall, as low as 130 mm per year and long stretches of drought. In India it thrives best in parts where normal rainfall ranges between 480 to 1 000 mm and maximum temperatures as high as 48° C.

Cultivation

Propagation

Seed propagation is the common method of growing neem trees. It can also be propagated easily by vegetative means, like root-and shoot-cuttings. Root-and shoot-cuttings can be made from 12-13 month old nursery plants. A success rate of 53% from root-shoot-cuttings is reported from Maharastra.

Nursery Raising

The seeds are collected from June-August, which coincides with the rainy season. The seeds remain viable for a short period of 3 to 5 weeks only. Hence, they should be sown immediately or within 2-3 weeks of collection. It is reported that the seeds obtained 10-12 weeks after flowering possess the maximum germination capacity and longevity. The seeds can remain viable up to 2 months when stored in airtight tins, in pots with wood-ash and in gunny bags. The seeds are depulped before sowing.

The nursery is raised in beds of rows 15 cm apart with the seeds 2.5 cm apart in a row. The beds are sparingly watered after sowing. The seedlings are transplanted from when they are about 2 months till 1-year-old. It is preferable to plant the seedlings when they are 7-10 cm in height. The nursery is protected against frost by providing screens. The seedlings can be raised in baskets and polythene bags also.

Planting

Direct sowing is easy and can be successfully done by dibbling, broadcast, sowing in lines or in tranches, depending on the site conditions. It is reported that, in Rajasthan, neem seed has been successfully dibbled under Euphorbia bushes in Ajmer district by placing 3-5 seeds in small pits and covering them with soil. In Maharashtra, neem is sown with 'babul'. While in the Bellary district of Karnataka sowing on mounds in rows 2.7 m apart on black soil has proved successful.

For planting the nursery-raised seedlings, the seedlings may be planted inside thorny bushes to provide initial protection from cattle damage. Neem can also be planted as a roadside avenue tree.

Stumps from 2-year-old plants have been reported to give a better survival and faster growth rate than those from 1-year-old plants. The stumps are prepared with 2.5 cm of shoot and 23 cm of root pieces and should be planted at the onset of the rains.

Neem in Agroforestry Systems

Neem is well suited for arid zones in India. It is the least affected by automobile exhaust and is best suited for roadside planting. It is also well-suited for afforestation of wastelands and for planting under agroforestry systems.

Neem is interplanted with groundnut, bean, and millets in farmlands. It is reported that neem trees can be planted in highly alkaline soils if the land is levelled, bunded and gypsum applied @ 10-12 t/ha over the whole surface in June July and a rice, wheat rotation followed for the next 4-5 years. The trees can then be grown along with agricultural crops.

Pests and Diseases

i) Pests

In India 38 insect species are reported on neem which include seed and flower insects (5), defoliators (13), root feeders (2), stem-and shoot-borer (1), sap-sucking insects (15), and mites (2). Apart from these insects, an unidentified species of mollusca also causes 15-20% damage to the seedlings in nurseries. Parasa hilaris has been reported to severely attack neem in Madurai. The mealy bug, Pseudococus gilberiensis, the scale insect, Parlatoria orientalis and the leafwebber, Loboschiza, koenigiana are reported to cause maximum damage in Tamil Nadu.

Among the other pests, the seed-and flower-insect Scirtothrips dorsalis prevents fruit development. The defoliating insects Boarmia variegata and Eurema spp. cause serious damage in nurseries in the arid and semi arid regions, respectively. The main sap-sucking insects of neem are Helopeltes antonii (tea mosquito) and Pulvinaria maxima. H. antonii is reported to cause 15% damage to neem plantations in Gujarat, it is also a key pest of cashew plantations.

Holotrichia consanguinea and termites, viz; Odontotermes obseus, are the prominent root-feeders of the neem tree.

To control the sap-suckers, including thrips, a systemic insecticide such as Dimethoate (0.01-0.2%) may be used. The larvae of the shoot-borer, L. koenigiana, can be controlled by 0.01-0.02% of Monocrotophos or Dimethoate. A mixture of 0.2% Dimethoate and Vipul (2ml/l) is also recommended. Against defoliators, 0.1-0.2% Folithion; and for termite control, mixing Aldrex in the soil before planting are recommended. The silvicultural measures and use of enemy complexes are also suggested.

ii) Diseases

The plant is not attacked by any disease of a serous nature.

Harvesting and Yield

The trees shed their leaves during February-March and a full-grown tree produces an estimated 350 kg of leaves. The fruits mature in June-July and produce about 50 kg/tree of berries. The fruit contains, skin: 23.8%, pulp :47.5%, shell:18.6% and kernel 10.1%. The fruits are dried in the shade and stored in airtight gunny bags or tin containers. The fruit gives on an average, 60% on a dry-weight basis. It must be ensured that the seeds do not contain moisture, basis. It must be ensured that the seeds do not contain moisture, which may otherwise invite fungal attack and lead to aflatoxin contamination . The kernel yields 45% of fixed oil.

Chapter 27

PARROT TREE

I. Introduction

Parrot tree is common medicinal tree found through out India. It is called by various name like Bastard teak, Flame of forest, Bengal Kino tree, Panat tree etc. Some common names of parrot tree are in different regional languages are given in table 1.

Table 1. Common names of parrot tree

No.	Language	Common name
1.	Hindi	Palas, Tesu, Dhak
2.	Bengali	Patas
3.	Gujrati	Khakno, Khakharo
4.	Sanskrit	Palasha
5.	Tamil	Palasu
6.	Urdu	Palash Papra
7.	Kannada	Muttuga
8.	Oriya	Porasu
9.	Telugu	Palasamu Mooduga
10.	English	Parrot tree, Flame of the forest

Parrot tree is a well known tree of India. Its scarlet and orange flowers come in such profusion that the tree has been very aptly called as "The flame of the forests." The tree is silviculturally important as it is one of the commonest among the trees in India and is capable of thriving where most species will not grow. Its leaves, flowers and seeds are widely used in ayurved. The bark and young roots make a strong coarse fibre.

The three leaflets are symbolic of 'Trimurti' the trinty of Brahma Vishnu and Shiva. So the tree have religious importance. The tree is highly valued as a host for the lac insect. The flowers yield a yellow dye. Leaves are largely used for making plates as well as for fodder for cattle.

II. Distribution

In is common throughout the greater part of India ascending the Himalayas upto 900 metre and in peninsular India upto 1,200 metre. Commonly found through out India, ascending the himalayas from metres high in the pennisular India. However it is rare in most arid regions. The tree is very typical of open grasslands as well as in the terai regions of North India. It can grow in water-logged situations on black cotton soils, even on saline, alkaline, badly drained soils and on barren lands. It is common in certain mixed deciduous forests.

III. Morphology

A deciduous tree of papilionacceade family having a some-what crooked trunk upto 15 m in height. Bark is bluish grey or light brown; leaves long petioled, three foliate leaflets broadly obovate from a cuneate or deltoid base. Leaves are glabrescent above and finely silky below.

Flower buds are dark blackish brown in colour, flowers are bright orange red in colour sometimes yellow. They grow in 15 cm long racemes on bare branches. Pods are pendulous, silky-tomentose, 10-13 cm long, containing one seed at its apex. Seeds are flat reniform 3.3-3.8 cm x 2.2-2.5 cm in size. The leaves fall during Nov-Dec, flowering beings in January and continues till end of April and pods ripen during May-June. Although the tree grows typically in open plains, it is capable of withstanding a fair amount of shade. It is frosthardy in its natural habitat and is highly drought resistant.

IV. Chemical Composition

The gum contains leucocyanidin, its tetramer, procyanidin gallic acid and mucilaginous material. It is rich in riboflavin (138.8 u microgram/gram) and also contains thiamine (4.3 micro gram/gram).

Analysis of bark gave 13.80% total water soluble extract, 5.82% tanins and 7.98% non tannins. Analysis of roots gave 45.4% moisture, 2.1% protein, 0.3% fat, 1.6% fibre, 50.0% carbohydrates, 0.6 g/100 g Calcium, 25 mg/gm phosphorus, 21 mg/g and energy 211 k cal/100 g. Glycine, a glycoside and an aromatic hydroxy compound are also found to be present in the roots. The leaves are reported to contain alkaloids.

The flowers contain butin, butein, butrin, isobutrin, polastirin, coreopsin, isocoreopsin, sulphurein, monospermoside and isomonospermiside. The major glycoside of the flower is butrin. The bright colour of the flowers is attributed to the presence of chalcones, and aurones.

The fresh seeds contain lipolytic and proteolytic enzymes. The latter is a mixture of plant proteinase and polypeptidase and behaves like "yeast trypsin." The presence of three alkaloids one of which is identified as monospermin, a new d-lactone of n-heneicosanoic acid and a phytolectin has been reported in the seeds. Palasonin is the anthelmintic principles present in the seeds. The seeds contain upto 20% of a fatty acid known as "moodooga oil" or "Kino tree oil". The fraction of oil rich in saturated glycerides may be used as a base for ointments and the other as a solvent for drugs.

V. Propagation

Progagation canbe made by sexual and a sexual or vegetative methods. The seeds germinate early in the rainy season not long after the pods fall to the ground. If moisture is plentifull and sustained germination takes place without difficulty. Owing to the hardiness of the seedlings their immunity to damage by grazing and their power of recovery from injury. Natural reproduction from seeds and suckers is profuse.

It can be effected by both the methods. Direct sowing and transplanting from the nursery. Though the former is undoubtadly the more successful and economic method. The young plants need protection from the pigs, porcupines and rats.

A. Direct sowing and after care

The direct sowing of the seeds can be done is several ways. The plants can be raised by line sowing under irrigated and unirrigated conditions with or without other field crops.

The seed are planted 25-30 cm apart along the lines and are lightly covered with soil. For ordinary afforestation a spacing of 3.0-3.6 m is maintained. Under irrigated conditions the seeds are sown in loose soil on the side of ridges of the irrigation of furrows which are made at the same distance as for the afforestation. For unirrigated line sowing the ground should be ploughed or hoed up to a width and depth of 30 cm, the best results can be obtained when the plants are grown with field crops. For lac cultivation, a spacing of 6 m is maintained to facilitate not only crown expansion but also the cultivation of other crops which help in controlling the weeds and protecting the young plants from pigs and porcupines.

The plants are thinned out, if congested, at the end of the first season and the operation is continued regularly. Weeding is done during the first year of proper development of the plants.

B. Transplantation

The trees can be raised with fair success by transplanting also. Transplanting is done in following steps.

1. Nursery raising

The plants are raised at 10 cm x 10 cm distance in the nursery by sowing the ripe seed long before the rainy season. Regular watering and weeding are carried out and the seedlings appear in7-15 days. The nursary bed is prepared facilitating well drainage system along with regularly intercultural operations. For the purpose a bed raised six inches above the ground the width of the bed should be kept 1.25 metre for facilitating the weeding. In areas where water stagnation is not a problem bed of same width and suitable length may be prepared on flat ground with drainage canals at the width of 1.25 metre.

2. Transplanting of seedlings

The seedlings are transplanted during the first rainy season after the stem is pruned to five cm and the taproot to 23 cm. Stumps can also be planted.

VI. Diseases and Pests

No serious disease has so far been reported on this tree though several fungi have been reported on it, including Pestalotia butea Panwar et al which causes leaf spots.

A number of pest are reported on this tree, some of which causes serious damage. Plocaederus obesus Gahan bores the wood and makes it useless. Removal of sick and dying trees and debarking of all fellings are recommended as remedial measures.

VII. Medicinal Value

Leaves, bark, gum exduate, roots, flowers and seeds all contain medicianlly important components which are used for treatment of various ailments. Almost all the parts of the plants are used medicinally.

A. Leaves

The leaves are astringent, diuretic, tonic and aphordisiac. They are given in diarrhea heart burn sweating of phthisis, (tuberculosis of the lungs) diabetes flatulent colic, piles and worms. The leaves induce a fall in the amount of blood sugar and so are given in glycosuria. Their infustion or decoction is given as a rectal enema in diarrhoea and dysentry, and as a vaginal douche in lecucorrhoea. Also used as mouth wash for septic and congested throat. The fresh juice is useful in phthisis (tuberculosis of the lungs) hemorrhagic affections for worms and fevers. A hot poultice of the leaves is applied to disperse boils, pimples, tumourous piles, ulcers, buboes and swellings. .

B. Bark

The bark is reported to possess astringent bitter pungent alternative aphrodisiac, and antihelmintic (destroys or expells intestinal worms) properties. Useful in tumours, bleeding piles, and ulcers. The decoction is prescribed in cold, cough, fever, various forms of haemorrhages, in menstrual disorders and in preparations of tonics and elixirs.

C. Roots

The root are useful in elephantiasis, and in curing night blindness, and other defects of sight. They are also reported to cause temporary sterility in women. The root bark is used as a aphrodisiac analgesic and nathelmintic. It is also applied in sprue, piles, ulcers, dropsy (disease marked by an excessive collection of watery fluid in the tissue or cavities of the body) and tumours).

D. Flowers

The flowers are reported to possess astringent, diuretic, depurative, aphrodisiac and tonic properties. They are used as emmenagogue, and as poultice in orchitis and to reduce swellings, for bruises and sprains. They are also effective in leprosy leucorrhoea, and gout. The petals are given to sheep for haematuria the decoction of flowers is given in diarrhoea and to puerperal women.

E. Seed

Seeds are reported to possess aperient (mild purgative) and rubefacient (reddening of the skin) properties. They are sometimes substituated for santonin. The seed are also used as vermifuge, in veterinary medicine. The freshly powdered seed give good results against Ascaris infecton. Maggots are killed by sprinkling the powder over them. A paste of the powdered seeds with lemon juice is applied as a cure for ring worm, and herpes. Seeds pounded with lemon juice are applied on "Dhobi"s itch."

F. Gum

It exudes the gum from the trunk. It is astringent and is a useful substiture for the true kino. Its action is mild and so it is suitable particularly for children and delicate women suffering from diarrhoea and dysentery. It is given in doses of 500 mg to 2 gram with a few grains of aromatics, in large doses of 2 to 2.5 grams the gum is given in phthisis and bleeding from the stomach and bladder. A solution of the gum is applied to bruises, erysipelatous inflammations ringworm etc.

VIII. Conclusion

Parrot tree is a multipurpose tree and can be cultivated even on barren land. It has got medicinal importance as well as other types of economic importance also. Its leaves are utilized for making leaf plates and are very much utilized as disposable plantes. Yellow dye yielded by the flowers popularly known as "Tesu" is the orange yellow colour which is fragrant and frequently used for festival "Holi".

The tree is an important host for rearing the lac insect Laccifer lacca which feeds on its sap. It is the most common host for "Rangeeni" strain and may be utilized for large scale production of lac. It is hardy type of tree and yields bunches of orange flowers so in large gardens it is preferred as a "Garden Tree". However, its properties and usages are still unknow to most people in our country.

Chapter 28

PERIWINKLE

English name	:	Periwinkle
Indian name	:	Madanah (Sanskrit) Mainphal Madan Sadabahar (Hindi) Kasikanagile Smashana Mallige Smashana Kanagale (Kannada) Madharai Marukkalankay (Tamil)
Distribution	:	India, Indo China, Indonesia, Israel, Madagascar, Philippines, South Africa, USA
Uses	:	Cosmetics, Drugs

Periwinkle (Chatharanthus roseus (L) G. Don) belonging to the family Apocynaceae is one of the few medicinal plants which has found mention in the folk medicinal literature as early as 2nd BC. The plants has been widely used as an abortificant purgative antidiabetic diuretic haemorrhagic antimalarial antidysentric and against skin diseases by the ancient people.

Modern investigations have shown that periwinkle contains more than 100 alkaloids distributed through all the parts of the plant. It has medicinal importance owing to the presence of alkaloids like ajmalicine (raubasin) serpentine and reserpine which are well known for their hypotensive and antispasmodic properties. Periwinkle gained further importance after the isolation of vincristine and vinblastine alkaloids which have importance in cancer therapy. Vincristine sulphate is being marked under the trade name ONCOVIN, which is used against acute leukemia, and vinblastine sulphate as VELBE to cure Hodgkin's disease and other lymphomas and choriocarcinomas. In addition to the above the alkaloids leurosidine, leurosovine and rovidine also possess anticancer properties, but they are not used clinically.

Distribution & Origin

The plant is a native of Madagascar and from there it has spread to India Indonesia, Indo-China, Philippines, South Africa, Israel, USA and other parts of the world. In India it is being grown in Tamil Nadu, Karnataka Andhra Pradesh, Madhya Pradesh, Gujarat and Assam in an area of about 3 000 ha. Farmers prefer it because of its wide adaptability and its ability to grow on marginal lands and drought-tolerance that rules out crop failure. The presence of alkaloids all over the plant body confers immunity to cattle- browsing and the crop due to pilferage.

USA is the world's largest user of this plant's raw material. A single frim which has the patent to manufacture Vinblastine and Vincristine sulphate have been consuming more than 1 000 t of leaves of the plant annually. Most of it has been imported from Malagasy and the remaining from India and Mozambique. Hungary is also been one of the major consumer of its leaves. West Germany, Italy, Netherlands and the UK are interested in the roots. They extract ajmalicine (raubasin), serpentine, etc. The total demand from these countries is more than 1000 t of roots annually.

Plant Description

C. roseus (2n=16) is a perennial herb which grows up to 90 cm high. The stem is erect lax branching with flexible long branches, purple or light-green in colour. The leaf is simple, opposite, exstipulate, petiolate. The inflorescence is racemose, with the flowers in axillary pairs. The flowers are rose-purple or white or white with a rose-purple spot in the centre pedicillate, hermaphrodite, complete, actinomorphic and hypogynous. There are five calyx-sepals, five corolla-petals-rose-purple or white or white with a rose-purple spot in the centre, tubular, swollen in the region of the anthers the throat of the corolla-tube is hairy, forming a corona-like structure. The androecium has five stamens included in the corolla tube the filaments are very small, spipetalous, the anthers forming a cone like structure above the stigma. The gynoecium has two carpels free below but united in the stylar region, two ovaries, free, single style with a dumbel-shaped stigma. After fertilization the carpels separate and form two fruits which form a pair of elongated follicles. The seeds are small, black in colour, 1 g contains about 835 seeds.

Types and Varieties

There are three variants in Periwinkle, those with (i) rose-purple flowers.,

(ii) white flowers and (iii) white flowers with a rose-purple spot in the centre. The first type is being cultivated because of its higher alkaloid content. Recently, two white-flowered varieties named 'Nirmal' and 'Dhawal' have been released by the CIMAP, Lucknow, which although, equal in active principles are reported to yield a higher biomass.

Soil

The crop is quite hardy and grows well on a wide variety of soils except those which are alkaline or water-logged. Deep sandy loam to loam soils of medium fertility are preferred for its large scale cultivation. Because in this soil there is not only a better development of roots, but it is also easy to take them out at harvest time.

Climate

The distribution of the plant shows that there is no specificity in its climatic requirements. It comes up well in tropical and subtropical areas. However, the growth in tropical areas is better than in the subtropical areas, where its growth is slow due to the low temperatures in winter. It can be successfully grown up to an elevation of 1 300 m above sea-level. A well distributed rainfall of 100 cm or more is ideal for raising this crop on a commercial scale under rainfed conditions.

Propagation

The plants can either be propagated by seeds or vegetatively through cuttings. Since plants propagated by cuttings flower earlier than the plants from seeds, it is recommended that for drug production the plants should be grown from seeds and for seed production from cuttings.

A) PROPAGATION BY SEEDS

Fresh seeds collected a few months in advance are referred for sowing, as they lose viability on long storage. In an experiment it was observed that the seeds had an initial viability of about 95 to 96% but when stored under uncontrolled conditions for two years there was no germination. The seeds can either be directly sown in the field, or a nursery can be raised and the seedlings transplanted.

i) Direct Sowing

This method is best suited for large areas where labour is expensive as it reduces the cost of production. For this purpose the land is ploughed twice and brought to a fine tilth. Weeds stubble and pebbles are removed. The field is divided into plots of convenient size and the soil is mixed with the recommended does of manures and fertilizers. The seeds at the rate of 2.5 kg/ha are broadcasted at the onset of the Monsoon in June-July in lines spaced 30-45 cm. apart and lightly covered. Since the seeds are very small for ease in handling and distribution, they are mixed with sand about 10 times their weight. Germination takes place about 7-8 days. After the germination is complete, the seedlings are thinned at a spacing of 30-40 cm within the row. The plant may grow upto a height of 120 cm and the flowering starts 40-45 days after sowing.

ii) Nursery Raising and Transplanting

When seed supply is short, this method can be followed. The other advantage of this method, in comparison to direct sowing, is that we can select the healthy and vigorously growing seedlings for our purpose and the inferior ones can be discarded. The seeds are sown in well prepared, raised nursery beds in March-April by broadcasting them in rows spaced at 8-10 cm apart and about 1.5 cm deep. They are then covered with a light soil and leaf-mould mixture and watered to keep the bed moist. About 500 g of seeds will be enough to raise seedlings to cover a one hectare area. In about 2 months time after germination, the seedlings are ready for transplanting into the field. The seedlings are transplanted at a spacing of 45 cm x 30 cm apart in the field. With this spacing, one hectare requires a population density of about 74 000 plants.

B) VEGETATIVE PROPAGATION

To raise the plants by this method, soft-wood cuttings obtained from the lateral roots have proved better than either the hard or semi-hard wood cuttings. Cuttings of about 10-15 cm length with a minimum of 5-6 nodes have been reported as being ideal and result in about 90% rooting. Soaking the cuttings over-night in NAA solution of 25 or 50 ppm concentration has been found to further improved rooting to the extent of 96%. This method can be profitably used for multiplying the clones which have high alkaloid content and also where we have to produce only the seeds.

Manures and Fertilizers

In areas where FYM is available, it is applied at the rate of 10-15 t/ha to obtain good growth and yield from periwinkle plants. If irrigation is available it is recommended to grow leguminous crops like sunhemp or horsegram and when they reach the flowering stage bury them inside the soil before sowing or transplanting periwinkle. Green manure will act as a substitute for FYM and is useful in the areas where it is either difficult to procure or it is very expensive. The seeds of the green manure crop should preferably be treated with bacterial innoculants prior to sowing to increase the development of root nodules which absorb atmospheric nitrogen and fix it in the soil. In case organic manure is not applied it is advisable to apply a basal dose of 20 kg N 30 kg P_2O_5 and 30 kg K_2O per hectare per year. In addition a top-dressing with 20 kg nitrogen can be given in two equal split doses during the season.

Irrigation

In places where rainfall is evenly distributed throughout the year the plants do not require any irrigation. However, in areas where rainfall in restricted to a few months in a particular period, about 4-5 irrigations will help the plants to give optimum yield.

Weed Control

This crop requires two weedings in the initial stages of its growth. The first weeding may be done after about 60 days of sowing and the second at 120 days of sowing. Mulching the field with cut-grass or rice-straw will also minimize the weed growth.

Application of the chemical weedicide Sinbar at 4-5 kg/ha as a pre-emergent spray is highly effective against all monocot weeds. Similarly, the application of a mixture of 2-4 D and Gramaxone at the rate of 25 kg/ ha to the soil before sowing keeps the weeds under control.

Insect Pests and Diseases

The plant is sufficiently hardy and practically free from the attack of insect pests and diseases. However the oleander hawk month is reported on this crop. Occasionally, some plants have been found to suffer from the 'little leaf' disease, due to infection by mycoplasma resulting in stunted growth and rosetting of the leaves of the plant. The disease can be effectively

checked by uprooting and destroying the affected plants.
Recently, another disease 'dieback' or twig blight or top rot caused by Pythium butleri Phytophthora nicotianae, P. debaryanum, Alternaria tenuissima and Colletotrichum dematium has been found to affact the crop during the monsoon in some parts of the country. The disease can be controlled by spraying Dithane Z-78 at an interval of 10-15 days. The other fungal diseases reported on this crop are Fusarium wilt caused by Fusarium solani and Sclerotium rolfsii blight caused by Pythium aphanidermatum as well as leaf-spot caused by Myrothesium roridum, A. tenuissima, A. alternata, Rhizoctonia solani, Ophiobolus catharanthicola Haplosporella marathwadenis and Glomerella cingulata.

Harvesting

i) Roots

The crop is harvested after 12 months of sowing. The plants are cut about 7.5 cm above the ground level and dried for the stems, leaves and seeds. The field is then copiously irrigated and when it reaches the proper condition for digging it is ploughed and the roots are collected. The roots are later washed well and dried in the shade.

ii) Leaves Stem and Seeds

If there is a demand for leaves two leaf strippings-the first after 6 months and the second after 9 months of sowing-can be taken. A third leaf stripping is also obtained when whole plant is harvested. After the plant is harvested, it is dried in the shade. Its seed-pods dehisce and release the seeds with a light threshing which can be used for the next sowing. The leaves and stems are also collected separately. It may be mentioned here, that the seeds collected in this way will have poor germination because they have been collected from pods in different degrees of maturity. Therefore, in order to obtain good seeds, it is advisable to collect them from mature pods two to three months before the harvest of the crop. The aerial part of the plant between 7.5 cm and about 25 cm above the ground level is taken as the stem for the purpose of marketing.

The total alkaloid content oin the leaf varies from 0.15 to 1.34% of which the average content of vinblastine is 0.002%, while that of vincristine is 0.005%.

Yield

Under irrigated conditions about 4 t/ha of leaves, 1.5 t/ha of stem and 1.5 t/ha of roots, on an air-dried basis may be obtained. Whereas, the yield under rainfed condition may be about 2 t/ha of leaves and 0.75 t/ha each of stem and roots on an air-dried basis.

Identification and Estimation of Vincaleukoblastine

Vincaleukoblastine (VLB) is a potent antineoplastic drug, present in the leaves. It is a dimeric alkaloid containing indole and incoline moieties. For the estimation of VLB the sample of leaves is dried at 60° C to constant weight and powdered in a dry grinder. Out of this, about 5 g leaf-powder is extracted with 50 ml methanol in a metabolic shaker at room temperature for one hour and left overnight. The extract is filtered and the residue is re- extracted three times with 50 ml methanol each time for half-an-hour. The combined methanol extract is concentrated to 20 ml in a vacuum diluted with 20 ml water acidified with 20 ml sulfuric acid and extracted twice with 20 ml ethyl acetate saturated with water. The ethyl acetate fraction is rejected. The aqueous phase is made alkaline with 10% ammonia and the liberated allkaloids are extracted with dichloromethane (3 x 50 ml). The combined dichloromethane extracts are dried over anhydrous sodium sulphate filtered and evaporated to dryness in a vacuum. The residue is dissolved in 20 ml benzene and extracted with 50 ml 0.1 M aqueous citric acid. The pH of the acidic solution is adjusted to 4.4 with 10% ammonia and the liberated alkaloids are extracted thrice with 50 ml of dichloromethane each time. The combined dichloromethane extract is dried over anhydrous sodium sulphate filtered and concentrated to dryness in a vacuum.

The residue containing the fraction of alkaloids liberate at pH 4.4 is dissolved in 2 ml chloroform and 0.2 ml of it is applied as a 3-4 band on precoated silica gel silgur-25 UV_{254} TLC Plates. The plates are developed in ethyl acetate-absolute ethanol (1:1). After development, the plates are air-dried in the dark and, when viewed under long wave ultraviolet light, a dull yellow fluorescent band at R 0.33 is observed which is identical with the R reported for VLB earler, under similar conditions of TLC (Cone et al. 3).

The band acquires the characteristic orange colour of alkaloids on spraying with Dragendorff's reagent. Corresponding bands from other plates are scraped along with blank silica gel portions of same area and eluted three times with a total of 10 ml ethanol. The measurement of optical density of the combined elutes at different wavelengths in a double-beam spectrophotometer show that the compound has maximum absorption at 214 nm. This, again, is a property which is characteristic of VLB. From the standard equivalence of optical density and the VLB concentration reported in literature, the VLB content of the leaves could be worked out as 6.8 mg/ 100 g on a dry-weight basis. The results are the average of estimations on a triplicate set of samples.

The 5 to 20 μof alkaloids extracted at pH 4.4, dissolved in acetonitrile and 0.01 M diammonium hydrogen orthophosphate which is also the mobile phase, is analysed by HPLC. The alkaloid fraction, thus analysed reveals the presence of a compound with the same retention volume reported for VLB similar conditions of HPLC.

Chapter 29

PRIMROSE

English name	:	Evening Primrose
Indian name	:	Dheriani (Hindi)
Distribution	:	India, temperate America
Uses	:	Cosmetics, Drugs, Health, food, Oil

Primrose (Oenothera lamarckiana) commonly called the evening primrose, belongs to the family Onagraceae. This is a beautiful biennial plant of hybrid orgin that has produced many other lovely varieties, and can best be described as a dwarfish form of Oenothera biennis only with much large flowers and bigger leaves, which are wide and crinkled. Its stems are reddish and the flower buds hairy. The name Oenothera is derived from the Greek word oinos (wine) and thera (hunt or chase). Plants of this genera are native to North and South America.

Evening primrose is grown for its seeds from which oil containing gamma linolenic acid (GLA) is extracted. The seed normally contains 20 to 25% oil, of which 8 to 10% is GLA. The GLA, rich oil is marketed principally as a health food that is used to treat various ailments such as cardiovascular disorders, metabolic disorders, dermatological conditions diabetes breast problems premenstural syndromes, actopic eczema, rheumatic arthritis and alcoholism.

Distribution

The genus Oenothera is distributed chiefly in temperate America, with some species occurring in the tropics. Some species have been introduced into Indian gardens, of which few have run wild.

Plant Description

It is a biennial herb. Parenchyma is present in submerged stems, mostly respiratory roots are present on the upperside of the submerged stem. The leaves are simple, alternate or opposite entire or have a toothed margin, the stipules are absent of caducous. The flowers are solitary, auxiliary or arranged in racemes, spikes or panicles.

The perianth is biseriate, the floral axis is elongated beyond the ovary into a calyx tube or hypanthium the calys has four sepals, which are free or the Hypanthium is extended above the ovary, is mostly persistent and valvate. The androecium consists of seven stamens the anthers are two- called dehiscing longitudinally. The gynoecium is composed of four carpels, rarely 2-5, is syncarpous, the ovary is inferior, axile placentation, the style is long and filiform, the stigmas are usually capitate. The fruit is a capsule, and the seed is endospermic with a straight embryo.

Soil

Although the crop can grow well on a wide range of soils, a fertile loam soil is considered ideal. The established crop has an excellent tolerance to drought and is capable of growing on soils of poor fertility. However, the plant is sensitive to water-logging and good drainage is critical for its survival. If the crop is being directly seeded, soils which are prone to crusting should be avoided.

Climate

It prefers a moderately cool climate for its successful growth. A soil temperature of 20° C is ideal for the yield and the quality of the oil. Higher temperatures not only decreases the seed yield but also the content of the gamma linolenic acid in them.

However in recent years, some high-temperature tolerant types have been isolated, leading the possibility of growing this crop in comparatively warmer regions also.

Cultivation

Propagation

Primrose can be directly seeded or transplanted. Although seeding is cheaper establishment problems and a higher potential for weed competition makes direct seeding more risky than transplanting.

a) Direct Seeding

To sow the crop by this method the field is throughly prepared to bring the soil to a fine tilth. It is later laid out into convenient-sized blocks to factilitate irrigation. The seeds are usually sown using a precision seeder, in early August. About 1 kg of seeds are enough to cover 1 ha area. Before sowing, the seeds are mixed with 10 kg of sand for easy distribution. The seeding depth should not exceed 1.5 cm. Low moisture content in the soil can severely reduce seed germination and affect seedling emergence. Light irrigation if available, should be given to supply the moisture necessary for germination.

The optimum density for this plant to grow and yield commercially is about 30 plants per spuare metre. Extremely dense population should be avoided as the crowded plants may not flower. Wherever such a situation is present the plants are thinned to achieve a population that will allow successful flowering. A thin population on the other hand, is of much less concern since the plant has the ability to produce many side branches.

The other method of direct sowing suggested is to dibble about 4-5 seeds at a spacing of 60 x 30 cm to thin out the seedlings, retaining one plant per spot after 20-25 days of sowing. About 1 kg of seeds are required to cover 1 ha for this method of sowing also.

b) Transplanting

The transplanting method although more costly, has certain advantages, like the crop is more easily established, the desired population is more readily achieved and weed control problems are minimized, and intra-row cultivation is possible.

For transplanting, 0.5 kg seed should be sown in well prepared, raised nurser- beds of convenient size during the month of August. When the seedlings are about 60 days old they are transplanted into the main field on ridges in such a way that a spacing of 90-100 cm between the rows and 30 between plants is maintained. A spacing of 60 x 30 cm is also recommended.

Manures and Fertilizers

As this is a newly domesticated crop very little information on the nutrient requirement of this crop is available and there is a need to work it out locally. However, in the absence of any other recommendation, FYM @ 2 t/ha and a fertilizer dose comprising of 40 kg N, 60 kg of superphosphate and 40 kg/ha of muriate of potash may by used to raise this crop.

Irrigation

It does not require much water. Initially, for 2-3 months irrigation is provided at 4 to 5 days, intervals. After this period, when the crop has developed the proper root system, the interval is increased to once in 10 days.

Cultural Operations

Weeds are kept under control through regular weeding and hoeing since there are no herbicides recommended for this crop. The crop must be kept free from weeds, because weed seeds are difficult to separate from the primrose seeds and they bring down the quality of the oil, making it unacceptable to the market.

Pests

Cut-worms are reported to attack the plants during the early period of growth, damaging the foliage seriously and causing a setback.

Tarnished plant bugs and aphids are the insects which appear in late June or early July and continue feeding throughout the remainder of the season, retarding the growth of the plant. Spraying the crop with Carbaryl @ 4 g/l of water controls these pests.

Diseases

Botrytis spp., a variety of fungus, may attack the new growth in early spring, resulting in the death of the plant. It is considered as a potential problem on crops caught with untimely heavy rains during the growth season. Drenching the soil with 0.2% of Bavistin helps to control the disease.

Harvesting and Yield

The specific growth habit of the plant indicates variance of seed maturity on each plant. The maturity of pods is observed at the bottom and the top ones are the least mature. As individual pods ripen, they begin to open and shed the seed. Thus, the timing of harvest must be carefully chosen to minimize losses and at the same time efforts must be made to allow as many seeds as possible to mature.

The best way to judge the stage of maturity of the crop is to observe the opening of the pods, progressively, from the base of the stem towards the top. Physiologically mature seeds at the bottom are dark reddish, brown or black in colour with rough surfaces, as you move up the boundary between mature and immature seeds. Mature seeds may also be present in green pods since the drying up of the pods is the last stage of the maturation process. The crop is normally considered ready for harvesting wehn the bottom 5 to 6 seed pods are split and start shedding seeds and the upper third of the plant is light-brown in colour.

The crop would normally be harvested in April-May. It must be harvested and allowed to dry for 5 to 7 days before threshing and winnowing. The seeds should contain not more than 10% moisture for safe storage. A well-maintained crop of primrose may yield about 800 to 1 000 kg/ha of dried seeds.

Chapter 30

PYRETHRUM

Family	:	Compositae, Asteraceae
English name	:	Pyrethrum
Species and	:	Chrysanthemum cinerariaefolium Vis.
varieties	:	Hansa, Jhelum, KKL - 1, Sel -2
Distribution	:	India, Algeria, Australia, Brazil, Bulgaria, California, China, Congo, Ecudor, England, France, Italy, Japan, Kenya, New Guinea, Persia, Russia, Rwanda, Spain, Switzerland, Tanzania, Yugoslovia
Uses	:	Insecticides, Repellents

The term pyrethrum is applied to the dried flower-heads of Chrysanthemum cinerariaefolium Vis. (Fam. compositae ; Asteraceae). The plant is cultivated for its flowers whose developing seeds or achenes consists of 3 pairs of esters: pyrethrin 1, cinerin I, Jasmolin I, Pyrethrin II, Cinerin II and Jasmolin II which are collectively referred to as pyrethrins. In addition to pyrethrins, the flowers also contain protocatechuic, isovaccnic, caproic, lauric, palmalic, and linodeic acids, choline and stachydrone. Pyrethrum is one of the safest insecticides known. It has very low mammalian toxicity and is metabolized if accidentally swallowed. It disturbs insects forcing them to move out of their hiding places. It also possesses an instantaneous "Knock-down effect". It is useful for the preservation of food grains in the preparation of insect-resistant packagings mosquito repellent aerosols and coils. Pyrethrum, being effective against wide range of insect pests, including mosquitoes cockroaches, flies and aphids, serves as an excellent household insecticide. Pyrethrum is also used for protecting dried fish and fish-meal against flies and in the tomato-canning industry against fruit files and in moushroom houses (farms) for the control of insect pests of the common mushroom (Agaricus biporus). Pyrethrum is indeed an ideal insecticide and it is therefore not surprising that the bulk of pyrethrum is used in or around homes. About 70% of the world's production finds its way into fly-sprays and insecticidal aerosols 20% is used in mosquito coils and the balance in other formulations-powder, liquid sprays, aerosols ointments and creams. Pyrethrum, however, is always used along with some synergist, the most popular being piperonyl butoxide, prepared from the oil sassafras, a natural product.

Origin and Distribution

C. cinerariaefolium is a native of Dalmatia, Herzegovina and Montenegro and is cultivated on a commercial scale in Algeria, Dalmatia, (Yugoslavia), Brazil, Bulgaria, Japan, Kenya, New Guinea, Congo, Tanzania, Ecuador, Australia, California, China, France, Italy, Persia, Russia, Spain, Switzerland, England, and India. Kenya and its neighbours Tanzania and Rwanda produce over 80% of the total pyrethrum produced in the world.

The experimental cultivation of pyrethrum in India was undertaken in Kashmir in 1931 and in the Nilgiri hills in the early years of World War II (1942). At present it is successfully grown in several parts of India (Kashmir, Kodaikanal Lucknow) on a commercial scale.

Description of the Plant

C. cinerariaefolium Vis. (2n=18) is a glaucous, perennial herb which grows up to 60 cm high. It has an unbrached stem with short, scattered hairs below the flower. The leaves are petiolate, long, finely-cut and silky beneath with distinct segments. Numerous flower-heads are borne which measure 6-9 mm when closed and 9-12 mm when open. The involucre consists of 2-3 mm of yellowish or greenish-yellow lanceolate hairy bracts. Each flomer head bears a receptacle 4 to 8 mm in diameter. This receptacle is nearly flat bears numberous yellow disc florets and a single row of cream-coloured ligulate ray-florets, 12 mm in length with 3 rounded teeth. The cream coloured floret looks like that of the field daisy (C. leucanthemum Linn) but differs from the latter in having the central teeth of ray-floret shorter than the adjacent ones.

Types and Varieties

C. cinerariaefolium, grown on the Eastern Coast of the Adriatic sea, is called the Dalmatian pyrethrum. While, the Japanese pyrethrum,, also derived from C. cinerariaefolium, is similar to the Dalmatian pyrethrum in appearance. The concentration of active principles (pyrethrin) in the

Dalmatian and Japanese type of pyrethrum flowers range from 0.38 to 0.58 and 0.58 to 1.21% respecctively. The pyrethrum grown in Kenya and other African countries, known as the Kenya pyrethrum, has a higher pyrethrin content of 1.43 to 1.89%.

There are three varieties of pyrethrum, viz : 'KKL 1', 'Hansa' and 'Jhelum' released by the CIMAP, Lucknow, for cultivation. Recently,' Sel-2' with 86% more flowers than 'Hansa' has been developed at the Kodaikanal Centre of CIMAP.

Soil

Pyrethrum thrives best on well-drained, sandy soil. Red laterite loams and light and medium loam soils are also suitable. The yields are considerably lower in poorly drained soils. It can grow on mountain slopes and wastelands but too rich soils and water-logged conditions are unfavourable for its growth.

Climate

Pyrethrum is a temperate crop. It grows best in areas which have a mild, cool, dry climate with a short, mild winter and a cool summer. A period of chilling, in which the temperature falls below 17° C, for about six weeks, is necessary for flower-bud initiation. In places where the winters are long (November to March) and the summers are warm, there is only one flush of flowering in May and June. In the highlands of Kenya where the maximum temperature is about 21° C three flushes of flowers are obtained because of three periods of flower-bud initiation during the year. The ideal temperature requirement for this crop is from 10° C to 24° C and it grows well in places where the annual average rainfall is about 1000 mm and the elevation between 1500 to 2400 m.

Season

Nurseries are raised either in spring (April-May) or in autumn (October-November) and in irrigated areas from March to November. The ideal time for planting is spring (March-April) or autumn (October-November). However, the seedlings can be planted during any time of the year, if irrigation facilities are available.

Land Preparation

The land is prepared well by 2 to 3 ploughings followed by planking, harrowing and clearing of weeds and stubble. Organic manure, if available, may be applied at the time of the last ploughing. It is desirable to make ridges 45-50 cm apart if the land is flat. In undulating land, the area should be terraced.

Cultivation

Propagation

Pyrethrum is propagated by seeds. However, it can also be raised vegetatively by splits. The seeds required for sowing should be gathered from selected plants when the flowers are fully mature and the seeds are about to be shed. The seeds tend to lose viability on storage. In case of vegetative propagation, healthy plants are pulled up from the ground the splits of which are used for planting. In certain areas it is better to plant the splits in nurseries before they are planted in the main field.

Nursery Raising

Seed-beds of convenient length and breadth and 15-18 cm in height are made in well-prepared land. FYM or poultry manure is added in the top 10 cm of the soil. The seeds are sown in rows 10 cm apart and covered with a layer of rice-straw wheat-straw or dried grass. The beds are watered frequently. The seeds germinate in5-10 days. The mulch is removed after the seeds have sprouted. The seed-beds should be kept weed-free by frequent irrigation. The seedlings will be ready for planting after 8-12 weeks.

Planting

The seedlings are planted at a distance of 27-45 cm in rows and 45-60 cm apart. Ridge-planting is preferred to flat-planting as it facilitates interculture and irrigation and avoids water-logging.

Application of Fertilizers

Fertilizer application is necessary to obtain good growth. But hardly any fertilizer was used earlier. The application of excessive doses of nitrogenous manure induces profuse heading but suppresses flowering. It has been found that 40-60 kg N, 40-50 kg/ha P and 50-80 kg/ha K is optimum for the good growth of pyrethrum in the first year. The entire quantity of P and K should be applied as a basal dose with 50% of the N at the time of planting and the remaining 50% of N is applied in split doses. The fertilizer application should be repeated every year. P and K are generally applied in spring at the time of the first harvest, while N is applied in two split doses in the months of March and April.

Experiments conducted at the CIMAP field station in Kodaikanal have established that the application of liquid phosphorus (30%P)@ 120 kg/ha increased the flower, yield by 28%. Liming the soil @ 1 t/ha and foliar application of P, resulted in 60% increase in the flower-yield over the control.

Interculture

Proper weeding and hoeing are necessary to obtain a good yield. Both can be done by a tractor-drawn cultivator and hand-hoes can be used in small terraces. The first hoeing can be done in autumn after the last crop is harvested, followed by two weedings and hoeings in spring.

Irrigation

Pyrethrum does not need irrigation if the rainfall is well distributed. However, under irrigated conditions, weekly irrigation during the peak season gives better results. Under irrigated conditions it is observed that the pyrethrum plants start flowering after 1 year instead of 2 years under unirrigated conditions. The crop should be irrigated frequently during the dry months of June, July and August. The crop should also be irrigated after the fertilizer application.

Pests and Diseases

A number of pests and diseases are reported from other countries. The crop is practically free pests and diseases of a serious nature under Indian conditions. Some of the major diseases of the crop reported from other countries are wilt caused by Fusarium spp. and Sclerortinia miner for which no control measures have been worked out, root-rot, caused by F. solani, can be controlled by drenching the nursery with 0.15% Benlate solution or Dithane - Z-78. Damping-off is caused by S. miner and S. sclerotium. The application of a solution of copper fungicide to the base of the plants can control this disease. Another disease, the bud disease, is reported to be caused by Rannularia belluniensis and this can be controlled by spraying Bordeaux mixture and Pereneox.

Harvesting

The plants flower within one year of transplanting. The crop gives a poor yield in the first year and the optimum yields are obtained only during the 2nd and 3rd year. In Kenya and the Nilgiris in India, three harvests of flowers are obtained as the flowering in these areas continues for 9 months. In temperate areas like Kashmir, the first harvest is obtained at the end of June or in the 1st week of July. The flowers should be picked when 2/3 rd of the disc-florests are open and the ray-florets are horizontal. The harvesting of immature or overmature flowers decreases their pyrethrin content. The flowers are picked at 10 to 14 days interval in Kenya, 14 to 18 days in Japan and once a week in Dalmatia. The flowers are picked at fortnighty intervals in India. There is a gradual fall in the pyrethrin content of harvested flowers after the third year of planting. The yields tend to become uneconomical after 3-4 years and replanting is necessary. Light pruning at the beginning of the dry season, after picking the flowers is required to keep the plant sturdy.

Drying

The harvested-flower heads are usually dried immediately in the sun. They are thinly spread on straw mats turned over frequently in order to avoid fermentation. At night they are kept under some kind of cover. Dehydration is complete in 5-7 days. The ideal method of drying is to use hot-air driers, in which the temperature should not exceed 80° C. The loss in weight will be about 65-75%. It is safer to dry it in the sun when the acreage is small and there is no chance of rain during the harvesting season. However, in larger farms the use of air-driers is essential in order to dry the harvested flowers in time.

Mechanical driers have been designed for drying pyrethrum flowers.

Yield of Flowers and Pyrethrin Content

The average annual yield in Kashmir is about 250 kg/ha against 700 kg/ha in Kenya and 500 kg/ha in Nilgiris. The yield in the first year, as reported from Kodaikanal, is abhout 450 kg/ha. The total pyrethrin content is reported to be 1.0-1.5% in India while the average content in Kenya is 1.4% and the highest is 2.1%.

Extraction and Storages of Oleoresin

Pyrethrins are extracted in the form of concentrated oleoresins by using a number of petroleum solvents, including petroleum ether and ethylene dichloride. The concentrated extract is used as such or, after refining, is used in a number of insecticide formulations.

After the addition of antioxidants, the pyrethrum concentrate should be stored in sealed containers.

Chapter 31

RAUVOLFIA

Family	:	Apocynaceae
Enlish name	:	Rauvolfia, root Serpentina root Serpentine root
Indian name	:	Sarpagandha, Chandrika (Sanskrit) Chandrabhaga, Chota chand (Hindi) Sarpagandha (Kannada) Sarppaganti, Sivan amalpodi (Tamil)
Species and	:	Rauvolgia serpantina Benth ex kurz
varieties	:	R. tetraphylla RS-1
Distribution	:	India, Andaman Islands, South east Asia Bangladesh, Burma, Indonesia, Malaysia, Sri Lanka
Uses	:	Drugs

Rauvolfia serpantina, Benth.ex Kurz (2n = 22) (Family :Apocynaceae), commonly referred to as Sarpagandha is one of the most important native medicinal plants of India. Apart from R. serpentina there is another species, R. tetraphylla which is also cultivated on a commercial scale. In India the root of sarpagandha has a 400 year history of use in treatment of snakebite insect stings, nervous disorders, mania and epilepsy, intractable skin disorders, such as psoriasis, excessive sweating and itching; gynaecological ointments for menopause toxic goitre and in conditons such as angina pectoris and to promote uterine contraction oin childbrith. The importance of the drug and the alkaloids obtained from it has been recognized by the allopathic system in the treatment of hypertension and as a sedative or tranquillizing agent.

The hypotensive properties of rauvolfia was first discovered by Chopra in 1953 but the attention of the Western countries was drawn to it only after the isolation and identification of its most active alkaloid 'Reseripine' by the Swiss scientists, Schiller and Mueller, of CIBA Pharmaceuticals in Switzerland in 1952. After that, there was a great demand for its roots, leading to its indiscriminate uprooting from wild sources where it grew luxuriantly. Intense collection brought the plant to the verge of extension. So in 1955, the Goivernment of India put a ban on the export of the raw drug and attempts to cultivate the plant were taken up at a number of places. About 30 alkaloids are known to exist in the plant. The most important among these are rescinamine, doserpidine reserpinine serpentine, serpentinine, ajmaline, ajmalicine, ajmalinine, rauvolfinine and yohimbine. The total alkaloid content varies from 1.7 to 3% of the dried roots. Detailed studies have been carried out on the chemistry of these alkaloids, their pharmacodynamics and their varying roles in essential hypertension and neuropsychiatric conditions.

Distribution & Origin

R. serpentina is indigenous to the moist deciduous forests of South East Asia including Burma, Bangladesh, Sri Lanka, Malaysia, the Andaman Islands and Indonesia. Most of the drug is obtained from wild sources in these countries. It is cultivated on a small scale in India and Bangladesh.

In India it is found in the central region, i.e. between Sirmor and the Gorakhpur district of Utter Pradesh in shady moist or sometimes swampy locatities. In the east in Bihar North Bengal and Assam as well as in Khasi Jaintia and Gharo Hills the plant is encountered more commonly on the forest margin of mixed deciduous forests. In the Western Ghats, R. serpentina occurs more frequently in Goa Coorg the North Kanara and Shimoga districts of Karnataka and Palghat, Calicut and Trichur in Kerala. In Orissa Andhra Pradesh and Himachal Pradesh the areas comprising the catchment of the river Godavari are the richest. The plant is chiefly associated with Sal (Shorea robusta) forests as well as bamboo brakes.

A major part of the commercial supply of this drug used in the USA and European countries originates from India, Pakistan, Sri Lanka, Myanmar (Burma) and Thailand with India being the major supplier. The present day commercial supplies of the roots of rauvolla are mostly from Uttar Pradesh Bihar, Orissa, West Bengal, Assam, Andhra Pradesh, Tamil Nadu, Kerala Karnataka and Maharastra. Rauvolfia roots exhibit more or less the same morphological features but they differ in their alkaloid content, not only in geographically distinct areas but also within the same geographical areas. The annual requirement of roots in the country for the manufactured rauvolfia extracts, simple and total alkaloids, have been estimated at about 650 t against the present annual supply of 30 t from all the sources. There is also a great demand for the alkaloids as well as the raw drug in the international market. The world requirement of dried rauvolfia roots is around 20 000 t/annum. The consumption of the raw drug is substantial in the indigenous drug market. Steps, therefore, will have to be taken to increase the present production to about 100-150 t/annum of dry roots. This is possible only if the plant is brought under large-scale cultivation in agroclimatically suitable areas.

Description of the plant

The plant is a perennial undershrub, growing to a height of 60-90 cm. Its leaves are simple 7.5-10 cm long and 3.5-5 cm broad, eliptic or lanceolate glabrous, bright-green above and pale-green beneath, pointed and occuring in whorls of 3-5. The inflcrescence is a many flowered corymb with white or pink flowers. The fruit is a drupe, 0.5 cm in diameter adn shiny black when fully ripe. The root system consists of a prominent, tuberous ,soft tap- root reaching a lenght of 30-50 cm in a 2-year-old plant. Its diameter at the thickest portion varies from 1.2 to 2.5 cm. The root-bark, which constitutes 40-60% of the whole root is rich in alkaloids. The fresh roots emit a characteristic acrid aroma and are very bitter in taste.

Varieties

As a result of the evaluation of six populations from different locations, a culture was purfied and designated as 'RS-1' and released for commercial cultivation by the Jawaharalal Nehru Krishi Vishwa Vidyalay, College of Agriculture, Indore. The RS-1 culture gives 50-60% seed germination even after storing it for seven months and the yield of air-dried root gives upto 25 q/ha, containing 1.641 to 2.94% of total alkaloid at eighteen months of age.

Soil

The plant grows in a wide variety of soils from sandy alluvid loam to red lateritic loam or stiff dark loam. In its natural habitat, it prefers clay or clayey loam with a large percentage of humus, and it does not grow well in soil having pH 8 or above. the ideal pH for this crop is from 4.6-6.2: generally the plant produces thicker roots in black stiff loam soils than in heavy clayey or sandy soil. Soils containing large quantities of sand, retand the growth of the plants and make them more susceptible to root and leaf diseases.

Climate

R. serpentina can be grown under a wide range of climatic conditions. It flourishes in hot, humid conditions and can be grown both in the sun and in partial shade. In its natural habitat, the plant thrives under the shade of forest trees. It prefers a tropical or subtropical belt, having the benefit of monsoon rains, preferably the South-West. Localities in the Deccan Peninsula which enjoy a more equitable climate throughout the year as compared to the sub-Himalayan tracts are said to be more suited for a profitable cultivation of this plant. A climate with a temperature range of 10-30° C seems to be well suited for this plant. The best areas for its growth are those which combine high rainfall with properly drained soil. Although it has been reported to grow naturally where rainfall measures about 250 cm annually, it grows well in areas with a rainfall of even 500 cm or more. In low rainfall areas the piant can be successfully cultivated, if irrigation is available during the drier months. Though the plant seems to be sensitive to water- logging it can withstand water for 2 to 3 days without too much damage. The plant sheds its leaves during the cold months in localities with severe winters. Frost kills the top tender green twigs only and fresh shoots sprout up with the advent of spring from the thicker shoots which can withstand the frost.

Cultivation

Propagation

Rauvolfia can be propagated by seeds and also by vegetative means like root-cuttings, root-stumps stem-cuttings and leaf-cuttings.

a) Seed Propagation

Commercially, the plant is usually propagated by seeds. Irregular and low percentage of germination of seeds is the main difficulty in the propagation of rauvolifia. The percentage of germination of seeds is quite variable, ranging from 10-60%. This is partly attributed to the adverse influence of the stony endocarp. Another serious factor is the absence of embryos though the fruits may appear perfectly normal externally. This may possibly be an effect of parthenocarpy or of deferred somato-plastic-sterility. The rate of germination, however, depends on the percentage of fully matured, heavy seeds in a particular lot. Fresh seeds, collected from ripe fruits and immediately sown, show a higher percentage of germination (58-74%). The ripe seeds collected from the beginning of June to the end of October or even November and stored in airtight bins, retained their viability for about 6 months. The viability of the seeds drops markedly with the increase in the interval of time between collection and sowing. The germination rate of the seed also differs under varying agroclimatic conditions.

The collection of mature seeds is usually done from September-February. Fruits mature between July-November. Only a few fruits ripen at a time and if they are not collected immediately, they shed and are lost. Therefore, the collection of ripe fruits twice a week is necessary. White this easy in case of plantations collection from plants growing in the wild is both laborious and costly owing to their scattered distribution over large areas. The fruits, after collection, are freed from their pulpy covering by rubbing them against old gunny bags or on rough flooring. The cleaned seeds are thoroughly dried in the sun and stored in dry places or in airtight containers. A yield of 100-120 kg of clean seeds can be obtained from one hectare of a 3-year-old plantation. An adequate supply of seeds can also be obtained by raising the plants vegetatively in compact areas, preferably by using stem-cuttings.

Direct sowing of the seeds in the field has not been successful and hence seedlings are raised in the nursery and transplanted into the field. The nursery should ideally be located in partially shaded areas with irrigation facilities. The land is cleared of weed and ploughed to a depth of 30 cm. raised beds are made, which should contain one-third quantity of well-rotted FYM and two thirds of fine soil. Seeds are sown in the middle of May. The seeds should be soaked in water overnight and the light seeds which float can be discarded. The seeds can be treated with Thiram at the rate of 3g/kg of seeds. About 5.5 kg of seeds sown in a 500 m^2 area will yield seedlings sufficient to plant one hectare. The germination is gradual and the growth of the seedlings is slow. Germination starts after 15-20 days and continues up to 40-50 days after sowing. The nursery should be kept moist throughout the germination period.

Transplanting

Seedlings of 40-50 days which have 4-6 leaves are ready for transplanting. The seedlings are carefully dug out and the tap-root should be cut. They are then dipped in a 0.1% solution of emisan fungicide before planting to protect them against soil-borne fungus causing damping-off disease. Well-rotted FYM at 25-30 t/ha is added during land preparation. The field is then divided into small plots for irrigation. About 15 cm deep furrows are dug at a distance of 45 cm. The seedlings are transplanted into the furrows, by making holes large enough to receive the seedlings along with the accompanying clump of earth. A spacing of 30 cm between the plants should be maintained. The seedlings are buried up to the first pair of leaves and the soil around them is lightly pressed. Irrigation after transplanting is essential, and should be continued at regular intervals until the seedlings are established.

b. Vegetative Propagation

As collection of seeds from wild sources is both laborious and costly vetgetative propagation by root, or shoot-cuttings has been advocated for raising plantations to collect the seeds, as well as to quickly multiply the genetically superior clones.

i) By root-cuttings

Large tap-roots with a few filiform lateral secondary rootlets are used. Cuttings of 2.5-5.0 cm length are planted in holes at the beginning of the monsoon and are almost completely covered with earth, leaving only 1 cm above the surface. Nearly 50% of the root-cuttings sprout in about a month. Trials have shown that under irrigated conditions, root cuttings of about 0.25 cm diameter planted during March-June give a 50-80% success rate. About 100 kg of root-cuttings are required to plant 1 ha. The high percentage of success obtained by using root-cuttings makes it more preferable than propagation by seeds. However, the recovery of roots from them has been found to be not as high as in plants raised from seeds.

ii) By root-stumps

Propagation by using about 5 cm of root with a portion of the stem above the collar has also been attempted. This method gives about 90-95% success, sometimes even 100%. Such plants transplanted in May-July into irrigated fields become well established by the end of September. This method has its limitations, as only one plant can be raised from a single stump.

iii) By stem-cuttings

Stem-cuttings taken from woody twigs have also been tried as a source of propagation. Hard-wood cuttings have been found better than soft-wood cuttings. Cuttings of 15-22 cm length with three in ternodes are the most suitable. Nearly 60-100% of rooting is obtained by treating hard-wood cuttings with β indole acetic acid solution of 30 ppm for 12 hrs and the treated cuttings root within 15 days. Stem-cuttings planted in the nursery during the early monsoon (June) and kept moist until they sprout, give about 40-65% success rate. Such cuttings though they start sprouting 3-4 days after planting, naturally strike roots mostly after about 75 days. Stem-cuttings have been found less statifactory than root-cuttings since many of them do not root easily.

Manuring

The use of organic manure, leaf-mould and compost has been recommended to increase the quantity of nutrients in the soil and improve the drainage. The plants respond better to chemical fertilizers than to organic manures. Nitrogenous fertilizers induce more vegetative growth followed by organic manure. Nitrogen seems to have a stunting effect on the root. But the combination of nitrogen either with FYM or phosphates results in better root growth than nitrogen alone. Application of phosphates induces more growth of thick as well as thin roots. Since good manure is in short supply and unecomomical, artificial fertilizers should, therefore, be preferably used.

In is better to apply 25-30 t of well-rotted FYM at the time of land preparation and 10 kg N, 60 kg P_2O_5 and 30 kg K_2O/ha as a basal dose. Later, two equal doses of N each of 10 kg/ha in moist soil is given at 50 days and 170 days after planting.

Irrigation

The crop may be irrigated fortnightly in the hot dry season and about once a month in winter. The crop can be cultivated under rainfed conditions also but the yield is considerably poorer.

Weeding and Interculture

In order to maintain the satisfactory development of roots about 2 weedings are necessary during the monsoon and one hoeing at the end of the growing season (December). This may be done in large plantations using a tractor-drawn cultivator which is cheaper than manual labour. Hoeing by means of a tractor drawn wheel-hoe, is the most economical.

Intercropping

It is possible to grow intercrops in rauvolfia plantations, particularly where good irrigation facilities are available. It is reported that although the yield of roots was higher under monoculture, the net returns were highest when rauvolfia intercropped with soyabeans and onions or soybeans and garlic.

Pests and Diseases

Insect Pests

1. Root knots appear as galls of various sizes, covering the root-system. Stunted growth of plants etiolation and decrease in leaf-size are the symptoms in the aerial portion. The galls on examination, show the presence of mites various soil fungi and namatodes (Heterodera sp). Generally, brown clay soils supporting the natural growth of R. serpentina are found to be infested with nematodes, while dark clay soils are free from them. Application of 25 kg of 3 G Carbofuran or 20 kg of 10 G. Phorate granules per hectare will control them.

2. A pyralid caterpillar (Glyphodes vertumnalis) causes appreciable damange to the leaves. The caterpillars roll leaf and feed on the green matter. Some other caterpillars (Daphnis nerii, L. and Deilophola nerii, L.) are also reported to feed on tender leaves, causing defoliation of the plant. They can be controlled by spraying 0.2% Rogor.

3. Cockchafer grubs (Anomala polita, Blanch) attack the seedlings about 2 cm below the hypocotyl, resulting in their drying up. To control the attack of grubs mix phorate granules with the soil at the time of nursery preparation. Haygrub (Scarabidae) is also reported on rauvolfia.

Diseases

1. Leaf-spot casued by Cercospora rauvolfiae manifests as dark-brown coloured spots on the upper surface of the leaf and yellowish-

brown on the lower surface. The affected leaves turn yellow, become dry and subsequently fall off, resulting in defoliation. To control this disease Dithane Z-78 or Dithane M-45 @ 0.2% is to be sprayed in early June, before the monsoons and repeated at monthly intervals until November.

2. Alternaria tenuis attacks the leaves, resulting in minute, brownish or dark-coloured circular spots with a yellowish margin on the ventral side of the leaves, these spots enlarge to form prominent dark brown circular lesions. The fungus also affects the flowers and fruits. The crop should be sprayed with 30 g Blitox in 10 litres of water, whenever the symptoms are seen.

3. Mosaic is a common disease on R. serpertina. The primary symptom comprises of vein-banding and the gradual yellowing of the leaves, later the leaves curl from the margin to the mid-rib on the abaxial surface and ultimately the leaves drop off. Strict selection of seedlings at the nursery stage helps in avoiding the disease.

The other diseases reported include target leaf-spot caused by Coryneospora cassicola and Pellicularia filamentosa leaf-blotch caused by Cercospora serpentina, anthracnose caused by Collitotrichum glocosporoides die-back caused by Collitotrichum dematium, powdery mildew caused by Leviellula taurica and fusarium wilt (Fusarium oxysporum f. rauvolfii). The root-knot nematode (Meloidogyne spp). is also reported on this crop.

Harvesting and Processing

The roots exploitable size are generally collected 2-3 years after planting i.e. from 18 months onward. It is reported that roots dug out in winter (December), when the plants have shed their leaves are richer in total content of alkaloids than the roots harvested in August. a light irrigation should be given in advance to facilitate easy digging of roots. The roots may be dug out carefully from the subsoil ,manually or by using a mould board plough. Care should be taken to keep the root-bark intact as the bark constitutes 40-56% of the whole root and has a higher alkaloid content. The roots are freed from the adhering soil washed if necessary and thoroughly air-dried till they become brittle and are usually packed in gunny bags. Roots containing 8% moisture keep better. They are stored in a cool, dry place to prevent mould. When the roots are to be stored for a short period, they may be packed in gunny bags or polythene bags pending disposal. But these must be periodically turned, to protect them from mould which is reported to reduce the total alkaloid content ranging from 5-25%. Under the present system, only tap-roots are selected for processing. It has been observed that the rootlets are also rich in alkaloids, so these should be included in the material.

Yield

Though R. serpentina can be propagated by various methods the optimum yield of roots (including thick, thin and fibrous) is obtained when the propagation is done by seeds. The yield of fresh roots per plant varies widely from 0.1-4 kg. With a spacing of 60 x 30 cm, the total yield of roots in the case of plants raised from seeds works out to about 1 175 kg/ha on an air-dried basis, as compared with 175 kg/ha in the case of plants raised from stem-cuttings and 345 kg/ha in the case of plants raised from root-cuttings. A yield of 2 200 kg/ha of air-dried roots has been obtained from a 2-year-old plantation and 3 300 kg/ha from a 3-year-old plantation, under irrigated conditions on sandy, clay loam soil.

Chapter 32

ROSELLE

English name : Hibiscus, Shoe, flower

Indian name : Lalambri, Patwa (Hindi), Pundi, Pundigida (Kannada) Pulichaikeerai, Gogu, Mandharam (Tamil)

Distribution : India, Central America, California, Cuba, Egypt Florida, Indonesia, Malaysia, Nigeria, Philippines Sri Lanka, Sudan, West Indias

Uses : Confectionery, Drugs, Foods, Wines

Roselle (Hibiscus sabadriffa L. var. sabdariffa) belonging to the family Malvaceae, is an important multipurpose annual under shrub preferred for its red, acid succulent calyces, young leaves, stem, fruits, seed and seed oil for food beverages and in Unani and modern systems of medicine throughout the tropics and subtropics, the world over. Apart from its wide range of uses, roselle is becoming increasingly important because of the growth in its export as a source of natural dye obtained from the dried calyces. The calyces which are valued as the main items of trade contain acids pectin mucilage crude protein, carbohydrates, ascorbic acid, anthocyanins and minerals.

The fresh calyces contain 88.26% moisture, 3.74-4% acid 3.19% pectin, 1.45% crude protein 1.97% ether extracts, 5.86& carbohydrates, crude fibre 0.87% ash, 0.108% calcium, 0.052% phosphorus, 0.021% iron, manganese aluminium, sodium and potassium in traces 0.82% reducing sugars, 0.29% sucrose, mucilage, gossypetin hibiscitin chloride, ascorbic acid and anthocyanins. The principal water-soluble acids present are citric acid, D.malic acid, tartaric acid and hibiscus acid. Hibiscitrin chloride on hydrolysis yields glucose-pentose and delphinidin chloride, Cyanidin-3-

glycoside, Delphinidin-pentoside glucoside, Delphinidin-3-sambubioside and cynadin- 3-sambubioside are the water-soluble pigments in the anthocyanins. Among these Delhinidin-3-sambubioside and cyandin-3-sambuioside are the major pigments. The other two are present only in traces.

The seeds contain 12.9% moisture, 3.29% nitrogen, 16.8% fatty oil 16.8% cellulose, 15.5% pentosans, 11.1% starch, myricetin, quercetin, 3.28% protein and 21.1% lipids. In addition, eighteen amino acids have also been identified and quantified. The most essential amino acids are leucine, lysine and phenyl-alanine. Tryptophan, valine isoleucine and threonine are the most limiting. Oleic acid is the most predominant fatty acid, followed by palmitic acid and stearic acid while potassium, sodium, magnesium and calcium are the major elements present in the seeds. Gossypol is found only as a trace.

The dried calyces have acquired a considerable reputation in the international trade as a substitute for tea and coffee and as a popular soft drink. The fresh calyces are used as a vegetable or eaten as salad or used in confectioneries, in the preparation of soups, curries, chutneys, sauces jams, jellies, squashes, tarts, tisanes and wines. The astringent herbal drink made from hibiscus, known as medicinal tea is used as a cure for fever, cold, cough, pneumonia and is said to possess diuretic demulscent emollient laxative, antiseptic, antiscorbutic, antispasmodic and choleretic properties. The drug is also used to cure heart and nerve diseases asthma and skin diseases. Besides the seeds contain fatty oil, proteins, starch and lipids. The seed-meal is made into soup. Medicinally the seeds are reported to have demulscent diuretic and tonic properties and are recommended in cases of dyspepsia, strangury and general debility. The oil of the seed is said to have antibacterial properties.

Origin and Distribution

Tropical Africa is considered as its place of origin. It is also being cultivated in warm countries particularly in the Philippines, Malaysia, Indonesia, India, Cuba, Central America, California, Florida, Egypt, Sudan, Nigeria, West Indies and Sri Lanka. In India it is cultivated in Punjab, Bihar, Uttar Pradesh, West Bengal, Assam, Orissa, Maharastra, Karnataka, Andhra Pradesh and Tamil Nadu.

Plant Description

Roselle is an erect, branched, glabrous undershrub, 0.5-1.8 m tall, with a strong tap-root. The stem is red or green in colour. The leaves are alternate, the stipules subulate, deciduous, 5-8 mm long. The lamina is variable. The lower leaves are often ovate and undivided, others palmately 3-5 lobed or rarely 7-lobed. The lobes are oblong, lanceolate, 7-15 cm long with the middle lobe being the longest the margin is serrate with a gland near the base the predominant mid-rib. The flowers are solitary, axillary, 3-5 cm long with a greyish-yellow corolla and an orange staminal column. The peduncle is short. The epicalyx has up to 10 linear, fleshy bracteoles. The calyx is 5-lobed, conical 1-2 cm long enlarging and becoming fleshly after anthesis. The epicalyx and calyx are red whitish or green in colour. There are 5 petals, 3-5 cm long.The staminal column is 1-2 cm long with numerous anthers. The stigma is 5-lobed. The fruit is a ovoid capsule, villous, 2-3 cm long closely invested with an enlarged, persistent fleshy calyx, dehiscing by 5 valves when ripe. The seeds are reniform dark-brown pilose 4-6 mm long and are 22-34 per capsule.

The flowers open late in the morning and close at mid-day, remaining open for more than three hours. The stigmas are flush with the opening of the staminal column and do not blow away into the air. The filaments are very short and the anthers burst around the opening of the column. Self-pollination is favoured by these arrangements and the completion the process is brought about by the closing of the flower.Flowering has a dual effect on growth. When floral induction is strong lateral buds develop into flowers and the number of branches will be proportionately reduced. When the first fruits are harvested early the resting flower buds grow and the total flowering period is lengthened.

Studies have revealed that Hibiscus sabdariffa L. var. sabdariffa has a chromosome number of 2n=4x=72 (2n=36 is also recorded) and is a tetraploid.

Soil

The crop is not very exacting in its requirements and can tolerate poor conditions and is well adapted for growth in a wide range of soils. But laterite soils and light soils deficient in humus have proven to be unsuitable for the satisfactory growth of this plant. Hence, the soil selected for its cultivation should be permeable not very compact and not subject to flooding. Sandy soils and heavy loam soils capable of retaining moisture are also suitable. However, for obtaining viable economic yields, a loamy soil with a good quantity of organic matter is ideal.

Climate

Roselle prefers a warm humid or dry climate with an even rainfall of 150 to 200 cm yearly and about 25 cm per month during the growing period. It can also grow in drier rainfed areas as an irrigated crop, but it cannot withstand heavy continuous rains, water-logging, winter cold and frost it is known to do well from locations at sea-level up to an elevation of 600-780 m. The monsoon crop is usually sown from the beginning of April to the end of May. In some places where the temperatures during winter do not go very low, it is also grown from October November.

Roselle is a short-day plant requiring 12-12.5 hours light in the period before flowering. It is found to show ambiphotoperiodic reaction flowering both in short days and in extremely long days remaining vegetative (at least at 21-25° C) in a 16-hour day.

Cultivation

Sowing

Roselle is usually propagated by sowing the seeds directly into the field. As the seeds lose the viability rapidly, seeds from the previous season's crop only should be used for sowing. About 2-3 kg of seed is required to cover one hectare.

Before sowing the field is thoroughly prepared by bringing the land to a fine tilth with repeated ploughings. It is then laid out into plots of convenient sizes by constructing bunds and channels. Generally, a plot of 6 m x 4.5 m size is preferred as it helps in the proper management of irrigation weeding and other intercultural operations. After the preparation of the plots the soil is incorporated with 5 t of well decomposed FYM or compost. Ridges and furrows are made at a spacing of 75 cm along the rows and the rows are irrigated lightly immediately after sowing. In some cases thin or thick medium-sized shoot-cuttings are also used for propagating it vegetatively.

Manures and Fertilizers

Roselle responds well to the application of manures and fertilizers. Well-decomposed FYM, at the rate of 5 t/ha, is incorporated into the soil at the time of land preparation. Subsequently a fertilizer dose of 50 kg N, 75 kg/ha each of P and K and is given at the time of sowing. An additional quantity of 200 kg N is applied in two equal split doses as top-dressing at 30 days and 70 days after sowing.

Irrigation

After sowing, the plots are immediately provided with light irrigation. Later, irrigation is given at regular intervals till the seedlings emerge and are well established. In the crop sown in the rainy season except during some long dry spells, practically no irrigation is required. However, the crop sown in October-November needs to be irrigated once in 7-8 days, depending on the weather conditions.

Interculture

Interculture in this crop is mostly confined to weeding. Two weedings during the early period of growth are enough to suppress the weeds. As it has a good canopy in the later stages the weeds do not get much of a chance to grow.

Pests and Diseases

Insect Pests

The crop is very hardy and there is no report of any serious insect pest in roselle. However some insect pests like capsule borer, flea beetle and the cotton stainer bug have been observed to affact the crop. Two sprays of 0.2% Quinolphos or 0.15% Monocrotophos will control the attack of the capsule borer and flea beetle. The spraying of any contact insecticide like 0.4% Carbaryl or 0.2% Enlosulphan will control the incidence of the cotton stainer bug.

Diseases

Black-foot or Stem-rot

This disease is caused by the fungus Phytophthora parasitaica var. sabdariffae due to which the plants suddenly wilt. It is usually severe at the reproductive stage, particularly when there is a high moisture content in the soil due to heavy-rains.

Root-rot

The soil fungus Rhizoctonia bataticola alone or with Fusarium oxysporum causes this disease. This is also severe under wet soil conditions.

Improving the soil drainage and controlling irrigation reduces the incidence of these diseases. Treating the seeds with 0.2% Captan or 0.1% Calixin or Kitazin before sowing and then drenching the plants with 0.1%, carbendiazimor 0.2%, diafoltan or 0.3% mancozeb chemicals a fortnight after germination, controls the disease.

A virus disease sometimes causes slight damage to the fruiting plants. The leaves of the affected plants become hard and crack when crushed. The affected plants may be uprooted and either burnt or buried to avoid further incidence of this disease.

Harvesting

Roselle is a 5-6 months duration crop. The plants come to the flowering stage after about 45-60 days of sowing and it extends over a period of 4 months. The capsules begin to mature progressively from the lower to the upper portion of the plant. The calyces grow rapidly and are ready for picking within 15-20 days of blooming. The growth of the calyx depends upon the production of phytohormones in the developing seeds.

While harvesting the whole fruits are plucked when they are tender, plump, fleshy, crisp and deep-red in colour. The calyces are then separated by hand. If the capsules are allowed to grow older the tissues become tough and harvesting is difficult. The calyx lobes gathered this way are placed fresh or dried in the shade for 12-15 days till a moisture level of 12% is reached. The harvesting season lasts for 2-3 months.

For seed production the calyces are picked while the capsule is still attached to the plant. After some time when a few of the lower and middle capsules turn dry and start splitting exhibiting well developed seeds, they are harvested separately or the plants are cut at ground-level. After harvest, the plants are allowed to dry in the field for some time. They are then brought to the threshing yard and the seeds are separated. These seeds are cleaned by winnowing and packed in airtight containers till they are marketed.

Extraction of Dye and Oil

Although the extraction of dye from the calyces on a commercial scale is yet to be exploited, on a small-scale it is being done, using small samples of fresh or dried calyces.

To extract the dye, the fresh calyces are ground in a wet grinder with water, boiled in an open contianer, strained and repeatedly washed with water and the filtrate is collected. The brilliant red filtrate is reduced to the required volume by boiling and is cooled and preserved in bottles or tins. However, for the extraction of dye from the dried calyces overnight soaking in water is necessary and there-after a procedure similar to the extraction of dye from fresh calyces is followed.

Organic solvents like ethanol and methanol can also be used in place of water for the extraction of the dye. The method for estimation of anthocyanin as suggested by Fuleki and Francis (1968) is the standard official method which may be followed.

Yield

An yield of 13-14 t/ha of fresh calyces which in turn may yield 1.8-2 t/ha dried calyces, may be obtained. The recovery of the water-soluble extracts containing the dye may be around 1.97% on a fresh-weight basis.

In addition a seed-yield of 2.5-3.0 t/ha, which contains 16.2% fatty oil, is also obtained from this crop.

Chapter 33

RUTIN BEARING EUCALYPTUS

English name	:	Red Stingy bark, Eucalyptus
Indian name	:	Nilaniryasa, Tailaparnah (Sanskrit), Yukeliptas (Hindi), Yukkalimaram (Tamil)
Species and	:	Eucalyptus macrorhyncha
varieties	:	E. youmani
Uses	:	Drugs Oils

Eucalyptus macrorhyncha, commonly called Red Stringy-bark Eucalyptus is one of the six thousand-and-odd species of the family Myrtaceae. It is considered to be the best source of rutin, both in terms of quantity and quality. This plant being perennial, and due to the ease of cultivation even on moderate soil under rainfed conditions, offers great advantage in commercializing its cultivation in India. There are vast areas and different regions in the country which can adopt this crop to meet the rutin reguirements indigenously. Furthermore, E. macrorhyncha is considered the best source of the drug, because the rutin produced from it is considerably purer and requires less capital outlay when compared with other sources. The leaf is the main source of rutin in this crop.

Rutin is being produced on large scale in Australia and New Zealand from E. macrorhycha and its sister species E. youmani. The rutin content in the leaves of these species is of the order of 8-10%.

Ruttin is an important pharmaceutical product, useful in the treatment of capillary fragility retinitis and possibly, rheumatic fever of haemorrhagic conditions. Generally, capillry fragility occurs in a significant number of cases of high blood pressure, diabetes and other conditions. It is also useful in the prevention of apolplexy and retinal haemorrhage in those cases where capillary fragility is concerned. It is used in cases of coronary thrombosis and for the purification of blood. Rutin also protects against the harmful effects of X-rays, indicating that it may be of use to persons exposed to dangerous atomic radiations. Under certain conditions, rutin can protect animals against histamine shock.

This pharmaceutical product is not found indigenously in sufficient quantities in our country. Presently, the rutin requirements of India is estimated at 7 t annually and is being met mainly through imports from Australia, involving huge sums of foreign exchange.

Origin

E. macrorhyncha is indigenous to the Central and Southwestern slopes of the New South Wales and Victoria provinces in Southern Australia.

Area and Production

In Australia E. macrorhyncha grows at 300-900 m elevation from MSL. At present this species is commercially cultivated on vast areas for rutin production. The product is exported to several countries of the world. In our country, its trial cultivation was carried out in the Palani Hills Tamil Nadu. The Regional Research Laboratory (RRL), Jammu, has recently taken up its cultivation at Palampur Station in Himachal Pradesh and has developed agrotechniques for its commercial cultivation. In Karnataka also, there are many potentially suitable areas for its successful cultivation on commercial scale.

Two units have been set up on Himachal Pradesh for the manufacture of rutin on a commercial scale with technical know-how from the RRL, Jammu. This new introduction in the country, if taken up for large-scale cultivation, will benefit both the growers and the country as a whole in meeting the indigenous needs of rutin as well as for export to other countries.

Plant Description

E. macrorhyncha is a perennial, medium-sized tree, attaining a height of 20-30 m, 1/2 to 1 m diameter, with a dark reddish to brown bark, which is persistent and stringy. The leaves of the mature tree are typical of the genus and the crown is moderately less dense. The leaves are alternate, petiolate, narrow, lanceolate and somewhat venulose the leaves have very thick cuticles and the laminae are borne vertically downwards. The leaves contain oil glands and tannin cells. The lifespan of the leaves is short in this species, compared with the evergreen trees of other genera. The mean life of the leaves is about 18 months. It varies with their position on the tree as on vigorous branches many leaves fall during the first year and most of the remainder fall with the new flush. Generally, the leaf-fall is a constant process and is greatest at the commencement of periods of fresh growth and when the fruit is forming.

Soil & Climate

E. macrorhyncha prefers altitudes between 300 and 900 m (under Australian conditions). Trials conducted at different elevations, in the range of 500 to 1 500 m MSL, to find the optimum altitude for large-scale plantations-show clearly that altitudes higher than 900 m are not favourable as the species does not exhibit the juvenile phase perfectly. In Australia, it is grown in less fertile lands in regions subject to hot spells and droughts. This species is reported to improve the texture and fertility of land. It is envisaged that in Karnataka, areas around Bangalore, Hassan and Chikmagalur which are less useful for other crop production can be profitably utilized for the cultivation of this species. The areas selected should be comparatively cooler and elevated.

Land Preparation and Planting

The main field is prepared well by clearing the weeds and stubble. One or two ploughings are given well before planting. The spuare method of planting is adopted. Pits of 15 cm are dug inthe field at a spacing of 1.5 x 1.5 m for the transplantation of the seedlings. On an average 4 400 /ha is the ideal plant population. About 6 to 12 g of Gramaxone should be incorporated in each pit along with FYM/compost mixture (2:1) before transplanting the seedling into the pits. The pits are well filled with the mixture at least one or two weeks before transplanting so that it settles down. Planting is done with utmost care, as the seedlings are delicate and small. The seedling begs are carefully kept in baskets and transported to the field and placed once near each pit in the main field. A hole is scooped out in the centre of the pit to the approximate volume of the beg containing the seedling. The polythene cover is carefully removed without disturbing the root-system. The seedling alongwith its ball of earth is planted in the hole and the soil pressed from sides to secure the seedling well in the pit. The planting in pits is done in late June-July when the nonsoon is in full swing.

Cultivation

Propagation and Raising of the Nursery

The crop is raised from seeds which are very small is size (720 seeds/g). The germination of seeds in this crop is very low even under ideal conditions, ranging only from 4 to 6%. The seeds normally lose viability on aging and so, fresh seeds are used for raising the nursery. Nursery, raising is necessary as the tiny plants require intensive care to protect them from frost, severe cold and winter rains. Further, it takes a pretty long time almost 6 months ıor the seedlings to be fit for transplanting, when they attain a height of 12-25 cm.

The nursery is started in January-February in shallow seed-pans or trays. The container is filled with a sand and soil mixture enriched with well-decomposed organic matter. The seeds are sown by broadcasting them in the container evenly and covering them with a thin layer of sand. The seeds sown deeper than 1 cm usually do not germinate. Generally, screening of healthy seeds is done before sowing. The seed-trays are well covered with paddy straw after sowing to ensure uniform watering and heat conservation.

The seedlings obtained from sowing during January February are quite healthy, less prone to diseases and attain a considerable height before transplantation in the mid-monsoon period. If sown during the hotter periods like April-May they suffer from damping-off, stunted growth and chlorosis. The germination is fairly good in the June-August period, but the plant growth is stunted in the nursery stages. Hence January-February sowing is recommended. The straw layer is removed immediately after the commencement of germination, after 20 to 25 days. The tiny seedlings having a pair of opposite leaves, are picked out tenderly and transplanted with care. A secondary nursery of polythene bags is also maintained. The plants are ready for transplanting into the main field in about 5-6 months' time.

Sometimes the seeds are sown shallow directly in the polythene bags packed with well-mixed soil and sand enriched with organic matter. An average of 10-12 seeds are sown individually in each bag to ensure that at least one germinates in each beg. The bags are covered with paddy straw until germination. In case more than one seed germinates in a bag the extra seedling is picked out in the early stage and transplanted into a separate bag. The seedlings are maintained in the bags for 5-6 months under intensive care and then transplanted into the main field at the right time.

Manures and Fertilizers

To supplement the nutrient requirements an adequate N, P, K mixture 15:15:15 at the rate of 10-15 g per plant is incorporated in the soil around the young seedling twice during January-February and again in August September each year during the first two years. From the third year onwards, nitrogen alone at the rate of 220 kg/ha/year in the form of urea is placed around individual plants in two split does after each harvest. Frequent foliar spray consisting of N, P, K and minerals at the rate of 0.5% concentration increases the foliage yield considerably.

Irrigation

Protective irrigation is essential during the dry periods of October-November and May-June. It also helps the plants' estabiishement and profuse growth. This two fold purpose is achieved by giving one or two irrigations during each dry season.

Weeding and Interculture

Weeding and hoeing are necessary during the first year after transplanting. The area around each plant is completely dug out, for better aeration to the root-zone and also to control weed growth.

These operations are carried out manually after the monsoon season is just over.

Training and Coppicing of Plants

Frequent coppicing (plucking of leaves from crown portion), is done in the second and third year, regularly. It is desirable to maintain the height of the plant at a moderate height of 2.0 m to2.5 m only, by pruning away the terminal shoots beyond 2.0 m. These two practices help in developing a denser crown and maximum foliage on maturity of the plant after three years, when it starts yielding economically.

Plant Protection

E. marcorhyncha is very susceptible to termite damage which increases when the plant loses vigour. To eliminate such attacks, doses of Chlordane or Heptachlor are incorporated in the soil repeatedly in the nursery stage. Such applications are sometimes needed after transplanting as well.

The leaf webber also attacks the plants during the monsoon and this can be easily controlled by spraying 0.1% Matacid during the pre-and-post harvest stage.

Harvesting and Yield

The growing trees yield the first harvest of foliage during the second year after the monsoon period and two harvests during the third year, before and after the monsoon. During the three years of plant growth and development, the plants are trained to a moderate height and dense crowns are developed. From the fourth year onwards, the plants successively yield three harvests of foliage in May-August and November-December depending upon the weather conditions. The plantation produces economic yields for 10 years after three years of initial growth and development. There are records of 93-year-old plantations yielding rutin from their foliage in Australia but with reduced rutin content.

A growing tree on an average yields 8 kg foliage per tree from the third year onwards. This amounts to 10to 12.5 t/ha of herbage.

Post-Harvest Handling of Leaves and Storage

The freshly harvested green leaves should not be stored for more than 3-4 days because of possible decomposition and attack by insect pests and diseases. The leaf material should be dried, spread out in thin layers on clean yards for a couple of days until the leaves are completely dried. The leaves may also be dried safely at temperatures of 80-100° C in artificial driers with adequate air-circulation systems. The dried leaves are then packed in polythene bags for longer periods of storage.

Yield of Rutin

The rutin content varies from leaf to leaf in a plant and also lengthwise within a leaf. The content is maximum (20%) in young leaves and tips and decreases gradually to 3% in the mature leaves. The July-August harvest of 3-year-old plants yields the maximum rutin content when compared to the other months of the year. Further, more, the rutin content decreases slightly with the aging of the plant. Nevertheless, the average rutin content on moisture-free leaves is 5%. The moisture content in the freshly harvested green leaves range between 51 and 58%.

Chapter 34

ROSE

Family	:	Rosaceae
English name	:	Damask Rose, Bulgarian Rose
Indian name	:	Shataputri (Sanskrit), Fasli Gulab (Hindi) Demask Gulabi (Kannada), Roja (Tamil)
Species and	:	Rosa damascena Mill
varieties	:	Kanzanlik, Bifera, Dofasali RSL-31, Noorjahan
Distribution	:	India, Afghanistan, Bulgaria, Europe, France, Iran, Italy, Middle East countries, Morocco, Russia, Turkey,
Uses	:	Confectionery, Drugs, Flavouring food and beverages, Liquors, Perfumary

Damask rose or Bulgarian rose (Rosa damascena) Mill) is a commercial source of rose oil, rose water, rose concrete absolute, rose attar, gulkand, gulroghan, pankhuri, otto of rose, etc. The total world production of rose oil is estimated to be about 19 t against the annual requirement which exceeds 25 t. Rose oil contains citronellol (0.4%) nonadecane (12.3%) geraniol (14.4%) henicosane (6.69%) βphenyl ethylalcohol (4.06%), 9 βeicosane hexanol, heptanol, αpinene βpinene myrcene cis-rose oxide trans-rose oxide terpinen 4 Ol αterpineol, β phenylethyl acetate, citral, eugenol, geranyl acetate, methyl eugenol βcaryophyllene αcadinene, docosane, heptadecane, farnesol tridecane hepta-cosone tetradecanol tricosane pentacosane and octadecane.

Rose oil is one of the most valuable perfumery materials from ancient times. All high-grade perfumes contain at least some quantities of rose oil. The best quality rose oil imparts characteristic flowery top-notes to perfumes, the absolute adds lasting tonalities and increases the fixation of odours.

The different products of rose are used in cosmetics beverages cold drinks foodstuffs, tobacco, flavouring like snuff and chewing tobacco fruit flavours, soft drinks, alcoholic liquors and medicines. It is reported that 3 drops of rose oil three times a day is useful for the treatment of gallstones. The rose flowers possess a laxative property due to the presence of a flavanoil glycoside.

Origin and Distribution

Basically, the rose is a temperate plant. The plant is indigenous to Europe and the Middle-Eastern countries especially, Iran, Afghanistan and Turkey. It is believed that the Damask rose originated in Damascus and was introduced into the European countries. The damask rose is cultivated in Bulgaria, Turkey, France, Itraly, Morocco, Russia, and India. Bulgaria, Turkey, and Morocco are the largest producers of rose oil in the world.

In India, scented rose cutlivation is mainly confined to the states of Uttar Pardesh, Rajasthan, Jammu and Kashmir and Himachal Pradesh, in an area of 3 000 ha. Out of this, Uttar Pradesh with 2 500 ha under rose cultivation is the leading rose growing state in the country. India is producing about 80 to 100 kg rose oil annually. At present, Rajasthan produces only rose water although a very high quality rose oil can be produced from the Haldighati plantation .

Description is the Plant and Genetics

R. damascena is a perennial shrub with a long lifespan of 20 to 30 years under cultivation. It grows to a height of 2.5-3 m. The stems possess numerous, moderately hooked, falcate prickles of unequal size, intermixed with glandular bristles the leaf is stipulate, compound and imparipinnate with 5-7 leaflets, the stipules are adnate. The leaflets are moderately large ovate to oblong and serrate. The flowers are borne in groups of 5 to 7 in axillary terminal corymbs. The flowers are sweet-scented, pink, red or sometimes white-striped. The pedicle possesses densely packed acicular and hispid glands. The sepals are leafy, pinnate, reflexed and persist after flowering. The petals are over seventy, light pink, fading to white. The fruit is pseudobacate made up of several hard achenes enclosed within a succulent calyx tube. The fruits (hips) are oviod, bright-red, pulpy and rich in Vitamin C.

The damask rose has many commercial varieties known in cultivation. R. damascena var. trigintipetala is called Kanzanlik rose and is grown in Bulgaria. This is similar to R. damascena which is grown in Aligarh district.

Another strian of R. damascena var. bifera is grown in the Kannuaj district of Uttar Pradesh. In the Aligarh district of Uttar Pradesh two other types are grown one of which flowers twice a year and is called 'Dofasali' the other flower only once as usual.

Varieties

Out of 567 local germplasms, in the evaluation trials at Aligarh a supperior clone RSL-31 was evolved as the best genotype, containing more geraniol and rhodinol + geranyl acetate in the oil as compared to the Bulgarian rose oil which is considered to be the best in the world. This has been named as 'Noorjahan' by the CIMAP, Lucknow. This variety yields 100% rhodinol + geraniol acetate, against 45.7% and 35% of the local check RSL -19 and Bulgarian rose, respectively.

Besides, the scientists at the Institute of Himalayan Bioresource Technology (IHBT), Palampur have developed two new varieties 'Jwala' and 'Himroz' for high flower and oil yields. 'Jwala' is suitable for cultivation in subtropical northern plains low hills and mild temperate regions up to 1 200 m altitude. It flowers in March-April and then in September and is tolerant to hailstorms rains and high velocity winds. Jwala bears short clusters of flowers in compact bunches, the weight of a single flower varies between 2.2 to 5.0 g.

'Himroz' is ideal for cultivation in mild temperate to cold temperate regions (1 200-2 500 m). It is winter tolerant and grows in cold areas without any visual sign of winter injury. It flowers for 22-25 days during the early summer and the weight of a single flower varies from 1.8 to 4.00 g.

A net profit of about Rs. 40-50, 000/ha can easily be realized from cultivation of the new varieties.

Soil

Scented roses can be grown on a wide range range of soils, however they prefers netural, well-drained, sandy loam soil. A pH range between 5.6 to 7.0 is considered favourable for rose cultivation.

Climate

Roses thrive well in temperate climate and for this reason the Kashmir Valley has been identified as being the most ideal for its cultivation. It can also be culuivated in the subtropical region of North India, where winters are pronounced. It is a photophyllous plant and is sensitive to frost and shade. Low atmospheric humidity during the flowering reduces the essential oil content in the flowers and high temperature leads to abscission of the flower-buds before blooming temperature ranging from0° to 5° C for a period of about 15 days prior to the start of blooming, enhances the quantity as well as the quality of the flowers. Therefore, regions with high atmospheric humidity (more than 60%) and moderate temperature (15-20°C) at the time of flowering are considered most favourable for a good flower yield. Bright morning conditions at conditions at the time of flowering is desirable as it prolongs the flowering duration and improves the quality of the oil.

Preparation of Land

Open land free from perennial grasses, with gradual slopes, facing south are the most suitable for rose plantations. The land is ploughed deep (30 cm) in order to minimize the weeds and finally levelled by planking. Pits of 0.45 cm in good soils and 60 cm in poor soils are dug a a spacing of 1.5 m x 1.5 m in temperate conditions, while the plants in the subtropical regions are spaced at 1 m x 1 m. They are filled with about 3 to 4 kg FYM, 20-25 g N, P and K mixture (18:32:16) 20 g Aldrin powder and soil mixture per pit before planting.

Cultivation

Propagation

Scented roses are vegetatively propagated by cuttings. They can also be propagated through the division of oil plants, lateral sprouts with roots and seeds.

Preparation of Nursery

A mixture of FYM (4:1) is added to the nursery-beds and mixed well into the soil. After levelling the field P_2O_5 and K_2O @ 20:40 kg/ha are also added as inorganic fertilizers.

The propagation material (cuttings) are taken from healthy, flowering bushes during November-December usually 25 to 30 cm-long stem cuttings with one year growth preferably the anterior portion with four to five nodes of 1 to 2 cm diameter, are taken. The basal end of the cuttings is treated with Indole Butyric Acid (IBA @ 200-250 ppm) solution for four hours before planting which helps in inducing roots. The beds are frequently irrigated. The cuttings begin to sprout after a months' time (30 to 35 days) and the beds are kept free from weeds. When the cuttings have attained a height of 10 to 15 cm a dose of 20 kg N/ha in the form of nitrogenous inorganic fertilizer is applied 4 to 5 cm away from the plants and mixed well into the soil. Monthly spraying of Benlate (0.1%) or Bavistin is done to keep away diseases.

Rooted cuttings are transplanted into the field after one year from mid November to mid-January. The rooting percentage of the cuttings from the year old shoot ranges from 50 to 60% whereas from the other shoots it is 25 to 30%.

Transplanting

Rooted cuttings are uprooted from the nursery and subjected to a treatment of 0.01% Bavistin for five minutes before planting them in the pits. The soil around the plants is compacted and irrigated immediately. Transplanting of rooted cuttings in sub tropical regions is also done in the same way during July-August.

Fertilizer Application

FYM @ 18-20 t/ha mixed with 100-125 kg N, P and K (18:32:16) mixed with fertilizers should be applied at the time of transplanting the rooted cuttings. Since rose plants remain economically viable for 15-20 years the soil around the plant must be sufficiently supplied with nutrients. Therefore, the need to apply fertilizer every year is evident. A total of 160 kg/ha N, 80 kg/ha each of P_2O_5 and K_2O should be applied each year in the form of inorganic fertilizers to get a good yield of flowers.

Fertilizers should be applied at a depth of 20-30 cm beside the rose-bushes, which is the peripherial zone containing most of the feeding roots. Phosphorus and potash are applied as a basal dose whereas, nitrogen is given in three equal splits during May July and September. The application of fertilizers along with NAA (20 ppm) spray and 1% micronutrient mixture (agromine) enhances the flower-yield.

Irrigation and Drainage

The crop requires frequent irrigation during the summer months. In all, about 10 to 12 irrigations are required in one year. Irrigation after pruning is necessary in order to protect the sprouting buds from withering away due to loss of water or damage by low temperature or frost. The field may be provided with proper drainage to drain out the excess rain water.

Weeding and Intercultivation

After every pruning weeding and hoeing should be done every year in January and February and the soil around the root-zone of each bush should be turned and pulverized well after each hoeing. At least three weeding and hoeings are essential during January and February. The weedicides, Simazine and Atrazine are used to control annual weeds.

Intercropping

Pulses and vegetables may be grown as intercrops in rose plantations during the first two years.

Pruning and Training

Rose plants require a dormant or resting period before flowering. Hence pruning is an essential operation for obtaining a good flower-yield. Its intensity and shape vary with the age of the plant. The first pruning is done after the plant attains two years of age. At 1.50 m height from the ground level, shoots and branches are removed with the help of secateur, leaving 8 to 10 primary branches in the shape of an umbrella. Whatever shoots appear during the growth phase are also removed, as they do not bear flowers. The time for pruning is during the first week of November to early December in temperate climates. In subtropical climates, heavy pruning at 30-45 cm of the plant-height is done during December-January and the soil around the base of the rose plants is dug up to bare the primary roots which facilitates the chilling of roots and, in February, the soil is again heaped at the base of the plant. The plants take about 70 to 90 days to flower after pruning. The other purpose of pruning is to train plants in the desired form, to keep the desired size to remove injured and diseased parts to remove the terminal buds and charge the growth habit, to encourage bushy roses to provide more horizontal expansion and finally to produce more flower-buds.

Pests and Diseases

Rose plantations are attacked by a number of pests among which the following are the important ones.

Pests

Aphids (Macrosiphum rosae)

Aphids attack the plants during the flowering period. They can be controlled effectively by prophylactic sprays at 15 days' interval with Methyl Demeton or Metasystox (0.1%) or Dimethoate (0.25%) or Phosphomedon (0.1%).

Caterpillars

The caterpillars of Operophtera frumata, Malacosoma neustria, Orgyia antiqua and Archips podana attack the foliage during the summer and the rainy resons. The caterpillars can be controlled by spraying Endosulphon (0.2%) or Quinalphos (0.15%) or Fenthion (0.12%).

Red Spider Mites (Tetranychus spp).

Heavy infestation results in the leaves becoming bronzed and falling prematurely. Wettable sulphur (0.4%) can be sprayed to control the mites.

Rose Thrips (Thrips fuscipennis)

Thrips attack is common during the flowering period. Heavy infestation causes a significant loss to the flower-yield. Sprays of Malathion (0.2%) or Sumithion (0.1%) at an interval of 10 days controls the attack of thrips.

Caspid Bugs (Lygocoris pubulinus)

These pale-green insects such the sap from the shoot-tips mainly from young flower-buds, causing the flower petals to develop small holes. The application of Carbofuron or Phorate @ 10kg/ha to the soil after pruning at the time of bud formation is recommended for the control of this insect.

Brown and Scurfy Rose Scale (Aulacaspis rosae)

the scales occur on the stems and suck the sap from the stems resulting in the drying up of the shoot. The incidence is more during the rainy/autumn season. For controlof this insect, foilar sprays of Monocrotophos (0.15%) or Carbaryl (0.3%) or Metasystox (0.15%) has been recommended.

The other pests of roses include aphide (Macrosiphum roseae) Eulecanium coryli, Podophylla fulho and Rhynchites hungaricus. Also, some insects that belong to Coleoptera, Hymanoptera, Diptera ,Neuroptera and Dermaptera specifically attack the flowers. These insects can be controlled by spraying any contact insecticide.

Diseases

Black Spot (Diplocarpon rosae)

The fungus causes black spots on the leaves, due to which the leaves will abscise. Fungicidal sprays with Captan (0.2%) or Benonmyl or Carbendazim (0.1%) is recommended for control of this disease.

Rust (Phrogmidium mucronatum)

This causes oranges-coloured pustules on the leaves, in summer and in antumn darker brown ones often develop on the same spot. Spraying fungicides like Plantavax (0.2%) or Mancozeb (0.3%) have been recommended for the control of rust.

Powdery Mildew (Sphaerotheca pannosa)

Small, white, powdery pustules of fungus appear on the leaves stems and occasionally on the flowers. Dinocap (0.1 to 0.15%) or wettable sulphur (0.4%) should be sprayed at 15 days' interval for the control of this disease.

Downy Mildew (Peronospora sparsa)

Small reddish-purple areas appear on the youngest leaves resulting in leaf distortion. Repeated sprays of Mancozeb (0.2%) or Captafal (0.3%) or Copper Oxychloride (0.3%) should be employed for effective control.

Virus Diseases

Rose mosaic is the most common virus disease. Control measures should be followed to kill the various virus vectors.

Rose Rust (Phragmidium subcorticium)

The disease attacks the leaves flowers and shoots and causes leaf-fall and abscission of buds. The most important control is to bury the fallen leaves under heaps of soil around the rose bush. The winter rust spores perish due to the development of antagonistic micro-organisms. The disease is chemically controlled by the spraying of Bavistin @ 0.1% twice during the flowering period (March and May). After the harvest Benlate @ 0.1% is sprayed periodically in order to check the disease.

Flowering

In northern India, the main season of flowering is 30-40 days during March April it reaches a peak in the middle of March and then starts declining. However, sporadic flowering does occur during September and October. Though the flowering starts in the second year after planting, it is always economical to harvest flowers from thirh year onwards. The flowers will have more then 70 to 80 petals per flower and the flower weight varies from 1.2 to 4 g. The flowers of the early crop are heavier than those received late in the season.

Harvesting

The flowers are hervested by hand in the early mornings, preferably before sunrise, when they start opening. The collected flowers should be distilled immediately as they lose their whole aroma within 25 hours of their opening.

Distillation of Flowers

A distillation apparatus made of stainless steel is the best for the production of quanlity rose oil. A weighed amount of fresh flowers along with six times its weight of cold water is fed into the churning tank, using a mechanical stirrer, till a uniform slurry of rose flowers is formed. This slurry is distilled for about four hours for the recovery of first rose water. The rose water is then prepared in the cohabitation tower for the recovery of water and oil through a packed column. The second rose water is also distilled in the same process. In subtropical climates an oil content ranging from 0.02 to 0.03 % on fresh-weight basis oof flowers is obtained. The yield of flowers and oil is also more in temperate climate than in subtropical climate.

Yield

The average yield of fresh flowers in moderately fertile soil under the temperate climate of Kashmir is 4.0-5.0 t/ha, which corresponds to 1.31-1.6 kg/ha/annum of oil Whereas, in the subtropics, the flower-yield reaches to about 1.2-2.0 t which corresponds to 0.3-0.4 kg/ha/annum of oil.

Rejuvenation

Yearly observations have shown that rose plantations do not have a uniform rate of production. In the first 5 to 6 years the flower yield rises, but after the sixth year the flower production declines. After 8-10 years, the roses become unprofitable, necessitating rejuvenation.

Antumn is the most favourable time for rejuvenation. The bushes are cut down to the base and on both sides of the rows trenches 18-20 cm deep are opened and the soil is spread in the inter-row space. In these rows 20-30 t of FYM along with 60 kg/ha each of P_2O_5 and K_2O are placed and covered with soil. In the spring, new shoots develop and out of them only six to eight vigorous branches are allowed to grow. After 2 years the yield of rose flowers reach the previous level and the life of plantation is increased by a further 8-10 years.

Chapter 35

SENNA

Indian name	:	Svarnapatri (Sanskrit) Sanay Sana ka Patt (Hindi) Nilavirai, Nelavakai (Tamil)
Species and	:	Cassia angustifolia Vahl.
		varieties C. acutifolia Del C. obovata C. italica C. abovata ALFT - 2, Sona
Distribution	:	India, Southern Arabia Yemen
Uses	:	Drugs

Senna (Cassia angustifolia Vahl). is a small perennial under-shrub, a native of Yemen, South Arabia. The leaves and pods contain Sennosides used for their laxative properties. It was introduced into Tamil Nadu in the eighteenth century where it is grown as an annual crop of 5 to 7 months duration in 8000 to 10 000 ha both under rainfed and irrigated conditions. Successful cultivations have also been demonstrated in Karnataka (Bangalore) Gujarat (Anand), Rajasthan (Jodhpur) and Delhi with comparable yield and quality of the produce but it is yet to establish itself as a cash crop there due to the lack of organized marketing. A major part of the produce is exported in the form of leaves, pods and sannoside concetrates, though several pharamaceutical houses utilize it for the manufacture of calcium sennoside granules, tablets and syrups for marketing within the country as well. Genmany, Hungary, Japan, Netherlands and the USA are the main markets. The export of leaves and pods from India is of the value of Rs. 20 million annually. In addition, the erstwhile USSR contries buy sennosides (concentrates) and the current annual export of the sennoside concentrate is around Rs. 20 million.

Senna is used in medicine as a cathartic. It is especially useful in habitual constipation. It increases the peristaltic movement of the colon. The pods have the tendency to gripe caused by senna may be obtained by combining it with an aromatic or a saline laxative. the laxative principles of senna are two glycosides, viz., sennoside A and sennoside B. The plant also contains sennosides C & D. A number of other glycocides have also been reported. It also contains beta sterol (0.33%) and flavanols-kaemferol, kaempferin and isorhamnetin. They are used in the form of decoctions, powders confections and many other household preparations. Senna extracts, on storage, lose biological activity more repidly than is revealed by chemical estimation. The leaves/pods as such or in powder form do not lose potency easily. The quantity administered in the form of infustion ranges from 0.6 to 2 g of leaves or pods soaked in 125 ml of warm water for about 12 hours, whereas, it is usually 30 mg of sennosides per tablet.

Distribution and Origin

Cassia is a pantropic genus comprising of 500 species, of which 20 are found in the native flora of India. There are two sources of the Senna drug, namely, Cassia augustifolia Vahl, and C. acutifolia. Del. C. angustifolia, commonly called tinnavelly senna, is indigenous to Somalia, Southern Arabia part of Sindh (Pakistan) and the Kutch area of Gujarat. In India it is cultivated in Gujarat, Rajasthan and Tamil Nadu. In Tamil Nadu it is caltivated in the districts of Tirunelveli, Ramannathapuram, Madurai, Salem and Tiruchirapalli in an area of about 10 000 hectares. C. acutifolia known as Alexandrian senna is indigenous to Sudan and Sinai. It is cultivated on a small scale in Sudan and Egypt and is mainly collected from wild plants of C. acutifolia whereas the Indian produce comes entirely from the cultivated crop of C. angustifolia, and their pods contain about 2.4-4.5 and 1.25 to 2.5% sennosides, respectively.

Plant Description

Cassia angustifolia (2n=28), belonging to the family Leguminosae, is a small perennial undershrub below 1 m in height with ascending branches. The leaves are large, compound and pinnate. The full grown leaflets are bluish-green to pale-green in colour and emit a characteristic fetid small when crushed. The flowers are bright yellow in colour, arranged in axillary, (on subterminal) erect many-flowered racemes. The flowers are not season bound and are borne between 35 to 70 days of age, depending upon the time of sowing, and its season of cultivation. The pods appear immediately after flowering, are slightly curved, 3.5 to 6.5 cm long and up to 1.5 cm broad-green in the beginning changing to greenish-brown to dark-brown on maturity and drying. Each pod has 5 to 7 ovate, compressed, smooth, dark-brown seeds.

The other species is very similar to C. angustifolia in morphology and growth except in the dimension of its leaflets and pods. The leaflets are shorter and narrow. The pods are distinctly short, flat and broad, oblong but slightly curved upwards and are broadly rounded at the two ends. Further, surface making on the testa (seed) and stomatal index (leaves) are remarkebly considered to distinguish between the two species. It has been found that Cassia obovata and C. italica also possess a fair to good percentage of anthraquinone compounds C, obovata is common all over India. C. italica grows on sandy, saline soils in west Rajasthan and Saurashtra (Gujarat) and is a potential new source of the senna drug.

Varieties

The Gujarat Agriculture University, under the All India Co-ordinated project on Medicinal and Aromatic Plants at Anand has released a late flowering type as 'ALFT-2' through selection which remains in a vegetative stage till 100 days and is suitable for growing exclusively as leaf-crop. The CIMAP, Lucknow, has also released a high-yielding variety named 'Sona'.

Soil

The crop can thrive on a variety of soils, but is largely grown on red loams, alluvial loams and the rich clayey rice fields. The texture of the soils which account for the major hectarage under senna crop varies from sandy loam to loam while the black cotton soils are heavier and more fertile. In general, these soils are more friable but less moisture retentive and of low fertility, usually, nitrogen and phosphoric acid are deficient throughout these soils. The average pH ranges from 7-8.5. It is very sensitive to water-logging and hence it is grown only on well drained soils.

Climate

Senna is a sun-loving crop and requires bright sunshine for its successful growth. The trials at Bangalore have shown that it can be grown as an early summer (Feb-March) or a winter (Oct-Nov) crop. However, sowing in the rainy season is not good, as the crop on harvest cannot be dried easily. Whereas, under North Indian conditions like Delhi and Gujarat, where the rainy season is short, it is reported to be the ideal time as the plants put on luxuriant growth. Heavy rains and cloudy weather during growth are harmful to the crop. An average rainfall of 25-40 cm, distributed from June to October is sufficient to yield good harvests.

Land Preparation

The land is preparad deep and exposed to the sun for 110-115 days to dry out the roots of perennial weeds, followed by two crossploughings, harrowing and levelling. FYM is incorporated into the soil at the time of the final cross-ploughing. Then the land is laid out into plots of convenient sizes with irrigation channels.

Cultivation

Propagation

The crop is raised from seeds. Since the seeds have a hard and tough seed-coat a certain amount of abrading of its surface is necessary to induce quick germination. This is achieved by pounding the seeds lightly with coarse and in a mortar.

Soaking the seeds for 10-12 hours before sowing is reported not only to give 100% germination but also the stand of the plants grown is even. About 20 kg of seeds are required to cover a hectare of land.

Sowing

The seeds are broadcast or more preferably, drilled at a distance of 30 cm in lines made at 30 cm apart at 1.5 to 2.5 cm depth on well-prepared land. The germination commences on the third day and is completed within a fortnight. Before sowing the field should be perfectly levelled lest it hamper uniform seed germination. It in found that treating the seeds with Thiram Captan or Agroson G.N. at 2.5 g/kg protects the seedlings from damping-off and seedling blight diseases which are common occurrences.

The seeds can also be dibbled on the inner sides of the ridges opened at 45 cm distance maintaining a plant-to-plant spacing of 30 cm. Only about 5 kg of seeds are required for this method of sowing.

Manures and Fertilizers

Farmers in Tamil Nadu use 4-5 cartloads (5-10 t/ha) of well-rotted FYM at the time of sowing. In most cases, it fully utilizes any leftover nutrient from the previous crop and, therefore, the nutrient requirement of senna is variable. However trials in India have shown that the crop in all, takes 50-100 kg of N 20-50 kg of P_2O_5 and about 30 kg of K_2O/ha in a growing period of 130-150 days depending upon the growth and number of pickings. In general, where specific soil nutrient status of the field is not readily found, 80 kg of N and 40 kg each of P_2O_5 and K_2O/ha may be applied for the optimum production of leaf, pod and total alkaloids. Of these, the entire dose of P and K and 50% of N should be applied at the time of sowing and the remianing 50% of N is to be applied 90 days after sowing.

Crop Rotation and Intercropping

In Tamil Nadu, senna is grown after the paddy and intercrop cultivation in between rosw of cotton, sesamum, chillies, brinjal, okra and tomatoes is popular. Studies conducted at Dehli showed that senna-mustard and senna coriander rotations gave higher profits and these rotations have proved superior.

Irrigation

Senna can be economically grown under rainfad conditions. In most years, the crop needs no irrigations except during prolonged drought. However when it is grown as semi-irrigated crop the yield increases considerably. In all about 5-8 light irrigations are enough to raise a good crop of senna as heavy irrigations are injurious to the crop.

Weeding and Interculture

When the plants begin to grow, once or twice interculturing is given after which the rows close up. The first weeding-cum-hoeing is done at 25-30 days a second at 75-80 days and a third at 110 days to keep to soil free from weeds. The use of Teeflan herbicide as a pre emergent spray at the rate of 4 kg/ha has been reported not only to increases the yield, but also the anthraquinone content.

Pests and Diseases

Pests

The larvae of several leaf-eating caterpillars feed on the green senna leaves. Usually, the syraying of Carbaryl (4 g/l) periodically in the growing season controls the infestation. The white butterfly (Catopsilia pyranthae) attack on this crop can be minimized by sowing the crop in March-April, instead of June-July in North India.

Another pest a pod borer is also reported to attack the pods and can be controlled by spraying Endosulphan (0.05%) or Carbaryl (0.25%) at an interval of 10-15 days.

Diseases

The leaf-spot disease is the most serious disease and causes severe damage to the crop. The infested leaves drop off resulting in poor yield. The disease is caused by Alternaria alternata (Fr) Keisel, Phyllosticta spp. and Cercospora spp. The sennoside content in the leaves is inversely proportional to the intensity of the disease. The spraying of 0.15% Dithane M-45 at fortnightly intervals 3 times in a period of 5-6 weeds has been found to control the disease effectively.

Damping-off of seedlings is the most devastating disease, which is caused by Rhizoctonia bataticola. The disease spreads rapidly if the fields are affected by stagnating moisture at this stage. Treatment with Thiram or Captan at 2.5 g/kg of seeds protects the growing seedlings. At a later stage its other physiological form, called Macrophomina phaseoli develops, it causes dry rot in the crop and kills the plant. The fields can be drenched with 0.2% Brassicol or 0.5 to 01.%. Rhizoctol, but this only gives partial control.

The leaf-blight disease is caused by Phyllosticta spp. usually occurring at the later stages of growth in September-October. Cloudy days and humid weather conditions favour the spread of the disease. The leaf-spot disease initially appears as small brown irregularly scattered lesions on leaves which grow bigger in size and turn black in colour at a later stage. The spraying of 0.15% Dithane M-45 at forthrightly intervals can control the disease.

Harvesting Processing and Storage

It has been found that young senna leaves and pods contain a high sennoside content but since the produce is sold on the basis of weight, a balance between weight and content hs to be made, to choose the right stage for harvest. It is also found that senna plants produce foliage containing higher sennosides between 50-90 days of sowing. The first picking of the foliage crop should be done at 50-70 days' age, depending upon the total plant growth. The picking of leaves is done by hand so that most of the growing tops are removed at harvest this also induces more branching which otherwise reduces the foliage growth consideraly. A second picking is taken at 90-100 days and the third picking between 130-150 days when the entire plants are removed, so that the harvested material includes both leaves and pods together.

The harvested crop should be spread in a thin layer in an open field to reduce its moisture. Further drying of the produce is done in well-ventilated drying sheds. It takes 10-12 days to dry completely. The dry leaves and pods should have a light-green to greenish-yellow colour. Improper and delayed drying changes the colour to black or brown which lowers the sennoside content and it fetches a lower price. A rapid mechanical drying at 40° C could also be attampted. The seeds contain no sennosides and only add weight to the produce. The pods are threshed during drying to remove the seeds. The produce is baled under hydraulic pressure and wrapped in gunny bags for export.

Yield

A good crop of senna can give 15 g/ha of dry leaves and 7 q/ha of pods, under irrigated and good management conditions. The yield, under rainfed conditions; is about 10 q/ha of leaves and 4 q/ha of pods.

Estimation of Sennosides

To 0.5 g (40 mesh) of accurtely weighed powder in a 100 ml flask and 50 ml of water swirl to mix, attach a reflux condenser and immerse the flask in a boiling water-bath with the water-level in the bath just above that of the liquid in the flask, for 15 minutes. Allow the mixture to cool. Decent and filter the extract into a volumetric flask (100 ml). Add 50 ml water to the residue and extract again in the boiling water-bath as above. The final volume in the flask is made up to 100 ml.

Transfer 20 ml of the clear supernatent liquid from the volumetric flask to a separating funnel, add 0.05 ml of hydrochloric acid and extract with two successive 15 ml portions of chloroform. Discard the chloroform extracts.

Transfer 20 ml of aqueous extract from the separating funnal to a 100 ml flask. Adjust the pH to 7-8 (with pH paper) with 5% w/v solution of sodium carbonate in water. Add 20 ml of 6.3% w/v freshly-prepared solution of ferric chloride ($FeCl_3$) in a water mix attach a reflux condensor to the flask and heat on a boiling water bath for 20 minutes and without cooling the liquid add 2 ml of HCI. Continue the heating for a further 20 minutes swirling the liquid in the flask frequently, to dissolve the precipitate and allow it to cool.

Transfer the liquid into a separating funnel, extract with three 25 ml portions of solvent ether, having used each portion to rinse the flask first. Wash the conbined etheral extracts with two 15 ml portions of water and dilute to 100 ml with solvent ether.

Evaporate 10 ml (exect) of the etheral solution to just -dryness on a water bath and dissolve the residue in 10 ml of 1N KOH. Then, immediately measure the extinction of 1 cm layer to 500 mm using water as a blank.

Chapter 36

STEROID BEARING SOLANUM

Indian name	:	Kasi Kateri (Hindi) Kasibadane (Kannada)
Species and	:	Solanum viarum Dunal.
varieties	:	Arka Mahima Arka Sanjeevini BARC Strain Galxo strain Pusa-1, RRL-20-2 RRL-GL-6
Distribution	:	India, Burma ,China
Uses	:	Drugs

Among the various plants which are being used as raw materials for the production of steroidal drugs, steroid-bearing solanum (Solanum viarum Dunal) holds an important place due to its quick growth and low initial investment in its commercial cultivation. It yields a glyco-alkaloid, solasodine, a nitrogen analogue of diosgenine. Solasodine through 16-dehydro pregenenolone (16 DPA) is converted to a group of compounds like testosterone and methyl testosterone and corticosteroids like predinisolone and hydrocortisone. These steroidal compounds have anti-inflammatory anabolic and antifertility properties, due to which they find large-scale use in health and family planning programmes all over the world.

Distribution

It is widely distributed in the subcontinent extending from sea-level up to 2 000 m and is reported from Khasi Jaintia and the Naga Hills of Assam and Manipur. It occurs in Sikkim, West Bengal, Orissa the Upper Gangetic Plains and in the Nilgiris, ascending to an altitude of 1 600 m. It is reported from North-east North-west southern as well as Central India and extends into Burma and China. Its commercial cultivation is mainly confined to the Akola-Jalgoan tract of Maharashtra in an area of about 3 000 ha.

Plant Description

Solanum viarum (2n=24) belonging to the family Solanaceae, is a stout, branched, woody shrub attaining a height of 0.75 to 1.5 m. The stem the spines, the leaves are ovate to lobed with spines on both the surfaces, the flowers are hermophrodite, borne on axillary clusters, white, the berries are yellowish when ripe or greenish, the seeds are small, brown in colour and abundant embedded in a sticky mucilage.

Varieties

Some of the promising less spiny strains developed in this crop are the Galxo strain, BARC Strain, Pusa-1, RRL-20-2 and RRL-GL-6, which is said to be completely spineless. 'Arka Sanjeevini' and 'Arka Mahima' are the two diploid and tetrapoloid varieties of this crop developed at the Indian Institute of Horticultural Research, Hessarghatta, Bangalore and released for cultivation.

Soil

Solanum viarum is a hardy plant and can be cultivated on a wide range of soils under various agroclimatic conditions, but it cannot withstand water-logging. Though it can be grown in all types of soils the best soil for its successful cultivation is red lateritic soil with a moderate quantity of organic matter. The plant does not perform well in very clayey soils.

Climate

It is found growing under different kinds of climates throughout the length and breadth of country, but prefers a moderate climate for its successful growth. The growth as well as development of the plants and, finally, the yield of fruits depend significantly on the climatic conditions. Depending upon the temperature, dry period length, rainfall and irrigation facilities, the sowing time may vary from June to September or October. The plants sown in late October to February are more susceptible to vrius diseases and sowing in March in not practicable as harvesting and drying will be hindered by the rainy season. Under rainfed conditions, the crop should be sown from mid-June to the first week of July. Under irrigated conditions, the sowing in September results in profuse flowering and berry formation during the winter months.

Land Preparation and Planting

Well before the time of transplanting, the field is thoroughly prepared, about 25 t/ha FYM is incorportated into the soil, it is divided into blocks of convenient sizes, and ridges are opened at a distance of 60 cm.

At the time of tranplanting, the seedlings uprooted from the beds are thoroughly cleaned of soil and dipped in 0.1% Bavistin solution for at least 5 minutes to overcome the wilt problem and, thereafter, transplanted at a distance of 45 cm within the row. Spacings of 50 x 50 cm, 75 x 75 cm and 90 x 120 cm are also recommended for this crop for different locations.

Cultivation

Nursery Raising and Transplanting

Although the crop can be raised by broadcasting the seeds directly into the field, it is advantageous to raise a nursery.

The seedlings are raised in nursery-beds of 10 m x 1 m size which are convenient for weeding, irrigation and removing seedlings. To each strip, 5 baskets of FYM and 1 kg of calcium ammonium nitrate are applied. Seeds which are presoaked in water in water for 24 hours are sown in lines of 1 to 1.5 cm-deep furrows, 10 cm apart and covered with a thin layer of soil. About 1.25 kg seeds sown in 5 nursery beds of the above size will provide enough seedlings for planting 1 ha of land. Their germination is completed in 7-10 days. Within 4-5 weeks, when the seedlings are 10-12 cm high and develop 6 leaves, they are ready for transplanting into the main field.

Manures and Fertilizers

Solanum viarum responds well to the application of manures and fertilizers. Green manuring before planting has been found to increase the yield by 20%. For better yields an application of 100:60 40 kg of P_2O_5 and K_2O/ha, depending upon the soil condition is recommended. The entire quantity of phosphorus, photassium and half of the nitrogen are applied at the time of land preparation. While the remaining half of the nitrogen is applied when the plants start flowering. A fertilizer dose of 65:40:40 kg of N, P_2O_5 and K_2O has been recommended under Banglaore conditions.

Irrigation

In the absence of sufficient moisture in the soil, the field should be immediately irrigated after transplanting. The crop is further irrigated at weekly intervals during the first month and then the interval is increased to once in fortnight, and later as and when required.

Interculture

After 2-3 weeks of transplanting the first weeding is done, and later when the crop is 2-3 months old. Afterwards, the crop puts on enough canopy to smother the surface and, hence, no growth of weeds takes place.

Pests and Diseases

Insect Pests

The plant is sufficiently hardy and, therefore, free from any of the serious pests. However, it is sometimes attacked by leaf-eating caterpillars and wingless hoppers. In case of severe attack, the crop may be sprayed with Endosulphan (3 ml/l) to control them. The fruit borer (Leucinodes orbonalis) and root-eating grubs are the other pests reported. Ekalux (2 ml/l) can be sprayed to control the fruit borer. Chloropyriphos may used to control grubs.

Diseases

Some of the diseases the crop is attacked by are powdery mildew collar rot bacterial blight, leaf-blight and damping-off.

Powdery mildew will be noticed during prolonged dry and warm period Bavistin (1 g/l) may be sprayed to control this disease.

Collar rot or Fusarium wilt can be overcome by keeping the field clean and planting the crop in a well drained soil. Dipping the roots of the seedlings in a 0.1% solution of Bavistin for 1 hour and drenching the seed-beds with 0.25% of copper oxychloride or 0.1% of Bavistin solution can control the disease.

Sometimes the plants are attacked by mosaic caused by three different viruses, which leads to stunted growth and chloratic leaves. Such plants are better removed and destroyed.

Bacterial blight is not a serious disease on this crop. However, under severe incidence, a treatment with the solution of 30 g of Streptocyclene and 30 g of Copper sulphate dissolved in 500 l of water per hectare controls this disease.

Leaf-blight is caused by Pythium butleri and is not a serious problem in this crop.

Seedlings may also be attacked by damping-off disease while growing in the nursery-beds. To control this the seeds are treated with Bavistin @ 3g /kg of seeds. Drenching the seed-beds 2-3 days after sowing and again when 50% of the seeds have germinated, with 0.1% of Bavistin or 0.25%of copper oxychloride solution, helps to check the further spread of the disease.

The occurrence of the chlorotic stunt disease and its association with the root-knot nematode (Meloidogye javanica), and the wilting of plants due to M. incognita have also been reported.

Harvesting and Processing of the Berries

Generally, the accumulation of glyco-alkaloid increases with the physiological age of the fruit and attains its peak value in the fruits of 50-60 days. This state of fruit growth coincides with the change in fruit colour from green to just yellow with streaks of green still present after which the glyco-alkaloid content falls gradually with the maturity of fruits. The alkaloid is distributed throughout the fruit. It is, however, established that about 60% of this is present in the seeds and the remaining 40% in the pericarop.

The crop takes about 6 months to be ready for harvesting. Harvesting is one of the labour-intensive operations in the cultivation of S. viarum. The spiny nature of the plant hampers plucking the berries at the right stage of maturity, which is very important. During the first part of the harvesting season, when the fruit is big, on an average, one person with gloves can pluck about 50 kg of berries, while working 8 hours a day. However, some good workers in the peak season when most of the berries are ready for harvest can pick even 80 kg of berries per day. The figure is reduced to 40 kg towards the closing season when the fruits become smaller in size. The picking operation spreads over 3 months, because the fruits mature at different times.

The processing of berries for marketing requires a lot of care. Fresh fruits contain about 80% moisture. The pharmaceutical firms need berries containing about 10% moisture. Hence, the berries must be dried in the sun.

Yield

When the crop is grown by adopting proper cultivation practices, it may yield nearly 10 000 kg/ha of fresh berries which, in turn, will give about 2 500 kg/ha of dried berries.

Chapter 37

SWEET FLAG

Indian name	:	Ugragandha (Sanskrit), Bacc Gorbacc (Hindi) Baje (Kannada), Vashampu (Tamil)
Species and	:	Acorus calamus L.
varieties	:	A. gramineus Soland
Distribution	:	India, North America, Asia, Central Europe Japan, Rumania USSR
Uses	:	Aromatics Confectionery, Drugs, Flavouring liquors, beer, gin, vinegar, snuff and various other preparations substitute for Ginger Insecticide

Sweet flag (Acorus calamus L) is a herb belonging to the family Aeraceae. The dried root (rhizome) has long been employed in medicinal preparations and for flavouring liquors. It contains a volatile yellowish-brown oil of peculiar, but pleasant, slightly sweet odour that can be isolated by steam distillation. The yield and physico chemical constituents and, consequently the composition of the 'calamus' oil depend upon the source from which the rihizomes are obtained. The European and American oils are similar in composition consisting of low amounts of 'asarone' which can be compared to the Indian oil. The rhizomes contain a high percentage of starch.

The plant is aromatic on account of the presence of an essential oil, which contains the glucosidic bitter principle, 'Acorin'. It has an expectorant action due to the presence of the essential oil and is commonly used as a remedy for asthma. It is also used as a remedy for chronic diarrhoea. The rhizome is an appetizer and is also useful in the treatment of epilepsy, delirium, hysteria and loss of memory. In Unani literature, the rhizome has been described as having a very bitter taste and is said to be useful as a brain tonic. The powdered rhizomes have been employed in combination with

Rauwolfia serpentina and other drugs in the treatment of neurosis, insomnia and hysteria. Because of the pleasant aromatic smell, the rihozmes are extensively used as an aromatic agent in agarbathies, dhoops and havana samagries. The powdered rhizome and the essential oil can be used as a safe insecticide against flies, mosquitoes, bed-bugs, moths and lice. This property is due to the presence of the 'trans isomer of asarone'. The leaves and rhiozmes are used to control lice. It's essential oil is used in flavouring liquors, beer, gin, vinegar, snuff and various other preparations. The "BACH" of commerce, which has many medicinal uses is prepared from the rhizomes. The fresh rhizomes are used in confectionery and also as a substitute for ginger. In moderate doses, the oil produces antispasmodial action on the involuntary muscle tissue, inhibiting the excessive peristaltic movements of the intestine.

Distribution and Origin

It grows wild on the edges of swamps, on the banks of rivers and ponds in North America, Europe and Asia. The countries growing this crop commercially are the USSR Central Europe Rumania India and Japan. In India, the leading states are Karnataka, Kashmir, Manipur, Arunachal Pradesh, Meghalaya and in the foothills of the Himalayas up to 1 800 m. In Karnataka, it is being grown in the Koratagere Taluk of Tumkur district in an area of 100 acres and the annual production is 400 t of dried rhizomes.

Description of the Plant

Sweet flag is a monocot plant.The plant is a herb, with narrow 0.75-1.5 m, long leaves. The breadth of the leaf is 2-4 cm and resembles the leaves of an iris. The leaves are bright green, thickered in the middle and the margin is wavy. The spathe is 6-30 cm long and the spadix is slightly curved. The fruit is a berry, yellow-green in colour, angular and 1-3 seeded.

The economic part of the plant is the underground rhizome. The rhizomes are horizontal and jointed, with a spongy texture. The rhizomes are 1.5-2.5 cm thick and sometimes up to 2 m long.

Species / Varieties

Acorus is a small genus of herbs, comprising 2 species.

1. Acorus gramineus Soland

It is a Japanese species, occasionally encountered in Sikkim (up to 1 800

m) and the Khasi hills (1 200 - 1 400 m). It is used for the same medicinal purpose as A. calamus. Here, the mid-rib of the leaf is absent. It is a semi-aquatic, perennial herb with creeping and many-branched aromatic rhizomes of spongy texture from 1.5 to 2.5 cm thickness and sometimes several metres long. The leaves are 10-22 cm in width and 0.60-1.8 m in length. The rhizome will be brown outside and white and sponge-lined inside.

2. Acorus calamus L.

It is a semi-aquatic perennial herb with a stout midrib with a creeping and many branched aromatic rhizome. It is found growing wild or cultivated throughout India and Sri Lanka ascending to 1 800 m in the Himalayas. The plant thrives in marshy places and moist situations, like the edges of lakes and banks of streams and rivers. It is plentiful in the marshy tracts of Kashmir and Sirmoor in Manipur and the Naga Hills. It is also grown in North America, Europe and Asia.

Soil

Sweet flag is cultivated in almost the same way as rice and may be grown in any part of the country where suitable irrigation facilities are avainable. Although calamus in the wild state grows in water, it may be cultivated in almost any good, but fairly moist soil. It is usually grown in areas where paddy can be grown. It is generally grown in the clayey loam and light alluvial soils of river banks.

Climate

Sweet flag is a hardy plant and is thus found growing from tropical to subtropical climate. However, it prefers an area with good and well-distributed rainfall throughout the year.

Planting Season

The best planting season is spring (March-April), but the crop may be planted almost at any time of the year taking into consideration the fact that plenty of sunshine should be available at harvest time to dry the rhizomes.

Land Preparation

The field is laid out exactly as for rice irrigated sufficiently and, after ploughing twice, is watered heavily and ploughed again. The field is then left alone for a few days and puddled. After that, it is levelled with a levelling board.

Cultivation

Propagation

The planting material consists of the live ends or tops of the previous crop. At harvest, the mature portion of the rhizome is cut off, which is the marketable part and the tender portion formed by the growing end is used for replanting and propagation. This propagating material can be planted at once or stored for about a week, by covering it whith straw or dried leaves. If it is required to be stored longer, this can be done by keeping it in open pits.

Planting

The recommended spacing for sweet flag is 30 cm x 30 cm the rhizomes pieces are pressed into the mud at a depth of about 5 cm inside the soil. The rhizomes are planted in such a way that the plant in the second row comes in-between the first row and not opposite to it.

Manures and Fertilizers

The field should be manured with green manure (10 to 12 t) and compost (15 t/ha). Along with this, 100 kg ammonium sulphate, 300 kg superphosphate and 100 kg muriate of potash should be added, or otherwise 125 kg N, P, and K/ha is recommended to be applied in 3 split doses.

Irrigation

The field must be regularly irrigated. About 5 cm of water is left standing in the field in the beginning. Later, the water level is increased to 10 cm the plant grows.

Weeding

Careful and regular weeding is required. In all, eight weedings are given and, at each weeding the growing plants are lightly pressed down into the soil.

Pests and Diseases

This crop is practically free from the attack of any pests or diseases of a serious nature, except mealy bugs, which infest the shoot and roots. The insect can be controlled by spraying the shoot and drenching the roots of grown plants with 0.1% Methyl Parathion or 0.15% Oxydemeton Methyl or 0.2% Quinolphos.

Harvesting and Yield

After about a year, the crop is ready for harvesting. The field is allowed to dry partially, so that sufficient moisture is retained to facilitate the necessary deep digging. The leaves start turning yellow and dry, indicative of maturity. The rhizomes will be at a depth of 60 cm and are about 30-60 cm long. Therefore, harvesting should be done carefully. The rhizomes, after harvest, are cut into short lengths of 5-7.5 cm and all the fibrous roots are removed. The pieces are then washed thoroughly and dried in the sun. The dried material is put into gunny bags and rubbed to free them of leafy scales. The yield of rhiozmes is about 10 t/ha.

The fresh rhizomes yield about 1.2% of dry rhizomes and 3-3.5% of essential oil which is bitter. The fresh aerial parts yield 0.125% oil. The rhizomes should not be peeled prior to drying, because peeling results in considerable loss of oil through evaporation and resinigication. The highest of oil are obtained from dried unpeeled rhizomes thet have been granulated immediately before they are put into the still. Peeled dried European calamus roots yield from 1.5-1.8% oil whereas the Japanese variety yields up to 5% of oil. The Indian roots growing in the plains yield about 3.1% and those growing in the Kashmir Valley yield not more than 1.4% of oil.

Chapter 38

SWEET WORM WOOD

Family	:	Asteraceae
English name	:	Sweet Worm Wood
Indian name	:	Dammakah (Sanskrit), Nagdona (Hindi), Sihivermwood (Kannada), Masipatri, Makkipu (Tamil)
Species and	:	Artemisia onnua Linn.
varieties	:	Asha
Distribution	:	India, Afghanistan, North eastern Asia, China, France, UK, USA
Uses	:	Cosmetics, Dermatology, Drugs, Perfumery

Artemisia annua Linn; commonly called 'sweet worm wood' or 'Annual worm wood', is a strongly scented annual belonging to the family Asteraceae. It is a native of China and has traditionally been grown in China as a medicinal plant with pronounced antimalerial activity. The medicinal property of the herb is attributed to the active constituent 'artimisinin' present in the extract. In China' it is commonly called 'Quinghao' and in Vietnam, 'Qinghaosu'.

The main constituent of the plant is artemisinin which varies from 0.05-0.17% with an average of 0.1%. Other constituents include the sweet smelling essential oil artimisilene arteannuin artemusinic acid phytene 1 2-diol, pinene, cineole, 1-camphor, scopoletin, scopolin, arteannuin quercetagetin, 6-7, 3, 4 tetramethyl ether, n-nonacosane, n-pentacosane amyrin acetate and qinghaosu (I).

It is reported that in China the artimisinin content in the regenerated plant is much higher (about 0.9%) compared to the original plant (0.6%) on a dry-weight basis.

The essential oil called the 'Artemisia', oil, is used in perfumery cosmetics and in dermatology. The artemisia oil has some specific antimycotic and antimicrobial action. It is useful in the treatment of skin moulds. Artemisinin, the antimalarial drug, has been recently introduced into the Indian market. It is very useful in cerebral malaria as well. Artimisinin is adminstered as an intramuscular injection and is also reported to have an inhibition rate of 100% against human gastric cancer-cell line SGC-7901 at 50 fg/ml.

Origin and Distribution

The plant is indigenous to China as mentioned earlier. It is found growing in India in the Punjab from Peshawar to Waziristan ascending to 5 000 ft. It also occurs in Afghanistan and Northeastern Asia ,USA, UK, and France. In India, it is cultivated in temperature as well as subtropical conditions in the Kashmir Valley and in the hills of Himachal Pradesh and Uttar Pradesh on a limited scale.

Description of the Plant

A. annua (2n=18) is an annual, determinate, erect herb with a very slender and glabrous stem. The branches are deeply grooved the leaves are broad 3-pinnatisect or decompound the segments are serrate or lobulate the heads are 2 mm in diameter, subglobose, secured in very slender panicled racemes, the pedicle is pendulous, the involucre bracts are glabrous the inner obicular is green and shiny with a scarious margin.

Varieties

A. annua is a highly cross-pollinated crop. Hence, the crop exhibits a large variation in maturity, leaf biomass yield and artemisinin content. The CIMAP, Lucknow, has developed a variety called 'Asha' through mass selection and this variety is recommended for cultivation.

'Jeevanraksha' and 'Suraksha' are the other two varieties recently released from the CIMAP, Lucknow. The variety Jeevanraksha represents an isolated population of A. annua selected for its artemisinin-rich foliage while the variety ,Suraksha, is a product of recurrent selection from Asha. A comparison of these three varieties is given in the table below.

Cultivar	Foliage colour	Flowering maturity	Capitulum size	Foliage content (%) of artemisinin	Foliage content (%) of artemisinic acid	Essential oil
Asha	Green	Early	Large	< 0.1	0.1-0.4	0.3
Jeeven-raksha	Dark green	Late	Small	0.5-0	<0.2	0.1
Suraksha	Light green	Early	Large	<0.2	0.2-1.2	0.3

Soil

The crop is adapted to a wide range of soil types from sandy loam to loam which are free from water-logging but a well-drained lightloam rich in organic matter, is reported to be the suited.

Climate

A. annua is a short-day temperate plant which requires a cold winter and a moderate summer. The critical photoperiod lies between 12 and 16 hours (13:31 hours). It can also be cultivated in subtropical areas as a winter crop. However it has been found that the artimisinin content is higher in plants grown in temperate climates than in the subtropical climates the extremes of too much shade or high temperature reduce the artimisinin content.

Season

Two crops can be grown under Indian conditions. The first crop during the late rainy season and the second during summer. The seeds can be sown in the nursery during September-October for the late rainy season crop and during December for the summer crop. For seed-production the rainy season-sown crop is advisable. The crop planted in November is reported to give the maximum oil-yield.

Land Preparation

The hand is ploughed and dised several times to produce a fine tilth before the seedlings are transplanted. For convenient management, it is laid out into beds, depending upon the local conditions, after applying the required dose of manures and fertilizers.

Cultivation

Propagation

The crop is propagated by seeds. The seeds are very small in size, therefore, direct sowing in the main field does not give good results. Hence the seedlings are raised in nursery-beds and then transplanted into the main field.

Nursery Raising

Nursery-beds of convenient sizes are prepared and well-decomposed FYM/ compost at the rate of 10 kg/bed is applied. Further, 250-500 g of seeds (sufficient to raise seedlings for 1 ha) mixed with sand are spread uniformly over the nursery-beds and covered with a thin layer of soil or sand. The beds are kept moist by frequent watering, with the help of a sprinkler or a rose-can. The seeds germinate in about 5-8 days. Freshly-collected seeds germinate early and the germination percentage is also high. The seedlings would be ready for transplanting after 6-8 weeds.

Planting

The beds are irrigated a day prior to transplanting. The seedlings withstand transplanting very well. Transplanting is done at a spacing of 30-40 cm or 60 cm between rows, and 45-60 cm between the plants. Usually, transplanting is done in the afternoon. The plots are given a light irrigation after transplanting. Gap-filling should be done within 8-10 days of planting. It is advisable to plant two seedlings per hill at the time of transplanting.

Fertilizers

The crop responds well to fertilizers. A fertilizer dose of 60-80 kg N, 40-60 kg P_2O_5 and 60 kg K_2O/ha may be applied for a good yield. The full dose of P_2O_5 and K_2O and two-third of N is incorporated into the soil at the time of land preparation. The remaining one-third of N is applied in two equal split doses at 30 and 60 days after transplanting. A. annua is highly sensitive to the deficiency of boron followed by iron; while zinc copper and manganese are reported to significantly decrease the growth and artemisninin content. Hence, a basal application of borax at the rate of 8 kg./ha is recommended a higher supply of copper and manganese are reported to have an inhibitory effect on the crop.

Interculture

The crop requires 2-3 weedings and hoeings during the growth period. The herbicides, Metachlor and Chloramben (2.2 kg/ha) as pre-emergent treatment and Trifluralin (6.5 kg/ha) as post-emergent treatment have been found useful for chemical weed control.

Irrigation

The field is irrigated frequently for establishment of the crop. Once established, only 3-4 irrigations are required in all.

Plant Protection

Insects : Ants

Diseases : Damping-off

Control

The ant menace can be minimized by mixing about 10 kg/ha of Carbaryl dust into the soil at the time of land preparation.

Damping-off disease can be overcome by adjusting the planting time so that bright weather prevails during the first few days in the early stages of establishment.

Harvesting Processing and Yield

The duration of this crop is about 4 1/2-5 months. The crop is harvested as soon as the flower initiation takes place. Delayed harvest or harvesting before the flowering, result in a low yield of artemisinin as well as essential oil. The crop is cut 15-30 cm above the ground-level with a sickle and dried in the shade. After the drying process is over, the leaves and flowers are separated from the stalks.

The fresh herbage yield is about 10-15 t/ha which, in turn gives 30-40 kg/ha of essential oil. The essential oil percentage generally varies from 0.2-0.4% under Indian conditions and 0.48-0.81% in Budapest. The essential oil content is found to be generally higher (0.34%) in the early sown crop (September) and it is known to decrease due to delay in sowing/ planting. The essential oil content is highest in the inflorescence. Further, the artimisinin content is found to be highest at the anthesis and declines after flowering. The yellow flowers are reported to contain 2-to-4 fold higher concentration of artemisinin as compared to the leaves.

Distillation of Oil

The essential oil from the fresh or dried leaves and flowers can be extracted by steam distillation or by solvent extraction method. For solvent extraction the solvent used is 'Hexane'.

Chapter 39

VALERIAN

Indian name	:	Tagarah Natah (Sanskrit), Tagar (Hindi), Takaram (Tamil)
Species and	:	Valeriana officinalis Linn
		varieties V. jatamansi Jones or V. wallichii DC
Distribution	:	India North and Southwest Asia Belgium China, Europe, France, Nepal, the Netherlands, USA
Uses	:	Drugs Flavouring tobacco and beer Ornamental purposes, Perfumes

Valeriana belonging to the family Valerineceae, is a perennial herb. Of the several species of the genus, the rhizomes stolons and roots of Valeriana officinalis Linn and V. jatamansi Jones (Syn. V. wallichii DC) constitute the official rhizomes stolons and roots of V. jatamansi, known as Indian valerian or 'muskhala' or 'tager' in trade, while V. officialis is used in Europe. The drug contains a number of epoxy-iridoid esters called valepotriates or valtrats which include valtrate, didrovaltrate acevaltrate, isovaltrate, isovaleroxy hydroxydidrovaltrate and the alkaloids chatinine valerianine and actinidien. The dried rhizomes stolons and roots on distillation also yield 0.5-1.9% volatile oil which contains bornylisovalerianate bornyl acetate bornyl, formate, eugenyl, isovaleriate, eugenol, terpenes and a sesquiterpene alcohol. The alkaloids possess, antiseptic, sedative, anti epileptic, hypotensive, cardiotonic and antidepressent properties. The drug is used in the treatment of hysteria hypochondriasis nervous disorders month ulcers epilepsy depression as a carminative and a tonic in the from of extract infusion and tincture. The essential oil is used as a tonic and stimulatin certain medicinal preparations. It is also used in perfumery for its musky woody balsamic notes which give interesting effects in modern chypre variations and in combinationn with many oils. It is also used for flavouring tobacco and beer.

Origin and Distribution

V. officinalis is indigenous to Europe, whereas, V. jatamansi is native to North and South-west Asian countries. The former is widely grown in Belgium France, Netherlands and also in the USA, for the drug as well as for ornamental purposes. V. jatamansi is found growing in India in limited quantities, only in Kashmir, Himachal Pradesh and Punjab. It is also found in Nepal and South-western China. The drug has an increasing demand in both India and abroad. It is, therefore, recommended to grow it on a large scale in Jammu and Kashmir, Himachal Pradesh Punjab Uttar Pradesh and whereas else the climate is suitable.

Description of the Plant

The genus Valeriana includes herbs with opposite leaves with no stipules. The calyx tube, adherent to the ovary, has one fertile 1-ovuled locule and two abortive or empty ones. The stamens are distinct, 1-3 in number are fewer than the lobes of the corolla and inserted on its tube. The corolla is tubular or funnel-shaped are 1-3, often irregular mostly 5-lobed the styles slender the stigmas are 1-3, the fruit is dehiscent and 1-seeded. The seed is suspended anatropous with a large embryo and no albumen. The flowers occur in panicled or clustered cymes. The roots are often ardous.

Description of Species

V. officinalis (2n=14,28 56) is a glabrous or pubescent, hardy, herbaceous perennial with a short rhizome producing subterranean stolons. The rhizomes of the wild plants are 2 cm thick and bear several roots 2-3 mm thick and 10-20 cm long. The rhizomes of the cultivated plants bear clusters of roots. These rhizomes are vertical, stoloniform, dull yellowish to dark brown in colour with a strong characteristic odour and sweetish, camporaceous and slightly bitter taste.

The leaves are imparipinnate with 7-21 lanceolate segments with dentate margins, whose flowering stalks attain a height of 90-120 cm and bear a loose head of small pinkish-white flowers. The flowering stems arising during the 2nd or 3rd year, are rounded and striated upto a height of 3-4 feet. The flowers are fragrant arranged in umbels and are small pink, and tubular.

V. jatamansi (2n=28) is a tetraploid, a slightly hairy, tuffed perennial herb which grows up to 60 cm in height. It has long, woody rhizomes producing roots covered with fibres. It is divided into a number of shaggy, scaly crowns from which the leaves are produced. The branches are erect, a few centimeters high, and downy. The leaves are obovate to lanceolate, 3-ribbed and downy. Those next to the root are acute, the upper ones are obtuse. The flowers are dark pink clustered in the axils of the upper leaves.

The Indian valerian closely resembles the valerian from V. officinalis in its properties.

Soil

The plant will grow in a variety to soils but thrives best in a moist rich and rather heavy loam. Some drought resistant forms also occur in chalky and limestone soils.

Climate

Valeriana is a temperate plant and prefers very cold winter and mild summer temperatures for its good growth. The plant is often found to flourish in damp and shady places. In the North-western Himalayas the Indian valerian grows naturally at an altitude of 1 800 to 3 000 m and, in Assam, between 1 200 to 1 800 m elevation .

Land Preparation

The land is prepared well and brought to a fine tilth by ploughing it several times. Later the field is divided into beds of convenient sizes and FYM is added at the rate of 15-20 t/ha.

Cultivation

Propagation

The plant is propagated by portions of the old root-stocks or rhizomes either in autumn or in spring. The plant may also be propagated from the seeds or seedlings of wild plants. The nursery is raised in July-August or April-May. At first, the nursery, raised seedlings are transplanted at a spacing of 18-20 cm in rows 30 cm apart. When the seedlings are 6-8 weeks old and 10-15 cm tall, they are transplanted to their permanent sites.

Planting

If the crop is raised through division of root-stocks or rhizomes, they are spaced at 30 cm x 40-90 cm. If the divisions are planted very early in autumn before the onset of frost a good crop may be harvested the following autmn. The summer cultivation requires the weeding of beds and cutting of all floral stalks to avoid exhaustion and to promote the formation of larger root-stocks. When seedlings are raised for growing the crop, the seedlings are transplanted at 30-40 cm x 40 cm spacing. The field is irrigated immediately after planting.

Manures and Fertilizers

Valerian responds well to the application of manure and fertilizers. FYM may be incorporated into the soil along with 50 kg/ha each of P and K at the time of land preparation while 150 kg/ha N is applied in 3-split doses at 4-month intervals.

Irrigation

This crop requires 2-3 irrigations during the dry period from June too September.

Weeding

The land is kept weed-free through regular weeding.

Interculture

The interspaces are harrowed to keep the soil loose and weed-free. A low ridge of soil is usually raised along the crop row to promote the formation of large root-stocks.

Pests and Diseases

Valerian is hardy crop. No serious pests and diseases have been reported to attack this crop.

Harvesting and Yield

Although the plants can be harvested after 1 year of planting it is advisable to harvest 2-year-old plants, since the yield of the under ground parts would be higher and so also their essential oil content. The plants can be harvested when they become dormant during November, exhibiting yellowing of leaves and withering of plants. The rhizomes and roots are pulled out by hand or sometimes mechanically. The harvested material is cleaned of adhering soil by thorough washing. This is done by placing them in baskets or perforated boxes, which are then suspended under running water. They are occasionally stirred to hasten the cleaning then the rhizomes and roots are dried under the sun or in Kilns and the longer rhizomes are longitudinally cut into pieces or into halves.

Under favourable conditions, a yield of 2 250 kg/ha of dried roots is obtained from a 2-year-old crop.

The fresh rhizomes, stolons and roots have practically no odour but, on drying they develop the characteristic valerian odour. Valerian occurs in trade as conical to cylindrical rhizomes 2-5 cm in length, and 1-2 cm in diameter dull yellowish-brown to dark-brown externally and whitish-internally, irregularly, divided-obliquely or longitudinally. The fracture is short and horny. The stolons are short, 3 cm long and 2-2.5 cm in diameter and are longitudinally striated.

Chapter 40

TUBERROSE

English name	:	Tuberose
Indian name	:	Rajanigandha, Gulshaba (Hindi) Sugandharaja (Kannada) Sampangi (Tamil)
Distribution	:	India, South Africa, America, Italy, Egypt, France, Mexico, Morocco, Taiwan
Uses	:	Boutonnieres, Cut flowers, Flavouring Ornamental purposes, Perfumery

Tuberose (Polianthus tuberosa L), belonging to the family Amaryllidaceae is essentially a florist flower a leading commerical crop because of its multifarious uses. The fleshy, white tubular flowers emit a strong odour and hence are cultivated on a large scale in some parts of the world for the extracton of highly valued natural flower oil, the tuberose oil. The predominant charcteristics of this crop are its lingering delightoful fragrance and excellent keeping quality.

The tuberose oil contains methylbenzoate methyl anthranilate benzyl alcohol, benzyl benzoate, butryic acid phenyl acetic acid, methyl salicylate eugenol, geraniol, nerol both free and as acetates, farnesol, methyl vanillin and piperomel. The leaves, flowers, bulbs and roots are reported to contain sterols, triterpenes carbohydrates saponins and traces of alkaloids. The leaves and flowers contain flavanoids also which is calculated as kempferol 3-0 oxidase in the air dried leaves was about 0.28%. The alkoloid present in the bulbs is lycorin which causes vomiting. The tubers yield sapogenins like hecogenin and tigenein. Two sapogenins hecogenin and 9-11 dehydrohecogenin and two sapogins becogin-3-0-glucoxyloside and 9-11-dehydrohecogenin 3-0 have been isolated from the bulbs. Besides, frucosans polyfructisons and transfructosidase have also been observed.

The tuberose flower oil of commerce is one of the most sought after the expensive raw materials in perfumery. The fresh flowers give a concrete yield of 0.08 to 0.11% of which nearly 18 to 23% constitutes the alcohol-soluble absolute. The essential oil is used in only the highest grade perfumes. Sometimes the oil is used in flavouring candy beverages and baked food.

The long flower spikes of tuberose are excellent cut-flowers when arranged in vases boquets and bowls. The individual florets or the loose flowers are used for making garlands ornaments for bridal makeup and for button holes (boutonnieres).

The bulbs possess diuretic and emetic properties. The powder of the dried bulbs is used as remedy for gonorrhoea. In the Konkan region the bulbs are rubbed with turmeric and butter and applied as a paste over the red pimples of infants.

Origin and Distribution

The tuberose is a native of Mexico. It is grown largely in the southern states of America Italy France Morocco South Africa Tarwan Egypt and many other tropical and subtropical areas in the world. In India tuberose is cultivated on a commercial scale in Ranaghat Kolaghat and Panskura in West Bengal Devanahalli Tumkur and Mysore in Karnataka the East Godavari Guntur Chittoor and Krishna districts of Andhra Pradesh Coimbatore in Tamil Nadu and Pune and Thane in Maharashtra. Reliable estimates on the total area under tuberose cultivation in India are not available.

Description of the Plant

P. tuberosa Linn. has a tuberous root stock and a mass of basal foliage. The leaves are pale green long narrow and very dense. The leaves at the base are 30 to 40 cm long 1.2 to 1.5 cm in width sometimes reddish near the base. The flowering stems are long and can reach a height of up to 100 cm although 60 to 75 cm is normal. It is approximately the top third of the stem which bears the pure white waxy textured raceme of bloows. The flowers are borne in pairs on a lax spike and are 3 to 6 cm in length. The segments are 1 to 2 cm long the tube is long narrow and funnel shaped slightly bent near the base.The filaments are attached to the upper part of the corolla. The ovary is 3 celled there are 3 stigmas which are ovate falcate. The fruit is crowned by a persistent perianthand the seeds are flat.

Species and Varieties

There are about fifteen species under this genus of which twelve species have been reported from Mexico and Central America. Of these nine species have white flowers one is white and red and two are red. With the exceptionof P. tuberosa L all the others are found growing wild.

There are three types of tuberoses named on the basis of the number of rows of petals they bear. Of the three types single semidouble double and variegated available the single type has the most fragrance. The flowers are pure white and are popular among the growers for the production of essential oil. Among the single varieties Calcutta Single and Single Mexican are grown in Tamil Nadu. Recently a single type variety Suvasini has been released by the IIHR Bangalore. Another single flowered variety Rajat Rekha a mutant has been released by the National Botanical Research Institute (NBRI) Lucknow. The Semi double type bears whicte flowers with two to three rows of corolla segments. The Double type has more than three rows of corolla segments and is white in colour. The flowers tiged with red in the Double type are known as Pearl. The variety Pearl Double has been assessed for flower yield and quality under different agroclimatic conditions in India. Another double variety Swarna Rekha a mutant has been released by the NBRI Lucknow. In this variety the leaf margin is streaked with golden yellow. Recently Shringar a double variety has been released by the IIHR Bangalore.

There are some streaked leaf forms known as variegated where as in others the flowers have little tinge of red in the bud stage which turns to white when fully open. Other varieties include Albinos and Excelsior.

Soil

Tuberose can be grown on wide variety of soils from light sandy loam to a clay loam. The soil should be at least 45 cm deep well drained friade rich in organic mater and nutrients with plenty of moisture in it. The soil should have a pH range from 6.5 to 7.5 with good aeration. The crop can be grown even in high saline alkaline soils with better agronomical practices. It is observed that the vegetative growth and flowering are affected by increasing the levels of NaCI and very a low concentration of $CaCI_2$.

Climate

The crop is best suited for cultivation in tropical to subtropical and temperate climates. The crop is reported to flower profusely throughout the year if the climate is mild and free from 20-30° C is considered ideal for this crop.

If the temperature is above 40° C the spike length and quality of the flowers are affected. Very low temperature and frost will damage the plants and flowers. Tuberoses grow well in a sunny situation. Although the plant is photosensitive exposure to a day length of about 16 hours appreciably promotes vegetative growth and enhances the emergence of the first flower spike by 10 days. The length of the flower spike also increases under long days.

Season

Tuberoses are generally planted in February March in the plants and April May in the hills. The bulbs can also be planted during July August. Tuberoses can be planted all year round in Bangalore but a higher flower yield is obtained from the April May planting. To obtain flowers almost throughout the year sequential planting can be practised.

Land Preparation

The land is ploughed deep twice, to a depth of 45 cm. The first ploughing is done in January and the second about a month before planting. At the time of the second ploughing 20-50 t/ha FYM is incorportated into the soil. Then the soil is brought to a fine tilth by breaking the clods and removing the weeds. The field is laid out into plots of convenient sizes with irrigation channels ridges and furrows at the recommended spacing.

Cultivation

Propagation

Tuberoses are propagated by bulbs, bulblets and seeds. Multiplication by using bulb segments and in vitro micropropagation from scale stem sections is also possible. The seeds are difficult to germinate and are seldom used for raising tuberose plants, except for the evolution of new varieties. Moreover, the plants raised from seeds take more time to come into bloom than the plants obtained from bulbs. Hence propagation by bulbs is the most common method practiced for the commercial multiplication of tuberoses. The bulbs remain dormant during the winter months in places where the temperature is low and if early planting is desired the dormancy can be successfully broken by dipping the bulbs in 4% Thiourea solution for one hour. Ethylene chlorohydrin can also be used for breaking the dormancy.

The bulbs are separated from the clumps by rubbing off the loose scales and the long roots should also be removed. Spindle shaped bulbs with a diameter of 2.6 to 3 cm size are used for planting. However, if the bulbs are very large they may be cut into 2-3 vertical sections each containing a bud and part of the basal plats. Each of these sections is treated with copper fungicide and planted vertically with their tips just showing above the surface. About 8-9 t (25 to 1.5 lakhs) of bulbs are required to plant an area of one hectare.

Planting

The density of planting markedly influences the yield and quality of the flowers. The planting distance varies with the soil and climatic conditions. About 1 00 000 to 2 00 000 bulbs are required for planting one hectare of land. Spacings of 15 x 20 cm (for Maharashtra), 25 x 25 cm (for West Bengal), 30 x 30 cm (for Lucknow), 30 x 22.5 cm (for Bangalore), and 20 x 20 cm (for South India) have been recommended for this crop. While planting the bulbs are planted at the recommended plant spacing 3.5 cm deep on the sides of the ridges. The plots are irrigated immediately after planting.

Fertilizer Application

The nutritional requirement of this crop varies with the soil type and climate. A fertilizer dose of 40 kg N and 60 kg P_2O_5/ha has been recommended for the Lucknow region. For the neutral clay soils of Tamil Nadu the recommendation is 100 kg N and 60 kg P_2O_5/ha. A fertilizer dose of 100 kg N, 50 kg each of P_2O_5 and K_2O has been recommended in Bengalore. For achieving increased essential oil content in flowers and for the maximum recovery of concrete a fertilizer dose of 80 kg N 60 kg P_2O_5 and 40 kg K_2O/ha has been recommended. Of the full recommended dose of fertilizers half the N the full dose of P and K are applied at the time of planting and the remaining half of N is given as a top dressing after 45 days of planting.

Apart from N, P and K, calcium magnesium, sulphur, iron, zinc, manganese, aluminium, boron and copper have also been found to influence the growth and flowering in tuberoses.

Growth Regulators

The application of CCC at 5 000 ppm and GA_3 at 1 000 ppm induces early flowering increased flower stalk production and inproves the quality of the flowers. Similarly enhanced flowering and increased number of inflorescences has been noticed as a result of foliar spray of Ancymidol. An early emergence of flower buds has been observed after GA^3 treatment at 100 ppm concentration. Ethrel spray at 2 000 ppm resulted in reduced stalk and rachis lengths and floret number. Three growth regulating chemicals viz. GA_3 (10 to 100 mg/l) CCC (0.02 ml/l) and IAA (10 mg/l) have been found to more effective in increasing the number of flower spikes when given as a foliar spray rather than as a soaking treatment.

Irrigation

Irrigation is given immediately after planting. Subsequently the crop is irrigated at 5-7 days intervals, taking into consideration the weather conditions. In the summer months irrigation is recommended twice a week.

Interculture

In order to keep the plots free of weeds and to avoid the exposure of bulbs the plots are weeded and earthed up once a month. Earthing up enables the spikes to grow erect despite strong winds and rains. The application of Atrazine (3 kg/ha) as a pre emergent weedicide keeps the plots weed free. A pre emergent treatment of Gramaxone (3 kg/ha) followed by three post emergent spraying at intervals of 110 days in between the rows also keeps the crop weed free. Mulching the plots with strips of black polythene dried grass and chopped straw is effective in controlling weeds. The flower spikes should be supported by stakes after about 2 ½ months of planting.

Pests and Diseases

Tuberoses are hardy crops and are not much affected by attacks of insects pests and diseases.

Pests

Aphids and grasshoppers are found to feed on flower buds and leaves. They can be controlled by a 0.1% spray of Malathion or Rogor at an interval of 15 days.

The leaves become yellow or bronze due to the sucking of spp by red spider mites. A spray of Metasystox (0.2%) wettable sulphur (0.3%) or Kelthane (0.5%) is recommended for effective control. The flowers also get deformed by thrips attack. The control measure suggested is to spray Nuvacron (0.1%) or the application of Thimet to the soil. Weevils feed on the leaves and shoots and cause considerable damage to the crops. The weevil larvae feed on the roots and funnel into the bulbs. Aldrex (20 kg/

ha) maybe applied to the soil at the time of planting for the effective control of the weevil larvae.

Root knot nematode (Meloidogyne incognita) and greasy streak nematode (Aphelencoides besseyi) are reported to cause damage to the crop, which is characterized by the stunted growth of the plants. The leaf size is reduced and the flowers look sikly and ultimately the roots rot. The application of Thimet or Furadan (20 kg/ha) to the soil has been recommended for control.

Diseases

The fungi, Scelerotium rolfsii deposits prominent coarse mycelial masses on the leaf surface or near the soil level. Later, the infested spots exhibit a light green colour due to rotting which extend and cover the whole leaf. In cases of severe damage, the plants become weak and bear fewer or no flowering shoots. Drenching the soil around the stem with Brassicol @ 1% and the soil with 0.3% have been recommended for control.

The fungi, Alternaria polyantha, causes leaf spot disease, which is characterized by the appearance of brown spots with faint concentric rings on the mid rib. Bordeaux mixture (0.4%) Zineb (0.5%) or Ziram spray will effectively control the disease. The other diseases reported are leaf spot and blight caused by Botrytis elliptica, rust and powdery mildew, which are not serious. Suitable fungicides may be adminstered to control them when the damage is noticed.

Harvesting and Yield

The tuberose is cultivated in India for the production of flower spikes and loose flowers. Flowers are ready for harvest in about 3 to 3 ½ months of planting. August-September is the peak period of flowering. Depending on the purpose harvesting is done by cutting the fully opened spikes from the base or single flowers are harvested as they open by day the picking of individual flowers should be completed by 8.00 a.m. The flowers have a shelf life of 3 days. To obtain a succession of flowers, the dormant bulbs should be planted at an interval of few weeks. Bulbs are collected after the flowering is over and the leaves have decayed and died. They are used as seed stock for the next season. Usually, the bulbs should be lifted every two or three years, rested and transplanted.

Normally, the tuberose begins to flower after 110-120 days of planting. It flowers during the summer and rainy seasons (April-September) in the plains of the eastern part of the of country on the hills it flowers in May July while in milder climates it flowers throughout the year. Harvesting is done in the early morning or late evening. The flowers are harvested with a portion of stalk when they are fully opened. About 17-18 t/ha flowers can be expected from a well maintained garden.

About 150 kg of flowers are required to produce 1 kg of the brown semi solid absolute of enfleurage. The extracted flowers will contain some natural perfume and are treated with petroleum ether to obtain the absolute of chassis as a valuable by product (yield 1.2-1.5%). In recent years, the process of enflurage has been partly replaced by solvent extraction, which requires much less labour though the yield of the absolute reduces considerably. The extracttion of the tuberose flowers with petrolum either yields 0.08-0.11% of concrete which gives 18-23% of absolute on treatment with alcohol and contains 3-6% steam distillate. The concrete yield is about 17-18 kg/ha which gives 3.5 kg absolute and 0.8 kg distillable oil.

Ratoon Cropping

After harvesting the main crop, the, flower stalks are headed back (cut to the base) and the plots are manured and irrigated. About 3-4 ratoon crops can be taken from a single planting.

Chapter 41

TULSI

I. Introduction

Tulsi often called as the Sacred basil has been widely used in religious rites by Hindus. Sweet basil or French basil oil is obtained from a flowering plant tops of ocimum basilicum L. Basil. It has been cultivated and used as medicinal and culinary herb for thousands of years. About 60 species are found to grow in tropical Asia Africa America and Subtropical regions of the world. The plant is considered most important for its sweet basil oil. It is known to have been cultivated for its sweet basic oil it is known to have been cultivated for over over 3000 years by Europeans and Asians for folk lore and religious rituals. The plant is showing a high degree of polymorphism in the species due to high cross pollination. A large number of sub species varieties and forms are available which may have made its nomenclature difficult. The genetic studies conducted to account the differences are not specific. This is due to differences in presence of certain genes the biogenetic pathways stage of oil synthesis etc. Hence keeping in view the great diversity various species and varieties have been classified in accordance with the chemical composition.

Four major types are identified which are as.

1. European Type

The main constituent of oil are methyl chavicol and linalool but no Camphor. Since it is of high quality it is great demand.

2. Reunion Type

The main constituents of the oil are methyl chavicol and camphor but no linalool.

3. Methyl Cinnamate Type

Though methyl chavicol and linalool are present in the oils methyl cinnamate is present in substantial amounts.

4. Eugenol Type

The principal constituent of the oil is eugenol. Nine species are recorded from India of which three are exotic.

II. Distribution

Basil or sweet basil is native to India and Asia and is extensively cultivated in France Egypt Hungary Indonesia Morocco USA (Califonia) and Greece. European type is cultivated all over the world for its oil quality. While Reunion types are restricted to Reunion Islands Comoros Madagascar and Synchelles. Methyl Cinnamate type is in large areas cultivated in Egypt Sicily Bulgaria and crestwhile British East India. Among Eugenol type species nine were fond to grown in India of which three are extotic. O. Sanitum called Holy Basil is planted and worshipped as a heavenly plant by Hindus. Ocimum basilicum Linn. alone is cultivated in India on a commercial Scale.

III. Botany

Ocimum basilicum Linn. occurring in nature as a tetraploid (2n=48) belongs to the family Labiateae. It is an erect almost glaborous herb reaching a height of 30-40 cms and cultivated in major parts of India. The plant has many oil glands which impart it a characteristic aromatic odour. Leaves ovate lanceolate 3.75-5 cm long entire or dentate. adexial and abaxial surfaces glabrous glandular Petiols very slender usually slightly hairy flowers 0.75-1.25 cm long borne in long terminal racemose inflorescence simple or much branched often thyrosoid bracts stalked ovate minute caducous.

Calyx - 5 toothed upper rounded shorter than others.

Corolla - white pink or pale purplish 2 lipped tube upper 4 lobed lower curved down.

Stamens-4 protrunding twice as long as corolla.

Ovary - bicarpellary syncarpous bilobular stigma bifid Fruits-nutlets 4 ellipsoid dark brown to nearly black oblong.

IV. Properties & Chemical Composition

The active constituents present in the oil obtained from flowers and other parts are Linalool 40% methyl clavicol 4-16% eugonol 10-12 per cent. The oil is extensively used in several European countries and USA for flavouring of food stuffs confectionery goods condiments and in other products. It finds a prominent place in flavouring of baked food spiced meats etc. In perfumery industry the oil is used for compounding certain popular perfumes eg. Jasmine blendings.

Various uses are attributed to different parts of the plant in indigenous system of medicine and homropathy. Thus an infusion of the plant is used for cephalalgia gouty joints and as a gargle for foul breath. The juice obtained from the leaves gives relief in irrigation of throat earache and ringworm. Seeds are used internally in constination and piles. Leaf juice is a domestic remedy for infantile cough bronchitis catarrh dysentery and a diarrhoea. Infusion of leaves is given in malaria in gastric diseases of children and hepatic infections. Tulsi is wiedely used as a specific for all kinds of fevers.

V. Soil

The plant thrives best in moderately fertile soil loamy or sandy loam with well drainage arragements. The clayey or sandy soils are not suitable for its cultivation. The best soils are those which are in good physical conditions and have good water holding capacity. The water logged lands must invariably be avoided for cultivation.

VI. Climate

The plants is rather susceptible to frost and the crop growth is adversely affected in areas which experience heavy and continuous rainfall. Therefore in the hilly areas of north India it is advisable to raise it as Kharif crop. In the plains of north or south India it can be grown in both kharif and rabi season. The crop thrives well between the temperature of 7° to 27° C with an annual rainfall of 600-1800 mm. The suitable soil pH for the crop is between 4.3 to 8.2. The crop may sustain and to some extent it is tolerant to the slight acidity salanity in the soil.

VII. Cultivation

The crop is raised through seeds but direct sowing of seeds in the field is not advised. The usual practices is to raise the seedlings in the narsery first and then transplant them in the field.

A. Field preparation

The field in which the crop is to be raised should be disc ploughed once followed by two cross harrowing and one planking. The operations are so arranged that the fields are ready in May and June and October November in north Indian plains and by end of March or latest by last week of April in hills for planting the seedlings. Soil may be prepard with removal of previous crop debris. Convenient size beds of 15mx15m may be laid out for planting.

VIII. Propagation

The crop is raised through seeds but direct sowing of seeds in the field is not advised. The usual practice is to raise seedling nurseries and then to plant them in fields.

1. Raising of nursery

The nurseries should have adequate irrigation facilities. A well prepared land is provided with well rotten farmyard marnure and leaf mould eash at the rate of 1 kg per sq. meter an soil is pulverised for removing any clods. The seed beds are prepared of convenient size of 1 mx4m with irrigation channel systems.

As the seeds are minutes they may be invariably mixed with fine sand or woodash to ensure even distribution. Seed rate of 10-15 gms per bed of 1mx4m bed is required. Since 1000 seeds weigh a little over 1 gm. and the germination percentage is 90-95 about 125 gm. seeds are required to give sufficient seedlings for one hectare.

The seeds may be sown in lines about 6 cm apart on the beds and covered with thin layer of sand and farmyard manure. The deep sowing of the seeds should be avoided as it affects germination. In north Indian plains sowing should be done in April May or August September and in the hilly areas in April. The germination of seed starts 3 days after sowing and is practically over within 10 days. The beds are covered with light straw to conserve moisture. In summer the seedlings are watered twice a day the seedling nurseries should be kept free from weeds. When the seedlings attain the height of 6-10 cms. they are ready for transplanting in the fields.

2. Transplanting

The field at the time of planting should have good tilth. If transplanting is to be done in summer the seedlings transplanted should be covered with green leaves or any other material for some time in the early stage. In summer transplanting is done in the evenings. Cloudy weather and fine drizzle are considered ideal of transplanting.

It is recommended to transplant the seedlings 40 cm apart in rows which are 60 cm apart.

IX. Irrigation

When raised in Kharif crop irrigation is required once in every week. With the onset of monsoon the rains meet the water requirements of the crop fully till september. Therefore irrigation is required once or twice in a month. Heavy irrigation and water accumulation may be avoided.

X. Fertilizer Application

In order to raise a good crop adequate supply of nutrients is essential. It is advisable to apply 20 kg N 40 kg P_2O_5 and 40 kg K_2O per hectare as a basal dose before planting and 40 kg nitrogen also is applied in top dressing in two split doses during the growing season. Increased yield of oil is obtained by application of nitrogen at the rate of 146 kg/ha north east India.

XI. Interulture and Weed Control

About 3 weedings and hoeings are required to keep the fields free from the weed. This can be done by hand or mechanically by a weeder or cultivator. The first weeding to the crop should be done about a month after planting. Second weeding may be followed after 4 weeks to be repeated in third month. After that plants become bushy and no further weeding is required. Earthing up of the plants is desirable but usually not done by growers.

XII. Diseases and Pests

Only a few diseases and pests affect the sweet basil plant.

A. Diseases

Most common diseases are blight and wilt of the plant.

1. Blight of basil caused by Alternaria sp.

It is an important disease affacting the aerial parts of the plant. The disease starts with a chlorotic appearance on the leaves which turn purple and finally black resulting in leafshedding.

Control : A spray of 0.2% Diathane Z-78 or Diathene M-45 once or twice is recommended. The diseased plants may be carefully removed and burnt to save healthy plants.

2. Leaf blight caused by Colletrotrichum capsiei (sp).

The disease appears as small chlortic spots on the leaves which enlarge rapidly coalesce and turn brown. Abundant acervuli are produced on the leaf surface. Older leaves appears to be more susceptible.

3. Basil Wilt caused by Fusarium oxysporum

The disease affects the plant at all stages of growth particularly in the rainy season. The disease appear initially by wilting of leaves and shoot tips on one or two branches but spreads soon to the whole plant. The plant finally dies.

Control : Before transplanting the seedlings should be dipped in a solution of some effective fungicide such as Tofason Asgalol etc.

B. Insect pest/leaf rollers

The larvae of the pest cause serious damage to the plants by sticking to the under surface of the leaves folding them from mid rib lengthwise and webbing them. The infected leaves finally fall off.

Control : It is recommended to spray the affected plants with Malathion or Thiodon diluted with water as required.

XIII. Harvesting and Yield

The crop is harvested when the plant is in full bloom and lower leaves tend to trun yellowish. Harvesting can be done with the help of hand sickles. Depending upon a number of factors the crop may come to full bloom 8-12 weeks after planting in different regions of the country. Corresponding to the parts harvested i.e. flowers or whole plants two grades of oil are obtained. The oil produced from flowers along is superior and fetches higher price. In order to have high grade quality oil only flowering tops may be harvested.

In the Terrain regions optimum yields of herb has been obtained by harvesting first four crops consisting of main as well as sub-inflorescences alone and last crop of whole herb. Of these four floral harvests first is taken when plants are in full bloom and second and subsequent after every 15-20 days interval thereafter with variations as in Jorhat (Assam) three harvest are taken. In certain areas whole plant has to harvested in one stage. About 13 to 14 tonnes of herbage per hectare is obtained. If the harvest after first bloom is followed by subsequent at the 1 month interval 18-20 tonnes/ha of herbage could be obtained.

On an average young inflorescene contain about 0.4 percent oil the whole herb contains 0.10 to 0.25 percent. In actual practice an yield of about 30-35 kg of oil/hectare corresponds to 12-13 kg of flower oil and 18-22 kg of whole plant herb oil. If only whole berb is harvested and distilled the yield obtained is in the range of 30 kg/hectare.

After the crop is harvested it is advisable to allow it to wilt in the field for 4-5 hours so as to reduce the moisture in the herb. This helps in reducing the bulk of herbage and it also makes easy to put it for extraction in distillation tanks. The herbage should not be exposed to sun for a prolonged period as it affects the quality of the oil. It may also be pointed out here that both yield adn percentage of oil may vary greatly depending directly on the fertility of soil and seasonal conditions. Further more bushy type of plants with less woody or smaller stems yield more oil than others. It is also reported that bright sunny weather immediately preceding the harvest increases the oil while cloudy or rainy weather decreases it.

XIV. Distillation

The oil of sweet basil is obtained on distillation of young inflorescences and/or whole herb by both hydro and steam distillation. The latter is considered definitely better than the former in that it takes less time and effects better recovery of oil contained in herb. While the former is carried on a direct fire still is cheaper and more handy for small plantations whereas the latter is preferred for large plantations.

In steam distillation the equipment consists of a boiler a distillation tub a condenser and 1-3 separators. The steam is generated in the boiler and led through a steam inlet pipe under a pressure of 18-32 kg. into the distillation tub filled with the charge to be distilled. Through the outlet pipe the water vapours along with the essential oil contained in the herb pass over to the condenser. As the distillation proceed the distillat goes on collecting in the separator.

The oil being lighter then water and insoluble in it floats on the surface and is periodically drained off. It is then decanted and filtered to get rid of impurities. About 1-1.5 hours are required to exhaust a charge completely. After the oil has been separated from the distillation water it is advisable to redistill the latter to recover small portions of oil held in suspension. The process of distillation requires more are and cleaning otherwise oil may get impure.

XV. Active Constituents and Uses

The variation in chemical constituents of basil oil is so much that it difficult to give a world standard for the oil produced in different areas. The main constituents of sweet basil oil of European origin are linalool (39-43%) methyl chavicol (23-31%) and fenchyal alcohol (5.2-9.2%). Minor constituents are alpha-pinene (0.11-0.17%) Camphene (0.02-0.07%) myreene (0.16-0.18%) limonaene (0.12-0.2%) 1.8-cineole + cisocimene (2.7-3.4%) alpha-terpinene (3 octanone + trans ocimene (0.46-0.7%) fenchyl acetate (0.07-1.0%) methyl eugenol (0.49-0.48%) methyl cinnamate (0.5%) and Eugenol (0.78%).

Basil oil is used as a perfume in products like dental cream mouth washes tooth pastes as well as perfumes. It is used as a flavour in food stuffs including confectionery special meats sausages tomato pastes sauces fancy vinegar pickles ketchups and pastries. It is also a traditional and folk medicine. An infusion of the plant is used for cephalalgia gouty joints and as a gargle for foul breath. The leaves juice gives relief in irritation of throat ear ache and ringworm. Seeds are used internally in constipation and piles.

Chapter 42

HERBS DRYING

Herb enter trade in several forms. Probably the most important are the dried form and it is these that are most common in international trade.

Most herbs enter international trade in the crude dried form world trade in processed herbs being relatively very small, although increasing rapidly. Further processing of herbs beyond the drying stage is almost invariably undertaken in the country of consumption. After drying, herbs are prepared for use either by grinding, chopping or crushing or by cleaning and packaging of the whole leaves stems or flower heads.

The most useful forms in which herbs are available to industrial food service or household user are as food service or household user are as follows.

(1) Whole leaf : this term is used for a product which has been cleaned but not cut or otherwise processed

(2) Chopped cut, cracked sliced etc : These term refer to leave that have been cut (rather than ground) into smaller pieces. Common particle sizes are about 3-6 mm but size is largely dependent upon buyer's specification. Bosil, barragom and sage are herbs available in the Chopped or cut forms.

(3) Rubbed : A traditional term for herb that has been subjected to only a minimum of grinding and then passed through a Coarse Sieve. Many users prefer this minimal processing because not only does it preserve flovour longer but also it enables easy blending of the product to be carried out. Rubbed herb are also referred to as crushed herb but these are not standeredised terms since the consistency can vary according to the processing procedures of the supplier.

(4) Ground or finely ground : In this case, the herbs have undergone more grinding than have rubbed herbs including pulverisation and fine sifting. There is no set particle size, this depending upon the purchaser's specification which in turn is dependent upon the use to which the herb will be freshly ground to conserve as many of the volatile principle as possible.

Grades and quality of Herb

There is no general system of herbs, quality considerations tending to vary from country to country and from herb to herb. The quality of herbs is dependent on several variable plant variety growing condition, cultural practices, drying and processing methods and storage and packaging.

The genetic characteristics of a particular plant variety may appear to be fairly obvious factor affecting quality, but in the past problems for producer have arisen from mislabelling, misunderstanding and ignorance and also from seed or cutting having been of the incorrect variety and less suitable for the required market, other important factor influencing quality include weather, soil condition, cultural practice; harvesting; drying and processing techniques, and packaging and storage.

PROCESS OF MANUFACTURE

Drying

Correct and proper drying is vital for the production of a satisfactory herb which is to be traded internationally. Drying involves reducing the moisture in the harvested herb to a maximum of 5-10 per cent, thus minimising spoilage. If properly dried a herb will retain much of its original colour, and this is an important criterion used by purchasers to judge quality. The method of drying will depend on the species of the plant and the parts of it to be dried. A considerable quantity of herbs is dried naturally in the shade, but artificial drying is increasingly being employed since it produces, according to some sources, a superior product, retaining much more of the original flavour and avoiding a hay-like taste. Modern methods now make it possible to dry some herbs which formerly could not be satisfactorily dried by natural methods. In all cases the drying area should be spotlessly clean, free of dust, and protected from animals and other sources of contamination. The drying room should also be well ventilated, and drying should take place or rust-free steel-method or firm fabric-meshed frames. Handling of the herbs should be limited to the absolute minimum to avoid crumbing. In most cases the herbs should be spread in thin layers to speed drying and to prevent spoilage by moisture condensation and overheating. However, some herbs can be dried by tying the aerial parts in bunches and hanging them up to dry. Tender leaf herbs, such as basil or mint, should be dried rapidly to avoid discoloration and mould.

The duration of drying varies according to the particular plant, its level of moisture content, and the drying temperature. Flowers and leaves tend to dry more quickly than stems. The drying temperature has a vital influence on quality. If herbs are dried naturally, it is preferable that it be special rooms where space is limited requires higher temperature, but for culinary herbs the flavour, are often lost at higher temperatures. The moisture level of herbs varies, and the drying ratio expresses the weight relationship between the fresh herb and the dried herb.

STORAGE AND PACKAGING OF DRIED HERB

Different type of storage can influence the quality of a herb considerably. Although herb can retain their aroma and flavour for a long period if kept under correct condition they tend to lose their flavour a little faster than spices such as pepper, ginger, llove etc.

Dried herb store best in the whole (or leaf) form, and consequently most buyer's choose this form of storage, while still turning over their stock fairly quickly. A further important consideration in storage is to limit contamination.

Dried herb is to be stored in airtight container in a dry dark place at a temperature not exceeding 18°C.

Satisfactory packaging material laminated paper bags, Cardboard containers, tins or hessian (Jute) sacks as well as various container made of other natural or artificial fibres.

PRECESS FLOW DIAGRAM

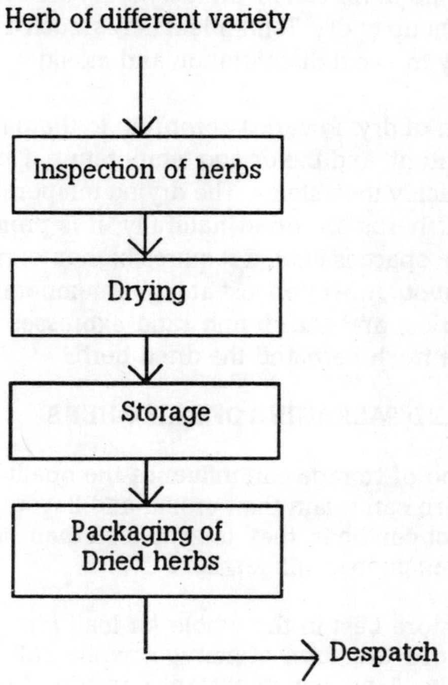

PLANT ECONOMICS

Rated Plant capacity = 1000.00 Kgs./Day

LAND & BUILDING

1. Land Area 500 Sq. Mt.	Rs.	12,00,000.00

PLANT & MACHINERY

1. Blower
2. Hot Air Convector
3. Steel mesh frames (Rust free)
4. Misc.

FIXED CAPITAL

1. Land & Building	Rs.	12,00,000.00
2. Plant & Machinery	Rs.	34,000.00
3. Other Fixed Assets	Rs.	30,000.00
TOTAL	Rs.	12,64,000.00

RAW MATERIALS

1. Herbs of Different Variety
2. Packaging Materials

TOTAL WORKING CAPITAL/MONTH

1. Raw Material	Rs.	50,75,000.00
2. Salary & Wages	Rs.	50,485.00
3. Utilities & Overheads	Rs.	35,200.00
TOTAL	Rs.	51,60,685.00

TOTAL CAPITAL INVESTMENT

Total Fixed Capital	Rs.	12,64,000.00
Total Working Capital for 3 Months Rs. 1,54,82,055.00		
TOTAL	Rs.	1,67,46,055.00

TURN OVER/ANNUM

1. Receipt by Sale of Dried Herbs of Different variety 300,000 Kgs.	Rs.	6,90,00,000.00

PROFIT SALES RATIO = Profit / Sales x 100 = 6.77 %

RATE OF RETURN = Operating profit / T.C.I x 100 = 27.64 %

BREAK EVEN POINT (B.E.P) = 37.10 %

Chapter 43

HERBS CULTIVATION

Sans-Sailaja, saileya; Hindi-Charila, pathar-ka-phul; Tel.-Ratipoovu; TAM.--Marappasi.

Punjab-Chalchalira, charcharila, ausneh, hiunsew; Bombay-Mota dagada phul, barik dagada phul.

Lichens constitute a class of small perennial plants, which are unique in that they are actually combinations of two organisms-a fungus and an alga-growing together in symbiotic association. The fungal element lives upon the food elaborated by the algae, while the algal element gets its moisture and mineral nutrients from the fungus; the fungus also protects the alga against desiccation and injury.

Thus we see that the fungus makes up over 90% of the lichen plant body or 'Thallus', entrapping within it the microscopic algae, the two types of organisms form a self supporting association in which one part, the chlorophyll containing algae component called the 'phycolrant' produces organic foods by photo synthesis, and the other, the heterotropic, fungus called the 'mycobiont' utilizes these foods without killing the other component. This type of association is a form of symbiosis and lichens are considered a perfect example of this phenomenon.

Lichens are widely distributed from the arctic to the tropics and are found on soil, barren rocks and tree trunks. They are not usually found in the neighborhood of large cities as they are sensitive to smoke and various gases.

The vegetative body of the lichen, called thallus, is composed of fungal mycelia which form a network enclosing algal cells or gonidia. The fungal component is the dominant participant and is usually a member of the Ascomycetes; less frequently and particularly in the tropical species, the fungal component is a Basidiomycetes. The algal component may belong to Myxophyceae (blue-green algae). The thalli in some lichen species are thin flat incrustations growing on the substratum; lichens of this type are called crustose. In foliose lichens, the thallus is flat, leathery, leaf-like and more or less deeply incised, growing in rosettes or irregularly spreading over the substratum. Fruticose lichens have erect or hanging, simple or branched, strap-shaped fronds which may be cylindrical or broadened to thin bands. The thallus may be very minute or large and the colour may be white, green, yellow, red, dark brown or black. The thallus surface may be smooth or rough due to the presence of vegetative outgrowths.

The greater part of the lichen thallus is composed of fungus hyphae woven together into a compact false tissue. In advanced forms, the thallus is differentiated into the upper cortex of compacted hyphae followed by the gonidial layer with algal cells, the medulla or loose hyphal tissue, and the lower cortex, which may be often absent.

Lichens reproduce by means of spores or by soredia. The ascospores or basidiospores of the fungal element are disseminated by wind and germinate in the presence of moisture into hyphae; each hypha, in its chance encounter with the requisite alga, forms a new lichen. Soredia are minute bits of lichen, composed of one or more algal cells together with a small mass of fungal hyphae, which feed on lichens; when deposited on suitable substrata, they develop into lichen thalli. Lichens have been produced artificially by growing the component organisms separately in pure cultures and bringing them together.

Lichens were recognized as distinct plants by the ancient Greeks and Romans, who used some of them as dyes. In the Middle, Ages they were collected for use as medicinal herbs. The modern study of lichens began with the work of the Swedish naturalist Carl Linnaeus, who described about 80 species in 1752. The dual nature of lichens was discovered in 1867 by the Swiss botanist Simon Schwendener. Before then, botanist thought that the green cells inside the lichen originated from the tip of the fungal filaments, or hyphae. They had not suspected any relationship between the green cells and free living algae. Today it is known that approximately 17.000 species of fungi-in fact, the majority of the inoperculate (nonpored) ascomycetes have successfully established symbiotic relationships with algae. However, only about 25 species of algae are known to occur in lichens.

It is believed that the earliest lichens were loose associations of algae and fungi, and that during the course of evolution, closer, more complex associations developed. There has been much argument over the exact nature of the algalfungus relationship, ranging from the theory of pure parasitism of the algae by the fungus to a kind of mutualism, where each component derives benefits from the other. Through physiological research, botanists are discovering that the truth lies somewhere between, perhaps a combination of symbiosis and controlled parasitism.

Importance Before the discovery of coal-tar dyes in the 19th century, lichens were gathered by the ton to make various dyes. They are still used as dyes in some rural communities in northern Europe, but the most important commercial use of lichen dye is in the manufacture of litmus paper, which is used by chemists to determine whether a solution is basic or acidic.

In southern Europe lichens are collected for their essential oils, which are used in making perfumes. In Scandinavia they are gathered for their usnic acid, a yellow pigment with antibiotic properties. Sold in Europe under the trade names Usno and Usniplant, the usnic acid is applied externally as a salve. It has also been used experimentally in the treatment of tuberculosis and in veterinary medicine to treat internal infections in cows. One type of lichen, Iceland moss (Cetraria islandica), is sold in drugstores in Sweden for use as an expectorant.

In nature, lichens play a significant role in the food chain since they are widely eaten by snails, slugs, insects, and other invertebrates. In arctic regions, caribou and reindeer live primarily on tundra lichens, especially reindeer moss (Cladonia), during the winter when other plants are dormant. In Lapland, lichens are harvested as fodder for domestic animals, and during famines lichens have been eaten by man. Today, however, they are at best considered an unusual delicacy, such as the rock tripes (Umbilicaria) eaten as salad in Japan. Because lichens grow very slowly, they will never be a major source of food for man.

MAJOR FORMS

When a lichen fungus is isolated and cultured separately, it forms a white cottony mycelium similar to that of a common mold. The alga done grows as a dense green colony indistinguishable from other algae. However, when combined in a symbiotic state, the fungus and alga from a complex thallus (body) with various growth forms that have no relation in size or scope to the isolated components-a unique feature of lichen symbiosis. Lichen growth forms are classified into three general types: crustose, close, and fruticose. Another form, squamulose, considered to be an intermediate between the crustose and foliose forms.

Crustose Lichens. These are the most primitive lichens, growing tightly attached to bark or a rock. The thallus, flat and crusty-looking, actually becomes an integral part of the substratum and is not easily removed from it. The lower layer of fungal filaments (hyphae) may penetrate a much as 0.4 inch (1 cm) deep between the subtratum's rock crystals or cork cells. In tropical regions, many species grow on the leaves of jungle trees and ferns, causing little or no damage to the plants. As a group, crustose lichens find to be rather small and inconspicuous, although some are bright yellow or orange.

Foliose Lichens. These lichens lie flat and are somewhat leaflike. The main thallus is usually divided into small, narrow, branching lobes from 0.2 to 0.8 inch (0,5-2 cm) wide. Although the lower surface often bears anchoring structures, all of these lichens can be peeled from their substrata.

Most species of foliose lichens grow from 2 to nearly 10 inches (5-25 cm) in diameter. Included in this group are the rock tripes, which are circular in outline and grow attached to rocks by a single central rootlike attachment (umbilicus). These leathery brown plants are known to grow about 3 feet (1meter) in diameter.

Squamulose Lichens. These lichens are intermediates between the crustose and foliose forms. Their thalli consist of numerous tiny lobes, or squamules, scattered on soil or bark. They lack the size and complexity of foliose forms and are not as tightly affixed to the substratum as the crustose forms.

Fruticose Lichens. The most highly developed lichens are the fruticose forms that hang from trees such as the old man's beard (Usnea). Some of these lichens are more than 3 yards (3 meters) long. Their thalli are usually round in cross section and may be abundantly branched.

The most common fruticose lichen is reindeer moss, which grows erect on soil and often has a primary squamulose thallus from which arises a hollow stalk (podetium) with spore-bearing structures (apothecia). Other common fruticose lichens are the red-capped British soldiers (Cladonia cristatella) and the cup lichens, such as Cladonia Chlorophea.

USES AND APPLICATION OF LICHENS

Lichens have been used from the earliest times as animal feeds and also as food for human consumption in times of scarcity; a few are consumed as delicacies. Cetraria islandica (Iceland Moss), Evernia prunastri (Linn.) Ach. and Lecanora esculenta Evers. (Biblical manna) are instances of lichens foods. Species of Umbilicaria and Gyrophora called Tripe de roche, have been consumed by arctic explorers. Gyrophora esculenta Miyosh. is prized as a food adjunct in China and japan. Some species of Parmelia, Peltigera, Ramalina and Usnea are reported to possess food value. Several lichens are used as fodder for reindeer, cattle, swine and goats, while all but gelatinous lichens are eaten by invertebrates, like caterpillars, snails and mites. Lichens, with few exceptions, are non-poisonous.

Lichens were once employed for dyeing wool and silk and colouring materials derived from them were highly valued before the advent of aniline dyes. Certain species of Roccella and Lecanora yield purple dyes, known in commerce as Orchil or Archil, Cudbear and Litmus. Lichen dyes are still employed in the production of high quality Harris Tweed cloth. Important dye yielding lichens are discussed in detail below.

Certain lichens containing volatile oil were once used in perfumery and cosmetic industries. Evernia prunastri, growing on the stems of oak trees and known as Oak Moss or Mousse de Chene, is highly esteemed by perfumers in Europe for scenting soaps and in compounding many popular scents. The chief odorous. principles of oak moss are α-and ß-thujone, along with some camphor, borneol and cineol.

Lichens were formerly used as sources of fermentable sugars for the production of ethyl alcohol. Cetraria islandica and Cladonia rangiferina yield up to 60% polysaccharides readily hydrolysed to glucose. Some species of Parmelia, Evernia and ramalina yield gums which found application in calico printing and in the production of parchment and cardboard. Many crustaceous lichens contain oxalic acid; pertusaria sp. is reported to be used in France in the manufacture of oxalic acid.

Several lichens possess medicinal properties. Cetraria islandica is considered useful in chest complaints. Some lichens belonging to Cladoniaceae, Parmeliaceae and Usneaceae elaborate substances which are active against Gram-positive bacteria. The active compounds are dibenzofurans of which usnic acid is the most important. Certain lactonic fatty acid and depsidones related to orcinol also show anti-bacterial activity. Usnic acid is active against streptococcus heamolyticus and Pneumococcus spp. and inhibits the growth of the tubercle bacillus. Barbatic acid and dibasic roccelic acid, in the form of its half esters of half amides. possess anti-tubercular activity. Atranorin is a fish poison.

PROCESS OF EXTRACTION OF LICHEN RESIN OIL

The process of extraction of Lichen Resin oil involves the following steps.

1. Cleaning of the botonical viz. lichen.
2. Washing
3. Drying
4. Steam Distillation
5. Bottling of Lichen Resin oil.

1. CLEANING

The botanical Lichen is cleared off the adhering soil or any other contaminants accompanying it.

2. WASHING

Lichen is then washed with water to wash off the remaining adhering dust or any other impurities.

3. DRYING

The process of drying of Lichen is carried out in the sun for economical reasons.

However, precautions are to be observed that the place where the stuff is kept for drying in the sun should be such that dust or dirt or any other foreign matter shouldn't get contaminated with it during the process of drying.

However, in the case of Lichen, prior to distillation process, it may be either partially dried or dried.

4. STEAM DISTILLATION

Distillation Process (For Handling Small batch)

Distillation is carried out in stills of copper or iron (150 gal), Lichen (240 lbs) is charged into the still through the manhole and fresh water (40 lbs) added to cover the material. The still is closed with a wooden plate and the joints sealed with mud paste. The vapours pass through a tube fixed to the lid, its long arm leading to a copper receiver immersed in the stream and held in position by a wooden frame work.

Distillation takes 4.5 hrs. The oil collected in the receiver is skimmed off, filled into galvanized iron containers of 2-4 gal capacity, and transported to the nearest place where the oil is separated from the water by decantation.

The oil is finally filtered through cloth into containers or drums of 45 gal. and despatched.

Galvanized iron drums are used as containers for exporting the oil.

A better quality of oil is obtained in higher yield by steam distillation.

Equally good results are obtained by the use of improved direct-fired stills with false bottoms.

ALTERNATIVE METHOD OF STEAM DISTILLATION

For extraction of Lichen Resin Oil from Lichen

The lichen, either, fresh or partially dried is used for distillation.

Distillation still consists of a cylindrical vessel 4 ft. height 2½ ft. diam, over which is placed a truncated cone, 1½ ft. height.

The charge (300-350 lbs) is introduced through a side opening in the cylinder and water is poured upto 10 in. below the side opening. The mixture of steam and volatile oil passes into a spiral condenser through a copper tube fixed to the cone and the condensed liquids are collected. The still is heated on an open wood fire and when steam begin to issue, 5-100 lbs or more of Lichen are introduced through the side opening which is then hermetically closed. Distillation is stopped when a test sample of the distillate is free from the oil.

The distillation takes 3-3½ hours, and 4-5 distillation are carried out in a day.

The upper layer of the distillate is collected in the receiver, constituting the oil, is labled out and stored in glass, copper or tin receptacles.

GENERAL STEAM DISTILLATION PROCESS

Steam distillation is by far the most common and important method of extraction whereas other process viz. extraction with cold fat (enflurage) or hot fat (maceration) is chiefly of historical importance.

Three different methods of steam distillation are practiced. In the oldest and simplest method a vessel containing water and the chopped or crushed plant material is heated by a direct flame, and the water vapour and volatile oil are recovered by a watercooled condenser.

This original method is being replaced by a process in which the plant material is suspended on a grid above the water level, and steam from a second vessel is introduced under the grid. The volatiles are condensed and the oil is separated.

In the third process, the vessel containing the plant material on a grid is heated to prevent condensation of steam, so that dry distillation is attained.

PLANT ECONOMICS

Rated Plant Capacity = 5.00 LTR/Day

LAND & BUILDING

1. Land area required, 1000 Sq.Mts.	Rs.	10,00,000.00

PLANT & MACHINERY

1. Distillation column
3. Mini pulveriser
4. Chopping machine
5. Baby boiler
6. Storage tank (S.S.)
7. Vacuum pump
8. Laboratory equipments
9. Small fractionating column
10. Pipes, pumps, valves and other miscellaneous

FIXED CAPITAL

1. Land & Building	Rs.	10,00,000.00
2. Plant & Machinery	Rs.	16,50,000.00
3. Other Fixed Assets	Rs.	3,00,000.00
TOTAL	Rs.	29,50,000.00

RAW MATERIALS

1. Lichens
2. Miscellaneous chemicals
3. Containers, glass bottles

TOTAL WORKING CAPITAL/MONTH

1. Raw Material	Rs.	12,71,250.00
2. Salary & Wages	Rs.	72,485.00
3. Utilities & Overheads	Rs.	71,400.00
TOTAL	Rs.	14,15,135.00

TOTAL CAPITAL INVESTMENT

Total Fixed Capital	Rs.	29,50,000.00
TOTAL WORKING CAPITAL FOR 2 MONTHS	Rs.	28,30,270.00
TOTAL	Rs.	57,80,270.00

TURN OVER/ANNUM

1. By sale of 1500 litres Lichen oil Rs. 2,25,00,000.00

PROFIT SALES RATIO = Profit / Sales x 100 = 18.82 %

RATE OF RETURN = Operating profit / T.C.I x 100 = 73.25 %

BREAK EVEN POINT (B.E.P) = 33.17 %

Chapter 44

SPIKENARD (JATAMANSI)

Sani-Jatamansi, Hindi-Jatamansi, Bal-chir, BENG-Jatamansi, MAR Jatamanshi, Guj-Jatamasi, Kaolichhad, Tel. Kan & Mal Jatamansi Tam-Jatamanshi.

It is an erect perennial herb 10-60 cm high, with long start woody rootstock fomed in the alpine Himalayas from Punjab to Sikkim and Bhutan, at altitudes of 3000 - 5000 m. Radical leaves elongate spathulate, cauline leaves sessile, few, oblong or sub-arate; flowers rosy, pale pink or blue, in dense cymes.

SPIKENARD

(Formed in the woods of Quebec, Gorgina, Kansas etc.)

Spikenard, a perennial plant, Aralia racemosa, found in woods from eastern Quebec to southeastern Manitoba and south to Georgia and Kansas. A member of the ginseng family, Araliaceae, the American spikenard grows from 3 to 6 feet (90-180 cm) tall. It has large compound leaves, sometimes nearly 3 feet (90 cm) long, with broad leaflets. The flowers, borne in much branched long clusters, are small and greenish yellow or greenish white. The dark purple berries are pleasantly flavored and may be made into a jelly. The stout roots have a spicy taste and have been used to flavour root beer. Certain North American Indians ate spikenard roots. And the drug aralia was prepared from dried spikenard roots.

The name "spikenard," or "nard," is also applied to an Indian plant, Nardostachys jatamansi, with rose-purple flowers. The roots and stems of this plant were once used to make an aromatic ointment, also called

spikenard, or nard.
The plant is propagated by cuttings of underground parts and sometimes by seeds. The drug (Jatamarshi or Nardus Root) consists of short, thick dark grey rhizomes crowned with reddish brown fibracs remains of the petioles of radical leaves. The rhizomes are collected from wild plants and sent to markets in the plains; the roots of valerian and cymbopogon schoenanthus are often mistaken for 'Jatamansi'. Recently roots and rhizomes of Selenium Vaginatum C.B. dark have been found as adulterants of Jatamansi.

PROCESS OF EXTRACTION OF SPIKENARD OIL (ESSENTIAL OIL)

From Rhizomes of spikenard (Nordostachys)

The process of extraction of essential oil spikenard oil involves the following steps.

1. Cleaning of the botanical Viz. rhizane.
2. Washing
3. Drying
4. Disintegrating into small chips
5. Steam distillation
6. Bottling of the essential oil

Cleaning

The spikenard rhizomes which occur within the soil, are dug out and cleared off the adhering soil or the rhizomes may be procured from the market where they are sent after collecting from wild plants.

Washing

The rhizomes are then be washed with water to wash off the adhering dust or any other impurities.

Drying

Then these rhizomes from which essential oil is to be extracted is dried.

This process of drying of the rhizomes is proposed to be carried out in the sun for economical reasons.

However, precautions are to be observed that the place where these items are kept for drying in the sun should be such that dust or dirt or any other foreign matter shouldn't get contaminated with them during drying.

Disintegrating into small chips

Prior to the distillation operation, the cleaned and dried rhizomes are disintegrated into small chips rather crushed to coarse powder.

Steam Distillation

The distillation is done with steam. The spikenard rhizomes are charged into the still filled with water and steam distillation operation is carried out for the purpose of extraction of oil.

The stills employed in industry are of copper, tin-lined copper or stainless steel and of capacity in accordance with the amount of material to be handled. They are provided with condensers of various sorts, tubular one being the more efficient, and with a separator for dividing the oily layer from the aqueous one.

However, a better procedure seems to be to construct the still with a perforated false plate lying just above the bottom. Underneath this false bottom are steam coils, both closed and perforated.

In operating these stills, the charge in heated by steam in both the open and closed pipes, thus effecting economical steam distillation.

The oil collected in the condensing vessel being heavier than water sinks to the bottom and the water cover prevents loss by evaporation.

The aqueous layer in the condensate frequents carries in solution, valuable constituents, and is consequently pumped back into the still to supply same of the necessary water.

Quality Testing

Quality testing of the essential oil i.e spikenard oil is done to ensure that it is of requisite quality.

Bottling

Then spikenard oil is filled in suitable containers and sent for marketing.

FLOW DIAGRAM FOR THE EXTRACTION OF SPIKENARD OIL FROM SPIKENARD RHIZOME

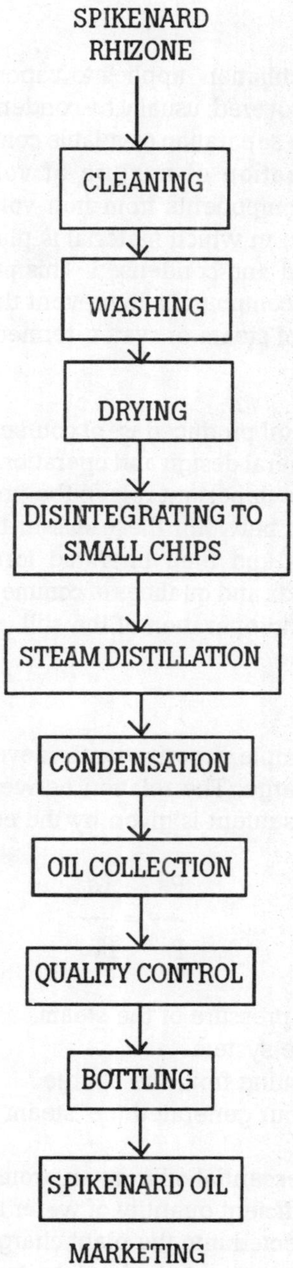

GENERAL DETAILED ASPECTS OF ESSENTIAL OIL PRODUCTION BY DISTILLATION

Introduction

In general, the term 'distillation' applies to vaporization process in which the vapour evolved is recovered, usually by condensation. The main purpose of distillation is either the separation of volatile components from nonvolatile materials or the separation of mixture of volatile components. The separation of volatile components from non-volatile materials is carried out by simple distillation in which material is placed in a still and heated and the vapour removed and condensed. This process is frequently used for high boiling organic compounds, to prevent thermal degradation of the product, with addition of steam or water, termed as water, steam/water, steam distillation.

The quality of essential oil produced is, of course, dependent on the plant material but also the general design and operation of distillation equipment. the distillation unit plays important role in the production of essential oils. It is the controlling link between these oils in their natural state within the tissues of the plant and their liberated form which are utilized for many purposes. The yields and qualities of commercial essential oils depend on the correct design and operation of the still.

Principle

Steam distillation is a simple vaporization achieved by letting in live steam directly through the charge. The relation between the quantity of steam and that of volatile constituent is given by the equation:

$$\frac{Ps}{P} = \frac{Ls}{LT}$$

Where Ps is the partial pressure of the steam.
P is total pressure of the system
Ls is moles of steam issuing from the charge
LT is total moles of vapour generated (i.e.,steam + volatile oil).

In order to isolate and essential oil from an aromatic plant, the material is packed into a still, a sufficient quantity of water is added and brought to a boil, or live steam is injected into the plant charge. Due to the influence of hot water and steam, the essential oil will be freed from the oil glands in the plant tissue. The vapour mixture of water and oil is condensed by indirect cooling with water. From the condenser, distillate flows into a separator, where oil separates automatically from the distillate water.

Mechanism of Distillation

Hydrodistillation of plant involves following main physico-chemical process:

i) Hydrodiffusion
ii) Hydrolysis
iii) Decomposition by heat.

Hydrodiffusion

Diffusion of essential oil and hot water through the plant membranes is known as hydrodiffusion. In steam distillation, the steam does not actually penetrate the dry cell membranes. Therefore, dry plant material can be exhausted with dry steam only when all the volatile oil has been freed from the oil bearing cells by first thorough comminution of the plants. But, when the plant material is soaked with water, exchange of vapours within the tissue is based on their permeability while in swollen condition. It has been studied that volatile oils are almost impermeable through membranes of plant cells. Therefore, in the actual process, at the temperature of boiling water a part of volatile oil dissolves in the water present within the glands, and this oil in water solution permeates, by osmosis, through swollen membranes and finally reaches the outer surface, where the oil is vaporized by passing steam.

Another aspect of hydrodiffusion is that the speed of oil vaporization is not influenced by the volatility of oil components but by their degree of solubility in water. therefore, the higher boiling but more water soluble constituents of an oil in the plant tissue, distill before the lower boiling but less water soluble constituents. Since hydrodiffusion rates are slow, distillation of uncomminuted material takes longer time than comminuted.

Hydrolysis

Hydrolysis in present context, can be defined as a chemical reaction between water and certain constituents of essential oils. Esters are part of constituents of essential oils. In presence of water, especially at high temperatures, esters tend to react with water to form acids and alcohols. However, reactions are not complete in either direction and the relationship between the molal concentration of various constituents at equilibrium is written as:

$$K = \frac{(\text{Alcohol}) \times (\text{Acid})}{(\text{Ester}) \times (\text{Water})}$$, Where K is equilibrium constant

Therefore, if the amount of water is large, the amounts of alcohol and acid will also be large resulting in decrease in the yield of essential oil.

Besides, being a time dependent reaction, the extent to which hydrolysis proceeds, depends upon the time of contact between oil and water. This is one of the disadvantages of water distillation.

Effect of heat

Almost all constituents of essential oils are unstable at high temperatures. To obtain best quality of oil, it is necessary that the distillation is resorted to low temperatures. The temperature in steam distillation is determined entirely by the operating pressure, whereas in case of water distillation and water steam distillation operating pressure is usually atmospheric.

All the above described there effects, i.e. hydrodiffusion, hydrolysis and thermal decomposition occur simultaneously and they affect one another. The rate of diffusion usually increases by higher temperatures and so also the solubility of essential oil in water. The same is true for rate and extent of hydrolysis. However, it has been observed that by (1) maintaining of low feasible temperature; (2) use of as little water as possible in case of steam distillation; and (3) through comminution of plant material before distillation and uniform packing, it is possible to obtain better yield and quality of oils.

Types of Distillation and Their Techniques

There are three types of hydrodistillation techniques for isolating essential oils from plant materials.

(1) Water distillation
(2) Water and steam distillation
(3) Direct steam distillation

Water Distillation

In this method, the material is completely immersed in water and water is boiled by applying heat either by direct fire or steam jacket or closed steam coil or open steam coil. the main characteristic of this process is that there is direct contact between boiling water and plant material.

Adequate precautions are necessary to prevent the charge from overheating when the still is heated by direct fire. When a steam jacket or closed steam coils are used, there is less danger of overheating and with open steam coils this danger is avoided. But with open steam, care must be taken to prevent accumulation of condensed water within the still. Therefore, still should be well insulated.

During watér distillation, all parts of the plant charge must be kept in motion by boiling water and this is possible when the distillation material is charged loosely and remains loose in the boiling water. For this reason only, water distillation possesses one distinct advantage that it permits processing of very finely powdered material or plant parts which by contact with live steam would easily form lumps through which the steam connot penetrate. other practical advantages of water distillation still are that these are cheap and easy to construct and suitable for field operation. These are still quite widely used with portable equipment in may countries.

The main disadvantage of water distillation is that complete extraction of material is not possible. Besides, certain esters are partly hydrolysed and sensitive substances like aldehydes tend to polymerize. Water distillation requires a greater number of still, more space and more fuel. It demands considerable experience and familiarity with the method. The high boiling and somewhat water soluble oil constituents cannot be completely vaporized or they require large quantities of steam. Thus the process becomes uneconomical. For these reasons, water distillation is used only in case where the plant material by its very nature cannot be processed by water and steam distillation or by direct steam distillation.

Water and Steam Distillation

In this method, the plant material is supported on a perforated grid or screen inserted some distance above the bottom of still. The lower part of the still is filled with water, to a level somewhat below this grid. The water is heated either by open fire, or by jacket steam, or steam coil or open steam. The saturated low pressure steam rises through plant material. The typical characteristics of this method are that the steam is always fully saturated, wet and never superheater and that the plant material is in contact with steam only and not with boiling water.

This method is generally employed by small producers using portable distillation equipment that can be moved from field to field, following the harvest. The smaller units are heated by direct fire and the larger ones by steam jacket or coil or open steam. When using direct fire, care is taken to ensure that only bottom of the still is heated, otherwise one one of the major advantage of this method over water distillation (no overheating of charge) will be lost.

Preparation of the plant material is also important factor in this method. Since steam contacts the material only by rising through it, the plant charge must be so dispersed that all parts of it are uniformly contacted by steam for obtaining high yields.

Compared with water distillation, water and steam distillation has many advantages, i.e., the decomposition of the oil is less, it requires less fuel, less time and yields more oil. If, however, a plant material (for instance, rose or orange blossoms) forms lumps under the influence of steam, the steam cannot penetrate the charge and reach every plant material. In such a case water distillation is opted.

One great disadvantage of water and steam distillation is that as a result of the low pressure of the rising steam, oils, of high boiling range require large quantities of steam for complete vaporization-hence long hours of distillation.

Water beneath the grid is usually discarded after the distillation is complete because water soluble materials of the plant charge accumulate in the water and they decompose during subsequent distillation imparting an objectionable note to the essential oil.

Steam Distillation at Reduced Pressure

This method is used when volatile oil is likely to decompose at high pressure, especially for oils containing esters. However, it should be noted that in case of distillation at reduced pressure the ratio of oil to water in the distillate is less than when some products are distilled at atmospheric pressure, because any lowering in the external pressure reduces the vapour pressure of all high boiling compounds relatively much more than that of water. Besides, at reduced pressure, because of lowering in temperature, effective log mean temperature between water and vapours will reduce and considerable oil losses may be expected by evaporation.

In order to achieve high rage of distillation at reduced pressure the empty space above the liquid in the vacuum still should be kept sufficiently large to permit the still content to boil without foaming into the condenser (this is particularly so in respect of hydrodistillation). Besides, the condenser surface must be larger, estimated to be 4 to 5 times than that required fro distillation at atmospheric pressure, because of high volumetric rates and low temperature difference.

Distillation at high pressure

Pressure in the still can be increased by inserting a throttling valve in the vapour line connecting the still and condenser. Steam distillation at high pressure is useful for certain purposes, for instances, for the hydrolysis of ester if so desired. There is another advantage, i.e., relative to steam pressure, the vapour pressure of higher boiling oil constituents increases more as the temperature rises resulting in better oil to water ratio in the distillate. However, from this viewpoint distillation with superheated steam is better because it vaporizes more oil without necessitating the high pressure of the former method, but hydrodiffusion in this case has be maintained by injecting wet steam, intermittently to obtain good yield.

Superheated steam distillation

In this method saturated steam may be superheated within the still by means of closed coils or jacket or outside the still in boiler. Usually the stills employed for distillation by superheated steam are constructed high with small diameter, well insulated and provided with jacket. this method is with mostly used for distilling all high boiling and chemically stable compounds and with the plants containing high moisture (60 -80%), because hydrodiffusion is automatically maintained by the presence of water in the plant material.

The operation can be carried out with superheated steam at reduced pressure as well. By this methods, it is possible to regulate the temperature of the oil vapours at will. According to degree of superheat, rise in vapour temperature will result which means a more favourable ratio of oil in the distillate than is the case when oil is merely steam distilled at reduced pressure without superheating. Injection of wet steam intermittently is necessary to maintain hydrodiffusion conditions.

Equipment

The equipment required for carrying out distillation of plant materials depends upon the size of the operation and the type of distillation to be used. But, however, in industrial practice, the following items are necessary:

i) Still
ii) Condenser
iii) Separator
iv) Steam generator
v) Labour saving devices

(i) Still:- This serves primarily as a container for the plant material where steam contacts the plant material and vaporizes the essential oil from the plant material. It is usually cylindrical, vertical tank equipped with a removable cover which can be clamped upon the cylindrical section. On or near the top of the cylindrical section a pipe is attached for leading the vapours to the condenser. Nearby the bottom, there is a grid or false bottom on which the material rests and live steam is introduced through a steam line, usually a perforated coil below false bottom.

The cylindrical section is slightly tapered to facilitate easy discharging of material manually or mechanically. The bottom of the still is provided with a drain valve so that any water condensing within the charge can be drawn off in the course of distillation.

Insulation:- The still, including the top should be well insulated to conserve heat. If insulation is neglected, excessive steam condensation occurs resulting in bumping of particles, higher steam consumption, prolonged distillation and inferior yield of oil. Usually all heated sections including steam lines are well insulated.

Condenser:- This serves to convert the steam and accompanying oil vapours into liquid. This requires the removal of an amount of heat equivalent to the heat of vaporization of the vapours plus steam, and cooling the distillate to near ambient temperatures. The rate which heat will be removed from the vapours is expressed by:

$$Q = UA\Delta t_{lm}$$

Where Q is heat removed per unit time
U is over all heat transfer coefficient
A is area of heat transfer
Δt_{lm} is long mean temperature difference between cooling medium and vapours.

Condenser design is important, the most efficient type being the multi-tubular condenser. It is compact, does not develop back pressure and permits higher distillation rate than the single coil or pipe condenser as U valves are much higher. Another point of importance in favour of shell and tube condenser is that when a distillation is carried out by cohobation, the condenser being compact, enables the distillates to be returned easily to the still from the oil separator without recourse to a high still head connection to the condenser.

(iii) Oil Separator:- Its function is to achieve a quick and complete separation of the oil from condensed water. Volatile oil and water are mutually insoluble. Because of the difference in their specific gravities two liquids form two separate layers. Since the total volume of water condensed is always greater than the quantity of oil, water is removed continuously. Various types of designs for separator area in practice and are designed on the basis of specific gravities and average flow rates.

Some of the prominent types of oil separators that are commonly used are discussed below:

(a) For oils lighter than water:- A smooth flow of condensate is assured by inserting a long stemmed funnel, the end turning upward. The distillate streaming from the condenser thus flows first through the funnel and oil droplets rise slowly towards the oil layer where they merge. Water is continuously removed through a siphon pipe.

(b) For oils heavier than water:- In this type also condensate is allowed to flow through the funnel steam ending in the middle of the separator chamber but there is no upward bend. The oil droplets which are heavier than water sink slowly to the bottom and get collected there. Water is allowed to flow continuously from the top.

When some of the essential oil fractions are lighter than water and some heavier, the separator is then so designed that both the heavy and light parts are collected separately.

In such cases, a cylindrical or rectangular chamber is divided into two parts by partition which ends a few inches from the bottom of the vessel. the condensate flows into the first chamber, oil lighter than water collects in the upper part of the first chamber and flows out from there, while oil heavier than water sinks to the bottom of the two chambers and is drawn off from there.

In some cases, when oil and water do not separate immediately in the oil separator, especially when the difference between specific gravities of water and oil is slight, one operational precaution must be taken into consideration that the condensate does not flow too rapidly and disturb the oil water layer. In such cases the chamber must be large enough to allow enough residence time for oil droplets. The stems of the inlet funnel and water outlet are bent upwards. The performance of the separator can also be improved by providing more compartments and bottom of the chamber partitions may be tapered to ensure quick and complete withdrawal of heavy oil. The same arrangement can be obtained by connecting serially several separators usually in the form of step like cascades.

The effect of condensate temperature:- When the oil specific gravity is slightly less than water, condensate should be allowed to flow hot through the separator, because with rising temperature the specific gravity of oil decreases relatively more than that of water. The resulting greater differential in the specific gravity between oil and water at elevated temperature causes the two layers to separate more rapidly. But in case of the specific gravity of oil at room temperature being slightly higher than water, the condensate should run as cold as possible. Any increase in the temperature would further decrease the already small differential between the specific gravity of the oil and water.

Steam generator:- Steam is most useful heating medium in process plant. In the initial stages of steam generation, water is evaporated and is in equilibrium with the boiling water at the pressure of generation. This water vapour is called saturated steam and any lowering of temperature or increasing of pressure will cause condensation to begin. High moisture in steam is undesirable, therefore, saturated steam passes through a heat exchanger called super-heater, which is located in a hot zone of the furnace. The steam is heated above its saturation temperature, so that it will be sufficiently dry to provide moisture-free steam.

A steam generator is composed of a furnace section which supplies the heat and a boiler section in which the heat is transformed to circulating water to form steam.

A steam generator is composed of a furnace section which supplies the heat and a boiler section in which the heat is transformed to circulating water to form steam.

Furnace:- Fuel is burnt under or adjacent to the boiler and the heat of combustion is transferred to the tubes by radiation and convection. The design of the furnace depends on the fuel to be used.

Solid fuels such as coal are all fed to the furnace manually or by mechanical means. These include the following:

a) Retort Stoker : Introduces fuel beneath the bed.
b) Spreader stoker : Distributes coal above burning bed.
c) Travelling grate
d) Pulverizer : Pulverized coal is mixed with air and distributed vertically/ horizo-ntally into the combustion zone.

Liquid fuels must be atomized so that drops of fuel will burn as completely as possible. A number of different types of burners can be obtained using either steam or mechanical atomization. In the first type, stem flows through nozzle with oil causing atomization. In the second type atomization is produced by forcing oil at high pressure through a spray type nozzle.

Types of boilers:- Boilers consist of surfaces through which heat is transferred and are designed for circulation and separation of water and steam. They may be classified generally as fire tube or water tube types.

Fire tube boilers:- I fire tube boilers, water circulation, steam formation and separation all take place in a large horizontal drum situated above the furnace floor so that it will receive both radiant and convective heat. Hot gases pass over the drum and then through the drum . Feed water is maintained above the top row of tubes. Fire tube boilers are low in initial cost and because of the large capacity of the drum operate will under fluctuating loads common to process plants. They are, however, limited to low capacities and pressure.

Water tube boilers:- In water tube boilers, water and steam flow inside the tubes and hot gases are directed across the tubes by baffles. They may be classified as straight tube and bent tube boilers. All large high pressure boilers are water tube types. Since the pressure is on the inside of the tubes instead of outside, the given thickness and diameter of the tube can withstand a higher pressure.

Standardized and packaged steam generators:- the boiler industry has standardized construction of many boiler styles in recent past. Standardized boilers are obtainable as packaged units which are completely assembled units that are ready fro installation. Fire tube units are built for capacities from 200 to 8000 kg/hr of saturated steam and pressure form 10 to 600 psig. Water tube units produce twice as much steam and upto 900 psig.

Packaged units are automatically controlled and are designed to operate efficiently both at low and high capacities. The locomotive type (oil fed) boiler is sometimes used for temporary installation in process plants.

(v) Labour saving devices:- In industrial large scale steam distillation practice, large-sized distillation stills in series are common. Labour and time requirement for charging and discharging the stills are very high if done manually. Therefore, in order to save both time and labour, the methods, of charging and discharging are mechanized. This is accomplished by installing a EOT Crane with suitable devices for lifting the top of the still and material. Automatic charging is done by placing the still sin such a position that truck or cart can directly empty the material in the still.

The false bottom or grid supporting the plant material, is usually circular in shape. Chains or heavy wires attached to three or four equally spaced points around the circumference of the grid, serve as handles so that the plant charge can be easily removed after distillation simply by lifting the grid. If charges in excess of one quintal are to be distilled, it will be convenient to use more than one such section, placing a new one on top of the first layer and continuing the charge above this section. This arrangement prevents excessive packing, assures better steam distribution, and facilitates discharging the spent material. Coarse and specifically lighter material can be packed higher, whereas fine and heavier material should not exceed a certain height.

Material of Construction

In the past copper was main choice for the still body, but mild steel and aluminium are used in many cases. There is increasing use of stainless steel as it offers many advantages, because it is non-reactive to the oils and has good mechanical strength. When mild steel constructed still is used, the condenser vapour lines and separator are constructed of aluminium for economy and maintaining the quality of oil.

Wood and concrete have been used in some instances, but because of their absorption characteristics, are suitable for distilling only one type of material. The use of plastic materials for lining purposes is not allowd. Where gaskets are necessary and come in contact with the oils, they should be constructed from compressed asbestos fibre. Rubber should never be used as packing material as it tends to be dissolved by essential oils.

Optimization

It is quite obvious that steam distillation parameters greatly influence the total cost of production therefore, for economic production on large scale it is always necessary to determine the optimum operating conditions so that the total cost of production per unit weight or volume of essential oil is minimum. The main parameters that should be considered before commercial scale production of essential oil by steam distillation are:

(a) Batch size
(b) Comminution of plant materials and handling
(c) Steam pressure and its saturation
(d) Steam injection rate
(e) Time of distillation.

For any particular type of plant material, the optimum values of the parameters can be determined only by experimentation and economic considerations; in essence, series of experiments are to be conducted by keeping all but one parameter constant and then studying the effect on overall cost of production. Detailed investigations on optimization studies on steam distillation of various plant materials like Mentha piperita, Eucalyptus citriodora, saussurea lappa roots, Himalayan Cedrus deodara wood, are available in literature and are discussed here in brief.

On pilot plant scale, studies were conducted by Narasimha et al. on steam distillation of M.piperita and E.citriodora by keeping batch size and steam pressure constant and it was found that at the steam injection rate of 1.2 kg/min for M. p;iperita (80kg/batch) and 1.3 kg/min for E.citriodora (175 kg/batch) and operation time of 45 minutes (which does not include charging, preheating and discharging time, etc.), the cost of production per unit weight of oil was found to be minimum. At this steam injection rate, cost of production for the total oil produced at the end of each interval was calculated. We get optimum distillation time. Similarly, for E. citriodora the percentage recovery vs time at different steam rates. At 1.3 kg/min percentage recovery is maximum. At this steam injection rate optimum distillation time can be graphically evaluated.

Chapter 45

MEDICINAL PLANT EXTRACTS

The terms alkaloids is applied to the members of a class of a basic nature, and is derived from the name of vegetable alkali, first applied to these substances. They all owe their basic nature to an amino nitrogen. They occur in leaves, seeds, roots and barks of the plants, particularly of the families papaveracease (poppies), papiteonacease (lapins) etc. from which they can be extracted by ethanol or after making it alkaline by ether or ethyl acetate. The separation of mixture of alkaloids so obtained may be accomplished by fractional crystallization, fractional precipitation, partial chromatography on column or by counter-current extraction.

EXTRACTION OF ALKALOIDS FROM SOLANUM KHASIANUM

Solanum is a large genus of herbs, shrubs & rarely tree, found throughout the temperates & tropical parts of the world. Over 50 species have been recorded in India & a few ornamental exaties have been & introduced into the gardens.

The genus is economically very important,as several species are sources of food, fodder & drugs. Some varieties are grown in gardens for ornament. The common potato is not only a prime food but also a source of starch, flow, dextrin, syrup, several alcohols, Fodder (especially for hags) & a host of other minor industrial products. Fruits of the eggplant or brinjalo are consumed as a summer vegetable all over India. Leaves of Black Nightshade have long been used in medicine for treatment of serofulous dyscrasias.

The presence of a particular alkaloid can be defected by a number of characteristic reactions, which are very important in Forensic medicine. Since Fredrich Serturner first extracted morphine from opium in 1805 the number of known substances of this type have increased enormously.

Medical demand has stimulated the search for alkaloids in the vegetable world. For they include some of the most potent drugs known.

EXTRACT OF STRYCHNINE AND BRUCINE NUX VOMICA SEEDS

Various species of the genus strychnos contain the alkaloids strychnine and brucine; strychnos nux vomica and strychnos ignatir are the most important and of these the former is official.

The alkaloid strychine is the pure state occurs as prismatic headle shaped or crystal and on account of this has been mistaken for certain non poisonous inorganic salts e.g. magnesium sulphate. It is an intensively bitter substance. The taste being appreciable even in a 600,000 solution in water.

Both strychnine and brucine are extracted from nux vomica seeds. Nux vomica is the dried ripe seed of strychnose nux vocmac. Its Indian name is Kuchila. It is disc shaped, sometimes irregularly bent 0.4 to 1 inch (10 to 30 mm) in diameter and 0.1 to 0.18 inch (4 to 6 mm) in thickness and slightly concavo-convex with rounded or some what acid margins and of ash grey colour. It has no smell but an extremely bitter taste.

Strychine was first introduced in medicine in 1540 but was not largely used until about two hundred years after. For many years it was frequently used as general tonic and considered to be a cardiorespiratory stimulant of great value but is now falling into the background. It is, however, of some value in norcotic poisoning as a respiratory stimulant.

EXTRACTION (PROCESS OF MANUFACTURE OF MEDICINAL PLANTS EXTRACTS)

Extraction of Alkaloids:-

From Vinca Rosea

EXTRACTION (PROCESS OF MANUFACTURE

In one general method for extraction and subsequent purification, water and alcohol is used either alone or mixed with dilute acid i.e. acetic acid, hydrochloric acid, sulphuric acid are not generally preferred in the availability of acetic acid, due to its complex salts formed by it.

Selective Extraction:-

The method of aqueous extraction aims, at extracting oil the alkaloids contained in the plant.

Purification of the Extract:-

This can be affected by a number of conventional methods and there is no procedure to which all alkaloids mixture will yield.

Direct Crystallization:-

The extract is evaporated to dryness and the residue is dissolved in a crystallizer which may be either a single solvent as methanol on partial evaporation of the solvent, i.e. some cases the pure base may crystallize out.

Chromatographic Technique

Wide choice of absorbents is available on the absorption chromatography, that includes the alumina, magnesia silica gel and carbon of these silica is finding the best use. The procedure involves charging a column of standarised alumina with a benzene solutions of the alkaloids to be separated.

Process of Isolation of Vinca Rosea

Ethanol extraction is best suited. The leaves of the plant vinca rosea are collected and then dried under the sun at temperature 50°C - 60°C. For there times a drier has be kept at ready disposal. After drying the material is then powdered in the pestle. This along with adequate ethanol is thoroughly extracted in big vessel. The extracted is concentrated in vacuum. This semi solid mass is then dissolved in 30 % of acetic acid and filtered. The precipitate which are left on the filter jar dissolved and precipitate one more in the same manner. The filtrate is basefied with ammonia solution. The crude glycoside is dissolved and crystallized in 80 percentage ethanol.

Alkaloid vinca rosea is hydrolyzed in ethanol as hydrochloride. The hydrochloride needless thus obtained are then suspended in dilute ammonia solution. The vinca rosea alkaloid is crystallized and recrystallized ethanol and weighed after drying.

PROCESS FLOW DIAGRAM

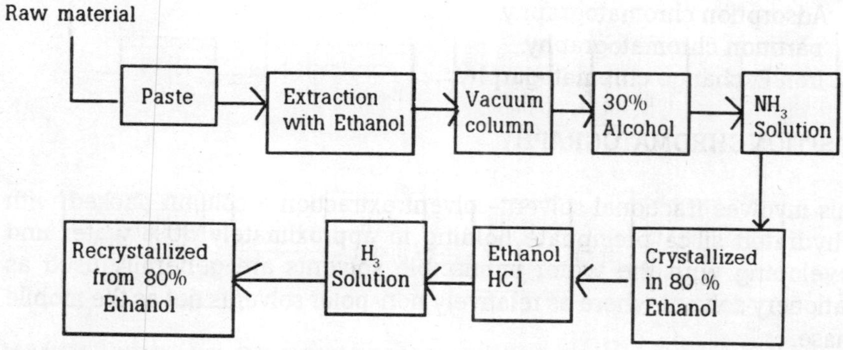

MANUFACTURING OF EXTRACTION OF ALKALOIDS FROM SOLANUM KHASIANUM

EXTRACTION :

SELECTIVE EXTRACTION

The extracting all the alkaloids contained in the plant. The other simple method consist essentially of separating the plant alkaloids into those whose trataraties are soluble in organic solvents and those which remain insoluble Extraction of the weak base from the basic crude drug is accomplished by benzene after the drug has first been pretreated with a solution of 2% tartaric acid. That is then made alkaline with ammonia and somewhat strong bases are extracted with benzene.

PURIFICATION OF THE EXTRACT

This can be effected by a number of conventional methods.

DIRECT CRYSTALLIZATION

The extract is evaporated to dryness and the residue is dissolved in a crystallizing which may be either a single solvent as methanol or acetone or a mixture of organic solvent, as acetone-emethanol, ethyl acetate-methanol and hexane-dry ether etc. On partial evaporation of the solvent, in some cases the pure base may crystallize out.

CHROMATOGRAPHIC TECHNIQUE

This is of three types :

1. Adsorption chromatography.
2. partition chromatography.
3. Iron Exchange chromatogarphy.

POSITION CHROMATOGRAPHY

This involves fractional solvent-solvent extraction a column packed with a hydrated silica precipitate holding in approximately 50% water and developing with the water immiscible solvents are generally used as stationery solvent where as relatively non-polar solvents not as the mobile phase.

PROCESS OF ISOLATION OF SOLASODINE

The ethanol extraction is best suited. Berriess from wild plant growing in the jungle are collected. These are cut into small pieces with the help of cutters. These are then dried under the sun at a temp. of 50-60°C. Berries can be put on the wooden trays and in turn can be stacked one above the other on a trolley or a truck. The trolley is then accommodated into a tunnel. This just fits in the tunnel. The currents of steam are passed through the tunnel there by drying the material

The dried material of berries is then powdered in the pestle. This alongwith adequate ethanol is thoroughly extracted in big vessel. The extract is concentrated. This semi-solid mass is then dissolved in acetic acid and filtered. The precipitate which is left on the filter is dissolved and precipitated once more in the same manner. The filtrate is justified with ammonia solution. The crude glycoside is dissolved and crystallized in ethanol. Solasodine thus obtained alongwith the additional crystal recovered from the mother liquor by subsequent treatment is hydrolysed in ethanol The hydrochloride needles thus obtained are then suspended in dilute ammonia solution at 100°C for one hour. The aglycone, solasodine is crystallised and recrystallised from 80% ethanol and weighed after drying.

FLOW DIAGRAM OF SOLANUM KHASIANUM ALKALOID EXTRACTION

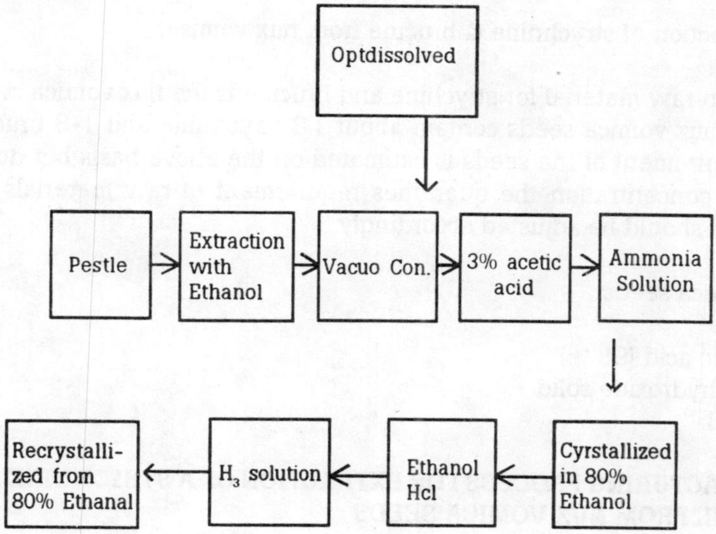

RAW MATERIAL REQUIREMENT

For extraction of strychnine & brucine from nux vomica.

The main raw material for strychine and brucine is the nux vomica seeds. Usually nux vomica seeds contain about 1.8 strychnine and 1-8 brucine. The requirement of the seeds is estimated on the above basis but due to varying concentration the quantities requirement of raw materials will vary and should be adjusted accordingly.

Nux vomica seeds
Benzene
Sulphuric acid (98 %)
Sodium hydroxide solid
Charcoal.

MANUFACTURING PROCESS FOR EXTRACTION OF A STRYCHNINE AND BRUCINE FROM NUX VOMICA SEEDS

Process of extracting strychinine and brucine from nux vomica seeds is very simple. It is extracted by solvent extraction method. Generally used solvent are organic aromatic solvent like benzene or toluene. The process of extraction involve, disintegration, blending, extraction, distillation, centrifugation, and filtering etc.

The starting step is the crushing and grinding of a nux vomica seeds. These crushed seeds are then ground in a ball mill.

After grinding the powder of the nux vomica seeds is grade by screening

The ground powder of nux vomica seeds is then subjected to solvent extraction. Two types of extraction units are available. First type is on batch type while the other is of continuous type. Here batch type extraction unit is preferred. The solid and benzene is mixed together after this dissolution the solids are transferred to the second stage and the fresh benzene is again agitated with the treated. With this operation, whole of the strychnine and brucine is dissolved in the benzene and thus separated from the vomical seeds.

The solution of strychnine and brucine is then concentrated in a distillation unit. The vapours thus formed are condensed in a condenser and collected for reuse. The solutions is concentrated to about 20% concentration.

The concentrated solution is then treated with sulphuric acid . The sulphuric acid is added to the concentrated solution of strychine and brucine very slowly with constant agitation.

The sulphuric acid reacts with strychine and forms strychnine sulphate precipitates and filtered. The precipitate contains pure strychnine. They filtrate from the reactor contains mostly brucine.

The precipitate of strychnine sulphate is decolarised with the help of animal charcoal. The solution of strychnine sulphate is distilled water is mixed with charcoal and boiled and then filtered in a filtered in a filter the decolourized struchine sulphate is then treated with sodium hydroxide. The sodium hydroxide reacts with strychine sulphate is then treated with sodium hydroxide. The sodium hydroxide reacts with strychine sulphate is then treated with sodium hydroxide. The sodium hydroxide reacts with strychine sulphate and forms sodium sulphate leaving behind pure strychine in solution. The solution is then evaporated to dryness; This dried strychine is packed in tin packaging in 100 grams packing.

The filtered obtained from the stainless steel reactor is fed to a distillation column. The brucine is separated as the overhead product and then dried and packed.

Sometimes the struchine separated from the centrifuge suitable and recommended method. The crystals of strychnine is separated with the help speed centrifuge the process flow sheet will clear the process.

PROCESS FLOW SHEET FOR THE MANUFACTURE OF STRYCHNINE AND BRUCINE

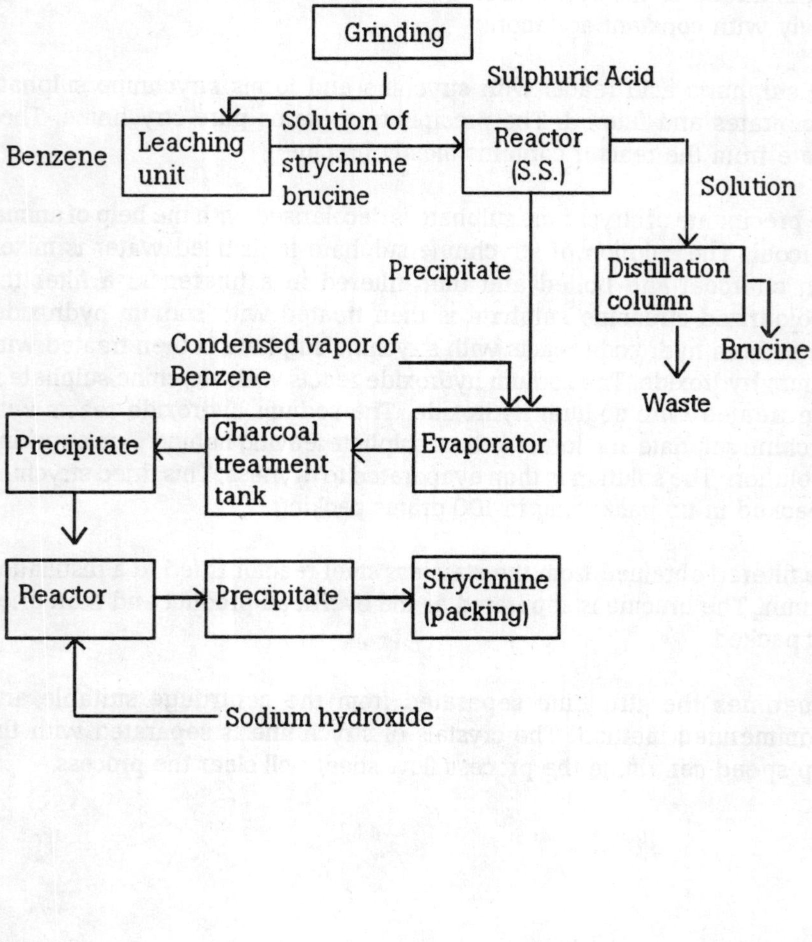

MEDICINAL PLANT EXTRACTS
PLANT ECONOMICS

Rated Plant Capacity

(A) 700 Kgs/annum
Alkaloids From Vinca Rosea.

(B) 600 Kgs/annum
Alkaloids from Solanum Khasianum.

(C) 600 Kgs/annum
Strychnine From Nux Vomica Seeds.

(D) 600 Kgs/annum
Brucine From Nux Vomica Seeds.

LAND & BUILDING

1. Total land required 1000 Sq.Mt. Rs. 13,52,000.00

PLANT & MACHINERY

1. **FOR MEDICINAL PLANT EXTRACTS.**
3. Solvent extraction unit
4. Column
5. Filter
6. Crystallizer
7. Storage tank
8. Drier
9. Circulation pump for solvent
10. Vacuum oven
11. **FOR EXTRACTION OF ALKALOIDS FROM SOLANUM KHASINUM.**
12. Solvent extraction unit
13. Column
14. Chaff cutter
15. Pulverizer
16. Tray drier
17. Circular pump for solvent
18. Storage tanks
19. **FOR EXTRACTION OF STRYCHNINE &BRUCINE FROM NUX VOMICA SEEDS.**
20. Solvent extraction unit
23. Filter
24. Reactor
25. Mini centrifuge
26. Evaporator
27. Charcoal treatment tank

28. Storage tank
29. Storage tank
30. Packing machine
31. Boiler steam generating
32. D.G.set
33. Lab equipments.
34. Process control & instrumentation.
35. Miscellaneous viz pipe fittings, valves, pumps, waters, etc.

FIXED CAPITAL

1. Land & Building	Rs.	13,52,000.00
2. Plant & Machinery	Rs.	43,25,000.07
3. Other Fixed Assets	Rs.	6,25,000.00
TOTAL	Rs.	63,02,000.07

RAW MATERIALS

1. FOR EXTRACTION OF ALKALOIDS FROM VINCA ROSEA.
2. Vinca rosea leaves
3. Chemicals, viz, ethanol, acetic acid, ammonia etc.

4. FOR EXTRACTION OF ALKALOIDS FROM SOLANUM KHASIANUM
5. Berries containing alkaloids
6. Chemicals viz ethanol, acetic acid,ammonia, etc.

7. FOR EXTRACTION OF STRYCHNINE & BRUCINE FROM NUX VOMICA SEEDS.
8. Nux vomica seeds
9. Benzene
10. Sulphuric acid
11. Charcoal
12. Sodium hydroxide
13. Packing material

TOTAL WORKING CAPITAL/MONTH

1. Raw Material	Rs.	1,25,680.04
2. Salary & Wages	Rs.	1,00,000.00
3. Utilities & Overheads	Rs.	39,700.00
TOTAL	Rs.	2,65,380.04

TOTAL CAPITAL INVESTMENT

Total Fixed Capital	Rs.	63,02,000.07
Total Working Capital for 3 Months	Rs.	7,96,140.12
TOTAL	Rs.	70,98,140.19

TURN OVER/ANNUM

1. Alkaloids from vinca rosea
2. Alkaloids from solanum khasianum
3. Strychnine from nux vomica seeds
4. Brucine from nux vomica seeds — Rs. 91,00,000.00

PROFIT SALES RATIO = Profit / Sales x 100 = 38.22 %

RATE OF RETURN = Operating profit / T.C.I x 100 = 49.00 %

BREAK EVEN POINT (B.E.P) = 47.19 %

Chapter 46

MANUFACTURERS/SUPPLIERS OF AGRICULTURAL EQUIPMENTS & IMPLEMENTS

American Spring & Pressing Works Ltd.
P.O.Box No.7602, ASPEE House
B.J. Patel Road, Malad (W)
Mumbai - 91(022)8822336
Ph:. 8822331,2,3,5* 882034
Mfrs. of : Aspee Sprayers & Dusters

A1-Sampatmal Manoj Kumar
9, Clive Row, Floor-2
Kolkata - 700001
Ph:. 2429093
Mfrs. of : Sprinklers, Teflon Washers Sheet Rubber Etc.

Ambica Cultivators
Ambawadia, Near Ranipur Village
Norol, Ahmedabad - 382405
Ph:. 5832298
Mfrs. of : Agriculture Equipments & All Types of general Fabrication

Ambica Industries
NR Shakti Estate, Narol-Isanpur Road
Ahmedabad
Ph:. 5352795
Mfrs. of : Agri Equipment, Tract/ Trailors

A.S. Mechanical Works
Railway Road, Morinda - 140101
(Rup Nagar) Punjab
Ph:. 01888-30539
Mfrs. of : Agricultural Implements

Azad Agros
Near Aam Khas Bagh
Bassi Road, Sirhind
Mandi - 14046 (Punjab)
Ph:. 01763-21376, 22376
Mfrs. of : All Kinds of Agricultural Implements & Sewing Machine Parts
Spl.in : Blades of All Kinds of Reapers & Combines

Atma Singh Engg. Works
Chandigarh Road
Samrala - 141114
(Ludhiana) Punjab
Ph:. 01628-62029
Mfrs. of : Haramba Threshers, Seed Drill & Patoli, High Class Sewing

Machine, Parts & Quality Parts & Quality Mark Agricultural Implements

Associated Agencies
21, Commercial Road
Ootacamund - 643001
Ph:. 0423-42398
Mfrs. of : Apee Sprayers, Dusters & Their Spares

Agro Sprayers
J-/16, Rajouri Garden
New Delhi - 110027
Ph:. 011-5190516
Mfrs. of : All kinds of Agriculture Sprayers, Spares Parts, Plastic & Brass Nozzels, Manual & Hand Operator Sprayers

Alfa-88
Sant Nagar, Basti Sheikh
Jalandhar (Punjab)
Ph:. 0181-251997, 205875, 205876
Fax: 91-181-255437
E-Mail : modspray@vsnl.com
Mfrs. of : Plant Protecton Equipments/ Sprayers, Anti-Malaria & Agricultural Sprayers (Single & Double Handle)

Aquapump Industries
Aquapump Engineering
Tudiyalur Post
Coimbatore - 641034
Ph:. 842484
Fax: 0422842128
Branch Off:Shop No.3 Palak Complex
Ramji Mandir Road, Maninagar
Ahmedabad - 380008
Ph:. 2114418
Mfrs. of : Domestic Pumps, Jet Pumps Electric Motors, Submersible Pumpsets Suitable for Bores

Amar Agriculture Equipment Works
Janta Nagar Gill Road
Ludhiana (Punjab)
Ph:. 0161-491780, 493128
Fax: 0161-491780
Mfrs. of : Seed Drill Etc.

Agrico Equipments (India) Pvt. Ltd.
S.K. Engineering Work
1753/129, Shanti Nagar
Tri Nagar, Delhi - 110035
Ph:. 011-71195099
Fax: 91-11-7104001
E-Mail : agrico@nda.vsnl.net.in
Mfrs. of : Asian Turbo, Asian Classic Asian Super, Asian Standard

Bir Singh & Sons
Chandigarh Road
Samrala - 141114
Ludhiana (Punjab)
Ph:. 01628-62316
Mfrs. of : Haramba Thresher, Seed Drill Land Pastoli Etc.

Bhajan Agriculture & Mechanical Works
Near Khem Singh Petrol Pump
G.T. Road, Doraha-141421 (Punjab)
Distt. Ludhiana
Ph:. 01628-41439

Bengal Metal Works
69A, Serpentine Lane
Kolkata - 700014
Ph:. 271533, 266514
Fax: 91-33-266514, 2489728
Mfrs. of : Trailers up to 100 Tonne, Tankers, Tractor Drawn Agricultural Implements, Towinc Winches, Dozer Front & Loaderws etc.

B.R. Enterprises
Shop No.16, Opp. Indra Market
Old Subzi Mandi
Delhi - 110007
Ph:. 011-3929120, 3962484
Fax: 011-3962484
Mfrs. Of : Agriculture Sprayers of All Kind & Their Spares, Plastic Nozzels Garden Tools, Flowers, Seed & All kinds of Vegetables Seeds

Beta Engineers
1534, Paposian, Narela
Delhi - 110040
Ph:. 011-7281507
Fax: 011-7281926
Mfrs. of : Agriculture Plant Protection Equipment/Anti-Malaria & other Pest Control Sprayers & Spare Parts

Bajaj Tempo Ltd.
Bombay Puna Road
Akurdi, Pune - 411035
Ph:. 0212-776380/81/82
Fax: 0212-773017
E-Mail : tempo-mktg@satyam.net.in

Brahma Styer Tractors Ltd.
33-34, Industrial Area
Phase-II
Chandigarh
Ph:. 652876, 652163
Fax: 652369
E-Mail : brahma@chl.vsnl.net.in
Mfrs. of : Tractors

Buhler (India) Ltd.
13D, Kiadb Industrial Area
Attibele - 562107
Bangalore Distt.
Ph:. 080-420212, 420413, 420315, 09844000115
Fax: 080-420314, 420317
E-Mail : buhlmktg@blr.vsnl.net.in
Mfrs. of : Colour Sorter Sortex 90003'& Vertical Whitener Dsrf

Carryon Trailers Pvt. Ltd.
259, Linghi Chetty Street
Chennai - 600001
Ph:. 6272711
Mfrs. of : Articulated Semi Trailers, Flat Bed Trailers, Semi Low Bed trailers, Low Bed/Well Bed Trailers with multiaxle Trailer, L.P.G. Trailer Running Gear

Champion Implements
Plot No. 32/3, HSIDC
Karnal - 132001
Ph:. 0184-261691
Fax: 91-0184-25211

Controlled Environments Ltd.
590, Beery Street
Winnipeg, Manitola R3HOS1
Canada
Ph:. 204-786-6451
Fax: 204-786-7736
Mfrs. of : Agriculture Machinery Brooders & Incubators, Constant Temperature Apparatus, Laboratory

Dashmesh Agriculture Works
Hind Agriculture Industries
Bhatinda Road
Rampura Phul - 151103
Ph:. 01651-20472
Mfrs. of : Wheat Thresher, Trolley Harrow, Cultivator Etc.

Droli Agriculture Works
D-33, Focal Point
Moga (Punjab)
Ph:. 01636-23101, 60031
Mfrs. of : Self Feeding Wheat

Threshes, Seed Drill, Automatic Potato, Planter, Potato Digger Straw Reaper

Darshan Agro Industries
Plot No.7052, ATI College
Backside, Kartar Chowk
Syan Street No. 14/2, Durga Nagar
Ludhiana - 141003
Ph:. 495910
Fax: 91-161-534150
Mfrs. of : V-Belt Pulley, Haramba Pulley, Combine Pulley, Reaper Pully, Motor Pulley, Slide Rail & Slit Pulley & All kinds Agriculture Machinery Pulleys

D.M. Enterprises
94, DSIDC, New Wazirpur Industrial Complex
Delhi - 110052
Ph:. 7247147, 7429383
Mfrs. of : Agro Sprayers & Spare Parts & Plastic Nozzels

Diplast Plastics Ltd.
C-36, Industrial Area, Phase-II
Mohali (Punjab)
Near Chandigarh - 160055
Ph:. 673942, 220876
Fax: 0172-670224
E-Mail : diplast@seekindia.com

Embassy of Spain
Commercial Office
2, Palam Marg, Vikas Marg
New Delhi - 110057
Ph:. 91-11-6145196/5205/5206
Fax: 91-11-6143217
E-Mail :
comoffice.spain@nuevadelhi.ofcomes,mex.es

Escorts Ltd.
Agriculture Machinery Group
18/4, Mathura Road
Faridabad - 121007
Ph:. 0129-284911
Fax: 0129-284839

Fine Engineering Works
Majestic Road
Moga - 142001 (Punjab)
Ph:. 01636-23060, 20141
(Wheat Threshers, Cutter Thresher, Disc. Harrow (Bearing Type) Seed Drill, Automatic Potato Planter etc.)

Frick India Ltd.
7/15, Kirtinagar Industrial Area
New Delhi - 110015
Ph:. 5463706, 5463798
Fax: 5154228, 5413119
E-Mail : frick.wiprobt.ems.vsnl.net.in
(Exposition to Potential Customers)

Gradex
808, Antriksh Bhawan
22, K.G. Marg
New Delhi - 110001
Ph:. 3715431
Fax: 3715096
(Comprehensive Range of Garden & Agriculture Tools Mattock Plks, Shovels, Pruners, Spades Forks, Hoes, Rakes, Hedge Shear European, American, British, African Models)

Gahir Agro Industries Pvt. Ltd.
Near Bus Stand
Sunam - 148028 (Punjab)
Ph:. 01676-20280, 22680
Fax: 20480
E-Mail : gahir@vsnl.com
(High Class Agriculture Implemented & Gahir Combine Harvester)

G.B. Agro Industries
1206/1, Rithala
Delhi - 110085
Ph:. 7046789
Fax: 7054143
(Power Sprayers & All Types of Plunger Pumps, HSP, HDP, HTP)

Green Nursery & Florist's
9, Pakhowal Road
Ludhiana
Ph:. 403957
(Marriage Palace & Home Decoration Welding Cars & Room Decoration, Bouquets Baskets, Jaimala, Vanie, Gazra & Garlands, Lawn Mowers, Garden Tools, Flower Seeds, Fancy Pots)

Greaves Ltd.
1, Dr. V.B. Gandhi Marg
Mumbai - 400001
Ph:. 2671524, 2674913
Fax: 2677850
E-Mail :
greaves@grvsbom.xeebom.seemail.ems.vsnl.net.in
(Engines, Gensets, Gear Boxes, Fluid Couplings, Rock Roller Bits, Pumps & Pumpsets Steam Traps)

Gem Engineering Pvt. Ltd.
P.B.No.1, Khandsa Road
Gurgaon - 122001
Ph:. 0091-124-6373701-06 (6 Lines)
Fax: 0091-124-6373708
E-Mail : gemengindia@yahoo.com
(Economical high performance Machinery for Storage Conveying)

Hymatic Agro Equipment Pvt. Ltd.
301, Kanchan House
Karampura Commercial Complex
New Delhi - 110015
Ph:. 5415868, 5421677, 5938130
Fax: 5458097, 5464933
(Agriculture Sprayers & Dusters etc.)

International Tractors Ltd.
Sonaloka House
283, AGCR Enclave
Karkarduma, Delhi - 110092
Ph:. 2163791
Fax: 2150492
Mfrs. of : Tractors, Multicrop Thresher, Submersible Pump, reper, Agri Equipments

International Tractors Ltd.
Sonaloka House
383, ACCR Enclave
Karkarduma, Delhi - 110092
Plant-Jalandhar Road
Industrial Estate
Hoshiarpur - 146001
Ph:. 2163785, 2163789, 2163791
Fax: 0091-11-2150492
E-Mail : lacjman@del2.vsnl.net.in
(Tractors, Threshers)

Jigar Enterprises
Khajurini Pole, Kadiakui, Relief Road
Ahmedabad - 1
Ph:. 334619, 339475
Mfrs. of : Chemical Process Pumps

Joginder Singh & Sons
Sugar Mill Road
Morinda (Ropar) Punjab
Ph:. 01888-30581
(High Class Agricultural Implements & Machinery Parts)

J.K. Agro Industries
Amloha Road, Near Petrol Pump

Mandi Gobind Garh - 147301
Ph:. 57906
(Head Gear, Combine Gears, Straw Reaper Gears)

Jagat Sukh Industries
Passi Chowk Pakhowal Road
Ludhiana - 141002
Ph:. 91-161-560919
E-Mail : jsukh@usa.net
(Charlie, Knapsack Sprayers)

John Flower India Ltd.
Sarjapur Road
Bangalore - 560034
Ph:. 080-5530026
Fax: 091-80-5533228
E-Mail : jfil@blr.vsnl.net.in
(Pre Cleaners,Fine Cleaners, Gravity Separators, Destoners, Seed Treators, Indent Cylinders, Z elevators, Seed/ Grain Processing Plants)

Kirloskar Brothers Ltd.
Udyog Bhavan, Tilak Road
Pune - 411002
Ph:. 0212-453455
Fax: 0212-434198, 431156
E-Mail : kbl@giaspn01.vsnl.net.in
Website : www.kirloskar-kbl.com

Madhur Agro Equipments Pvt. Ltd.
34, Friends Colony
Chambaghat - 173213
Solan (H.P)
Ph:. 01792-30336, 30436, 20536, 24436
Fax: 01792-24436
E-Mail : madhurae@nde.vsnl.net.in
Website : www.business.vsnl.com/madhursprayers
Mfrs. of : Quality Agricultural Sprayers

Mahalaxmi Precision Works
214, Madhani Industrial Estate
Senapati Bapat Marg, Dadar
Mumbai - 400028
Ph:. 4220647, 4228823
(Agriculture Implements such as Naspak Sprayer, Rotary Duster, Steel & Wooden Furnitures H.S.S. Reamer, End Mills Slot Drills Extra-Long & Other Special Cutting Tools)

Mitushi Enterprises
F-168-C, Rajouri Garden
New Delhi - 110027
Fact.: C-323, Maya Puri, Phase-II
New Delhi - 110064
Ph:. 5194836, 5422290
Fax: 011-5110341
E-Mail : mitushienterprises@hotmail.com
(Agriculture Sprayers & Dusters)

Naveen Industries
80, Vijay Nagar, Near Bye Pass
Delhi Side, G.T. Road
Karnal (Haryana)
Ph:. 262745, 262962
(Massey Type, Escort Type Pin to Pin Type-Cultivator & Harrow)

New Solar Engineering Works
174, Hapur Road
Ghaziabad - 201001
Ph:. 545-732867
Fax: 575-711948

Osaw Agro Industries
P.O.Box No. 5
Osaw Complex, Jagadhri Road
Ambala Cantt - 133001
Ph:. 91-171-652154, 652167, 652147

Fax: 91-171-652018, 652102
(Other seed Processing & Testing Equipment)

Ocean Agro (India) Ltd.
76 GIDC Nandesari
Baroda - 391340
Ph:. 0265-840307
Fax: 0265-840407
E-Mail : oail@ad.1.vsnl.net.in
(Natural Viricide, Plant Growth Promotors Enzymes, Garden products Soil Applications Drip, Sprinkler & Pipe)

Punjab Tractors Ltd.
Sahibzada Ajit Singh
Nagar - 160055
(Near to Chandigarh)
Mfrs. of : Swaraj 8100 combine Harvestor

Pritam Singh & Sons
B-12, Maya Puri Phase-I
New Delhi - 110064
Ph:. 5130970, 5142916
Fax: 91-11-5139027
(Harrows, Disc Plough, M.B. Plough Tillers)

Phoel Industries
G-8, Kripa Bhawan
Model Town-III
Delhi - 110009
Ph:. 7116973
Fax: 7436974
Mfrs. of : Sprinkler, Irrigation System & Drip Irrigation System, Special Irrigation System Available for Green House/Farm House

Pal Agro Industries
Kularan Road
Sunam - 148028 (Punjab)
Ph:. 20527
(Self Propelled Combine Tractor Mounted Combine Straw Reaper)

Panesar Repairing Works
Wathinda Road, Chima Mandi
Distt. Sangrur)Punjab)
Ph:. 01676-84251 (P.P)
(Hydraulic Trolley, Cultivator, Seed Drill & All Types of Agriculture Implements)

Punjab Agriculture Industries
Near P.W.D. Resi House
Rampura, Phul - 151103
Bhatinda (Punjab)
Ph:. 01651-20462
(Cutter Thresher Etc.)

Punjab Agro Engineers
Railway Road
Sirhind - 140406
Dist. Fathgarh
Sahib (Punjab)
Ph:. 01763-20107
(Agriculture Implements as per BIS)

Paramjit Engineering Works
C-5, Basement, Rajouri Garden
New Delhi - 110027
Ph:. 5418584, 5430245
(Quality Tractor Implements, Linkage Parts & Replacement Parts for Road Massey, Escorts & HMT)

Pardesi Industries
Palahi Gate, Street No. 10
Phagwara (Punjab)
Ph:. 01824-62508
Supplier of : Oil Engine & Spray Parts)

Punjab Agro Industries Co. Ltd.
2-A, Sector 28-A
Madhya Marg, Chandigarh
Ph:. 651561, 656241, 656242, 651576
Fax: 651561, 657398, 656270
E-Mail : pbagro@ch1.vsnl.net.in
(Marketing of Agriculture inputs i.e. Fertilizers, Pesticides, Tractors of Agro based Industries in the areas of food processing agro residues utilization, Agro chemicals & agro products & procurement of foodgrains)

R.K. Sprayer Equipments Pvt. Ltd.
138, Transport Centre
New Subzi Mandi
Azadpur, Delhi - 110033
Ph:. 7139788, 7450772, 7442633
E-Mail : koul@bol.net.in
(Aspee sprayer with honda GK-200 Engine, Honda Water Pump)

R.S. Products Pvt. Ltd.
A-22, Okhla Industrial Area
Phase-I, New Delhi - 110020
Ph:. 6813189, 6810413
Fax: 011-6466134
(Irrigation Equipments, Drip, Micro Sprinklers, Mini Sprinklers, Foggers, Mister, Prop Sprinklers etc.)

Swastik Wheels India
Ami Nagar, Sarai Road
Barut - 250611
Ph:. 62461, 64840
Mfrs. of : All Kinds of A.D.V. Wheels, Axles, Double Plate Wheels & other Agricultural Goods

Super Agro Industry
2/110, Daya Basti
New Rohtak Road
New Delhi - 110005
Ph:. 5758743, 5758937
Mfrs. of : All types of sprinkler & Accessories, Foot Betton, Lachen Clump, Pipe Fitting & Aluminium

Surendra Earthmovers
GF-4, B3/4, Ansal Building
Dr. Mukherjee Nagar
Commercial Complex
Delhi - 110009
Ph:. 7653711, 7651717
Fax: 7258990
Mfrs. of : Mitsubishi Shakti Power Tilers, Tractors & Implements

Surendra Agro Equipment
Anaz Mandi, Samraj Road
Khanna - 141401
Mfrs. of : Mitsubishi shaki Power Tilers, Tractors & Implements

Shah Irrigation Systems
111/113, Vithalwadi, Kalbadevi
Mumbai - 400002
Ph:. 2018174
Mfrs. of : Distr. Rain Bird (America) Drip & Sprinkler Systems for Garden Landscape, Golf & Agriculture

Spraywell Industries
4659, Roshanara Road
(Near Jaipur Tyres)
Delhi - 110007
Ph:. 3918995, 232449
Mfrs. of : Agriculture Sprayers & spare parts

Sonalika Agriculture Industries
704, Nirmal Tower
Barakhamba Road
New Delhi - 110001
Ph:. 3318911

Fax: 3714768
Mfrs. of : Tractors, Multicrop, Threshers, Submersible I.E. Pumps, Agri-Implements

Sprayers India
16/10, 181-82, Bhagwandass House
Chowk Gurudwara Road
Ph:. 5734384, 5710856
Fax: 5755812, 5781052
(Sprayers & Spare Parts for power Sprayers Cum Duster, Manual & Hand Operated Sprayers Serving Indian)

Shivalik Agro Engineers
S.C.O. 148-149, 1st Floor
Sub City Centre, Sector 34-A
Chandigarh - 160022
Ph:. 0172-645927, 603714
Fax: 0174-609898
Head Office : Near DAV School
Bye Pass Road
Solan - 173212 (H.P)
Ph:. 01792-21861, 20494, 20604
Fax: 01792-21859
Mfrs. of : Sprinkler & Drip Irrigation Systems, Green Houses & Poly Tunnels, Green House & Poly Tunnels, Mulching, Cannal/Pond lining, General Covering etc.

Thomson Agro Industries
82/2, Phase-I, Vatva GIDC
Ahmedabad - 445
Ph:. 5503837
Mfrs. of : Agriculture, Pesticide Sprayer, Helispray Super Battery Operated Sprayer

Thomson Equipments
3, Sheela Apt. B/H Kamal Colony
Navrangpura, Ahmedabad - 9
Ph:. 6562896
Mfrs. of : All type of Agri Pesticide Sprayers-Hell Spray Htp Sprayer

Tractors & Farm Equipment Ltd.
35, Nungambakkam High Road
Chennai - 600034
(Tractors/Agro Based Machine)

Yeshika Irrigation Systems Pvt. Ltd.
D-122A (Post Office Street)
Shakarpur, Delhi - 110092
Ph:. 2051795, 2225030
Fax: 2225040
(Turnkey Projects on Overhead, Pop-Up, Micro Irrigation Systems, Lawn Mowers, Turf Maint. Equipment)

117. MANUFACTURE OF TIN CONTAINERS
118. MANUFACTURE OF STORAGE TANKS, PRESSURE VESSELS. HEAT EXCHANGERS
119. MARK II HAND PUMPS
120. MARUTI WORKSHOP CUM - SERVICE STATION
121. MECHANICAL JACKS
122. METAL CUTTING DIE DESIGN
123. METAL CUTTING OF AND GRINDING WHEELS (ABBRASIVE CUTTING WHEELS)
124. METAL HOOKS & CLIPS
125. METAL SEPARATION (COPPER, TIN, LEAD) FROM SPENT WASH ACID
126. METALLIC RING JOINTS
127. METALLIC GASKET (SPIRAL WOUND)
128. MICROVEE & ABSOLUTE FILTER
129. MICROWAVE OVEN
130. MILD STEEL INGOTS
131. MINI STEEL PLANT
132. MODERN VEHICLE WORKSHOP
133. MOPED
134. M.S.HINGES
135. M.S.INGOT AND HR. STEEL STRUCTURALS
136. M.S.INGOT BY INDUCTION FURNACES
137. M.S.PIPES
138. M.S. WELDING ELECTRODE
139. MUFFLERS & SILENCERS FOR THREE WHEELERS
140. NAIL CUTTER WITH FILER & MANICURE
141. NICHROME WIRE
142. NICKEL LINED SCREENS
143. NON-FERROUS ALLOY ROLLING
144. NON-FERROUS FORGING
145. NON-FERROUS FOUNDRY
146. NON PRESSURE
147. INCANDESCENT LAMP
148. NUMBEP COMBINATION LOCKS FOR LUGGAGES
149. NUTS & BOLTS
150. PAPER COATED ALUMINIUM AND COPPER WIRE
151. PETROMAX CONTAINER
152. PHOTO ETCHING OF STAINLESS STEEL PLATES
153. PIPE GALVANIZING PLANT
154. PISTON RING-AUTOMOBILE
155. PLANT PROTECTION EQUIPMENTS
156. PLATINUM LABORATORY APPARATUS
157. PRESSURE COOKER & ALUMINIUM UTENSILS
158. PRESSURE COOKER (ALUMINIUM)
159. PRESSURE DIE CASTING
160. PRINTED ALUMINIUM COLLAPSIBLE TUBES
161 PRINTED TIN CONTAINERS
162. PRINTING PRESS (CYLINDER MACHINE)
163 PUMPS FOR CHEMICAL INDUSTRY (SPECIAL)
164 RAILWAY SLEEPERS (M.S.)
165 RAZOR TWIN BLADE
166. R.C.C SPUN PIPES
167. RECONDITIONING OF M.S. DRUMS/BARRELS
168. RE-ROLLING COPPER AND BRASS SHEET AND RODS
169. RE-ROLLING MILLS
170. RESIN COATED SAND
171. RESIN CORED SOFT SOLDER WIRES
172. ROLLING MILL (BY INDUCTION FURNACE) & MANUFACTURE OF BARS, ANGLES, SQUARES, TUBES AND OTHERS
173. ROLLER BEARING & FORGING
174. ROLLING OF STAINLESS STEEL PATTA
175. RUBBER INSULATED PLIERS (HAND TOOLS)
176. RUBBING COMPOUND FOR AUTOMOBILES
177. SCIENTIFIC LABORATORY EQUIPMENTS
178. SCOOTER ASSEMBLING
179. SECONDARY LEAD EXTRACTION BY SCRAP BATTERY PLATES, PIPES & SHEET
180. SEAMLESS M.S. TUBES & PIPES
181. SELF TAPPING STEEL SCREW
182. SEWING NEEDLES
183. S.G. IRON & ALLOY STEEL
184. SHEET METAL PRODUCTS, (FERROUS/NON-FERROUS)
185. SHIP/MARINE CONTAINER
186. SHOCK ABSORBERS
187. SHOE EYELETS
188. SHOT AND GRITS BY AUTOMIZATION PROCESS
189. SHOVELS
190. SILICO MANGANESE ALLOYS
191. SILENCERS (MUFFLERS). EXHAUST & TAIL PIPE FOR ALL TYPES OF VEHICLES
192. SINTERED BEARING
193. SINTERED BUSHES
194. SINTERED METAL PRODUCTS
195. SOFT AND HARD FERRITES
196. SPANNERS
197. SPARK PLUGS
198. STEEL PLANT (ELECTRIC ARC FURNACE BASED- EAF)
199. SPHERIODAL GRAPHITE CAST IRON
200. SPRAY DRYER
201. STAINLESS STEEL HINGES
202. STAINLESS STEEL SHEET ROLLING TO PRODUCE STAINLESS STEEL UTENSILS
203. STAINLESS STEEL UTENSILS
204. STAPLE PINS, PAPER PIN, GEM CLIPS ETC.
205. STEEL CASTINGS
206. STEEL CHAIN
207. STEEL FOUNDRY
208. STEEL FURNITURES AND ELECTRICAL APPLIANCES
209. STEEL PLANT (MINI)
210. STEEL RODS AND COILS FROM SCRAPS
211. STEEL ROLLING MILL
212. STEEL STRIPS (COLD ROLLED) SILICON WITH GRAIN RIENTED FOR ELECTRIC USE
213. STEEL TRANSMISSION LINE TOWERS & ROLLING MILL TO PRODUCE STEEL SECTION
214. STEEL FURNITURES AND ELECTRICAL APPLIANCES
215. STEEL WIRE DRAWING AND GALVANIZING
216. STEEL WOOL
217. SUBMERGED ARC WELDED PIPES
218. SUBMERSIBLE PUMP MANUFACTURING
219. SUPER ENAMELLED COPPER WIRE
220. THREE WHEELERS
221. TIE-ROD ENDS
222. TIN CONTAINERS
223. TOOLROOM AND SHEET METAL PRODUCTS
224. TRACTOR TRAILERS
225. TRANSMISSION POWER FITTING
226. TUBULAR POLES
227. SUPER ENAMELLED COPPER WIRES
228. TUBULAR POLES FOR ELECTRICAL TRANSMISSION (BY FABRICATION PROCESS)
229. TUBULAR POLES OF M.S. & HIGH TENSILE STEEL
230. VACUUM CLEANERS
231. VACUUM FLASK (STAINLESS STEEL)
232. VALVES FOR REFRIGERATION AND AIR-CONDITION
233. VEHICLE WELDING & PAINTING
234. VENETION BLIND
235. WASHING MACHINES (AUTOMATIC & COMPUTERISED)
236. WATER CONTROLLER (AUTOMATIC)
237. WATCH STRAPS/CHAINS/ BRACELETS/BELT BRASS & STAINLESS STEEL
238. WATER COOLERS
239. WELDED WIRE MESH
240. WELDING ELECTRODES
241. WICK STOVES
242. WIND MILL WINDOW FRAME (FERROUS & NON-FERROUS)
243. WRIST WATCH

359. DI ETHYL OXALATE
360. DI METHYL ORTHOPHTHALATE
361. DI-METHYL PHTHALATE
362. DICLOFENAC GEL
363. DIOCTYL PHTHALATE (DOP)
364. DI PHENYL GLYCERINE
365. DI PHENYL OXIDE
366. DINITRO-CHLORO BENZENE
367. DISTILLED WATER
368. DODECYL BENZENE SULPHONATE
369. DUSTLESS CHALK
370. EDTA & ITS SALTS
371. ELECTROLESS NICKEL PLATING ON PLASTICS
372. ENDOSULFAN
373. EPOXY RESIN BASED COMPOUND
374. ETHYL ACETATE
375. EHTYL ETHER
376. ETHYL ALCOHOL (POTABLE LIQUOR)
377. ETHYL HEXANOL
378. EXTRACTION OF ESSENTIAL OILS BY SUGAR CRITICAL FLUID (CARBON DIOXIDE) METHOD FROM FLOWERS, HERBAL & SPICES
379. FERRIC ALUM
380. FERRO CHROME LIGNO SULPHONATE
381. FERRO MANGANESE
382. FERRO SILICONE
383. FERRO VANADIUM FROM VANADIUM SLUDGE
384. FERROUS SILICATE
385. FERROUS SULPHATE
386. FERTILIZER FROM ANIMAL BLOOD & LEATHER WASTE
387. FLUORESCENT TUBE LIGHT POWDER
388. FOAMED PVC COMPOUNDING & ITS PRODUCTS
389. FORMALDEHYDE
390. FRACTIONAL DISTILLATION OF D.M.O (DEMENTHOLIZED OIL)
391. FRACTIONAL DISTILLATION OF ESSENTIAL OIL & MEDICINAL PLANT EXTRACT
392. FRICTION DUST (LIQUID & POWDER) FROM CNSL
393. FRUIT FLAVOURS
394. FURFURAL FROM RICE HUSK
395. GARLIC ACID
396. GASKET SHELLAC COMPOUND
397. GEAR OIL
398. GIBBERELLIC ACID
399. GLASS PUTTY
400. GLYCERINE
401. GOSSYPOL (POLY PHENOL) FROM COTTON SEED OIL
402. GUAR GUM POWDER
403. HAIR FIXER (HAIR GEL TYPE)
404. H - ACID
405. HENNA PASTE MAKING
406. HEPTAL DEHYDE
407. HIGH CARBON FERRO CHROME
408. HYDRATED CALCIUM SILICATE BRICK
409. HYDRATED LIME FROM SEA SHELL
410. HYDROCHLORIC ACID
411. HYDRO FLUORIC ACID
412. HYDROGEN PEROXIDE (BY AUTO-OXIDATION PROCESS)
413. ICE PACKS (SOLUTIONS TYPE, WHITE GEL TYPE, VIOLET SEMI SOLID POLYMER TYPE)
414. IMPROVING DROP POINT PARAFFIN WAX FROM 45-50°C TO 75-80°C
415. INDUSTRIAL ALCOHOL
416. INTEGERATED COMPLEX OF EASTER & ALLIED PRODUCTS (D.O.P, D.B.P, ETHYL ACETATE WIRE ENAMEL & CABLE JELLY)
417. IMFL (WHISKY) & COUNTRY LIQUOR
418. IRON OXIDE FOR MAKING FERITTE
419. IRON SULPHIDE
420. JUTE BATCHING OIL
421. KESH KALA TEL (HAIR DYE LOTION) (VASMOL 33, BLACK NITE TYPE)
422. L-LYSINE MONOHYDROCHLORIDE
423. LACTIC ACID FROM WHITE SUGAR BY FERMENTATION PROCESS
424. LDPE GRANULES FROM VIRGIN (LDPE RESIN)
425. LEAD EXTRACTION FROM BATTERY SCRAP
426. LEAD OXIDE (A) LEAD MONOXIDE (B) LEAD TETRA OXIDE (C) GREYLEAD OXIDE
427. LIQUID GLUCOSE & ITS BY PRODUCTS
428. LIQUID OXYGEN BOTTLING PLANT
429. LIQUID SHOE POLISH
430. LIQUID.FLOOR POLISH
431. LUBE OIL VISCOSITY IMPROVED FOR P.P.G/P.E.G.
432. LUBRICANTS ASHLESS 100% COMBUSTION
433. MAGNESIUM CARBONATE AND MAGNESIUM BICARMONATE
434. MAGNESIUM HYDROXIDE POWDER
435. MAGNESIUM SILICATE
436. MAGNESIUM SULPHATE
437. MALACHITE GREEN
438. MALEIC ANHYDRIDE
439. MANGANESE SULPHATE
440. MANUFACTURING OF CARBON MONO-OXIDE WATER GAS
441. MENTHOL BOLD CRYSTALS FROM FLAKES
442. MENTHOL CRYSTAL & MENTHA OIL
443. MERCURIC OXIDE
444. METAL PRE-TREATMENT CHEMICALS
445. METHANE GAS BY SODIUM ACETATE & SODA LIME
446. METHYL ACETYL RICINOLATE
447. METOL
448. METOL FROM HYDROQUI-NONE & METHYLAMINE
449. MICANITE
450. MICRO NUTRIENT MIXTURE
451. MINERAL WATER
452. MINERAL WATER AND PET BOTTILNG PLANT
453. MINERAL WATER IN BOTTLES, GLASS AND POUCHES
454. MINI CEMENT PLANT (BY ROTARY KILN PROCESS)
455. MIXED FERTILIZER
456. MOSQUITO & FLIES REPELLENT AGARBATTI (INCENSE STICKS)
457. MONO CHLORO ACETIC ACID
458. MONOCROTOPHOS (TECHNICAL)
459. MOSQUITO COIL
460. MOSQUITO COIL & MAT
461. MOSQUITO MAT
462. MOTHER TINCTURE & BIO CHEMIC MEDICINES
463. NAPHTHALENE & PHENYL (INTEGRATED UNIT)
464. NATURAL MINERAL WATER BY REVERSE OSMOSIS PROCESS
465. NICKEL PLATING BRIGHTNER (PRIMARY OR CARRIER BRIGHTNER & SECONDARY BRIGHTNER)
466. NICKEL SULPHATE
467. NICOTINE FROM TOBACCO WASTE
468. NICOTINE SULPHATE FROM TOBACCO WASTE
469. NITRO BENZENE
470. NITRO CELLULOSE SANDING SEALER/LACQUER
471. NITRO MUSK
472. NITROGEN & OXYGEN GAS PLANT
473. NON-IONIC SURFACTANT (WETTING AGENT)
474. NO-CARB PASTE
475. OCTANOL
476. ORTHO NITRO PHENOL
477. OXALIC ACID FROM MOLASSES
478. OXALIC ACID FROMRICE HUSK
479. OXALIC ACID FROM TREE BARK
470. OXALIC ACID FROM WASTE VEGETABLES
471. OXYGEN GAS PLANT
472. OXYGEN GAS PLANT (AIR SEPERATION METHOD)
473. PARA-AMINO BENZOIC ACID
474. PARA-AMINO PHENOL
475. PARA TOLUENE SULPHONIC ACID
476. PECTIN FROM RAW PAPAYA
477. PERFUME (LEMON & OTHERS)

CRUDE NAPHTHA
570. TRIMETHYL AMMONIUM CHLORIDE
571. TRIPHENYL PHOSPHITE (T.P.P)
572. ULTRAMARINE BLUE (LIQUID)
573. UREA FORMALDEHYDE & MELAMINE FORMALDEHYDE POWDER
574. UNDECYLINIC ACID
575. VINYL ACETATE MONOMER
576. VITAMIN C
577. VITAMIN E
578. WASTE WATER TREATMENT PLANT FOR INDUSTRIAL SECTOR IN INDIA (ONLY MARKER SURVEY)
579. WIRE DRAWING LUBRICANT
580. WIRE ENAMEL
581. XANTHATES
582. YELLOW DEXTRIN
583. ZINC CHLORIDE
584. ZINC OXIDE
585. ZINC PHOSPHATING BY COLD PROCESS
586. ZINC SILICATE
587. ZINC STEARATE
588. ZINC SULPHATE
589. ZINC SULPHATE MONOHYDRATE
590. ACID BLACK
591. AURAMINE'O'
592. AZO DYES STUFF
593. DYE & DYE INTERMEDIATE
594. DYE INTERMEDIATES
595. MALACHITE GREEN
596. METHYLENE BLUE
597. PHTHALOCYANINE BLUE
598. PHTHALOCYANINE BLUE & GREEN
599. REACTIVE DYES
600. SULPHUR BLACK DYE
601. VAT DYES
602. WATER CHILLING PLANT
603. WADDING OIL (100%) FOR WADDING OF COTTON HOSIERY CLOTH IN THE DYEING PROCESS
604. WHITE OIL
605. WAX FLOOR POLISH

ELECTRICAL, ELECTONICS, COMPUTERS AND INFOTECH/IT PROJECTS

606. AIR CONDITIONING
607. ALUMINIUM ALLOY CONDUCTOR
608. ALUMINIUM CABLE
609. ALUMINIUM ELECTROYTIC CAPACITORS
610. AUDIO CASSETTE ASSEMBLING & RECORDING
611. AUDIO CASSETTES DUPLICATING RECORDING
612. AUDIO CASSETTES & AUDIO STUDIO
613. AUDIO CASSETTES PLANE & RECORDED
614. AUDIO MAGNETIC HEADS
615. AUDIO MAGNETIC TAPE
616. AUDIO/VIDEO CASSETTES
617. AUTO BULB/LAMPS
618. AUTOMATIC VOLTAGE STABILIZER
619. BATTERY PLATES
620. BACK OFFICE (Rs. 5000/-)
621. B/W TV & COMPUTER MONITOR PICTURE TUBE
622. BREAD BOARDS
623. CALL CENTRE
624. CAMERA (35 MM)
625. CAPACITORS
626. CARBON ELECTRODE USED FOR BATTERY CELL
627. CARBON POTETIOMETERS
628. CEILING FAN
629. CERAMIC INSULATOR
630. CHILDREN INFOTECH TRAINING INSTITUTE (Rs. 5000/-)
631. CHOKE AND PATTI
632. CHOKE AND STARTER
633. CHOKE USED FOR FLUORESCENT LAMPS
634. COLOUR TELEVISION
635. COLOUR AND BLACK & WHITE TELEVISION
636. COMPACT DISC
637. COMPACT DISC PLAYER (AUDIO/VIDEO)
638. COMPUTER EDUCATION INSTITUTE
639. COMPUTER ASSEMBLY
640. COMPUTER HARDWARE
641. COMPUTER KEYBOARD
642. COMPUTER PERIPHERALS
643. COMPUTER PRINTERS
644. COMPUTER RIBBON
645. COMPUTER RIBBON REINKING OR REFILLING
646. COMPUTER STATIONERY
647. COMPUTER STATIONERY &

IMPORTED HARDWARE PARTS
648. COMPUTER TERMINALS
649. COMPUTERISED WASHING MACHINE (AUTOMATIC)
650. COMPUTER SOFTWARE
651. CONDENSER FOR MOTOR USING MPP FILM
652. CONTENT DEVELOPMENT CENTRE (EOU) (Rs. 5000/-)
653. CONTROL PANEL BOARD
654. COOLING COIL FOR AIR CONDITIONERS
655. COPPER STRIP COIL FROM SCRAP
656. CORDLESS TELEPHONES
657. CYBER CAFE
658. CYBERKIOSK (Rs. 5000/-)
659. DATA PROCESSING CENTRE (Rs. 5000/-)
660. D.C. MICRO MOTORS
661. D.G.SETS
662. DISH ANTENNA AND CABLE T.V. NETWORK EQUIPMENT
663. DISTRIBUTION TRANSFORMERS & REPAIRS
664. DOMESTIC ELECTRICAL APPLIANCES- ROOM COOLER, WASHING MACHINE, WATER HEATER, ELECTRIC ROOM HEATER
665. E-SCHOOL
666. E-COMMERCE/BUSINESS
667. ELECTRIC ENERGY METER
668. ELECTRIC FANS
669. ELECTRIC HORN FOR AUTOMOBILE
670. ELECTRIC LAMP/GLS (INCANDESCENT LAMP)
671. ELECTRIC MIXER
672. ELECTRIC MOTORS UP TO 10 HP. REWINDING OF ALL TYPES OF MOTORS WATER PUMPS
673. ELECTRIC MOTOR WINDING (FOR FAN, MIXIES, ETC.)
674. ELECTRIC STEAM IRON
675. ELECTRICAL APPLIANCES
676. ELECTRICAL FIXTURES
677. ELECTRICAL STAMPING
678. ELECTROLYTIC CAPACITORS
679. ELECTROMAGNETIC RELAY
680. ELECTRONIC BALAST/CHOK
681. ELECTRICAL CHOKE
682. ELECTRONIC DIGITAL WATCHES
683. ELECTRONIC DIGITAL WEIGHING MACHINE
684. ELECTRONIC FIRE ALARM
685. ELECTRONIC GAS STOVE LIGHTERS
686. ELECTRONIC PRESSURE INDICATORS, ELECTRICALS, ELECTRONIC LIQUID LEVEL INDICATORS, ELECTRONIC TEMPERATURE INDICATOR, DIGITAL TACHOMETER
687. ELECTRONIC TELEPHONE INSTRUMENTS
688. ELECTRONIC TOYS
689. ELECTRONIC WATCHES & CLOCKS
690. FAX MACHINES
691. F.H.P MOTORS
692. FLOPPY DISKETTES
693. FLUORESCENT LAMP STARTER
694. FLUORESCENT TUBULAR

Price Rs. 3675/- for each "Detailed Project Report" Payable in advance through Draft/Cash/M.O. in favour of *"ENGINEERS INDIA RESEARCH INSTITUTE"*. 4449, Nai Sarak (D), Main Road Delhi - 110 006 *OR Ask by V.P.P.* ● Ph : 3918117, 391 6431, 392 0361, 396 0797 ●Fax : 91-11- 391 6431 ●E-Mail : eirisidi@bol.net.in ● WebSite : www.startindustry.com

LAMPS WITH INTRODUCTION TO MERCURY VAPOUR LAMP
695. FRANCHISEE COMPUTER EDUCATION CENTRE (Rs. 5000)
696. GAS DETECTOR (L.P.G)
697. GENERATOR SET & PUMP SETS
698. GENERATOR (BATTERY OPERATED)
699. GIS SERVICE CENTRE (GEOGRAPHICAL INFORMATION SYSTEMS)
700. HARDWARE FITTING FOR TRANSMISSION LINE OVERHEAD LINE MATERIAL
701. HEADERS FOR TRANSISTOR ICS SEMI CONDUCTOR
702. H.T & L.T INSULATORS
703. H.T & M.V INDUSTRIAL CUBICAL SWITCH BOARD
704. INFORMATION MOVING DISPLAY (L.E.D TYPE)
705. INSURANCE CLAIM PROCESSING CENTRE (EOU) (Rs. 5000/-)
706. INTEGRATED CIRCUITS
707. INTERNET BASED STOCK TRADING (Rs. 5000/-)
708. INTERNET SERVICE PROVIDER (I.S.P.)
709. JELLY FILLED TELEPHONE CABLES
710. LAP TOP COMPUTERS
711. LEAD ACID BATTERIES
712. LEAD ACID BATTERY PLATES AND ASSEMBLING OF BATTERY
713. LEGAL TRANSCRIPTION & SECRETARIAL SERVICES CENTER (EOU)(Rs. 5000/-)
714. LIGHT EMITTING DIODES (L.E.D)
715. LINEAR ICS TRAINER KIT
716. LOUD SPEAKER
717. L.T TRANSFORMER REPAIRING
718. MEDICAL TRANSCRIPTION CENTRE
719. METAL FILM RESISTORS
720. METALLISED POLYPROPYLENE, POLYESTER FILM CAPACITOR
721. MICA BASE ELECTRONIC COMPONENTS
722. MICA PAPER WASTE PAPER FROM MICA WASTE
723. MICRO PROCESSORS TRAINER KITS BASED ON MICRO PROCESSORS
724. MINI COMPUTER (PERSONAL COMPUTER)
725. MINIATURE CIRCUIT BREAKER (M.C.B)
726. MINIATURE WATCH BATTERIES (BUTTON CELL)
727. MIXER/GRINDER (MIXI)
728. MONO CHROME COMPUTER MONITOR
729. MOTOR START ELECTROLYTIC CAPACITOR
730. MULTI LAYER P.C.B
731. MULTIPLE RELAY FOR LOW VOLTAGE
732. NEON INDICATOR
733. NEON SIGN MANUFACTURE
734. OPTICAL FIBRE CABLES
735. ON LINE SHOPPING MALL (Rs. 5000/-)
736. OPTO MECHANICAL & ELECTRICAL EQUIPMENTS
737. PHOTO COLOUR LAB
738. PICTURE TUBE (B/W)
739. PLAIN PAPER COPIER
740. PLASTIC FILM CAPACITORS
741. POLYESTER CAPACITORS
742. PORTABLE GENERATOR SET
743. PORTAL
744. PORTABLE TELEVISION(TV)
745. POWER CAPACITORS
746. POWER INVERTERS
747. POWER PLANT
748. POWER TRANSFORMERS UP TO 600 KVA
749. PRINTED CIRCUIT BOARD
750. PVC WIRES & CABLES
751. RE-CONDITIONING OF PICTURE TUBE
752. RESIN CAST CT & PT (1 KV)
753. SEMI CONDUCTOR DEVICE
754. SEMI CONDUCTORS FOR TRANSISTORS & DIODES
755. SETTING UP OF A VIDEO STUDIO
756. SMOKE DETECTORS
757. SOLAR CELLS
758. SOLAR MODULES
759. SOLAR PHOTO VOLTAIC SYSTEM
760. SOLDER FLUXES
761. SOLAR WATER HEATING PANELS
762. STEEL FURNITURE & ELECTRICAL APPLIANCES
763. STEREO AMPLIFIERS
764. STEREO CASSETTE RECORDERS/PLAYERS
765. STREET LIGHT FITTINGS SURGE SUPPRESSOR
766. TANTALUM CAPACITORS
767. TEFLON COATED ELECTRIC CABLE
768. TELEMEDICINE (DISTANCE HEALTH CARE) (Rs. 5000/-)
769. TELEPHONE CORD/CABLE
770. TELEPHONE (PUSH BUTTON TYPE)
771. TELEPHONE (PUSH BUTTON & CORDLESS)
772. TELEVISION (CTV & B/W)
773. TELEVISION (3-D)
774. TELEVISION DEFLECTION COMPONENTS
775. TELEVISION SIGNAL BOOSTERS
776. TELEVISION TUNERS
777. TRACTION BATTERIES
778. TRAINING INSTITUTE OF MEDICAL TRANSCRIPTION
779. TRANSFORMER FOR B/W TV
780. TRANSFORMER FOR VOLTAGE STABILIZER & E.H.T
781. TRANSMISSION POWER LINE FITTING
782. TRANSMISSION TOWER FITTING
783. TV AUDIO EQUIPMENT CABINETS & THEIR ASSEMBLING UNIT
784. UN-INTERRUPTED POWER SUPPLY (U.P.S)
785. VARIABLE FREQUENCY
786. VARIABLE VOLTAGE A.C. DRIVE
787. VIDEO CASSETTES (COMPLETE MANUFACTURING & ASSEMBLING)
788. VIDEO CASSETTES RECORDER (V.C.R)
789. VIDEO FILM STUDIO
790. VOLTAGE REGULATOR FOR AUTOMOBILES
791. VOLTAGE STABILIZERS
792. VOLTAGE STABLIZER & T.V. GAIN BOOSTER
793. WAX AND CHEMICAL COATED, BRAIDED TINSEL WIRE
794. WEBSITE DESIGN & E-MAIL REGISTERING
795. WELDING ELECTRODES
796. WIND ENERGY POWER PROJECT (10 MW) WIRE WOUND POTENTIOMETERS

FOOD, AGRO FOOD, PROCESSED FOOD, AGRO PLANTATION, CULTIVATION, FARMING, DAIRY/MILK, TOBACCO/PAN MASALA, BREWERY & DISTILLERY, EDIBLE OILS, EOU FOOD PRODUCTS AND ALLIED PRODUCTS

797. ALCOHOLIC BEVERAGES & VENEGAR FROM COCONUT WATER
798. ALCOHOL DRINKS FROM ETHYL ALCOHOL BY MIXING OF VARIOUS FLAVOURS
799. ANTI SCALE COMPOUND FOR ADDING INTO SUGAR JUICE BOILING
800. APPLE JUICE CONCENTRATED & DEHYDRATED FRUIT & VEGETABLES
801. ARTIFICIAL FISH MEAL FOR POULTRY FEED
802. AUTOMATIC BISCUIT PLANT
803. BABY CEREAL FOOD AND MILK POWDER
804. BACTERIA FOR CANE JUICE
805. BAKER'S YEAST
806. BAKERY INDUSTRY
807. BANANA PUREE
808. BEER & WINE
809. BEER PLANT (BREWERY)
810. BIDI
811. BIDI & CIGARETTE
812. BISCUIT PLANT

813. BREAD (AUTOMATIC PLANT)
814. BLACK PEPPER (SPICES)
815. BREAD AND BISCUITS
816. BREEDING FARM
817. BROILER CHICKEN
819. BUTTON MUSHROOM CULTIVATION & PROCESSING
820. CANNING OF RASAGULLAS IN METAL CANS
821. CAFFEIN FROM TEA WASTE
822. CANNING OF FRUITS & VEGETABLES
823. CASEIN AND BY-PRODUCTS
824. CASHEW FRUIT JUICE FROM CASHEW FRUIT APPLE
825. CASHEWNUT KERNEL EXTRACTION FROM CASHEWNUT FRUIT
826. CASHEWNUT SHELL LIQUID & KERNEL PROCESSING
827. CASHEW FENI
828. CATECHEU (BY CHEMICAL PROCESS)
829. CATTLE FEED FROM TAPIOCA
830. CHEWING & BUBBLE GUM
831. CHICKEN/SHEEP MEAT PROCESSING
832. CHOCOLATE (MILK)
833. CIGARETTE AND BEEDIES
834. COCOA BUTTER FROM COCOA MASS
835. COCONUT PRODUCTS & BY PRODUCTS PROCESS COMPLEX
836. COLD/SOFT DRINKS
837. COLLECTION OF MILK AND MILK MAKING POWDER
838. COLLECTION OF MILK AND PACKING IN POLYTHENE POUCH (1/2 KG. 1 KG. & 2 KG.)
839. CONDENSED MILK (SWEETNED)
840. CONFECTIONERY INDUSTRY (TOFFEE & CANDY, SEMI-AUTOMATIC PLANT)
841. COUNTRY LIQUOR FROM MOLASSES
842. CIGARETTE
843. DAIRY FARM AND DAIRY (MILK) PRODUCTS (PASTEURISED MILK, BUTTER, GHEE, PANEER)
844. DAIRY FARM TO PRODUCE MILK & PACKING IN POUCHES (50%) & CAN (50%)
845. DAIRY FOR MILK PROCESSING
846. DAIRY FARM (BUFALO)
847. DAL (PULSE) MILL UNIT
848. DEHYDRATION OF CARROT & GARLIC
849. DEHYDRATION & CANNING OF FRUITS & VEGETABLES
850. DEHYDRATION OF FIGS
851. DEHYDRATION OF FRUITS AND VEGETABLES
852. DEHYDRATED ONIONS AND ONION POWDER
853. DRY ICE BY BREAKING OF AIR
854. DRYING OF RED CHILLIES, HALDI, DHANIA, AND GREEN PEAS
855. EGG POWDER (40,000 EGGS PROCESSING PER DAY)
856. EXPORT OF PROCESSED FOODS AND MARINE PRODUCTS
857. FISH CANNING & POUCHING
859. FISH FARMING (PRAWN & OTHER MARINE PRODUCTS)
860. FISH MEAL
861. FLOUR MILL AND MUSTARD OIL
862. FOOD COLOUR & ORASTED GROUNDNUT GRAM PEAS, ETC IN POUCHES
863. FROG LEGS PROCESSING
864. FROZEN MEATS PROCESSING
865. FOOD FLAVOURS (WHISKY) VODKA, GRAPE, BUTTER SCOTCH)
866. FOOD PRODUCTS COMPLEX (DEHYDRATED ONIONS, GARLIC POWDER & FLAKES, CATTLE FEED, TOMATO POWDER, TOMATO PRODUCTS, CANNED FRUITS & VEGETABLES, TOMATO PURE, GROUN NUT OIL, REFIND OIL, DEHYDRATED GRAPES, BANANA POWDER & WAFFERS)
867. FRUIT JUICE, JAM, JELLIES & ALLIED PRODUCTS
868. FRUIT JUICE, PICKLES PROCESSING AND CANNING
869. FRUIT JUICE MAKING & PACKING IN PLASTIC CONTAINER/POUCHES
870. FRUIT PROCESSING (JAM & JELLIES)
871. FRUIT PULP & JUICE CONCENTRATES
872. FRUIT & VEGETABLE DRYING (FREEZE DRYING METHOD)
873. GOAT & SHEEP FARMING
874. GRAM DALL/PULSE MILL
875. GRAPE DEHYDRATION
876. HARD BOILED CANDY (TOFFEE & CANDY)
877. HERBAL CIGARETTES
878. HONEY PROCESSING & PACKAGING
879. ICE CREAM OF DIFFERENT FLAVOURS
880. ICE CREAM STABILIZER
881. ICE MAKING PLANT
882. INDIAN MADE FOREIGN LIQUOR (I.M.F.L)
883. INSTANT FOOD (IDLI MIX, DOSA MIX, GULAB JAMUN MIX)
884. INSTANT FOOD (INSTANT FOOD & FAST FOOD PARLOUR)
885. INSTANT NOODLES
886. INSTANT TEA
887. INSTANT TEA FROM BLACK TEA
888. INTEGERATED STARCH BAKING POWDER/YEAST INDUSTRY
889. IODIZED SALT
890. IODIZED SALT (ORDINARY MOISTURE-LESS/FREE FLOWING IN PLASTIC BAGS AND CONTAINERS)
891. JAM, JELLIES, FRUIT JUICE & ALLIED PRODUCTS
892. KATHA AND CUTCH
893. KHANDSARI SUGAR
894. KHANDSARI SUGAR & IMFL
895. LACTIC ACID FROM WHITE SUGAR BY FERMENTATION PROCESS
896. LACTOSE & BY PRODUCTS PROCESSING FROM MILK
897. LIQUID GLUCOSE AND ITS BYE PRODUCTS
898. MACRONI AND VERMICILLI
899. MALT EXTRACTION FROM BARLEY
900. MANGO PROCESSING (MANGO PULP, JUICE & SLICES)
901. MAYUR BRAND TYPE CHEWING TOBACCO
902. MINERAL WATER
903. MILK PRESERVATION & MARKETING TO WHOLE SELLERS (INPOUCH PACKING BY UHT TECHNOLOGY)
904. MILK PROCESSING AND PACKAGING OF MILK PRODUCTS
905. MILK PRODUCTS (CASEIN, LACTOSE, GHEE & WHEY POWDER)
906. MILK TOFFEE
907. MINI FLOUR MILL
908. MINI SUGAR PLANT
909. MISRI (PEARL SUGAR CANDIES)
910. MODERN RICE MILL
911. MURABBA
912. MUSTARD OIL EXTRACTION & REFINING
913. MUTTON TALLOW
914. NAMKEEN INDUSTRY (BHUJIA, CHANA CHUR ETC.)
915. NAMKEEN & SWEETS
916. NON-BASMATI RICE FROM PADDY
917. OLEORESIN, ESSENTIAL OIL, DYES & POWDER OF SPICES
918. OLEORESIN EXTRACTION FROM DIPTERO-CARPUT TURMINATUS AND PINUS KHASYANA
919. OLEORESIN EXTRACTION FROM CHILLI
920. PAN MASALA AND POUCH

1059. BUFFALO HORN TIP, HOOF
1060. BANQUET HALL
1061. BUTTON
1062. CALCINED PETROLEUM (C.P) COKE
1063. CANVAS SHOES
1064. CANVAS SHOES, JUNGLE BOOTS
1065. CARBON BRUSH, BRUSH HOLDER & SLIP RING
1066. CEMENT SHEETS WITH COIR FIBRE & OTHER SEGMENTS
1067. CERAMIC TILES (GLAZED) BY DOUBLE FIRING/HEATING
1068. CHILDREN RECREATION CENTRE
1069. COAL BRIQUETTES
1070. COLD STORAGE & ICE
1071. COLD STORAGE FOR FRUITS AND VEGETABLES
1072. COMPRESSOR (HERMETIC) FOR AIR CONDITIONER
1073. COSTUME JEWELLERY/ IMITATION JEWELLERY
1074. DECORATIVE LAMINATED SHEET (SUNMICA)
1075. DIAMOND CUTTING & EXPORTS
1076. DRINKING STRAW FROM PROPYLENE
1077. ENGINEERING COLLEGE
1078. ENTERTAINMENT CLUB
1079. FASHION TECHNOLOGY INSTITUTE
1080. FAST FOOD PARLOUR
1081. FAST FOOD (INSTANT FOOD & FAST FOOD PARLOUR)
1082. FIRE EXTINGUISHERS (SODA ACID TYPE)
1083. FISH NET
1084. FLORICULTURE (CUT FLOWER ROSE) WITH GREEN HOUSE
1085. FLOOR COVERING SHEET
1086. FILM STUDIO (VIDEO)
1087. FLUSH DOOR, CHIP BOARD, WOOD WOOL & OTHER INSULATING BOARDS
1088. GAS DETECTORS OF L.P.G
1089. GEMS MANUFACTURING
1090. GLASS BOTTLE BY SCRAP
1092. GOAT & SHEEP FARMING
1093. GOLD ELECTROPLATING
1094. GOLD JEWELLERY (E.O.U)
1095. GOLD PLATED SILVER JEWELLERY & CUTLERY
1096. GRANITE SLAB AND TILES
1097. GREEN HOUSE
1098. HARD CHROMIUM PLATING
1099. HEALTH CLUB AND BEAUTY PARLOUR CUM HAIR SALOON WITH SONA BATH
1100. HEALTH CLUB CUM BEAUTY PARLOUR TRAININGINSTITUTE
1101. HORN TIP,HOOVE BUTTON
1102. HOSPITAL
1103. HOSPITAL (100 BEDS)
1104. HOSPITAL (200 BEDS)
1105. ICE MAKING PLANT
1106. IMITATION AND COSTUME
1107. JEWELLERY (NECKLACE, EARRINGS EAR TOP ETC.)
1108. INITMATE SCENT CHEMICALS FROM ALL TYPES OF FLAVOUR
1109. INVESTMENT CASTING
1110. JUTE, COIR, GLASS ROPE/ SUTLI
1111. JUTE TWINE
1112. L.P.G BOTTLING PLANT
1113. L.P.G REGULATOR (DOMESTIC PURPOSE)
1114. LAMINATED PARTICLE BOARD & HARD BOARD
1115. LAMINATED SAFETY AND TOUGHENED GLASS
1116. LEASING & HIRE PURCHASE
1117. LICHEN (CHARILA)
1118. MANILA ROPES
1119. MEDICAL COLLEGE
1120. MATCH UNIT FROM WAXED PAPER
1121. MEDIUM DENSITY FIBRE BOARD
1122. MELAMINE CROCKERY
1123. MINERAL WATER
1124. MINI CEMENT PLANT
1125. MIRROR SILVER, GOLDEN, PINK, BLACK & SMOKES
1126. MODERN ADVERTISING AGENCY WITH DTP & FILM STUDIO
1127. MOTEL/SMALL HOTEL
1128. MULTI COLOUR PRINTING
1129. MULTI STOREY COMMERCIAL COMPLEX ALONGWITH RESIDENTIAL AND DELUX FLATS FOR FOREIGN TOURISTS & REVOLVING RESTAURENT AT THE TOP
1130. MULTIPLE LAMINATION INDUSTRY
1131. MUSHROOM GROWING AND PROCESSING (BY DEEP FREEZING METHOD)
1132. NEWS PAPER PRINTING
1133. NICKEL LINED INDUSTRIAL SCREEN
1134. OFFSET COLOUR PRINTING PRESS (SIX COLOUR)
1135. OFFSET PRINTING PRESS
1136. P.C.C ELECTRIC POLES
1137. PHOTOGRAPHIC DEVELOPER & FIXER
1138. PVC EXTRUSION PROFILE (DOOR & WINDOWS)
1139. POP-CORN
1140. PHOTO ETCHING OF S.S.
1141. PRE STRESSED CEMENT CONCRETE PIPES
1142. PILFER PROOF CAPS
1143. PILFER PROOF CAPS AND CROWN CAP
1144. POUCH MAKING & GRAVURE PRINTING (ROTO PRINTING)
1145. POULTRY & FISH FARMING (INTEGERATED UNIT)
1146. PRINTING OF TIN SHEETS
1147. READYMADE GARMENTS
1148. RESTAURANT
1149. ROSE PLANTATION AND ROSE OIL EXTRACTION
1150. ROTOGRAVURE PRINTING
1151. SAFETY BELTS
1152. SAFETY MATCHES
1153. SHOE LACES
1154. SILK COCOON CULTIVATION (GROWING OF SILK COCOON WARM)
1155. SILK SCREEN PRINTING FORMULATIONS FOR PLASTIC, PAPER & CLOTH
1156. SPIKENARD (JATAMANSI)
1157. STENCIL COATING SOLUTION
1158. SUGAR CANDY (MISRI)
1159. SUGAR CANE PLANTATION
1160. SUGAR CANE JUICE PRESERVATION
1161. SURAT ZARI
1162. SYNTHETIC SHOES & SOLES
1163. TEA PACKAGING INDUSTRY
1164. TENNIS BALLS
1165. THREE STAR HOTEL
1166. TRAVELLING AGENCY
1167. TRAYS, TROLLEYS FOR HOSPITAL WITH SCRATCHLESS COATING
1168. WAX EXTRACTS (TANNING POWDER)
1169. WIRE ROPE SLINGS
1170. WOOD WOOL SLAB
1171. WOODEN CANE FURNITURE WITH EXPORT POTENTIAL
1172. WOODEN FURNITURE
1173. WOODEN PANEL INCLUDING KILN SEASONING
1174. WOODEN FURNITURE
1175. WATCH CASE BUFFING
1176. WATCH DIAL
1177. WRIST WATCHES
1178. WATCHES (ELECTRONIC)
1179. ZEDOARY (KACHUR)

EDIBLE OILS, ESSENTIAL OILS LURICATIING OILS, GREASES, VEGETABLE OILS, WAXES, CAMPHOR, PERFUMES & PERFUMERY COMPOUNDS AND REFINED OILS ETC.

1180. AROMATIC PERFUMERY COMPOUND
1181. AEROSOL
1182. AGARBATTI PERFUMERY COMPOUND
1183. BEES WAX MANUFACTURE
1184. CAMPHOR
1185. CARDANOL FROM CASHEW NUT SHELL LIQUID
1186. CASTOR OIL
1187. CASTOR OIL DERIVATIVE OLEORESINS
1188. CHILLI OIL
1189. CITRONELLA OILS
1190. CLOVE OIL
1191. CONCENTRATE OF ROSE JASMINE & LILY ETC.
1192. COLOURED FLAME CANDLE

1193. CANDLES (SEMI-AUTOMATIC)
1194. CORN OIL (MAIZE OIL)
1195. DEHYDRATED CASTOR OIL
1196. EUGENOL FROM CINNAMON LEAF OIL
1197. EXTRACTION OF ESSENTIAL OIL (CARDAMON, JEERA, AJOWAN, GINGER OILS ETC. & PACKAGING OF GROUND SPICES)
1198. EXTRACTION OF JASMINE ESSENCE
1199. EXTRACTION OF ESSENTIAL OILS BY SUPER CRITICAL FLUID METHOD FROM FLOWERS, HERBS & SPICES
1200. EUCALYPTUS OIL
1201. EXTRACTION OF OIL FROM OIL SEED EXPANDEREXTRUSION TECHNOLOGY)
1202. FAT LIQUOR SULPHATED OIL
1203. FLAVOURS FOR FOOD
1204. GARLIC OIL & POWDER
1205. GINGER OIL, SANDALWOOD OIL AND NAGARMOTHA OIL
1206. GINGER OIL
1207. GINGER OIL & GINGER DUST
1208. INTEGERATED WAX COMPLEX
1209. IONONE FROM LEMON GRASS OIL
1210. JASMINE & LILLY FLOWER OIL
1211. LEMON GRASS OIL
1212. LIQUID PARAFFIN
1213. LUBE OIL & GREASE
1214. LUBRICATING OIL
1215. MENTHOL CRYSTALS
1216. MENTHOL OIL & CRYSTAL
1217. MICRO CRYSTALLINE WAX
1218. MUSTARD OIL (EDIBLE OIL)
1219. OIL FROM ARTEMISIA HERBS
1220. PALM OIL CRUSHING UNIT
1221. PAN MASALA
1222. PARAFFIN WAX
1223. PARAFFIN WAX FROM SLACK WAX
1224. REFINED OIL-SUN FLOWER OIL, GROUNDNUT OIL, STAFF FLOWER OIL & COTTON SEED OIL
1225. REFINED VEGETABLE OIL
1226. RECLAMATION OF USED ENGINE OIL
1227. RICE BRAN OIL (R.B.O)
1228. ROSE OIL EXTRACTION
1229. SMOKE LESS CANDLE
1230. SPICE OIL & OLEORESINS
1231. SOLVENT EXTRACTION PLANT (OIL CAKE BASED)
1232. SYNTHETIC ALMOND OIL
1233. SYNTHETIC TALLOW
1234. SYNTHETIC GHEE
1235. VEGETABLE OIL EXTRACTION & REFINING
1236. WADDING OIL (100%) FOR WADDING OF COTTON HOSIERY CLOTH IN DYEING PROCESS
1237. WAX EMULSION FOR TEXTILE
1238. WAX FLOOR POLISH

PAINT, ENAMEL, SOLVENTS, THINNERS, INKS & VARNISH

1239. ACRYLIC EMULSION PAINTS
1240. ALUMINIUM PAINT
1241. AUTOMOBILE PAINTS
1242. BALL POINT PEN REFILL INK
1243. BITUMINIOUS ROAD EMULSION
1244. BITUMEN
1245. BITUMINIOUS FELTS FOR WATER & DAMP PROOFING
1246. BITUMINIOUS ROAD EMULSION RAPID MEDIUM & SLOW SETTING
1247. BUFFING & POLISHING
1248. CEMENT PAINT FOR WHITE & GREY CEMENT

1249. DISPERSANT
1250. DRY DISTEMPER
1251. DRY DISTEMPER & CEMENT PAINT
1252. DUPLICATING INK BLACK FOR GESTNER DUPLICATOR
1255. EMULSION PAINTS (WATER BASED)
1256. HAMMERTONE PAINT
1257. INSULATING VARNISH & WIRE ENAMEL
1258. IRON OXIDE PIGMENTS
1259. INSULATING VARNISH (POLY VINYL BUTYRAL BASED, FFC GRADE)
1260. LIME COLOUR (CEMENT COLOUR)
1261. SYNTHETIC RED OXIDE FOR FLOORINGS
1262. SOLVENT & THINNERS
1263. MARKING INKS (WATER PROOF)
1264. METAL NAPHTHANATE (AS DRIER FOR PAINTS)
1265. N.C.PUTTY
1266. OFFSET PRINTING INK
1267. OIL BOUND DISTEMPER PAINT
1268. PAINT BRUSHES
1269. PAINT REMOVERS
1270. PAINT INDUSTRY
1271. PAINT & VARNISH
1272. PICTURE VARNISH
1273. POWDER COATING PAINT
1274. PRINTING INKS (OFFSET, FLEXO & ROTO GRAVURE)
1275. PRIMER PAINT & ENAMEL PAINT
1276. PUTTY & WATER PROOFING PAINT
1277. PRINTING INKS (FLEXO-GRAPHIC INK)
1278. PUTTY (METAL CASEMENT)
1279. RED OXIDE PRIMER (ANTI CORROSIVE)
1280. REFRECTORY PAINT (GRAPHITE BASED)
1281. SCREEN PRINTING INKS
1282. SILK SCREEN PRINTING INK FORMULATION FOR PLASTIC, PAPER, CLOTH
1283. STAMP & PAD INK
1284. STOVING PAINT
1285. SPIRIT SOLUBLE MALEIC RESIN
1286. TEXTURE PAINT
1287. THINNERS AND ITS ALLIED PRODUCTS
1288. TONER INK
1289. VARNISH THINNER (SOLVENT)
1290. VACUUM METALLIZING LACQUERS
1291. WOOD PRIMER

PHARMACEUTICAL, DRUGS, AYURVEDIC/HERBAL COSMETICS & MEDICINES, HOMOEOPATHIC MEDICINES, DISPOSABLE SYRINGE, DENTAL COLLEGE & FINE CHEMICALS ETC.

1292. AROMATIC PILLS
1293. ASPIRIN
1294. AYURVEDIC PAIN BALM OINTMENTS
1295. AYURVEDIC CHURAN AND TABLETS
1296. AYURVEDIC TABLETS (HAJMOLA TYPE)
1297. AYURVEDIC/HERBAL PHARMACY
1298. AYURVEDIC SHERBATS
1299. AYURVEDIC PRODUCTS
1300. BULK DRUGS (E.O.U)
1301. BLOOD BAGS
1302. CALCIUM GLUCONATE
1303. CAPSULE, TABLET & INJECTION WITH MODERN INSTRUMENTS
1304. CASHEW FENI
1305. CHLOROQUINONE PHOSPHATE (BULK DRUGS)
1306. CLINICAL THERMOMETER
1307. DENTAL CLINIC

1308. DENTAL COLLEGE
1309. DENTAL GRADE EUGENOL
1310. DEXTROSE MONOHYDRATE, LIQUID GLUCOSE
1311. DEHYDRATED ONION & ONION POWDER
1312. DEXTROSE POWDER (ANHYDROUS FROM STARCH)
1314. DEXTROSE SALINE SOLUTION
1315. DISTILLERY (I.M.F.L)
1316. DISPOSABLE NEEDLES FOR SYRINGES
1317. DISPRIN
1318. DISTILLED WATER
1319. EMPTY HARD GELATINE CAPSULES
1320. FILLING & PACKING OF CAPSULES
1321. GLUCOSE - D - POWDER
1322. GLYCERINE
1323. HERBAL COSMETICS
1324. HERBAL SHAMPOO
1325. HERBAL HAIR OILS (AYURVEDIC)
1326. HOMOE & BIO-MEDICINES WITH MOTHER TINCTURE
1327. HOMOEPATHIC MEDICINES
1328. HYPODERMIC NEEDLES
1329. I.V. FLUIDS
1330. IBUPROFEN
1331. INFUSION & TRANSFUSION SETS (I.V. SET)
1332. INJECTABLE FOR PHARMACEUTICALS
1333. INJECTION AMPOULES PACKAGING BOX
1334. INTEGERATED SURGICAL COTTON
1335. ICE MAKING PLANT
1336. ICE & COLD STORAGE
1337. LACTOSE & BY PRODUCTS PROCESSING FROM MILK
1338. LICHEN (JATAMANSI CHARILA)
1339. LIQUID GLUCOSE AND ITS BY-PRODUCTS
1340. L-LYSINE MONOHYDRO CHLORIDE
1341. LIQUID GLUCOSE FROM POTATOES
1342. MEDICAL COLLEGE
1343. NICOTINE FROM TOBACCO WASTE
1344. OINTMENT-AYURVEDIC (YELLOW & WHITE)
1345. PHARMACEUTICAL AND FOOD GRADE GELATINE
1346. PHARMACEUTICAL INDUSTRY (TABLETS, CAPSULES, LIQUID, GEL, OINTMENT POWDER INJECTABLE)
1347. PHARMACEUTICAL UNIT (EOU) WITH FORMULA TIONS, INJECTABLES, ETC. PYRIDINE & DERIVATIVES
1348. SALT (IODIZED SALT)
1349 SALINE & INJECTION WATER
1350. SALINE WATER & DEXTROSE SOLUTION (I.V.FLUID IN PLASTIC BOTTLES)
1351. SORBITOL
1352. STARCH (MAIZE)
1353. SURGICAL ADHESIVE PLASTER
1354. SURGICAL BANDAGES
1355. SURGICAL GLOVES
1357. SURGICAL COTTON
1358. SURGICAL COTTON AND BANDAGE
1359. SYNTHETIC CAMPHOR POWDER
1360. TABLETS & CAPSULES
1361. TISSUE CULTURE
1362. TINCTURE FROM RECTIFIED SPIRIT
1363. TRIMETHOPIME
1364. VETERENARY MEDICINES (ONLY FORMULATIONS)
1365. VITAMIN 'C', SORBITOL' ANHYDROUS DEXTROSE, STARCH

PULP, PAPER, STRAW/GREY BOARD, KRAFT PAPER, PACKAGING, PAPER CARRY BAGE, PAPER FROM AGRO WASTE & STATIONERY ETC.

1366. AMMONIA PAPER
1367. AUTOMATIC BOOK BINDING
1368. ADHESIVE (FEVICOL TYPE)
1369. ALL PIN & GEM CLIPS
1370. CARBON PAPER
1371. CARD BOARD
1372. CARBON LESS PAPER
1373. CELLPHANE PAPER
1374. COMPUTER FORMS & SECURITY PRINTING PRESS
1375. CORRUGATED BOARD & BOX (PRINTED & LAMINATED)
1376. CORRUGATED BOARD AND BOXES FROM FROM CARD BOARDS
1377. CORRUGATED CARTONS FROM PLAIN PAPERS
1378. CORRUGATRED PACKING & MATERIAL (BULB & TUBES PACKING)
1379. DESK TOP PUBLISHING
1380. DEFOAMING AGENT FOR PAPER PLANT
1381. DRINKING STRAW PAPER
1382. D.T.P CUM OFFSET PRESS
1383. EGG TRAYS
1384. EXERCISE NOTE BOOK, REGISTER AND PAD
1385. FLEXOGRAPHIC INK
1386. GREETING CARD BY OFFSET PRESS
1387. HAND MADE PAPER FILTER PAPER
1388. HARD BOARD
1389. INJECTION AMPOULES PACKAGING BOXES
1390. INSULATIING PAPER
1391. KRAFT PAPER
1392. KRAFT PAPER FROM BAGASSE
1393. LAMINATED PACKAGING PAPER WITH PRINTING
1394. LAMINATION & COATING ON PAPER
1395. M.G. PAPER FROM WASTE PAPER
1396. MILL PAPER FROM WASTE PAPER
1397. MILL BOARD FROM RICE & WHEAT STRAWS
1398. MILL BOARD FROM WASTE PAPER
1399. MINI PAPER PLANT FROM SISAL
1400. MINI PAPER PLANT
1401. MULTI WALL PAPER SACKS
1402. NEWS PAPER FOR CHILDREN
1403. NEWS PRINT PAPER FROM RICE STRAW BAGASSE
1404. NEWS PAPER CHILDRENS
1405. NEWS PRINT PAPER
1406. OFFSET AND TREADLE TYPE PRINTING PRESS
1407. MILL BOARD BASED ON RICE STRAW
1408. PAPER AND BOARD FROM STRAW
1409. PAPER & PAPER PRODUCTS
1410. PAPER ENVELOPES
1411. PAPER CARRY BAGS
1412. PAPER BOARD CARTON
1413. PAPER CONES FOR LOUD SPEAKERS
1414. PAPER FROM AKRA
1415. PAPER FROM BAGASSE WITH CORRUGATED BOARD & BOXES
1416. PAPER FROM BAMBOO
1417. PAPER GLASSES FOR BEVERAGES
1418. PAPER FROM RICE HUSK & WHEAT HUSK
1419. PAPER FROM TREE BARK, EUCALYPRUS WOOD
1420. PAPER PRODUCTS
1421. PAPER PLANT (WHITE WRITING & NEWS PAPER FOR PULP & WASTE PAPER)
1422. PAPER PLATES, PAPER GLASS
1423. PAPER CONES & TUBES
1425. PAPER PLANT WITH DTP & PRINTING & PUBLISHING UNIT
1426. PAPER BASED PHENOLIC SHEET
1427. PAPER CUP FOR ICE CREAM
1428. PAPER TUBES SPIRAL WINDING COMPOSIT CONTAINER
1429. PAPER LABLE FOR BEER BOTTLES
1430. PARTICLE BOARD & BLACK BOARD WITH SANDING & LAMINATION OF PARTICLE BOARD
1431. PARTICLE BOARD FROM RICE HUSK
1432. POUCH FILLING & MAKING FOR TOMATO SAUCE
1433. POUCH MAKING &

INSULATION & SHEETS GRADES)
1550. P.V.C GRANULES FROM PVC SCRAPS (WITH POLLUTION CONTROL)
1551. P.V.C HOSES
1552. P.V.C LEATHER CLOTH
1553. P.V.C FLEXIBLE PIPES
1554. P.V.C PIPES AND FITTINGS
1555. POLYTHENE BAGS (PRINTED)
1556. PVC PLASTICS FILM SHEET SOFT/RIGID
1557. PVC RESIN AND COMPOUND
1558. PVC RULAR
1559. PVC STABLIZERS (SINGLE PACK SYSTEM)
1560. PVC WIRE AND CABLES
1561. PAPER BASED PHENOLIC SHEET FOR ELECTRICAL
1562. PHENOL FORMALDEHYDE RESIN
1563. PHENOLIC RESIN
1564. PLASTIC BEADS FROM PLASTIC SCRAPS
1565. PLASTIC BUTTONS
1566. PLASTIC CANS
1567. PLASTIC COLLAPSIBLE TUBE
1568. PLASTIC CORRUGATED SHEET & BOXES
1569. PLASTIC FILM AND SHEETS WITH PRINTING FLEXO & ROTO/LDPE/HDPE/PP/HM/PVC
1570. PLASTIC FILTER MASTER BATCH & OTHER MASTER BATCHES FOR VARIOUS PLASTICS
1571. PLASTIC JERRY CANS
1572. PLASTIC GRANULES OR POWDER FROM PLASTIC SCRAP
1573. PLASTIC INJECTION MOULDED T.V. CABINETS
1574. PLASTIC ITEMS MANUFAC TURE FROM POWDER MELAMINE
1575. PLASTIC GOODS
1576. PLASTIC PIPES & TARPAULINES
1577. PLASTIC SHEET FROM SCRAP
1578. PLASTIC PLANT (BLOW MOULDING & INJECTION MOULDING)
1579. PLASTIC PRODUCTS (GOLD, SILVER, NICKEL)
1580. PLASTIC TOYS
1581. POLYESTER BEADING
1582. POLYESTER FILM
1583. POLYTHENE BAGS & AUTOMATIC PRINTING
1584. POLYTHENE PRINTED BAGS
1585. POLYURETHANE FOAM AND ITS PRODUCTS
1586. PROPYLENE FILM (PRINTED) & BAG MANUFACTURING
1587. PLASTIC MATS
1588. RAINBOW COLOUR ON PVC FILM & SHEET
1589. RED MUD PVC PIPES AND FITTINGS
1590. RE-RUBBERISED OF SOLID TYPE
1591 RESIN COATED SAND REXINE
1592 REXINE CLOTH & ALLIED PRODUCTS
1593 RUBBER ADHESIVE
1594. RUBBER AUTO PARTS
1595. RUBBER BELTING
1596. RUBBER MOULDING UNIT INCLUDING LINING RUBBER SHEETING
1597. RUBBER RECLAIMING
1598. RUBBER ROLLERS FOR TEXTILE MILLS & PAPER INDUSTRIES
1599 RUBBER & PLASTIC SHEETS, MATS & FLAPS
1600. RUBBER SHEET AND ALLIED HOSPITAL RUBBER GOODS
1601. RUBBERIZED PVC GASKET
1602. RUBBERISED COIR
1603. RUBBER COMPOUND FOR AUTOMOBILES
1604. SAFETY BELTS
1605. SILVER AND GOLD PLATING ON PVC AND NYLON-6
1606. SILICONE RUBBER NIPPLES/ TEATS
1607. SPECTACLE FRAMES (PLASTIC)
1608. SPUNGE RUBBER
1609. SURGICAL EXAMINATION GLOVES
1610. SYNTHETIC PEARL COATING ON POLYSTYRENE BEADS
1611. SYNTHETIC RUBBER ADHESIVE
1612. TEFLON MANUFACTURING
1613. TEFLON TAPE
1614. TEFLON TAPES & CABLES
1615. THERMOCOLE SHEET AND MOULDED PRODUCTS EXPANDED POLYESTERENE EXTRUSION PROFILES
1616. THERMOFORMED PACKAGING (BLISTER PACKAGING & POUCH PACKAGING)
1617. THERMOPLASTIC POLYURETHANE
1618. THERMOFORMED CUPS, PLATES & GLASS WITH HIPS SHEET
1619. THERMOCOLE
1620. THERMOCOLE BASED DISPOSABLE GLASS, CUPS & PLATES
1621. TOOTH BRUSHES
1622. TOY BALLOON, DECORA TIVE & INDUSTRIAL BALLOONS
1623. TREAD RUBBER
1624. TYRE RETREADING (HOT)
1625. TYRE RETREADING BY COLD PROCESS
1626. TYRE TUBES & FLAPS
1627. TYRE & TUBES
1628. UNSATURATED POLYESTER FOR REXINE
1629. V-BELT AND FAN BELT
1630. VINYL ASBESTOS AND PVC WALL PAPER
1631 VITON (FLUORO ELASTOMER)

SOAP, COSMETICS & PERFUMS

1632. ACID SLURRY, SYNTHETIC DETERGENT POWDER
1632. ACID SLURRY
1633. AGARBATTI SYNTHETIC, PERFUMERY COMPOUND
1634. AFTER SHAVE LOTION
1635. ANTISEPTIC CREAM
1636. BETA IONONE
1637. BLEACHING POWDER
1638. BLUE DETERGENT POWDER
1639. CLEANING POWDER (VIMTYPE)
1640. COLD CREAM
1641. COLOURED FLAME & PERFUMED CANDLES (RED, BLUE, GREEN FLAME)
1642. COSMETIC INDUSTRY (MODERN)
1643. COSMETIC INDUSTRY (SHAMPOO, SPRAY PERFUME, TALCUM POWDER
1644. DETERGENT POWDER (ARIEL TYPE)
1645. DETERGENT POWDER (NIRMA TYPE) FULLY AUTOMATIC PLANT
1646. DETERGENT WASHING POWDER
1647. FISH OIL SOAP
1648. GLYCERINE TRANSPARENT SOAP
1649. HAIR REMOVING CREAM
1650. HERBAL COSMETICS
1651. HERBAL SHAMPO & CREAM
1652. HERBAL/AYURVEDIC COSMETICS
1653. INCENSE POWDER, INCENSE STICKS & INCENSE CAKE
1654. OPTICAL WHITENERS
1655. ROSE OIL EXTRACTION
1656. SHAMPOOS (COCONUT OIL BASED COLD PROCESS)
1657. SHAVING CREAM
1658. SINDUR (KUMKUM)
1659. SOAP COATED PAPER
1660. SPRAY DRIED DETERGENT POWDER
1661. STAIN REMOVER
1662. TALCUM POWDER (FACE & TOILET POWDER)
1663. TOILET AND HERBAL SOAP
1664. TOOTH PASTE & POWDER
1665. WASHING DETERGENT POWDER AND WASHING SOAP
1666. WASHING POWDER LIQUID DETERGENTS, LOTION & SHAMPOO

ENTERTAINMENT CLUB WITH 4 STAR HOTEL
1779. HOSPITALS
1780. ICE CREAM PARLOUR
1781. INTERNET SERVICE PROVIDER (I.S.P.)
1782. MEDICAL COLLEGE
1783. MEDICAL COLLEGE, HOSPITAL & RESEARCH INSTITUTE
1784. MEDICAL TRANSCRIPTION CENTRE
1785. MENTAL RETARDATION HOSPITAL & CEREBRAL PALSY
1786. MOTEL/SMALL HOTEL
1787. MULTISTOREY COMMERCIAL COMPLEX
1788. MULTISTOREY RESIDENTIAL COMPLEX
1789. NURSERY SCHOOL
1790. NATURE CARE CENTRE
1791. NURSING HOME
1792. ONLINE SHOPPING MALL (RS. 5000/- REPORT)
1793. PORTAL
1794. REHABILITATION CENTRE FOR AGED & NEEDY PERSONS
1795. RESIDENTIAL CUM COMMERCIAL COMPLEX
1796. RESTAURANT
1797. RESTAURANT WITH PUB
1798. SCHOOL (PRIMARY)
1799. SCHOOL (HIGHER SECONDARY)
1800. THREE STAR HOTEL
1801. TOURIST CLUB
1802. TRAINING INSTITUTE FOR MEDICAL TRANSCRIPTION
1803. VIDEO FILM STUDIO
1804. WARE HOUSE
1805. WEBSITE DESIGN & E-MAIL REGISTERING

AGRO BASED INDUSTRIES

1806. COAL BRIQUETTES FROM AGROWASTE
1807. FURFURALFROM RICEHULL
1808. MUSHROOM CULTIVATION & PROCESSING (BUTTON)
1809. MUSHROOM GROWING & PROCESSING WITH AIR CONDITIONING
1810. MUSHROOM CULTIVATION & PROCESSING UNIT DEHYDRATION & PACKAGING OF OYSTER & PADDY STRAW MUSHROOMS
1811. ORGANIC MANURE
1812. PAPAYA CULTIVATION
1813. PAPAYA & TOMATO CULTIVATION
1814. PROCESSING & UTILISATION OF COCONUT
1815. PROCESSING OF SHEEP HAIR TO PRODUCE WOOL

BAKERY, CONFECTIONERY & FOOD PRODUCTS

1816. AGROLACTOR SOYA MILK
1817. APPLE FRUIT JUICE WITH CANNING BOTTLING
1818. AYURVEDIC SHARBAT
1819. BAKERY UNIT (PASTRIES, BREAD, BUNS, CAKE, TOFFEE ETC.)
1820. BAKING POWDER
1821. BANANA & ITS BY PRODUCTS
1822. BANANA POWDER
1823. BANANA WAFERS
1824. BANANA CULTIVATION
1825. BEER INDUSTRY
1826. DEHULLING OF JAUN FOR BEER
1827. BEER & WINE
1828. BEER, ALCOHOL, IMFL
1829. BESEN PLANT
1830. BISCUIT PLANT
1831. BREAD & BISCUIT PLANT
1832. BOTTLING PLANT COUNTRY LIQUOR FROM RECTIFIED SPIRIT
1833. BRANDY
1834. BREAD RUSKS
1835. CANNED FRUITS & VEGETABLES
1836. CANNING & PRESERVATION OF MEAT
1837. CANNING & PRESERVATION OF VEGETABLES
1838. CANNING OF MANGO PULP & MANGO SLICES
1839. CARBONATED BEVERAGS
1840. CASHEW FENI
1841. CASHEW NUT (DRIED & FRIED)
1842. CATTLE BREEDING
1843. CATTLE BREEDING & DAIRY FARM TO PRODUCE MILK
1844. CATTLE FEED FROM TAPIOCA
1845. CHEWING GINGER & AMLOKI
1846. CHEWING GUM
1847. CHILLI SAUCE
1848. CHILLI POWDER
1849. CHOCOLATE
1850. CIDER PLANT
1851. COCOA POWDER
1852. COCOA BUTTER & COCOA POWDER
1853. COCONUT SHELL POWDER
1854. COCONUT WATER
1855. COCONUT SWEET (WATERY)
1856. COCONUT MILK POWDER (DEHYDRATED)
1857. COCONUT PRODUCTS & BY PRODUCTS (INTEGRATED PLANT)
1858. COLD DRINK
1859. CURRY POWDER
1860. DAIRY FOR MILK PROCESSING (GHEE, BUTTER & PANEER)
1861. DAIRY PRODUCTS
1862. DAIRY PRODUCTS MILK PACKAGING IN POUCH (GHEE, BUTTER, ETC.
1863. DAIRY FARM TO PRDUCE MILK WITH PACKAGING (COW)
1864. DAIRY FARM TO PRDUCE MILK WITH PACKAGING (BUFALLOE)
1865. DAIRY FARM & MILK PRODUCTS
1866. DAL MOTH, CHANACHUR & BHUJIYA
1867. DEHYDRATION OF FRUITS & VEGETABLE
1868. DESICCATED COCONUT POWDER FROM COCONUTS
1869. DEHYDRATION & CANNINGOF FRUITS & VEGETABLES
1870. DRY FRUIT ROASTING & PACKAGING
1871. DRYING OF RED CHILLIES, HALDI, DHANIYA, PEAS & GROUND NUT
1872. EGG POWDER
1873. FISH CANNING IN TIN & POUCHES
1874. FISH DEHYRATION (DRYING OF FISH)
1875. FISH MEAL
1876. FISH PROCESSING (BEAST FREEZING PROCESSES)
1877. FLAVOURS FOR FOOD INDUSTRIES
1878. FLOUR MILL (ROLLER)
1879. FROZEN MEAT
1880. FOOD DEHYDRATION (FRUITS & VEGETABLES)
1881. FRIED & ROASTED GROUND NUT, GRAMS, PEAR ETC.
1882. FRUIT JUICE MAKING & PACKAGING IN PLASTIC CONTAINER
1883. FRUIT JUICE IN TETRA PACK (DRINKS)
1884. FRUIT JUICE, SQUASHES, SAUCE & KETCHUP, JAM, JELLY, VINEGAR ETC.
1885. GARLIC FLAKES
1886. GARLIC POWDER
1887. GHEE & BUTTER
1888. GINGER (PULVERISED)
1889. GINGER GLAZING & PRESERVATION
1890. GINGER STORAGE
1891. GINGER PROCESSING
1892. GINGER OIL & GINGER DUST
1893. GINGER POWDER (DRY) & OLEORESIN
1894. GRAPE DEHYDRATION
1895. GRAPE CULTIVATION
1896. GRAPE JUICE
1897. HONEY PROCESSING & PACKAGING
1898. ICE CREAM & ICE CANDY
1899. ICE CUBE
1900. INVERT SUGAR
1901. IDLI MIX, DOSA MIX SAMBHAR MIX, VADA MIX, GULAB JAMUN MIX
1902. INSTANT COFFEE & INSTANT TEA

1903. INSTANT NOODLES
1904. INSTANT SOUPS
1905. IODIZED SALT FROM CRUDE SALT
1906. JAM CHUTNEY PICKLES & SQUASHES
1907. KATHA MANUFACTURING
1908. LECITHIN (SOYA BASED)
1909. LEMON & ITS PRODUCTS
1910. MACARONI MANUFACTURING
1911. MACARONI, SPAGHETTI, VERMICELLI & NOODLES
1912. MAIZE & ITS BY PRODUCTS MALTING PLANT
1913. MANGO PAPPAD (AAM PAPPAD)
1914. MANGO POWDER RIPE
1915. MANGO POWDER
1916. MANGO PROCESSING & CANNING (MANGO PULP)
1917. MEAT PROCESSING (CHICKEN MUTTON)
1918. MEAT PROCESSING (BUFFALO)
1919. MENTHOL BOLD FROM MENTHOL FLAKES
1020. MILK POWDER
1921. MILK POWDER & GHEE
1922. MILK POWDER, GHEE & SPICES
1923. MILK PRESERVATION & MARKETING TO WHOLE SELLERS
1924. MILK PRESERVATION & MARKETING TO WHOLE SELLERS (IN POUCHES)
1925. MILK TOFFEE MANUFACTURES
1926. MINERAL WATER
1927. MINERAL WATER IN POUCHES
1928. MINI FLOUR MILL ATTA MAIDA, SUJI & WHEAT BRAN
1929. MITHAI/HALWAI (SWEET & NAMKEEN)
1930. MUTTON PROCESSING
1931. PAN MASALA (MEETHA, SADA, ZARDA) MAKING & PACKING
1932. PAN MASALA AND POUCH MAKING
1933. PANEER (CHEESE)
1934. PAPAD & BARIYAN
1935. PAPAD PLANT
1936. PEPSICOLA IN POLYTUBES
1937. PETHA PACKAGING
1938. PICKLES
1939. PIGGERY/MEAT/CHICKEN PROCESSING
1940. PINE APPLE JUICE CANNING
1941. POTATO & ONION POWDER
1942. POTATO & ONION FLAKES
1943. POTATO CHIPS
1944. POTATO GRANULES
1945. POUCH FILLING FOR SAUNF SUPARI ILAICHI ETC.
1946. PRESERVATION OF RAWS MANGO JUICE
1947. PROCESSED CHEESE & MARINE PDTS.
1948. PULP FROM TARMARIND
1949. READYMATE PROCESSED FOOD
1950. RICE & CORN FLAKES
1951. RICE BASMATI (TRADING)
1952. RICE POLISHING & PACKAGING IN POUCH
1953. ROASTED/SALTED/MASALA/ CASHEW NUTS ALMONDS & PEA NUT
1954. ROLLER FLOUR MILL

INFOTECH/IT PROJECTS

1955. MEDICAL TRANSCRIPTION
1956. E-COMMERCE
1957. CYBERCAFE
1958. INTERNET SERVICE PROVIDER (ISP)
1959. COMPUTER EDUCATION CENTRE
1960. PORTAL (WEBSITE DESIGN)
1961. CALL CENTRE

TERMS AND CONDITIONS

FOR INDIA

1. Price Rs. 3,675/- (Rs. Three Thousand Six Hundred Seventy Five Only) for Each *Market Survey Cum Detailed Techno Economic Feasibility Report.* Payable in advance through Draft/M.O./Cash in favour of 'ENGINEERS INDIA RESEARCH INSTITUTE', Delhi. Delivery by Regd.post within 2 Days. (Postage Free)

2. Reputed Firms/Companies may place their orders by V.P.P. for full amount in India Only.

FOR OVERSEAS

1. Price US$ 250/- (US Dollars Two Hundred Fifty Only) for Each *Market Survey Cum Detailed Techno Economic Feasibility Report.*

2. Payable fully in advance through Draft in favour of 'ENGINEERS INDIA RESEARCH INSTITUTE', Delhi (Payable in India) Delivery by Regd. Air Mail Post within 2 Days.

ENGINEERS INDIA RESEARCH INSTITUTE

4449, Nai Sarak (D), Main Road, Delhi - 110 006 (India)
Ph:. 91-11- 3918117, 3916431, 3920361, 3960797
Fax: 91-11- 3916431 E-Mail : eirisidi@bol.net.in
Website:www.startindustry.com
Also at : 4/27, Roop Nagar, Near Roop Nagar No. 1 School, Delhi - 110 007 (India) Ph:. 396 0797, 392 0361

Modern Packaging Technology for

Processed Food , Bakery, Snack Foods, Spices & Allied Food Products

With Directory of Suppliers of Packaging Materials, Machinery & Equipments and other Important Relevant Addresses

The Book covers latest & Updated technology for food packaging including process food, fruits & vegetables, meat poultry & fish, edible oils, vanaspati & ghee, spices, biscuits, confectionery, snack foods, drinking water. Packaging laws & regulations, National standards of packaging code for food stuffs & perishables, food packaging, International Standards.

Fruits & Vegetables Processing Hand Book

The book covers Canning in Commercial Scale, Canning of Fruits, Canning of Vegetables, Fruit Juices, Squashes & Cordials, Fruit Beverages, Jams & Jellies, Tomato Products, Pickles, Sauces & Chutneys, Cashew Fruit Juice, Dehydration of Fruits & Vegetables, Frozen Foods, Fruits & Vegetables Juice with Other Products etc.

Hand Book of Perfume & Flavours

(With Directory of Plant & Equipment, Raw Material & Manufacturer/Exporters/ Suppliers of Perfumes)

The book covers new formulaes of various kinds of perfumes & flavours. The major chapters of the book are Perfume, Formulary of Perfume, Formulary of Flavour, Chemicals Specifications for Perfume & Flavour Components, Plant & Equipment Suppliers, Suppliers of Raw Materials, Manufacturer/Exporters/Suppliers of Perfumes. At the end of the book the last but not the least chapter project profiles has also included for the benefits of the new entrepreneurs.

Hand Book of Essential Oils Manufacturing & Aromatic Plants

The book covers trade of essential oils, rose oil distillation method, cultivation of matricaria chamomilla, extraction of essential oils, essential chemical constituents profile in tree spice, folk medicinal, essential oil bearing plants status, promising aromatic plants of industrial value, essential oil industry waste utilization, fractionation of essential oil in perfumery & turpentine industry, citronella oil, ginger oil, jasmine rose & lily oil, jasmine flower oil etc.

Hand Book of Spices & Packaging with Formulaes

(With Directories of Plant & Equipments & Importers/ Exporters/Mfrs. of Spices)

The Book covers new formulaes of various kinds of Spices. The major chapters of the book are Ajowan, Amchur, Aniseed, Asafoetida, Chilli, Caraway, Cardamom, Cassia, Celery Seed, Cinnamon, Clove, Coriander, Cumin Seed, Fennel, Fenugreek, Garlic, Ginger, Nutmeg, Pepper, Tamarind, Turmeric, Drying of Red Chilli, Dry Ginger, Onion Dehydration, Garlic Powder, Mustard Powder, Turmeric Powder, Formulaes of Different Kinds of Ground Spices, Packaging of Spices, Methods of Tests, Agmark, Details of Machinery, National Standards, Importers/Exporters of Spices, Plant & Equipment Suppliers & Manufacturers of Spices

Hand Book of Electroplating, Anodizing & Surface Finishing Technology

The book covers New & latest technology of Electroplating, Anodizing & Metal Treatments. Various Project Profiles including Aluminium Anodizing, Gold Plating, Nickle Plating Brightner, Precious Metal Plating, Mirror, Hard Anodizing on Aluminium, Barrel Electroplating, Chrome Plating, Zinc Electroplating Brightner, Electrolating on Silver & Gold, Copper Plating on Metallic Parts etc.

ENGINEERS INDIA RESEARCH INSTITUTE

4449, Nai Sarak, Main Road, Delhi - 110 006 (INDIA)

Ph. : 391 8117, 391 6431, 396 0797, 392 0361 • Fax :91-11-391 6431

E-Mail:eirisidi@bol.net.in • Website:www.startindustry.com